# The American Design Adventure

W9-BRG-202

The MIT Press

Cambridge, Massachusetts

London, England

# The American Design Adventure

1940–1975

Arthur J. Pulos

First MIT Press paperback edition, 1990

© 1988 Massachusetts Institute of Technology

This book was set in Helvetica by Achorn Graphic Services and printed and bound by Halliday Lithograph in the United States of America.

Library of Congress Cataloging-in-Publication Data
Pulos, Arthur J.
The American design adventure
Bibliography: p.
Includes index.
1. Design, Industrial—United States—History—20th century.   I. Title.
NK1404.P85 1988   745.2′0973   87-26266
ISBN  0-262-16106-0  (hardcover)
        0-262-66068-7  (paperback)

# Contents

**Note on Citations**

In citations of sources—for example, (25, 37)—the first number indicates the source's position in the bibliography and the second indicates the page in the source.

## Introduction

The products of nature follow cycles of conception, birth, service, death, and renewal, with each product dedicated to the survival of its species. All living things are temporal—only the species aspires to eternity by maintaining homeostatic balance with the environment of which it is a part.

The technological products of man are in no wise different. They, too, are temporal rather than eternal, with survival of the species dependent upon constant renewal. Manufactured things, all their applied symbols of value and pretenses of permanence notwithstanding, are transitory in character. They are constantly being made obsolete by advancing technology and changes in public need and fancy. Useful products are conceived to serve their purpose as humanely as possible and then, like those of nature, to disappear without encumbering living spaces or burdening future generations.

Products come into being as a consequence of an intuitive spark and an innate capacity for synthesis that enables one to draw a unique and useful concept from what may appear to others to have been disassociated experiences. This activity, while not exclusive with any one country, has found particularly fertile ground in the United States as part of the American design adventure that founded this country and continues to sustain it.

The things that people make are expected to provide services that cannot be performed better by other means. Whether the products are animal skins or nylons, sandals or jets, caves or condominiums, the exchange contributes to survival in an essentially hostile environment, with one person offering energy abstracted as money for the energy of another crystallized into the form of a useful product. Adam Smith noted that this propensity to barter—unique to humans—is the fundamental source of their survival on this planet.

Design, as one of the instruments of this exchange, has a commitment to human service beyond the cold touch of science and the predatory grasp of commerce. The role of the designer, as the humane and aesthetic conscience of industry, is that of a surrogate for the consumer. He senses the pattern of evolutionary factors in manufactured products and directs the object toward the perfection of its typeform.

It is natural that the invented form of a product should be based on the technology and the skills available to the inventor. If the service it performs comes up to expectations, people will accept it and may even find beauty in it. Once the object has come into being and has demonstrated its value, it will enter a pattern of ascending improvements to meet increasing competition. From time to time, however, it may reach a plateau where technology and function are in equilibrium. Such a plateau may be either comforting or discomforting to the manufacturer—comforting because, in its stable state, it may be repeated *ad infinitum* with little further investment; discomforting because it may find itself locked in competition to reduce price at the risk of deterioration of quality. Manufacturers may then seek to give it a semblance of progress by reliance on arbitrary form and other superficial implications of change. Although such promises of progress may confuse and even frustrate consumers, in the end they build pressure for genuine improvement, forcing the product off the plateau and on its way upward again. When the purpose for a particular product evaporates, or it is superseded by a better concept, production will cease and it will fall back to become a relic of the taste and technology of its time. Should it, however, possess a unique quality of expressive form, it may, in time, transcend its period to be cherished as an artifact for cultural and aesthetic values beyond its original purposes.

*The American Design Adventure* traces manufactured products through the dynamic decades of the post–World War II era, noting the vigor of their evolution, their excesses, and their aspirations to eternal value.

# The American Design Adventure

*. . . these men . . . know all about the prob-
lems, the dreams, and the realities that the
future has in store for us. They are trained to
think ahead; they know tomorrow like their
own stream-lined pockets. . . .*

Vogue, 1939 (188)

The New York World's Fair of 1939–1940 was
conceived as an exposition of technological
advances that would emphasize social and
historical relevance, as a "fair of the future,"
and as a unified whole that would represent
all the interrelated activities and interests of
the American way of life. The industrial
designers Walter Dorwin Teague and Gilbert
Rohde were members of the original group
that in 1935 organized a meeting of some 100
architects, urban planners, artists, designers,
and educators to discuss with businessmen
and sociologists the idea of a fair that would
address contemporary social problems. Lewis
Mumford set the early theme for the fair by
hoping that it would "lay the pattern for a way
of life which would have an enormous impact
in times to come" (17, 4). In 1936 a seven-
member design board was formed to refine
the theme of the fair and to set its plan and
general character so as to balance architectural values with those of commerce and
industry. The board was also empowered to
recommend designers, architects, and
engineers and to give final approval to all
construction.

Industrial designers—"men believed to be in
touch with the realities of the machine yet
capable of speaking the public's language"—
have been credited with having contributed a
great deal to the fair's final theme, "Building
the World of Tomorrow" (17, 6). The development of the theme and the design of the focal
exhibits were assigned to a group of industrial
designers who were riding the crest of popularity for having contributed to the country's
victory over the Depression and whose imagination inspired the board of design to reach
out for the future as no fair had done before.
Henry Dreyfuss designed "Democracity," the
theme exhibit of the Perisphere. Raymond
Loewy's "Transportation" exhibit depicted a
"Rocketport" for transatlantic flights to London. Gilbert Rohde took on two focal exhibits,
"Man in the Community" and "Home Furnishings." Egmont Arens designed "Production
and Distribution," Donald Deskey "Communication," and Russel Wright "Food." Teague
served as a member of the design board, and
his office designed pavilions for Kodak and
U.S. Steel. He and many other designers
created exhibits for various companies and
agencies represented at the fair. For General
Motors, Norman Bel Geddes conceived and
built Futurama, the fair's most popular exhibit.
(In response to public criticism of the 1939
version of Futurama, Bel Geddes was obliged
to add a university and many more churches
and temples to Futurama's model landscape
for 1940.)

Futurama's prediction that in the future the
United States would be laced with superhighways on which a driver would be able to cross
the country at high speed without once being
stopped by a traffic light has, of course, come
true. At the time, however, Robert Moses, New
York City's Parks Commissioner, was not convinced. At a meeting of the American Society
of Civil Engineers, he declared that the whole
question of great transcontinental highways
was irrelevant and that they were a needless
and expensive luxury. Bel Geddes responded
that Moses was short-sighted. "Under the
present system," he said, "highways are outmoded before they are completed—not only a
vicious circle but a silly one." In the face of an
annual death toll of 32,000 and enormous
property losses, he could not, he said, be as
calm as Mr. Moses. "I have great respect for
him as Park Commissioner," said Bel Geddes,
"for setting bushes and making playgrounds,
but landscaping along a highway does not
make it safe for present-day travel." (163)
Today, a half-century after this public argument, the nation is indeed overlaid with
superhighways. However, in contradiction to
Bel Geddes's position that planning can
foresee and ease traffic problems, it seems
that bigger and better highways only encour-

age urban sprawl; they stimulate the production of automobiles and discourage the development of mass-transit systems and the building of satellite towns.

After the World's Fair, General Motors put together a traveling show based on Futurama. A poleless "Aerodrome" tent, and twenty-two "Futurliner" tractor-trailer units, many of them containing portions of the original exhibit, toured the country in 1941, gleaning publicity for GM. Bel Geddes also traded on the exhibit by designing a "Futurama" line of furniture, which was exhibited and sold at the Abraham and Straus store in New York.

A prediction was made at the 1939 World Automotive Engineering Congress of the Society of Automotive Engineers that the interior of the car of the future would be, in effect, a comfortable room, with light, movable chairs on a wide, flat floor. Part of the roof would be made of curved, translucent material that would eliminate glare without cutting out the health-giving rays of the sun. Temperature and humidity would be controlled by buttons. A bed would be concealed in a partition between the passenger compartment and the engine compartments, and there would even be lavatory facilities. The car would be drivable from any seat. Alfred P. Sloan, Jr., entered the prediction stakes by declaring that the cars of 1960 would be as different from those of 1941 as the '41 models were from those of 1913, and Charles F. Kettering suggested that the automobile industry would benefit by studying the clothing industry: "Maybe we could learn from the dressmakers who change styles with every season," he observed. "They carry over only a very little from the past and obsolete their product four times a year." (61)

Early in 1939, the first year of the World's Fair, *Vogue* magazine got into the act by asking nine prominent industrial designers who were working on exhibits and buildings at the fair to each create a costume for the future. The editors qualified their interest in industrial designers by pointing out that the "men who shape our destinies and our kitchen sinks,

streamline our telephones and our skyscrapers, men who brought surrealism to the department stores and the be-Tryloned Perisphere to Long Island . . . know all about the problems, the dreams, and the realities that the future has in store for us. They are trained to think ahead; they know tomorrow like their own stream-lined pockets. . . . " "Let them have some fun," proclaimed *Vogue*, "with the Clothes of Tomorrow." (188) These nine designers—Donald Deskey, Gilbert Rohde, Russel Wright, Raymond Loewy, Egmont Arens, Walter Dorwin Teague, George Sakier, Henry Dreyfuss, and Joseph Platt—took on the assignment in the spirit in which it had been presented. They conceived garments that combined their knowledge of technological advances with serio-whimsical predictions of a new society for the year 2000. Their designs were executed by leading fashion houses in New York and illustrated in *Vogue*'s February 1939 issue.

Even though the first season of the fair and its gleaming promises for the future had been dimmed by September's outbreak of war in Europe, it was decided that the fair should be continued. As a number of countries were obliged to close their pavilions, the World's Fair Board elected to play down the international in favor of the national. It was announced that for 1940 the World's Fair would be more like a county fair. The area left vacant when the Soviet pavilion was taken down was renamed the American Common and graced with a bandstand. Many of the exhibits were modified or replaced. The Consumer's Building became the World of Fashion, and model homes built to the Federal Housing Administration's standards were put up near the Electrified Farm.

In order to make up for the fact that the Town of Tomorrow had paid scant attention to contemporary living, an exhibit entitled America at Home was added to the fair for 1940. It consisted of a group of rooms, each designed and furnished by an architect, a decorator, or an industrial designer. The rooms were arranged asymmetrically by Shepard Vogelgesang

"Highways and Horizons,"
designed by Albert Kahn
Associates for the Gen-
eral Motors complex at the
1939 New York World's
Fair. Credit: Albert Kahn
Associates.

The "Rocketport,"
designed for the 1939
New York World's Fair by
Raymond Loewy. Credit:
Underwood and Under-
wood/Bettmann Archives.

The "Parade of Progress"
was a traveling exposition
condensed by L. R. Kiefer
and B. Bergman from
General Motors' pavilion
at the 1939 New York
World's Fair. It toured the
country in 1941. Credit:
Antonin Heythum papers,
George Arents Research
Library, Syracuse
University.

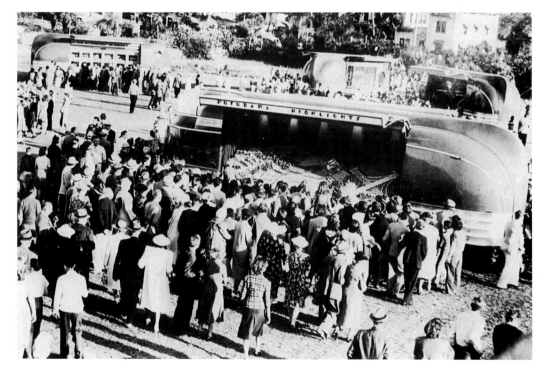

around a central "Unit for Living" designed by Gilbert Rohde. John Vassos's "Musicorner" featured a built-in audio system and a television, and Russel Wright's contribution was a "Winter Hideout in the Adirondacks."

The World's Fair was thus transformed into a promotion of the American way of life, echoing Russel Wright's 1939 attempts to market modern home furnishings under the title American Way. *House and Garden* observed that the new ideas expressed in the exhibition rooms would "surely bend the collective American mind to a much more widespread acceptance of the modern idiom—in architecture, decoration, and landscaping" (91). As Warren Sussman has observed, "For the people, the World of Tomorrow projected not a new world, but a new fantasy world based on the possibilities of modern technology, a world that could be enjoyed because it could be controlled—a veritable Disneyland." (17, 27)

The Metropolitan Museum of Art blithely continued its series of Contemporary American Industrial Art exhibitions in 1940 with a series of room displays created by architects and designers, each of whom followed the "ensemble" concept of the 1925 Paris Exposition. Two displays of particular interest here were retreats from the threatening problems of the day. One, a handicrafted haven called Pennsylvania Hill House, was a collaborative effort of the architect George Howe and the sculptor-craftsman Wharton Esherick. Talbot Hamlin applauded their effort: "The joy of making things for one's self is a very real satisfaction; and when this is joined to that creative imagination in the handling of wood . . . which runs through this room . . . the result is not only beautiful but eminently timeless." (182) The second retreat was Donald Deskey's Sportshack, a prefabricated cabin whose furnishings were multi-functional to serve in turn living, dining, and sleeping needs. (The walls of the Sportshack were paneled with Douglas Fir plywood that had been scraped mechanically to transform the wild grain of the peeled veneer surface into

*The "Musicorner" designed by John Vassos for the "American Home Pavilion" at the 1940 New York World's Fair. Credit: John Vassos papers, George Arents Research Library, Syracuse University.*

Wharton Esherick's interior for the Pennsylvania Hill House at the 1940 New York World's Fair. Credit: Wharton Esherick Museum, Paoli, Pennsylvania.

Donald Deskey's furnishings for the "Sportshack" were designed for mass production. The walls were of "striated" plywood, patented by Deskey. "Cheese-hole" wall decorations were the decorative cliché of the time. Credit: Metropolitan Museum of Art.

parallel yet random striations—a process patented by Deskey in 1942. In texture and color the surfaces suggested the "barnwood" siding and paneling that became popular in the postwar era.)

The editors of *Art Digest* suggested that the Metropolitan Museum's design shows were beginning to show their age by depending too much on established designers, and that "now that the first blush of romance is passing out of industrial design, maybe a few younger designers could turn in a better showing" (60).

The center of focus on modern design was shifting to the Museum of Modern Art, which was beginning to exercise its charter commitment to monitor, shape, and elevate the quality of the man-made environment. In the wake of its successful Machine Art (1934) and Bauhaus (1938) exhibitions, MOMA had initiated a series of annual exhibitions of "Useful Objects." For these exhibitions (usually staged during the Christmas season), the museum selected a variety of products in order to acquaint the public with inexpensive but well-designed items available on the open market. The concept was undoubtedly an extension of a classroom assignment conceived by Alfred H. Barr, Jr., who sent his Wellesley students out to purchase well-designed products selling for between 5 and 25 cents. The idea was introduced at MOMA in 1938 by John McAndrews, curator of architecture and industrial arts. His exhibition "Useful Objects under $5.00" was enthusiastically received by visitors as a buying guide. This exhibit also set the stage for the collaborative Good Design shows held by MOMA and the Merchandise Mart in the early 1950s.

McAndrews, in MOMA's bulletin covering the 1940 exhibition "Useful Objects Under Ten Dollars," proposed a set of standards that would acknowledge that such products were not examples of fine art and should not be judged in aesthetic terms. But McAndrews—although he noted that suitability to purpose, to material, and to manufacturing method were important—still put the primary emphasis on aesthetic quality, as judged by the museum. This point of view helped establish a distinct style that supported MOMA's elitist notion of good taste.

## Preparing for War

*Nor do we believe that an aluminum or stainless steel alloy cocktail shaker is necessary to maintain the morale of the worker on the home front.*

Harvey A. Anderson, 1942 (153)

By 1940, memories of the Depression were fading fast. A housing boom was underway, with some 360,000 new homes built since 1936 and a commensurate increase in the manufacture of domestic furnishings, appliances, and tableware. American manufacturers were gearing up to produce an even greater volume of consumer products and automobiles when the government began its defense program. For a while there was a surge in manufacturing, in anticipation that the production of civilian goods might be curtailed. Despite the fact that prices had gone up, sales of major electrical appliances were more than 30 percent greater than in the same period of the previous year. Throughout the appliance industry, as in the auto industry and other industries likely to be restricted by defense priorities, there was a lively scramble for shares of the market. Then, as the federal government began awarding generous defense contracts that guaranteed profits, production shifted from civilian goods to war materiel.

The high salaries and other inducements offered to war workers put nearly 20 million Americans on the road. Some headed for the steel mills and factories in or near the cities and for the shipyards along the coast, but most headed for defense plants, which were distributed across the country. New "defense towns" boomed into existence almost overnight, creating an unprecedented demand for homes, fixtures, appliances, and automobiles, which the new prosperity had promised. Although wartime restrictions now made many such civilian goods unobtainable, most Americans who remained stateside joined in the patriotic spirit of the day. They took part in bond drives, collected everything from metal scraps to grease for the war effort, and toler-

ated rationing of sugar and gasoline and other impositions on their freedom in order to assure freedom for themselves and others after the war.

The Museum of Modern Art's 1942 exhibition, "Useful Objects in Wartime," was divided into a display of household products made of non-priority materials, a display of products that had been asked for by men and women in the military, and a display of equipment essential for civilian defense. The exhibition did not include products using steel, chromium, tin, aluminum, copper, or nickel, all of which were essential to the war effort. Even plastics, such as acrylic, nylon, and Bakelite, were excluded if they had replaced critical materials. Harvey A. Anderson, chief of the Conservation Division of the War Production Board, had written to the museum's acting director of industrial design, Alice M. Carson, recommending that every effort be made to conserve critical materials:

Our conviction is that men in America's Armed Forces would prefer to see used in the armaments many of the metals ordinarily used in gifts. . . . Nor do we believe that an aluminum or stainless steel alloy cocktail shaker is necessary to maintain the morale of the worker on the home front. . . . These are the convictions you gain when you examine the casualty lists. . . . the manufacturing of non-essentials, the wholesaling of them, the consumer's purchase of them, and the tacit recommendation (through exhibition of them) that they be purchased as a demonstration of "doing your bit," "boosting morale," etc., [has] often come to be regarded as a convenient excuse for "business as usual." (156)

As a result, the exhibition concentrated on products made of glass, ceramics, paper, and plywood. A good percentage of the glass products were either imported items or laboratory glassware now proposed for domestic use. (The latter set off a fashion preference that continued for some years after the war—witness the success of Peter Schlumbohm's Chemex coffeemaker.) Of particular interest were Corning's Pyrex cooking vessels, some of which are now in MOMA's permanent collection. The more elegant glassware produced

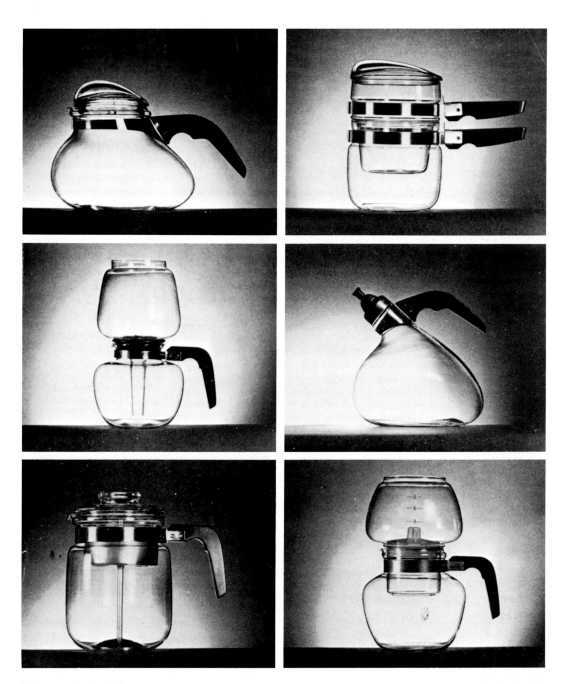

Glassware designed by
Dave Chapman as a war-
time substitute for the
Club Aluminum Products
Company. Credit: (39).

for the Club Aluminum company as its own wartime substitute was not included in either.

The ceramic products in the 1942 exhibition ranged from the handmade decorative bowls of the Natzlers to Steubenville's low-cost line of earthenware (designed by Russel Wright). There was very little representation from the major ceramic manufacturers; either they were too involved in war production to bother or their products were not considered aesthetically suitable.

The substitution of sheet materials such as plywood for furniture and paperboard for toys in the exhibition was a logical wartime expedient. In the case of furniture, the "discovery" of plywood as a convenient way of building furniture, with the least investment in tooling and assembly, lent itself to the flat, amoeba-like "free forms" that were characteristic of the moment and remained in fashion into the postwar era.

The *MOMA Bulletin* describing the 1942 Useful Objects exhibition remarked that Americans had been trained to expect a new version of a product every year and offered discouraging evidence of the " 'conspicuous waste' for which Americans are noted" in the fact that a good design had been superseded by new and inferior "styling" (154). The catch phrase "all change is not progress" was used in a comparison of a toaster that had been presented in the 1934 Machine Art exhibition as forthright and simple versus a 1940 Toastmaster described as being "streamlined as if it were intended to hurtle through the air at 200 miles an hour" (157). In fact, however, the 1934 toaster was a rather crude box, wasteful of materials, labor, and energy, clumsy to use, and difficult to clean. That the 1940 toaster was superior in all these aspects would not be apparent to one who did not understand the challenge of manufacturing products in large quantities with a minimum of energy and materials.

As might be expected, MOMA's survey of the needs of men and women in the service came up with a list of prosaic items that are taken for granted in civilian life but seem to take on great value in extraordinary circumstances—clothespins, hangers, sewing kits, handkerchiefs, scuffs, and so on. There were many requests for small traveling bags that would make it possible (as one WAVE put it) "to boil living and traveling space down so that if alone you went to an airplane, you could carry your own and it wouldn't weigh too much" (155).

The civilian-defense items in the 1942 exhibition included a kerosene lantern, a first-aid kit, a stirrup pump, a water pail, and a wooden sand pail. These stark items contrasted eloquently with the more extravagant forms of the consumer products. In the same year, MOMA staged at least two other exhibitions related to the war effort: Camouflage for Civilian Defense (originally held at the Addison Gallery of American Art, and prepared with the assistance of Pratt Institute) and Posters for Defense (during which visitors were encouraged by the Office of War Information to vote for their favorite).

In 1932, as part of the National Recovery Act, President Roosevelt had established "floors" on the prices of manufactured products in order to help manufacturers already hit hard by the Depression to avoid price-cutting wars. One result was that manufacturers, forbidden to complete on the basis of price, turned their attention to improving the appearance of their products. In 1942 Roosevelt acted in the opposite direction, authorizing the Office of Price Administration (OPA) to establish price "ceilings" on manufactured products. Price limits had already been set on automobiles to coincide with the War Production Board's order to cut production. Now the OPA, in order to keep short supplies from leading to unreasonable retail prices (and thus to inflation) ruled that price limits should be placed on refrigerators, heating and cooking stoves and ranges, washing machines, irons, radio sets, phonographs, and typewriters. This disrupted the normal swing, in a free economy, between

In 1941 the Museum of
Modern Art held an exhi-
bition of award-winning
posters on defense sub-
jects to attract the government's attention to the role
that such posters could
play in what Time maga-
zine called the "pro-
paganda of patriotism."
Included was this power-
ful poster by Jean Carlu.
Credit: Offset Lithograph.

a buyer's market (which favors the consumer) and a seller's market (which, as has been demonstrated again and again in Third World and socialist countries, substantially reduces pressure on the manufacturer to improve his product and deprives the citizens of the freedom of choice). In this case, however, because it was evident to producer and consumer alike that the postwar era would bring a sharp swing back to a buyer's market, the tendency was to continue product improvement and development as much as the price ceilings permitted.

In a few cases it was suggested that the pent-up demand could be met, at least in part, by importing products from countries that were not involved, or not deeply involved, in the war. Raymond Loewy returned from a three-month trip to Latin America with the announcement that a " 'very important' nation" had created a post in its Ministry of Production for an American industrial designer, who would provide advice on how to style products for American consumers. Loewy told the *New York Times* that this country was willing to make a capital investment in manufacturing products for the United States on the condition that Americans would continue buying its products after the war and that the U.S. government would not erect trade barriers to impede the flow.

The Federal Reserve Board, in order to control price inflation brought on by the developing shortages and to conserve national resources for the defense program, imposed limits on instalment purchases of consumer goods. Sales of new and used automobiles—which accounted for half of all instalment buying—were affected immediately as down-payment requirements were raised and loan terms were shortened, and sales of refrigerators, radios, furniture, and other comparatively expensive consumer products were also affected. The theory was that consumers tended to purchase as much as their credit ratings would allow. Then, when they became burdened with instalment payments on relatively expensive products and were unable to make essential

purchases, a drop in the national economy would result. Manufacturers would then be compelled to lower either the quality of a product or its selling price in order to bring it within the consumer's financial reach, thereby jeopardizing their companies and undermining the confidence of their stockholders. Even if the manufacturer decided to maintain the quality of his product but to reduce the quantity produced, both manufacturer and consumer would be penalized and inflation would continue to rise.

It was thought that a manufacturer who found it difficult to reduce production might be compelled to increase his promotional budget in an attempt to persuade people to buy his product even though they might be unable to afford it. Again, the result would be an increase in the rate of inflation. Thus, any change that disturbed the natural flow of products threatened to induce inflation or to create pent-up demand (which carried an inflationary charge of its own). Nevertheless, the government was obligated to increase its control of the nation's material resources if it was to meet the goals that had been set for the defense program. Specifications were written for replacing materials considered essential for military preparedness with substitutes. For example, to conserve lumber for building military cantonments and temporary housing for workers, the military substituted corrugated and solid-fiber board for wood in its shipping containers. In another case, the Office of Priority Management put aluminum under rigid controls. It ruled, for example, that the number of aluminum ice trays that could be sold with a refrigerator would be restricted according to the size of the refrigerator, with one tray allowed for a small unit and four for the largest one. To compensate for the inconvenience, a research agency was commissioned to explore the possibility of plastic ice trays.

In another move to control the volume and the types of products that could be manufactured, the War Production Board reduced the variety of enameled kitchen wares from a peacetime total of 450 different items to 25 in order to

Wurlitzer's Model 850 jukebox, designed by Paul Fuller in 1941. Baroque ornamentation notwithstanding, this machine reigned supreme until the postwar "bubble" model was introduced.

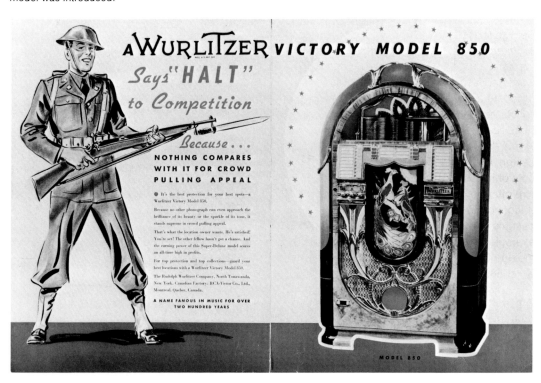

conserve steel. However, no such restrictions were placed on glassware. As a result, glass percolators, frying pans, casseroles, and the like appeared on the market as temporary replacements for steel ones. The technological necessity of departing from traditional typeforms resulted in many handsome new forms, some of which permanently replaced the forms of their steel predecessors. Moreover, Pyrex—a tempered glass that could withstand impact and changes in temperature—became popular. Many products conceived as a result of the emergency entered everyday use in this way.

In other cases, the WPB *encouraged* the manufacture of a particular product because of its value to the defense program. For example, in order to conserve the steel that would have gone into food cans, a bank of materials was established for the manufacture of large commercial dehydrators that would preserve food by drying. The WPB also agreed to permit limited quantities of plywood, heaters, and smaller motors to be drawn from this bank for the manufacture of some 106,000 small dehydrators to be used by farmers and victory gardeners.

George Nelson, a contributing editor to *Architectural Forum* at the time, found philosophical comfort in the observation that, in wartime, designers were, "after decades of functionalist preaching," at last producing functionally designed objects on a tremendous scale. "In an extreme emergency," he wrote, "we turn unquestionably to functional design. It is important to note that . . . products of ingenuity, economy, and utmost exploitation of limited materials have quite unconsciously become the most satisfying designs of our machine civilization." (55) The examples that accompanied this statement included a Bakelite gun-turret seat, a Lucite bomber nose, and a celluloid gas-mask lens.

Jukeboxes continued to be manufactured; in fact, they were considered essential to wartime morale. (Although coin-operated, electrically amplified record-playing machines had appeared on the market in 1927, it was not until 1934, when the Wurlitzer company introduced its extravagantly designed machines, that the name *jukebox* came into common use.) The jukebox reached its peak popularity during the war, when it became a focal point in the social lives of soldiers away from home and war workers seeking relaxation and companionship. It reached its ultimate typeform in 1946 with Wurlitzer's model 1015, designed by Paul Fuller.

## The War Effort

The Jeep (General Purpose vehicle), one of the most memorable vehicles to come out of World War II, became a symbol of no-nonsense ingenuity and daring military adventure. It looked like the work of a mechanic, but the conviction of its proportions and the strength and consistency of its detailing elevated it into an ideal typeform that any industrial designer would have been proud to take credit for. Its form still echoes in the scout vehicles of almost every country. General George C. Marshall described it as America's greatest contribution to modern warfare.

The Jeep's development began in 1929 when Sir Herbert Austin contracted with a group organized as the American Austin Company to build his English automobile in the United States. Since the Austin was considered too conservative-looking for American tastes, Alexis de Sakhnoffsky, a prominent stylist of custom automobiles, was hired to modify the car's rounded, toylike appearance.

From the moment of its introduction, the American Austin was popular with movie actors as an amusing plaything. It was a subject of conversation, comment, cartoons, and radio gags. Everybody talked about it, but few bought it. The company filed for bankruptcy in 1934 and was bought at auction by Ron Evans, a sales entrepreneur, at a cost lower than the salvage value of the factory. Evans reorganized the company in 1936 as the Bantam Automobile Company and hired Sakhnoffsky a second time to give the car an even more rakish appearance. Once again, however, it failed to attract enough customers to survive, despite the dedication of a band of small-car enthusiasts. Nor did it help sales that the Bantam was used for advertising purposes by Coca-Cola, Firestone, and other companies, or that it was chosen to lead the parade that kicked off the New York World's Fair.

However, the Bantam company had supplied the Pennsylvania National Guard with several roadsters for use during its field maneuvers in 1939, and the military brass realized that a

*"Nose art" on an Army Air Forces B-26 bomber. Credit: Randall Bond.*

Bantam came close enough to the government's specifications and deadlines to be awarded the first production contract for the Jeep. With its soft, rounded hood, radiator, and form details, the product did not inspire confidence at first. Credit: National Automotive History Collection, Detroit Public Library.

The Willys prototype, with an additional six weeks for development, had the Bantam Jeep as a design target. It met the technical requirements and surpassed the Bantam version in character, with a squared-off form and powerful-looking details. Credit: Library of Congress.

mechanized army would need a small, versatile, powerful, and durable command and reconnaissance vehicle.

In mid-1940 the Army released specifications to more than 100 manufacturers asking for bids on a four-wheel-drive vehicle that could operate at a low speed of 3 miles per hour if necessary, with a maximum weight of 1,300 pounds and a 500-pound payload. Only two companies responded: Willys and Bantam. It appears in retrospect that Bantam may have had the advantage, because the initial specifications seem to have been drafted around the Bantam roadster.

The Jeep was designed by a committee of military and civilian engineers who managed to suppress personal bias and, under the threat of war, to conceive a landmark vehicle. In order to put an end to the controversy about its origin, the Federal Trade Commission announced that "the idea of creating the Jeep was originated by the American Bantam Company of Butler, Pennsylvania, in collaboration with certain officers in the United States Army." The Willys company was ordered by the FTC to "cease and desist from representing" that it had "created and designed the automotive vehicle known as the Jeep" (62). (Willys was permitted, however, to advertise that it had contributed to the Jeep's development.)

The Bantam prototype was tested and accepted. However, since the Bantam company could not meet the Army's demand for 75 Jeeps a day, production contracts were also awarded to Willys and to Ford. Several Ford components, and a more powerful and dependable engine developed by Delmar B. Roos of Willys, replaced the original Bantam equivalents. By mid 1941, Willys and Ford had virtually taken over Jeep production, with orders between them amounting eventually to some 650,000. Bantam, unable to keep up, produced only 3,000 Jeeps—some of which were shipped to the USSR. Ironically, the company that had originally created the Jeep survived until 1946 primarily by building trailers for Jeeps produced by other companies.

The first-generation industrial designers (those born around 1900) had been active in illustration and theatre design before they began to direct their creative attention to the products they had been illustrating. Somehow, they found a narrow foothold between architecture and arts and crafts. With their reputation enhanced by the dramatic market success of some of their products during the Depression, they were extolled as wizards of aesthetics with a down-to-earth approach to marketing.

As the war clouds gathered in Europe, the U.S. government looked to Henry Dreyfuss, Raymond Loewy, and Walter Dorwin Teague to design strategy rooms for the Joint Chiefs of Staff. The military planning and strategy facility consisted of two identical large rooms and a small workshop for the preparation and storage of materials. One of the large rooms was fitted with a world map painted on a curved surface 12 feet high and 25 feet long; the other was equipped for the projection of movies, slides, and diagrams. On a deadline of six weeks, the furnishings were built in the loft of an old brewery in New York and then transported to Washington for installation in the Public Health Service Building. This project was to serve as a prototype for the planning facilities of many transportation authorities and utility companies.

Dreyfuss and his associates also took on the assignment to design and build four rotating globes, each 13 feet in diameter—one for Roosevelt, one for Churchill, one for Stalin, and one for the Joint Chiefs of Staff. (Because of the restrictions on aluminum, the globes were constructed of laminated hoops of cherrywood.) The Dreyfuss office was also assigned to restudy the cumbersome 105-millimeter anti-aircraft gun. By reorganizing the components, the designers were able to reduce the critical field-setup time of the weapon from 15 to 3½ minutes. Other military

projects taken on by this office included work on trailer-mounted field equipment for aircraft detection, radar tactical instruments for bombers, and (later) launch platforms for Nike missiles. By the end of World War II, Dreyfuss had also worked on over 100 communication projects for Bell Laboratories.

Some of the first wartime projects assigned to the Loewy office were to provide assistance to the Office of Strategic Services in the Department of Visual Presentation. Other work included development of new ideas for the Medical and Engineering Corps, for Ordnance, and for the Quartermaster General. For the Medical Air Corps they modified a military glider into a field hospital that could be towed into a combat area, landed, and set up for operation. They also designed tents, swamp shoes, and a comprehensive first-aid kit for airborne troops. When Paris was liberated, Loewy—a naturalized American citizen—spoke on the radio to his former countrymen.

Teague and his associates worked for the armed forces (principally for the Naval Bureau of Ordnance) from 1942 into the postwar period. In 1946 they received a citation from the Navy for their outstanding work on more than 150 projects.

*This photo of Walter Dorwin Teague (at left) in his orderly drafting room supports his view of "this new profession of industrial design in which one man of restless mind and many interests assembles around him a group of variously trained co-workers." Credit: (40, 227). Photograph by Stowe Myers.*

The first steps toward a "science" of design are evident in the successful attempts of these and other designers to improve the combat effectiveness of military products. They demonstrated that the designer's understanding of human psychology could be applied to making the interiors of military vehicles, bunkers, barracks, and hospital wards more functional and more hospitable. For example, Egmont Arens recommended ways that certain colors could be used to make important controls and instruments stand out and, on the other hand, how other colors could be used to make bomb shelters, command centers, and factories more bearable and efficient. He also recommended color-coding the wiring, the hydraulic lines, and the control systems of aircraft. William Purcell, who joined Henry Dreyfuss's firm in 1946, writes that "human factors research began in earnest in the decade of 1940 . . . encouraged by military requirements and the recognition of industry that this was a new and potent sales feature to be added to its products" (199).

George Cushing, who (with Thomas G. W. Nevell as partner and Raymond Spilman as chief designer) worked on nondetectable mines, walkie-talkie radios, radar, shelters, and other equipment for the Signal Corps during the war years, writes that "perhaps the greatest contribution by the company was in the field of educational communication . . . we developed visual aids, training aids, technical books and manuals for all branches of the service" (194). George Kosmak and William Pahlman were involved in camouflage or in the design and installation of military and medical installations. Though most of his colleagues served the war effort as civilians, John Vassos "joined the Armed Forces and went to war as Captain in the Engineering Corps in charge of camouflage at the Third Air Force Headquarters" (223).

During World War I, Norman Bel Geddes had invented a chess-like war game in which toy soldiers and model vehicles and combat equipment (including some weapons that were to become a reality in World War

II) "fought" on a panoramic "battlefield" mounted on a large board at shoulder level. In the 1930s, as the war clouds were gathering over Europe, it became a popular evening pastime in New York City among certain luminaries from the theater, literature, and architecture and certain diplomats, manufacturers, politicians, and military personnel. This game led to assignments to devise techniques for recording naval and military battles through the use of model photography. Bel Geddes developed a bank of scale-model fighting ships, airplanes, tanks, and other military equipment of many nations. Many of the models were made in sterling silver by Cartier craftsmen (as the model automobiles in the Futurama had been). Using these models and realistic panoramas, the Bel Geddes office developed photographic recognition training programs for the Army and the Navy. Other war-related model assignments for the Bel Geddes office included the simulation of a shoreline near Tunis (used in 1944 to brief landing forces) and a number of pre-invasion models for events that never occurred, such as a battle of Gibraltar, landings on the north coast of Germany, and a tank battle in the USSR. There were also assignments from *Life* magazine to build models of several naval and military battles in order to dramatize these events for its readers. A 1944 exhibition at the Museum of Modern Art featured enlargements of some of the *Life* photographs and a team of Bel Geddes employees working on a model of a hypothetical battle along a river bank. After the war, Bel Geddes was asked by the Navy to contribute to the official record of the Battle of Midway and commissioned by the *Encyclopaedia Brittanica* to build and photograph models of the building of the Great Pyramid and the Panama Canal.

The second generation of industrial designers may be taken to include those born around 1910, who had recently completed or were in the process of completing their formal education in areas peripheral to industrial design when the bottom fell out of the stock market. By and large they were more broadly educated than the first generation. With their senior colleagues, many managed to stay in practice during World War II by turning to problems involving the safety and efficiency of human operators, to the development of substitutes for priority materials, to communications, to technical publications, to models, or to camouflage.

Between the two world wars, a number of European designers, disillusioned with political and economic affairs in Europe, had decided to take their chances in the United States, despite the Depression. Many of their younger American colleagues were graduates in architecture who, finding jobs or commissions scarce during the Depression, had gone into industrial design, whose star was ascending and whose academic base was as yet undeveloped.

Raymond S. Sandin, who had come to the United States from Sweden in 1926 to study architecture and design at the Armour Institute of Technology in Chicago, took a position with the Albert Peck company as a designer of restaurant, hotel, and institutional kitchens and equipment. In 1935 he joined the Hotpoint company as a designer in the commercial cooking equipment division. During World War II his major work consisted of kitchen planning. (At one time, he had twenty young women under his direction.) He remained with Hotpoint as an industrial design manager after the company became part of General Electric.

Dave Chapman (1909–1978), also an architecture graduate of the Armour Institute of Technology, was on the design staff for Chicago's Century of Progress Exposition until 1933, when he joined the Montgomery Ward company as an architect. When Ann Swainson was hired away from Revere Copper and Brass as a "fashion coordinator" to develop Ward's corporate design department, she had Chapman transferred to the new department as head of product design. By 1935 Chapman had eighteen designers working for him, most of them architects. Chapman credits Ann Swainson with having also fostered the

careers of Joseph Palma, Fred Preiss, and Richard Latham, who went on to become important industrial designers on their own. In 1936 Chapman left Montgomery Ward to establish an independent design practice. His first employee was William Goldsmith, who would later become a partner in the firm (along with Kim Yamasaki and Paul Specht). Chapman continued to practice design during World War II, working primarily with Knapp-Monarch, Apex Washers, and Club Aluminum in adapting their products to materials that were not under wartime control.

Robert H. Hose (1915–1977) was graduated from the University of Minnesota in 1937 and took a master's degree in architecture at the Massachusetts Institute of Technology. In 1939 he went to work at the Bell Telephone Laboratories, working in a small industrial design laboratory for which Henry Dreyfuss was serving as a consultant. During the war Hose and Dreyfuss worked together on some 115 communications projects, and in 1946 Dreyfuss invited Hose to join his firm as an associate. After becoming a partner, Hose left the Dreyfuss office in 1961 to open his own consulting firm.

Montgomery Ferar (1910–1982) also studied architecture at MIT. Upon graduation he went to work as a designer at General Motors, where he met and worked with Carl Sundberg (1911–1982), whose background was in custom car bodies. In 1934 the two of them left GM to begin a lifelong partnership in industrial design. The success of their first product—a plastic mousetrap named the Mouseoleum—enabled them to move their operation out of Sundberg's basement. Sundberg and Ferar's earliest design assignments were for small plastic parts for various manufacturers who used their concepts to interest prospective clients in molded plastics. In 1940 they established their own comprehensive model shop, in which the three-dimensional presentations for which the firm became well known were produced. During the war, their firm continued to design major appliances for

Sears, Roebuck and Whirlpool, and industrial and commercial equipment for the Square D company. Sundberg and Ferar were also employed by IBM to assist that company's engineers and designers in the development of typewriters and early electronic calculating equipment.

Other second-generation designers, whose academic specialties ranged from engineering to the fine arts, were assigned (whether as employees of corporations, as civilian employees of the military, or as members of the armed forces) to the development of two- and three-dimensional training, technical, and tactical aids and manuals for the war effort. Theodore G. Clement, for example, began his career in industry in the industrial engineering department of Kodak Park Works. After he became aware of the potential for design at Kodak, and with encouragement from Walter Dorwin Teague, who was serving as a consultant to the company, he applied for a position in the camera works and was taken on as a renderer. During the war, he wrote and illustrated manuals for military equipment. For a time, he worked on the design of equipment for the Manhattan Project. "I found myself," he writes, " 'streamlining' components much as we did on consumer products but for electronic reasons, not aesthetic." (193) Harper Landell (1918–) also made his way into industrial design by way of engineering. During the war he worked for the Baldwin company on the design of the M-3 tank and of tank destroyers, and then for the Eastern Aircraft Division of General Motors, where he established and headed the technical publications section for the FM-2 carrier fighter. After the war Landell joined the firm of Harold Van Doren; after Van Doren's death Landell opened his own design office.

George Beck (1908–1977), a graduate of the Chicago Academy of Fine Arts, worked under Ann Swainson in the fledgling design department at Sears, Roebuck in the middle of the Depression (an era he once called the "heyday of industrial design"). Between 1936 and 1942 he was assistant director of design, under Ray Patten, at General Electric in Bridgeport,

Connecticut; then he became manager of industrial design in GE's new electronics department. During the war, he produced technical publications for the government while, on his own, designing radios and televisions for the postwar era. (Some of his radio and TV designs were made up in plaster in GE's model shop.) Soon after the war, Beck and his department moved to GE's new Electronics Park at Syracuse.

William F. H. Purcell (1911–), a South African, had studied engineering at Cambridge University before coming to the United States in 1937 to study architecture at MIT. During the war he served in Washington in the Canadian government's Department of Munitions and Supply. At war's end he joined the office of Henry Dreyfuss, and he became a partner in 1949.

The U.S. Department of the Navy had a particular interest in the contribution that designers could make to its part in the war effort. Victor Schreckengost was made head of design in its Department of Training Devices, where he was joined by Henry Glass and Paul MacAlister. Francis Braun, a 1935 "art in industry" graduate of the Applied Arts department of the University of Cincinnati, served in the Navy's Office of Research and Invention in Washington, which was responsible for training materials. He was also assigned as a designer to coordinate the appearance and the function of aircraft cockpits. Robert Zeidman, one of the first graduates of the pioneering program in industrial design at the Carnegie Institute of Technology, served in the Navy the Pacific arena, designing and producing foam relief maps and models of coast lines and other training devices. William Renwick, a graduate architect, served in the Navy as a materials engineer. Arthur BecVar (1911–), a fine arts graduate of Notre Dame with master's work at Charles University in Prague and engineering courses at Purdue, left his design job at Revere Copper and Brass to work in the Navy's Ordnance Department.

Several designers were employed by the federal government in one or another of its wartime administrative agencies. Edward Wormley (1908–) worked for two years as chief of the Furnishings Unit of the Office of Price Administration; Alfred Auerbach, under whom Wormley served, credited him with attaining price stabilization in the furniture industry during the period when shortages of materials and machines made it extremely difficult for that industry, because of the highly variable styles and contents of its merchandise, to meet the demands put upon it by the wartime housing program. Gordon Obrig served with the Federal Housing Authority at the planning level.

George Nelson, Eliot Noyes, and Charles Eames were young architects who did not go into architecture or industrial design immediately upon graduation. Instead, they found positions in related areas from which they were to make contributions to the quality and character of the practice of design in the United States—one through an architectural magazine, one through a museum, and one by means of innovative furniture.

Upon graduating from Yale, George Nelson (1908–1986) was awarded the Rome Prize, which took him abroad for a year early in the Depression. On his return from Rome, where he had become acquainted with the nature and the quality of design on the Continent, he found a challenging position as an assistant editor of *Architectural Forum*. In 1943 he was named co-managing editor of that publication and head of the *Fortune, Forum* experimental department of Time, Incorporated. During the war, *Architectural Forum* reflected Nelson's interest in the broader impact of design. He suggested that some materials developed for military purposes might be adapted to civilian use. For example, he proposed that the new process used to produce lightweight ammunition boxes, in which a laminate of plastic and fabric was molded in long sections around a rectangular mandrel, could be used to manufacture household storage cabinets "so inexpensive that they could be discarded without a twinge of the owner's conscience when they have served their purpose" (56).

Eliot Noyes (1910–1977) went to New York in 1940, fresh from his architectural studies at Harvard and a brief apprenticeship with Walter Gropius and Marcel Breuer in Cambridge, to take a position as director of the new department of industrial design at the Museum of Modern Art. His appointment was an inspired one because, despite his lack of curatorial experience, he had an innate sense of the best in American material culture and an ability to cross effortlessly the senseless boundaries that suspicion had erected between the various design specializations. Noyes's most important effort in this vein was the organization and staging—in collaboration with several major department stores—of a competition entitled Organic Design in Home Furnishings. His proclaimed goal for this 1940 exhibition was to discover a group of designers capable of creating a "useful and beautiful environment for today's living in terms of furniture, lighting and fabrics" (151).

The principal awards in Noyes's competition went to Cranbrook Academy graduates and staff members Charles Eames (1907–1978) and Eero Saarinen (1910–1961) for a combination of chairs and storage pieces. (Saarinen was as distinguished as Nelson, Noyes, or Eames; however, despite his forays into furniture design, his forte was architecture.) Eames and Saarinen's use of layered veneers in their chairs echoed methods that were being developed for other mass-produced products, and their cabinetry advanced the principles of standardization, interchangeability, and functional adaptability. The chairs, it was said in *Architectural Forum*, offered "the most convincing glimpse of the future, when such pieces may well be squeezed out on huge presses like Henry Ford's new plastic fenders" (49).

The Museum of Modern Art and its collaborating department stores had committed themselves to see through to production the award winners in the Organic Design competition, but the furniture industry did not have the technology to produce the unconventional molded plywood chairs at a price within the

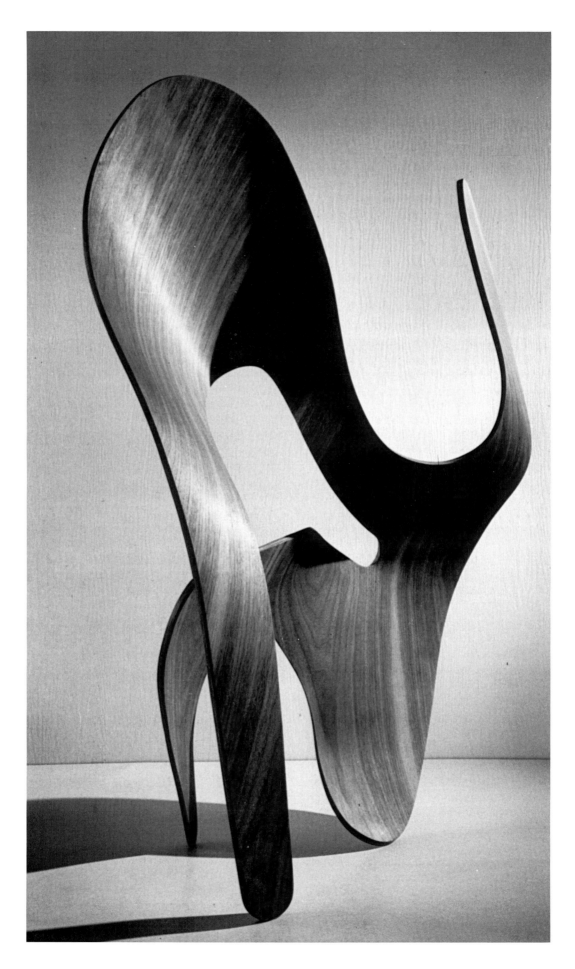

A laminated-wood sculpture created by Ray Eames in 1942. Experiments such as this established the formal and technical base from which laminated furniture would be developed. Credit: Ray Eames. Photograph by Charles Eames.

The Eameses' experiments with laminated wood resulted in a commission from the Navy to produce these molded-wood splints. Credit: Ray Eames. Photograph by Charles Eames.

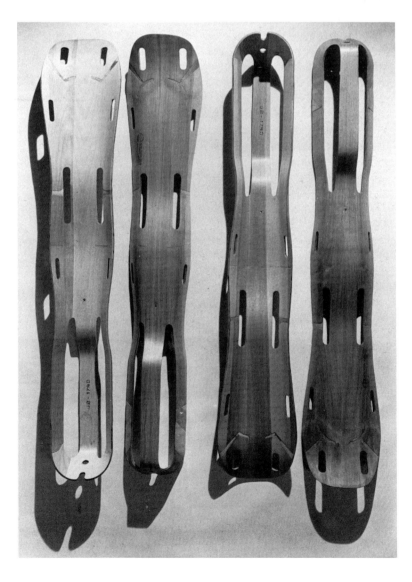

reach of its intended public, and did not seem interested in developing it. Neither Eames nor Saarinen, however, lost faith in the ultimate value of their concept, and its impact on the industry and on the design-conscious community was strong enough to start preparing the way for the postwar acceptance of a fresh character in American products. The new forms were in harmony with the movement in the plastic arts toward amorphism, and with the social commitment to simplicity and modularity.

In 1941, Eames and his wife Ray Kaiser (who had worked with Eames and Saarinen at Cranbrook) moved to California, where Eames had taken a job at the MGM Studios. They continued to experiment with molded laminated wood for furniture, sculpture, and other applications, building a press and molds and developing methods for shaping and gluing veneers with pressure supplied by sandbags and a bicycle pump. With the inspired naiveté of all inventors, they developed the processes that would eventually be used for mass production.

Eames's contact with personnel connected with the Naval Hospital in San Diego led to the idea of replacing the awkward and uncomfortable padded metal splint then used to set and hold broken legs with a light, shallow wooden trough. The Navy was impressed enough with the Eames Splint to place an order in 1942 for 5,000 units. To meet this commitment, Eames formed a company with John Entenza, then editor and publisher of the magazine *California Arts and Architecture*. With Marion Overby (a sculptor who had been an assistant to Carl Milles at Cranbrook), Gregory Ain (an architect), and Herbert Matter (an artist and photographer), they transformed three empty stores in Venice, California, into a factory, designed and built production equipment, and trained local housewives and itinerant workers. The order was filled within three months.

After the Eames Splint was brought to the attention of Colonel E. S. Evans, whose company, Evans Products of Detroit, was interested in molded plywood, the original company became the Molded Products Division of Evans Products and the production of the Eames Splint was increased. Other products followed, including a molded plywood stretcher and components for gliders and prefabricated houses. The Venice factory was kept in operation as a research laboratory for experiments in wood lamination, glue chemistry, and electronic heating.

After the Organic Design competition, Eliot Noyes took leave of his position at MOMA to enter the Army Air Forces as a major. Before the war he had been an amateur glider pilot, and he spent the war years in Washington helping to establish and administer the armed forces' glider program. In the Pentagon he met Thomas J. Watson, Jr., who became interested in sailplanes and friendly with Noyes. Later, Watson would bring Noyes in as consultant design director for the IBM Corporation.

# The Housing Front

*They are out designing all these things, pioneering ahead of us and making us rapidly obsolete.*

Eugene Raskin (181)

Particularly after waterproof synthetic resins replaced animal glue as a bonding agent in the late 1930s, plywood sheets with various surface treatments came into use as stressed skin panels in buses, such as the Victory Liners manufactured for Santa Fe Trailways. Plywood was also used in Howard Hughes's huge "Spruce Goose" transport airplane. Temporary housing, and especially prefabricated housing, depended so heavily on plywood paneling that it became identified in the public mind as a hasty and cheap substitute—even though, with waterproof glue, it proved superior to solid wood.

Any reservations that Americans had about plywood should have been assuaged by the handsome furniture and other items that Swedish and Finnish designers were creating with veneers of birch, beech, and other hardwoods native to northern Europe. At the New York World's Fair, the Aaltos' dramatic Finnish exhibit and Sven Markelius's masterful Swedish pavilion, along with furniture by Aalto and by Karl Matthson, brought aesthetic respectability to modern design in laminated wood. Scandinavian architects and designers had developed a cohesive modern style that went beyond the clinical austerity of the German functionalists. Their innovative furniture of bent and molded veneer layers had something democratic about it; it offered escape from the presumptive aristocracy of dark mahogany and walnut styles that had dominated American furniture for so long.

In addition to Eames and Saarinen, Russel Wright and Gilbert Rohde were designing and seeing to the manufacture of light wood furniture in the United States, and other Americans were designing and building prototypes of furniture that could be band-sawn from plywood sheets and shipped knocked down for on-site assembly. (Experiments with plywood provided a favorite academic exercise during the war and for some years afterward.) The new concept of standardized components (e.g. tops, side panels, and legs) that could be assembled into a variety of finished pieces was entirely in harmony with the philosophy of prefabricated housing and has since become established practice in the manufacture of office furniture. The movement toward systemized, mass-produced furniture carried the Herman Miller company away from traditional furniture design and construction, provided the basis for the founding of the Knoll company, and eventually influenced many major American office and institutional furniture companies to move into modern furniture design.

John McAndrews of the Museum of Modern Art was frustrated by the unwillingness of the housing industry to learn from mass production. He believed that, with standardization and mass-production practices already familiar to other industries, efficient and well-equipped kitchens and bathrooms could be produced and made available at reasonable cost. The crucial problem facing American architects, he proposed, was not so much a matter of construction or of aesthetics; it was the humanitarian and social challenge of satisfying the demand for adequate housing. McAndrews suggested that if skyscrapers were the monuments of the 1920s, housing developments might be the monuments of the 1940s. To a maddening degree his prediction was realized, not as a result of peacetime accountability but rather as a desperate answer to the severe housing problems brought on by the war.

The wartime housing shortage was due not only to the fact that hundreds of thousands of military personnel were on the move but also to the fact that workers and their families were caught up in the greatest labor migration the United States had ever known. Hundreds of new communities were established, many in out-of-the-way locations. Site preparation was often inadequate, and there was little time for the establishment of community centers, fire and police departments, and schools. Whether site-built or prefabricated, the housing was modest, often hastily built, and inevitably looked upon as a war-related inconvenience. The need for a morale-building program to draw the American public into a cohesive force working toward the common goal was evident.

One attempt to increase public, professional, and political awareness of the housing problem was a major exhibition staged in 1942 by the Museum of Modern Art, sponsored by the National Committee on the Housing Emergency in cooperation with the National Housing Authority, and supported by the Farm Security Administration. The exhibition was designed and assembled by Eliot Noyes, with George Nelson and Edgar Kaufmann, Jr., as advisors. Its premise was that "an appreciation of the necessity for providing a war worker with the comfort of a proper home for himself and his family will lead to close cooperation between Federal officials and the officials and citizens of different localities in the United States" (152).

The profession of architecture was in disarray. Still feeling the effects of the Depression in building, and disturbed by the attention given to industrial design at the New York World's Fair (which some considered an invasion of their sacred precinct), architects were now being hit with restrictions on private building handed down by the newly established Federal Defense Construction Administration (FDCA). With a few notable exceptions, architects found it difficult if not impossible to work under the FDCA's controls on the design and building of air, sea, and ground bases, cantonments and training facilities, defense factories, and housing for workers. Those who tried to join the preparedness program often found their attempts complicated by federal employees who were jealous of their new prerogatives. Furthermore, few architects had any interest in low-cost housing. Most looked upon prefabrication as threatening the sanctity of their craft. Edwin Bergstrom, president of the American Institute of Architects, empathized with those of his colleagues who

were reluctant to apply their professional skills to low-cost housing; nevertheless, he observed that they were being forced by circumstances to modify their historic individualism and broaden their area of activity.

The critic Douglas Haskell suggested that industrial design offered alternative employment for architects who were not involved or interested in low-cost housing. "Do you believe," Architectural Record had asked its readers in a May 1940 survey, "you could improve your economic condition if existing ethical restraints were liberalized, thereby permitting you to duplicate all services offered by industrial designers?" (57) To support his response, Haskell pointed to the success of two exhibitions: "America at Home" at the New York World's Fair and "Contemporary American Industrial Art" at the Metropolitan Museum of Art. His position was that no one was better qualified to design furnishings and household accessories than the architects of the buildings that contained them. He concluded, with understandable and mistaken bias, that "the design of household objects led historically to the creation of the whole realm of industrial design" (57). Haskell was manifesting the general concern among architects that industrial designers were taking work away from them. Industrial designers, the architect Eugene Raskin complained, "realize that people use not only buildings, but furniture, autos, ships, trains, planes, clothes, canned goods, fountain pens— and so on through the whole list of material goods. . . . They are out designing all these things, pioneering ahead of us, and making us rapidly obsolete." (181)

William Lescaze, a Swiss-born architect who had tried in the 1930s to walk a line between the two professions, was convinced that the architect "did the job of the industrial designer." "The architect," he wrote in 1942, "used the same techniques he had developed for architectural problems, the technique of requirements and the technique of materials, and he started the improvement of the design situation even though the objects he designed were not at that time manufactured in large quantities and were, therefore, expensive. Concentrating on the whole, he didn't try to market his designs for the accessories—for his own financial gain. He should have." (21, 172–173) Therein lies the rub. Industrial design is more than the development of products for a prepaid or captive market. It serves an open, competitive market in which the designer must—before a financial exchange is made—take into equal consideration the fitting of a product to human expectations and needs and the adaptation of the product to economical yet safe manufacturing processes.

The architects might have responded to the challenge of wartime housing with the daring and imagination that the crisis demanded. Instead, they either ignored it altogether, ridiculed the design attempts of the federal housing agencies, or complained that they were not getting their share of the action.

Although mass production was being welcomed in every other realm, the thought of houses rolling off production lines was too much for most architects. In 1943 *Architectural Forum* tried to allay their concern by suggesting that they could look forward to being retained by prefabricators as competition in the field increased. S. W. Morgan, dean of the school of architecture at Princeton, observed that the history of automobile design promised many opportunities for architects. Those who would control the design of "models" coming out of the factories, he observed, would be "part of a hierarchy, rather than independent professionals," but they would "be well paid and have the security which group action brings" (51).

Prefabricated housing was regarded as primarily a means of providing minimal shelter for oil-field laborers, migrant farm workers, and the like. Even the housing shortages of the Depression had not, it seems, convinced the general public that low-cost factory-made dwellings were fit habitation. Furthermore, the notion of putting workers into housing manufactured under government subsidy was considered by some to be socialistic and, therefore, inimical to the American way. Even

so, the possibilities of prefabrication of one sort or another were explored by the Farm Security Administration, the Forest Products Laboratory, and other Federal agencies. In addition, the Purdue University Research Foundation and other respected private organizations, such as the Albert F. Bemis Foundation and the John B. Pierce Foundation, carried on research into alternative structural methods. The Army and the Navy entered the defense housing program, walking a thin line between the American Federation of Labor (which was protecting the interests of building craftsmen) and the Congress of Industrial Organizations (which was equally concerned with the interests of factory workers). Established manufacturers of prefabricated houses were left to scramble for the remainder of the market while the architectural profession stood apart, unwilling to sacrifice the monumentality upon which architectural reputations were built for the anonymity of human service. Architects were (and remain) reluctant to accept mass production as a sensible way of meeting public needs. The detractors of prefabrication rejected the premise that it was motivated by social conscience, claiming that hastily erected prefab communities were instant slums.

The trailer (or "mobile home"), thought of during the war as a temporary expedient, became the dominant form of low-cost housing, preempting the role that prefabrication had been expected to play. In 1941, the year in which the federal government approved a program for a flying squadron of trailers to meet housing emergencies, a parade of fifty trailers built by the Alma company passed in review before government officials in Washington. By 1943, more than 125,000 of the country's 200,000 trailers had been subsidized by the government to meet war-related housing shortages. When the National Housing Authority declared that the housing crisis had passed, it ruled (undoubtedly with a nod to the contracting establishment) that, since trailers were factory-built, they did not qualify as houses and therefore could no longer be purchased with federal housing funds. As a

*Neighbors calling on new tenants in one of the houses built in 1941 on a hastily prepared site near a defense plant in Connecticut. Credit: Library of Congress.*

*This housing for war workers near the Martin Aircraft plant was more permanent and showed the results of research in prefabrication technology. Credit: Library of Congress.*

*These trailer homes were ordered by the Farm Security Administration to provide emergency housing for civilian shipyard workers. Credit: UPI/Bettman Archives.*

result, the number of trailer manufacturers dropped from 105 to fewer than 50. Even so, the mobile home had found itself a place in American society. The architects did not see it as a threat.

The wartime need for housing attracted the attention of a few innovative designers and architects, whose proposals stimulated interest in alternative materials and methods for building and equipping a home. These innovators helped pave the way for new technologies that found their way into housing (often in the guise of traditional styles).

Among the innovators was Walter Neff, who in 1941 proposed a structure that would be created by inflating a hemispherical rubber balloon and then spraying it with Gunite concrete over wire-mesh reinforcement. Neff claimed that the resulting shell-like form would be easier to camouflage than a conventional house and would provide more protection from bombs and incendiary devices. Although several prototypes were erected, the idea proved too expensive for further consideration. Martin Wagner, an émigré from Berlin, proposed a monocoque metal structure of similar shape, which he had originally conceived as a shelter for Turkish earthquake survivors; it, too, proved to be too expensive.

P. N. Nissen, a Canadian Army engineer, is responsible for the steel half-cylinder that came to be known in the United States as the Quonset hut (after the naval base where the first one was built). A variant called the Victory House, developed by the Pierce Foundation, proved too spartan for further consideration.

One would have thought that the International Style would be most appropriate for emergency housing. Indeed, many dwellings in that style were put up; however, they were universally rejected as inhospitable, even as temporary shelters.

The German émigrés Konrad Wachsmann and Walter Gropius established the General Panel Corporation to manufacture a prefabricated

One of the patent drawings for the Dymaxion Deployment Unit. Credit: U.S. Patent Office.

The Dymaxion Deployment Unit. Credit: Library of Congress.

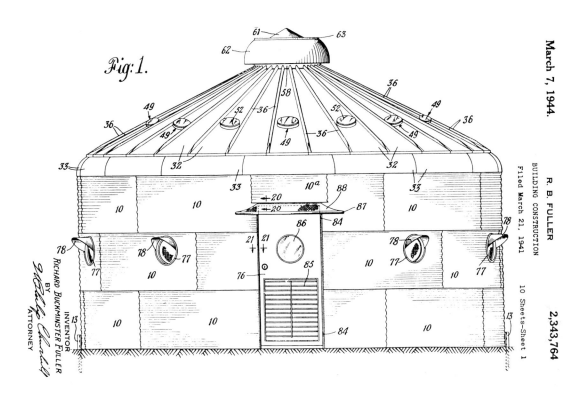

March 7, 1944.

R. B. FULLER

BUILDING CONSTRUCTION

Filed March 21, 1941

2,343,764

10 Sheets-Sheet 1

Fig: 1.

house made up of six standard panels that could be assembled (with ingeniously designed wedge-shaped connectors) in a variety of ways. Despite the promising concept and the ample funding, only a few examples were built; it seems that the concept came along too late. Even so, Gropius must be credited with influencing the federal government's decision to support research in prefabrication. In a paper presented to a select committee of Congress (which was investigating "national defense migration"), he offered a long-term decentralization plan based on prefabrication. As a result of this proposal, more than 100,000 prefabricated houses were built with federal support during the war.

Only one of the truly innovative proposals for temporary housing came anywhere near fruition: that of R. Buckminster Fuller. Driving through the midwest, Fuller was struck by the possibility that the corrugated-steel grain bins he saw could be transformed into inexpensive, weatherproof, and fireproof dwellings. The manufacturer, the Butler company of Kansas City, agreed with him and provided drawings and technical support for a test of the idea. Like Fuller's original Dymaxion House of 1927 (which was never more than an experimental model), this house was built from a mast through a hole in the conical roof; later the hole was closed with a ventilator. A prototype, christened the Dymaxion Deployment Unit (DDU), was shipped to Washington in 1941 for study by government representatives. It was lived in for a time by the head of the department of architecture at the University of Michigan, Walter Sanders, and his wife, who found it comfortable and convenient enough. During the autumn of 1941, two DDUs, one 20 feet and the other 15 feet in diameter, were exhibited in the sculpture garden of the Museum of Modern Art. Though they attracted a great deal of attention, most visitors were apparently unable to think of them as real houses. The DDU's chief drawback was that it required some 1,800 pounds of steel and 1,200 pounds of other materials that were important to the defense program. Although it was argued that workers' housing deserved a high priority, the government

decided to contract the Butler company to build DDUs for military use only. Hundreds were used by the Signal Corps and the Army Air Force as radar huts and housing in the Pacific Islands and the Persian Gulf region.

Fuller's commitment to the Dymaxion house came closer to realization with the Wichita House project for the Beech Aircraft company. The aircraft manufacturers were hit by a labor shortage in 1944 as many workers, realizing that airplane orders were beginning to fall off, left their jobs to look for work in other parts of the country. In order to hold them, as well as to prepare for a transition to postwar manufactures, the management of the Beech company agreed to a request from labor leaders to invite Fuller to design and see to the production of an adaptation of his original Dymaxion house. Fuller, who was offered space in the company's plants plus tools and the loan of experienced engineers and mechanics at nominal costs, accepted the challenge, resigned his government position, and moved to Wichita to work on the new Dymaxion house. This had an immediately positive effect on employment in the aircraft industry. "It was the consensus of the War Production Board, War Manpower Commission, the Air Force, and the aircraft labor unions, that the reversal of the labor situation in Wichita was directly attributable to the introduction of Fuller's house project to the aircraft industry." (26, 37)

The opening of the first Wichita house, as it came to be called, was generally successful, with considerable interest shown in purchasing at an expected price of about $6,500. The Air Force ordered two houses for immediate use, and the War Production Board and War Manpower Commission gave the project the highest priority in terms of materials and men. Then suddenly the war ended, and the Beech company abandoned the project to concentrate on the production of private aircraft. They were convinced that the demand for small private planes would be considerable, whereas trying to market Fuller's unusual house would be risky.

## Postwar Promises

*It is my firm conviction . . . that as soon as production can be resumed after victory, the public will be offered new and greatly improved models in most, if not all, lines of consumer goods. . . . new products will appear which will make the fanciful predictions that decorate our advertising pages seem commonplace.*

Walter Dorwin Teague, 1943 (169)

A year and a half after Pearl Harbor, America's war-related production was exceeding all expectations. Warehouses of military supplies were approaching capacity, and it seemed a certainty that they could be kept full. At the peak of wartime production at Ford's Willow Run plant, one B24 bomber was coming off the assembly line every minute, and at the Chrysler plant fifty tanks were being produced each day. The shift to a war economy had led to the construction of many new factories across the country, many expecting to be adapted to the manufacture of consumer products after the war.

The War Production Board announced in 1943 that "the nation has the plants and tools needed to build production to beat the Axis and is ordering a cut-back on contracts. The job of equipping the military forces to their maximum for the final phase of the war is done." (184) The National Resource Planning Board had already earmarked nearly 8 billion dollars for postwar construction projects, which were intended as a buffer against recession. The NRPB considered such planning for peacetime essential to "sustain the American concept of living, for full employment, security and the pursuit of happiness" (54). Thus, the door was opened for industry to begin thinking about reconversion.

While noting (rather awkwardly) that no letup in the war effort was called for, the federal government encouraged industry to begin planning for postwar production of civilian goods. It was hoped that a gradual increase in the availability of domestic products would re-

duce the pressure from a growing reservoir of purchasing power, thus helping to offset inflation and, at the same time, offering employment to returning veterans. The Department of Commerce tried to allay concerns about the planned dismantling of some 98 percent of the temporary wartime housing at the end of the war by suggesting that new housing would take up the slack. Several million families were also expected to become able to afford to purchase homes. Furthermore, it was pointed out that a family's postwar spending on products and furnishings for its new home might easily exceed the cost of the house.

By 1943 it was realized that industries that had been producing consumer goods before the war would have to decide whether or not to resume production of the same goods when the war ended. In many instances, production tools had been set aside for the duration of the war and needed considerable work before they could be returned to service. It was also realized that a company that decided to swing into production quickly by going back to its old designs might find itself reentering the market with obsolete products and having to compete with companies that had been recently formed—and equipped with up-to-date machinery—to meet the needs of the war. Yet a company (new or old) that decided to make radical changes in its products in order to take advantage of new technologies and materials might face risky delays in coming into an increasingly competitive market.

Manufacturers and government officials cautioned that reconversion would have to be accomplished with a minimal reduction in employment. The public would have to understand that keeping the labor force intact might mean producing prewar models while new models were readied. In industries (such as the auto industry) that had switched over completely to military production, reconversion would take a while. It was, however, evident that technological development moved much more quickly under the pressures of war. The fact that the production of many consumer goods had stopped abruptly did not mean that the manufacturers did not have advanced models ready to go at first opportunity.

All American companies, moreover, were presented with a situation that was unique to the circumstances of the war. A number of industries in other contries whose manufacturing plants had been severely damaged or destroyed during the war were certain to transform their tragedy into a blessing in disguise. They had not only to clear away the rubble and outmoded production methods, but also to generate a freshly determined management that was above the autocracy that had led them to disaster. These facts, plus a grim determination to regain social and economic esteem, developed formidable competition for the United States, particularly from the very countries whose industries it had helped level. A similar brutal catharsis would engulf the United States in the agonizing social revolts of the 1960s and the sad but inevitable decline of the smokestack industries in the 1970s.

In 1943, however, the U.S. government's primary concern for the postwar period was not competition from foreign manufacturers but, rather, a transition from military to consumer products. The Office of Price Administration, especially concerned about impending inflation, proposed a plan for postwar delivery of certain major products (such as automobiles, major appliances, and pianos) that took into account their scarcity under wartime restrictions and the temporary character of wartime housing. Under this plan, consumers would be encouraged during wartime to purchase certificates that could be applied to the postwar price of a product. Moreover, the certificate-holder would be given a priority and a discount. The certificates would be issued and honored by established dealer organizations. This OPA proposal, which was endorsed by a national committee of important government representatives, economists, and industrial leaders, was a virtual duplicate of Adolf Hitler's promise of postwar Volkswagens to Ger-

man citizens who purchased certificates for them. Fortunately for the American consumer, neither proposal was carried out.

Eighteen months after Pearl Harbor, the *New York Times,* in its annual report on American industry, observed that the nation was over the hump of preparing for and serving the needs of war. The *Times* noted that most major companies had already established special departments of postwar planning, and predicted: "[A boom] will come from those three stalwarts of the first World War—railroad rehabilitation, automobiles and housing—with added fillips from revolutionary synthetics such as nylon, rubber and plastics, the light metals, electronics, planes and new types of food." (52)

In 1942, *Fortune* predicted: "The first [postwar] contribution of the railroad [will] be an enormous demand for steel (and aluminum) to replace rolling stock and repair roadbeds. Competition [will] force an ambitious program of modernization, and the railroads [will] for once have the money to do it."(87) In fact, however, America's railroads, which had proved invaluable during the war, went into decline, owing largely to the highway program, the trucking industry, and the airlines. *Fortune*'s other predictions, however, turned out to be more accurate: Plastics indeed began to lose their prewar notoriety as new formulations (particularly nylon, which became precious during the war in the form of stockings) developed their own identities; aluminum found its way from warplanes to architectural panels, furniture frames, and luggage; stainless steel virtually displaced sterling silver in flatware and holloware; electronics miniaturized business machines and revolutionized the acquisition of information; and fast foods became enormously popular. (Atomic energy, nuclear medicine, and space exploration seem to have been beyond the vision of *Fortune*'s savants.)

Perceptive humor based on modern design and materials characterized Alan Dunn's cartoons of the 1940s. This is one of a series published in Architectural Record and in a collection of his work. Credit: (14).

Stockings made from nylon, introduced by Dupont at the 1939 Golden Gate Exposition in San Francisco, proved superior to those made from other materials. When material shortages were lifted toward the war's end, some could not wait to try them on. Credit: Hagley Museum and Library.

"We thank Thee, O Lord, for neoprene, sulphanilamide and nylon, and we beseech Thee now for aluminum, manganese and tin."

While the war was still on, some companies began to promote prefabricated houses with advertisements featuring the ideas of industrial designers. In *Architectural Forum,* the Barrett company promoted an idea, developed and illustrated by George Nelson, for selling prefabricated houses in department stores like any other manufactured product. The Durez Plastics and Chemicals company hired Walter Dorwin Teague to tell readers of the *Architectural Record* about the prospect of plywood prefabricated houses. Teague suggested that "postwar development of the prefabricated house [would] revolutionize the housing problem for the average man just as efficiently as the automobile [had] solved his transportation difficulties. Right off the assembly line . . . it [would] come complete with built-in kitchen, automatic heat and air conditioning, refrigeration, radio and telephone." (58) Teague also predicted, on the behalf of the Revere Copper and Brass company, that the only way to meet the demand for postwar housing for the average American family with an income of less than $2,000 a year would be to produce modular houses. A manufactured house, Teague believed, could be reduced to a small number of interchangeable parts, each designed for efficient production. The various sections could be rearranged, added to, subtracted from, or dismantled and transported. A major service unit would contain all the necessary utilities. In one day a newly assembled house would be "ready to move into—sparkling, clean-cut, handsome as a new car" (167).

*Business Week* reported in 1940 that Norman Bel Geddes, a "streamline enthusiast and industrial designer," had "entered the housing sweepstakes with plans for a low-cost prefabricated metal house" for the Housing Corporation of America (63). Although experimental models were built, this house never went into production; it did, however, focus attention on the potential of prefabrication. In a 1941 advertisement in *Time* for Revere Copper and Brass, Bel Geddes revived his prefabrication concept (which was, in fact, quite similar to Teague's). Bel Geddes believed that homes could be mass produced that would

*Major manufacturers in material-based industries expected to have excess capacity at their disposal after the war. Many turned to prominent architects and industrial designers for assistance in conceiving and promoting new applications. Credit:* Architectural Forum *(May 1943).*

meet government and housing inspection regulations and still not be standardized in design. He claimed that if consumers could get as much for their money in a house as they did in a modern radio or automobile, even the poor would be able to live like royalty. "Today," he wrote, "we have an opportunity to change over from old-fashioned and costly methods to the modern mass-production way of building better homes at lower cost. This is the first time such an opportunity has ever fully opened before us and America need not pass it by." (166)

In the late 1930s, *McCall's* magazine had held a series of annual "Home of Tomorrow" contests in which readers had been invited to submit essays on their preferences for the layout and the furnishings of various rooms in their homes. In addition, they had been asked to complete a questionnaire asking for information about themselves, their families, and their actual living environments. The winning essays and a summary of the results of the questionnaires were published, and more detailed questionnaire results were made available to the magazine's advertisers. These contests were revived in 1943—with an admonition from the editors that, because of the war, the readers should not expect to purchase the goods discussed. In each of the last four issues of the year, a conventional living room, dining room, kitchen, or bedroom was compared with an advanced design. Readers' comments were invited. The editors hoped that the results would provide insight into trends in taste and into consumers' postwar plans. Again the results were published and made available to manufacturers. The National Association of Home Builders, perhaps motivated in part by concern about the strong interest in prefabrication, accused advertising copywriters and magazine editors of overstimulating consumers' expectations by placing too much emphasis on "dream products." The extensive publicity given to plastics and electronics, the NAHB claimed, may have been good for circulation; however, it whetted

the public's appetite for products that were still either too expensive or too far in the future. Of some 500 families surveyed by the NAHB, a large majority expected complete air conditioning and electronic controls to be available within a year after the war, and most expected that they would soon be able to purchase prefabricated rooms.

For many, homes in the postwar era were not to be found in decaying cities but rather in the new suburbs, where easier credit would bring them within reach. New technology, lower land prices, and less restrictive building codes made living outside the cities more attractive. The move was already underway as the increasingly affluent acquired the means and an automobile of whatever vintage. The earliest moves had been modest ones to previously unkempt urban edges. Urban planners hoped to keep residents in the city by replacing run-down districts with housing projects.

There was, however, a question in the minds of some about the ability of developers and contractors to meet the great demand for housing that was expected to arise in the immediate postwar period. If the supply of new housing could not keep up with demand, it was suggested in *Architectural Forum,* some of the income that might once have been used for housing and furnishings would be diverted to automobiles, recreational equipment, television sets, and whatever other manufactured treasures might be available. In other words, the idea of disposable income was beginning to emerge, owing partly to the fact that many wives had gone to work during the war and were likely to continue working and partly, perhaps, to the idea that people would want to reward themselves for having done the chores of war well.

The anticipation of security and prosperity, and the taste for travel that had been stimulated by the decentralization of industry and by military service, combined to make a mobile home seem more attractive to many people than the conventional home, which was tied to the land and to whatever means of livelihood were available nearby. Many felt that the mobile home would make them free to follow the lures of opportunity and pleasure. It was also expected that the coming generation might be reluctant to be as burdened by property as its parents were.

The kitchen—the traditional center of household activity—was used by numerous companies and designers as a showcase for the introduction of new design concepts and products for the postwar world. For the Revere Copper and Brass company, J. Gordon Lippincott designed a kitchen made up of several modules: a corner sink, with a garbage disposal, a sprayer, and a revolving cabinet; a cooking module with a high-mounted oven, a pull-out broiler, three burners, a well, and a dishwasher; a four-compartment refrigerator; and a storage wall and appliance center.

The Libbey-Owens-Ford glass company revived a decade-old dream with its "Kitchen of Tomorrow," developed under the direction of H. Creston Doner (1902–). This particularly successful prototype kitchen was built in two full-scale models that were shown in major department stores across the country, beginning in 1944 at Macy's in New York. Visitors were asked to vote for the features they wanted most to see become available. The wood cabinetry and the covers for various appliances suggested that this kitchen was less like a laboratory and more like a family center. The refrigerator cabinet, which was accessible from both sides, formed a partition between the kitchen and a dining alcove. The stove had become a cooking center, with an oven, a griddle, a barbecue, a deep well, a roaster, a waffle iron, and separate wells for cooking glass-packed foods in their original containers. Though LOF was not in the appliance business, it expected the "Kitchen of Tomorrow" to acquaint the public with its name and trademark and to impress other manufacturers with the advantages of using glass in their products.

*The Kitchen of Tomorrow set a precedent for other experimental and promotional kitchens that followed. Credit: H. Creston Doner.*

*The most revolutionary product in the Kitchen of Tomorrow was the stove. Broken down into its separate functions, it was predictive of a wave of portable cooking appliances and separate oven and surface units that would come onto the market in the next few years. Credit: H. Creston Doner.*

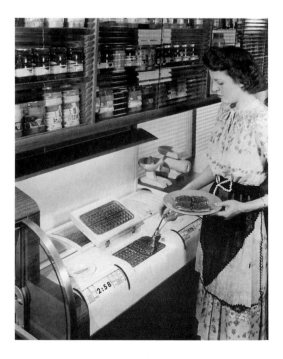

Peter Müller-Munk (1904–1967) was commissioned in 1943 by the Dow Chemical Company to work with Dow engineers and sales specialists to stimulate public interest in plastics by suggesting original ideas for postwar products. He used the opportunity to explore the idea of the kitchen as a domestic production line combining factory efficiency with elements of "charm and livability" that would make working in it "a pleasure rather than a chore" (150). Appliances would be part of the architecture of the kitchen rather than independent units—refrigeration, cooking, dishwashing, and garbage-disposal units, as well as air conditioning and lighting, would disappear into walls, counters, and ceilings. The woman who had worked in industry, the company prophesied, would no longer "be frightened by the complexities of mechanical construction"; indeed, she would "insist that her household appliances be as functionally perfect as the tools or weapons she [had] been handling during the war period and as easy to keep in good repair" (150).

At the American Furniture Summer Market in 1944, John Wicht, General Electric executive and president of the American Washer and Ironer Association, declared that he had no "jet-propelled" irons. Still, he estimated that there was an existing market for over 4 million washing machines, and he expected the industry to produce and sell more than 2 million that year. He warned, though, that the first machines available would be 1941 models—"not like the beautiful artwork in the magazines" (170). "Customer conditioning" through advertising was proposed by W. A. Grove, GE's sales manager of appliances, as a method of preparing the public for the realities of the postwar period. Grove, too, saw danger to the economy in the way that advertising had been misleading the public with glorified ideas and futuristic plans for "dream" products. Arguing that a public led to expect too much and finding the products not immediately available would put off buying, thereby setting off a postwar depression

that would push new products even further into the future, he recommended that the public should put its money into war bonds earmarked for special purchases at maturity.

The public was not put off by such words of caution. A survey of the postwar plans of families taken by the U.S. Chamber of Commerce showed them accumulating savings on a vast scale and arranging financing to begin buying as soon as they could. It was estimated that of some 24 million families who were ready to buy, 10 percent were planning to purchase an automobile first. Another 15 percent were ready to purchase electrical appliances and radios, and another 5 percent would be shopping for furniture and other items for the home. The Department of Commerce estimated that non-farm incomes in 1943 were 60 percent above those of 1939, largely because of the greater prevalence of the two-income family. The demand for better housing was also fueled by the Federal Housing Administration, which was making it possible for veterans to buy homes with only 5 percent down and with 4.5 percent interest spread over 25 years.

Although it was obvious that there would be a seller's market in every product area, manufacturers were already jostling one other to get to the market first. They were using the hunger for postwar products to attract attention to their wares, and they were surveying the responses to new ideas as a guide to product planning and development. The manufacturers and their designers continued to serve their defense-contract obligations first, but they were allocating more and more time and energy to the planning of products for the postwar market. Consultants suggested that postwar competition would best be met with better products. Voices echoing Horatio Greenough's philosophy that fashion stimulates progress were warning manufacturers that many companies had been brought down in the past by short-sighted adherence to outmoded product design. A strong recommendation was made by management consultants that the anticipated postwar clamor for new products offered an excellent opportunity for manufacturers to improve both appearance and functional quality. Moreover, the acceleration of technology brought on by the war effort was expected to provide considerable resources for industry to draw upon in the development of new products for the postwar market. It was also pointed out that companies should exploit their trademarks and reputations in order to ensure the acceptance of new products.

Whereas at one time the engineers were assumed to be the source of new or improved products, now that responsibility appeared to be shifting to the sales and marketing departments. This was a compliment, in a way, to the advances in scientific and technological capability; it was now felt that any product that could be conceived could be engineered and produced. It also gave credibility to the idea that industry now had the capacity to produce more than could be consumed, even by a product-starved populace, and that therefore salesmanship and promotion were going to be more important than before. Promotional competitions and advertisements rose to an unprecedented level in the latter years of the war. Some of the competitions were organized by the manufacturers; others were conceived by advertising agencies, magazines, newspapers, and radio stations.

Industrial designers played an important part in stimulating the popular interest in potential postwar products, not only by participating in advertising campaigns sponsored by manufacturers and promoting prospects for the future to professional and lay organizations but also by working as consultants or as corporate designers. In some cases they simply restyled and added features to products that would be produced with prewar tools and dies. In other cases they helped companies conduct surveys of consumer preferences and designed products to fit the findings. And sometimes a designer explored the entire range of a company's field and suggested new lines of products or ventures into new areas.

Durez Plastics and Chemicals was in the forefront of the companies that were primarily producers of materials and that used the trade and professional press to promote their materials as suitable for tomorrow's products. Over a period of several months, this company ran a series of magazine advertisements featuring proposals by prominent industrial designers for innovative products whose production was said to have been made possible by Durez plastics. And designers, apparently flattered by the request to predict the forms of the future, responded with models and illustrations. The designer Jean Reinecke (1909–) suggests that "the plastics industry and the industrial design profession grew up together." "The plastics group," he writes, "recognized the value of design to its products, and designers saw the new design opportunities provided by the materials." (200) Egmont Arens (1888–1966) contributed to the Durez series a design for a cylindrical refrigerator with wings, which was to be made of shaped plywood bonded and coated with plastic. The cylinder was to be used for food preservation, with refrigeration at the top and "Violet Ray" sterilization at the bottom. One of the wings was for bottles; the other was to contain an ice-cube maker and a cold-water faucet. "Some day in the not-so-far-off future," the advertisement prophesied, "you'll be recommending Durez plastics and resins to Allah for getting this dream refrigerator off the blueprints and onto the production lines." (53) In another advertisement for Durez, Peter Müller-Munk proposed that the use of plastics would reduce the weight of a sewing machine substantially. Perhaps more important, Müller-Munk suggested that a lustrous finish and handsome integral colors would provide a sales advantage. (In actuality, although plastic shells for products became an immediate reality after the war, they were not widely accepted by consumers as replacements for iron and aluminum for several years.) In another Durez ad, Donald Deskey (1894–) foresaw pushbutton and cordless telephones, intercom systems, and the replacement of printed telephone directories with microfilm.

Another promotional scheme was a collaborative effort sponsored in 1945 by the American Stove company and *Architectural Forum*. The assignment to design the "Gas Range of Tomorrow" was organized by George Nelson, consultant editor to the magazine at the time, who also served as professional advisor to a jury composed of economists, architects, and designers. The sponsors were convinced that a general invitation to the public to tell what was wanted was a better way of finding out what was in the housewife's mind (most of the entries did, in fact, come from housewives) than a conventional survey would be. They also believed that a person outside the stove industry was just as likely to come up with a successful concept as a professional engineer. The sponsors of the competition attracted favorable public attention as well as getting a relatively inexpensive look at a cross section of public and professional minds that had an interest in the area.

In a 1944 lecture to the Society of Automotive Engineers, Henry Dreyfuss proposed that airlines offer world cruises consisting of long flights and shorter helicopter jaunts to obscure places. For the long-distance planes, he advocated private staterooms and suites, dining salons, and card, television, and radio rooms. He was particularly concerned with the development of comfortable seats for airliners. Indeed, Dreyfuss—more than any other industrial designer of his generation—identified himself and the work of his office with design that was considerate of the relationship between human beings and their machines.

Henry Dreyfuss recalls in his book *Designing for People* that the Crane company, a manufacturer of bathroom fixtures, asked him to cancel their agreement for the duration of the war. However, the Crane company wanted to continue to pay the retainer fee so that the Dreyfuss office would not work for a competitor. Dreyfuss agreed to reserve his services for Crane but refused to be paid for doing so. A short time later, however, the president of the company admitted he was wrong in canceling

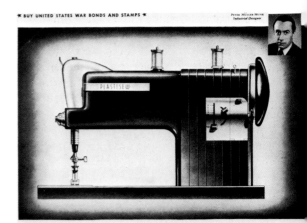

*Plastic substitutes for metal components were promoted for years before synthetic formulations and properties came into balance with performance and public acceptance. With this design, Peter Müller-Munk suggested using Durez material for the shell rather than for structural purposes. Credit: Fortune (July 1943).*

the contract and asked Dreyfuss to continue his services to Crane by researching and designing the products that the company would make after the war. As a result, Dreyfuss set up a satellite office in the Crane building in Chicago during the war to study the company's entire line. He and his employees selected products that should be carried over and designed new products to fill the gaps that were left in the company's catalog, making full-scale models in wood and finishing them to look like porcelain. "By the end of hostilities," Dreyfuss writes, "Crane's postwar line of products was in readiness for manufacture. Thanks to the company's foresight, it gained a substantial time advantage in the market." (11, 174)

Donald Deskey was contracted by the Brunswick, Balke and Collender company to conduct research into new product areas for the postwar years. His first assignment was to come up with new concepts for billiard tables, but this was soon expanded to an investigation of the idea of turning billiard parlors into recreational facilities for both men and women. Of particular importance, however, was a report (dated January 14, 1944) to the company of his services, linking it to a "national program of postwar recreation for the American Community" in anticipation of a strong possibility that a 5-billion-dollar postwar building program would stimulate the construction of suburban shopping centers and recreational facilities. Deskey's vision that bowling centers built and furnished by the company would attract not only young men (who had patronized bowling alleys in the past) but also whole families became a successful reality, particularly after automatic pin-setting was introduced by the American Machine and Foundry company. Proposals developed by Deskey with Edgar Lynch (Brunswick's company architect) set the typeform for the hundreds of bowling centers that were built in the postwar era.

Despite the federal government's caution, and despite the reluctance of a few industries to

invest in new ideas and new tooling, consumers were aware that the products of 1942 were obsolete. The wave of optimism stirred up by advertisements illustrating dream automobiles, homes, and appliances was not about to be calmed by the self-serving conservatism of old-line industries or by caution in Washington.

In a *New York Times* debate between Walter Dorwin Teague and Raymond Loewy, entitled "What of the Promised Postwar World—Is It Just a Dream, Or Will It Come True?," Teague had taken the optimistic position that American manufacturers were eager to show what they could do with the new materials and technologies that the war had brought within their reach, that at the end of the war there would be a perfect seller's market, and that competition—the driving force behind progress in a free economy—should be expected to be intense after the war. Shipbuilders would be making prefabricated houses, automobile manufacturers would be making airplanes, and airplane manufacturers would be making household appliances. "It is my firm conviction," Teague had written, "that as soon as production can be resumed after victory, the public will be offered new and greatly improved models in most, if not all, lines of consumer goods. . . . new products will appear which will make the fanciful predictions that decorate our advertising pages seem commonplace." (169) Loewy had acknowledged the publicity value of "bluesky" designs, their positive effect on the public morale, and the hope that the development of new products would boost postwar employment and thus help to offset the predicted depression; however, he had protested that consumers were "being misinformed systematically about the wonders that await them in their dealer's windows on the day when 'Johnny comes marching home,' " and that "every writer with an extra sheet of paper in his typewriter has dashed off a tale of the 'dream world of the future,' more because he knew that such a story would make good reading than because it bears any relation to fact" (168).

# The Modern (?) House

*Do our homes really express the ideals of democracy and individualism we all profess?*

Mary and Russel Wright, 1955 (42, 1)

In the period immediately after World War II, housing was the major problem facing the country. One war plant after another closed down, and the displaced workers and their families were unable to move because no housing was readily available elsewhere. The situation was compounded by the great numbers of discharged veterans who were also competing for what little housing there was. Within a year after the end of the war, 12 million men were demobilized to return to private life, with promises that the Federal Housing Administration would help them buy houses if any were to be found. In many cases the best way for a veteran to get a place to live was to attend college under the G.I. Bill, which guaranteed housing as well as tuition.

As was mentioned above, the federal government had purchased thousands of trailers to be used as temporary housing near war plants, many of which were in remote parts of the country. The building establishment tolerated the invasion of these trailers only with the promise that they would be disposed of as soon as the emergency was over. Many of them were scrapped; others were sold to municipalities to be used for purposes other than housing. Some 13,000 trailers were rented or given to colleges and universities to provide emergency housing for married veterans. (Many of them were still in use more than a decade later.) Columbia University established a "trailer campus" across the Hudson River from its main campus. The university, it seems, had borrowed the trailers from the FHA and was renting them to veterans at $25 a month, including utilities. Other programs to provide veterans with housing involved the rehabilitation, often with questionable success, of facilities originally built for military purposes. One magazine's description of a converted barracks mentioned apartments "each with its living room–kitchen door opening right into the mud, dust and desolation of a typical barracks stamping ground." "Construction," it was noted, "is flimsy, facilities are mighty few and the veteran . . . might be tempted to wonder what he had been fighting for." (120) Some innovative people moved into Quonset huts, considered to be a practical answer to housing if one could find a site that was free of zoning against their unconventional shape. More unusual (and, in some ways, more romantic) challenges involved the transformation of barns, buses, railroad cars, or trolleys.

The idea of prefabrication attracted the attention of some manufacturers who had expanded their facilities to meet the country's military needs and now were searching for new products to make. The Harman Corporation of Philadelphia transformed a system developed for building heavy steel truck bodies into one for manufacturing homes. The homes were designed, with help from the architect Oscar Stonorov, to be constructed of steel panels that could be assembled on site with a power screwdriver. The electrical wiring and the plumbing systems were designed for installation as complete units like the electrical "harnesses" and hydraulic systems used in airplanes. The company expected to build 10,000 houses a year in a former shipbuilding plant, leased from the Navy, in Wilmington, Delaware. The United States Steel company bought out the Gunnison Corporation of New Albany, Indiana (which had been producing prefabricated homes since the early 1930s), and proceeded to increase the amount of steel in each house. Other manufacturers of prefabricated housing chose to maintain their independence by seeking financial support from the Reconstruction Finance Corporation to expand and improve their products.

Donald Deskey had preceded his industrial design colleagues into manufactured housing with his Sportshack (discussed in chapter 1). The prototype had provided Deskey with evidence that the Sportshack could be expanded to meet the need for low-cost housing, and in 1946 he established a company, Shelter Industries, to begin manufacturing units ranging in price from $4,000 to $6,000. Expecting to manufacture about 200 completely equipped houses per month, he displayed a full-size model at the 1946 New York Housing Exposition. The first production model, manufactured at Southampton, New York, and erected in Lyndon, New Jersey, had a utility unit, developed by the Ingersoll division of the Borg-Warner company, that was similar to the utility core that Deskey had conceived for the Sportshack; however, the Ingersoll Utility Core had been developed independently as a result of Roy Ingersoll's search for a new product to be manufactured in his company's war-expanded facilities. (The publicity-minded Deskey, who had been retained by Ingersoll in 1945 to assist in the design and promotion of the Utility Core, had recommended that the company create a showplace to introduce it to the public, and on his advice twelve houses—each designed by a prominent architect—had been built in a suburb of Kalamazoo.)

The Manhattan site on which Frank Lloyd Wright's Solomon R. Guggenheim Museum was soon to be built was used for the temporary display of a prototype "Usonian house" designed by Wright, who hoped to prove that houses of high architectural quality could be inexpensive and easily reproduced. However, although Wright's original estimate for the house was $15,000, its final cost—even with much of the labor provided by students and apprentices—was $46,000. In a statement written for the opening of the house in 1953, Wright supported its open plan as one in which a housewife could "operate in gracious relation to her own home, instead of being a kitchen-mechanic behind closed doors" (175).

In 1947 the Consolidated Vultee company of California, determined to convert its aircraft plants to produce prefabricated houses, commissioned Henry Dreyfuss and Edward L. Barnes to work with its aeronautical engineers on the design of a two-bedroom unit. The design they came up with was particularly suitable for Southern California. It was to be manufactured from panels consisting of a kraft-paper honeycomb core faced with sheet aluminum, and to be completed on site by conventional tradesmen.

Dreyfuss was convinced that prefabrication was the long-range solution to the American housing problem. No other country, in his opinion, was as well prepared to mass-produce houses of quality. He acknowledged that the Consolidated Vultee house may not have been the ultimate, but he saw it as a step in the right direction. Although prefabrication was still struggling for recognition in 1949, he was certain that Americans would accept it.

Walter Dorwin Teague became involved with prefabricated housing in 1948 when he was commissioned by *Look* to develop a house suited to the needs of the average war veteran and his family—needs which the magazine had determined by conducting a survey, the results of which were turned over to Teague and his staff. The house was expected to be one that could be financed by the Federal Housing Authority at a price within the reach of a veteran earning the typical weekly wage of $100. *Look* displayed a prototype of the house in New York in April 1948 as part of the Museum of Science and Industry's "Modern Living" exhibition. The so-called *Look* House, designed for manufacture and sale by the Adirondack Homes company, was to be made of conventional materials prefabricated in sections delivered to the site to be finished locally.

One of the most ingenious prefabricated houses of the postwar period, and the only one that came close to succeeding as an alternative to homes built by traditional methods, was the Lustron house. Invented by Carl Strandlund in 1946, it was built much like the standard kitchen stove of the era. That is to say, its structure was a steel frame upon which porcelain-enameled steel panels (in any one of six colors) were mounted providing both inner and outer wall surfaces. The house was fireproof, rustproof, and termite-proof, and could withstand the elements without chipping. It had built-in radiant heating, and it came equipped with everything except a stove and a refrigerator. The standard five-room, two-bedroom model was priced at $7,000. After unsuccessful attempts to begin production in Chicago in 1947, the Lustron company

*The Lustron house was traditional in appearance despite its new materials and construction methods. Credit:* Architectural Forum *(June 1947).*

*The interior of the Lustron house was conservatively modern. Credit:* Architectural Forum *(June 1947).*

moved into the former Curtis-Wright aircraft factory in Columbus, Ohio, and began operations in 1948, with production goals of 17,500 units in that year and 40,000 in 1949. It was the biggest prefabrication venture of the postwar days. However, costly modifications and production problems delayed the start of production until February 1949. Beginning with a rate of 25 units a day, the company hoped to increase the daily production rate to 100 by mid-year, with 3,200 men working in three shifts. By early autumn, production still had not come up to the expected rate. The Reconstruction Finance Corporation, wanting to give the venture every opportunity to succeed, extended additional loans of 35.5 million dollars. However, the Lustron company did not survive. Only some 3,000 houses were built over the five years that the company was in operation. (Most of them are still in use.)

Undaunted by the failure of the aluminum and steel industries' ventures into housing, some producers of plastics set about developing plastic equivalents for traditional materials used in housebuilding. At the National Plastics Exhibition in 1956, the B. F. Goodrich company showed a cutaway "House of Today" that used vinyl in nearly 100 applications, from the roofs and the siding to the ceilings, walls, and floors to the kitchen sink. The Armstrong Cork company developed a revolutionary process of combining opaque blocks of vinyl with a clear vinyl grout to make a virtually indestructable replacement for asphalt, rubber, cork, and linoleum flooring.

The Monsanto company went even further. Perhaps as much for publicity as for the experience, it commissioned the Massachusetts Institute of Technology in 1954 to research the use of plastics as building materials. The architects, Richard Hamilton and Marvin Goody, conceived a cruciform structure consisting of four fiberglass-reinforced polyester rooms attached to a cast-concrete core. (In many ways the concept was an extension of R. Buckminster Fuller's original Dymaxion house.) Each of the four plastic units was made of two molded sections, one providing

the roof and the upper half of the wall and the other providing the lower part of the wall and the floor. The two molded bathrooms (one for adults and one for children) were developed by Henry Dreyfuss in collaboration with the engineers of the Crane company, and the kitchen appliances were designed in collaboration with the Kelvinator company and other manufacturers. A model was presented at the 1957 Plastics Show, and in that same year a full-scale version was built and tested by Lunn Laminates (the company that made the plastic body of the Chevrolet Corvette) and shipped to California to be set up at Disneyland. The project cost Monsanto over a million dollars.

The producers of light metals were as eager as the plastics industry to attract attention to their materials. The Dow Chemical Company promoted magnesium, while Kaiser, Reynolds, and the Aluminum Company of America (Alcoa) tried to interest designers and the public in aluminum. In 1958 Alcoa built the Care Free House, designed by the architect Charles Goodman, to demonstrate the use of aluminum in a residence.

The Monsanto and Alcoa houses were advertisements for the materials manufactured by their sponsors rather than a commitment to the manufacture of houses. After all the promises and the activity in that area, only a handful of struggling companies continued to manufacture prefabricated houses, which were stigmatized as cheap and temporary and banished to undesirable sites by defensive building codes. Only the prefabricated houses designed by Carl Koch in collaboration with John Bemis were able to achieve respectability. The Acorn House of 1950 and the Tech-built House of 1952 had been conceived with sensitivity and imagination in forms that dissociated them from other prefabs and managed to be acceptable in middle-class suburbs, although most of the buyers found more interesting sites.

Prefabrication found more use in the elegant corporate palaces that were built in the 1950s and afterwards. Among the first such build-

With this "House of the Future," Monsanto explored the use of plastics on a large scale with the cooperation of twelve leading companies in the fields of building supplies and equipment. The house became a popular attraction at Disneyland. Credit: Library of Congress.

The Techbuilt house appeared to be custom designed and built rather than prefabricated. Moreover, variability of form and adaptability to interesting sites enhanced its appeal. Credit: Akron Art Museum and Carl Koch.

ings to employ the new technology were the corporate headquarters of Alcoa, in Pittsburgh, and Lever House (the headquarters of Lever Brothers), in New York. In 1952 Alcoa commissioned Wallace A. Harrison and Max Abramowitz to design its corporate headquarters, using aluminum wherever possible to demonstrate its architectural potential. The most distinguishing feature of the Alcoa building was the use of preformed aluminum panels instead of glass for the curtain walls. The panels were inset with small TV-shaped windows that could be turned inside for cleaning. Aluminum was also used for virtually all of the building's hardware and accessories.

Lever House, also built in 1952, was one of the first International Style buildings to celebrate the emergence of American commerce and industry as patrons of modern architecture and design. Designed by Gordon Bunshaft of Skidmore, Owings and Merrill, it was considered daring in that it occupied only 25 percent of the space allowed by Manhattan's building code. By leaving open space in the most expensive area of the city, Lever House set the pattern for the urban plazas that were to follow.

Lever House and Ludwig Mies van der Rohe's Seagram Building (1959) are eloquent examples of the International Style steel-frame building with glass curtain walls. The facade of Lever House is made up of aluminum framing and blue-green glass; the Seagram Building has bronze framing and amber-tinted glass. In effect, these buildings were constructed from prefabricated components that were trucked to the site. They could have been duplicated ad infinitum. The waning of the International Style is due as much to the reduction of architecture to the assembly of Tinkertoy-like parts, which could be accomplished with or without taste or judgment, as to anything else.

In the realm of housing, the quest for a middle ground between prefabrication and traditional construction that would satisfy local building codes and financial interests and would soften

The Alcoa building (1952) was designed as a showcase for aluminum in architecture. It was the prototype for some 300 aluminum-curtained buildings that followed. The x-shaped creases in the panels were used by the Harley Earl office as the basis for the company's new trademark. Credit: Industrial Design (December 1955).

Lever House (1952) set the prototype for buildings that were to transform the architecture of Park Avenue from one of dense stone walls to one of transparent glass cells. In 1982 the building was honored as an architectural monument by the Landmark Preservation Commission of New York. Credit: Lever Brothers. Photograph by Harry Wilks.

*The American Institute of Architects selected the Seagram Building (1959) for its 25-year award in 1984, calling it "the standard against which all modern steel architecture is measured." Credit: Ezra Stoller, Esto Photographics, Inc. Courtesy of Seagram & Sons.*

the resistance of the building trades led the Small Homes Council of the University of Illinois to plan and build six prototype "engineered" houses for testing. This study was supported by grants from the Producers' Council, the National Retail Lumber Association, 42 other business organizations, and the U.S. Department of Commerce. Another engineered house was built, with collaborative support from the Westinghouse Electric Company, the Hartford Electric Light Company, and the Hartford *Times,* as a guide for home designers and builders.

The New York State Housing Authority conducted a statewide design competition for low-cost housing, with William Lescaze representing the American Institute of Architects as a professional advisor. Out of more than 300 designs submitted, 43 were selected as award winners to be recommended for single- or multiple-family housing to be sold outright or rented to lower-income families.

The first major entrepreneurial builder of housing for veterans and middle-class consumers was William J. Levitt. Before the war he had built conventional homes on Long Island's North Shore, and during the war he had built some 2,400 rental units for the Navy at Norfolk, Virginia. By 1946, the firm of Levitt and Sons was building the first Levittown on a 1,400-acre former potato farm on Long Island.

Levittown and its spinoffs succeeded because of the G.I. Bill and the growth of the highway system. The virtually identical houses were built on a kind of moving production line. Using precut lumber and prebuilt components, gangs of masons, carpenters, plumbers, and electricians followed one another down the new streets and around the curves of the expanding suburbs. Within ten years the Levitts were completing 100 houses a week.

Daniel Boorstin described the middle-class suburbs as being primarily for folks moving "rapidly about the country and up the ladder of consumption." There was, however, virtu-

ally no social ladder in these suburbs—every family was in about the same age and income group. "One does not move up in a one-class suburb," Russell Lynes wrote, "one moves out." (25, 253) It is fashionable to condemn the Levittowns, yet they provided first homes for many families of modest income. These suburbs provided the primary market for postwar products, as well as the most logical solution to the housing crisis.

On the West Coast, Henry J. Kaiser (whose company had built ships during the war) and Fritz B. Burns (who had already built some 7,000 houses) joined forces in 1945 to form the Kaiser Community Home Company. Their goal was to build as many as 10,000 houses a year in collaboration with local builders. By 1947 a converted Kaiser war-materiel factory near Los Angeles was building houses on a production line similar to those used to build automobiles. There were two basic chassis, on each of which one of three styles—the Suburban, the Palm Springs, or the New Englander—could be built.

By the autumn of 1949 it appeared that the housing shortage was being resolved. Home ownership had increased by 25 percent, and for the first time since the war the public was being offered a choice of housing. The market was shifting to the advantage of the buyer, and it was becoming evident that the seller would have to work harder to attract customers than before. Moreover, the public had apparently accepted some of the houses, products, and furnishings that designers and museums had been promoting and were demanding that they be made available to everyone at affordable prices.

The number of annual housing starts grew from 200,000 in 1945 to 1,154,000 in 1950, and every new home increased the demand for new appliances and furnishings. Factories rushed into full production as soon as materials became available. In 1939 there had been 9 million Americans out of work, but by 1945 a shortage of labor to meet and serve the promises that had been made was developing. In-

dustrial design was expanding rapidly into a
glamorous professional career for those who
saw in it opportunities for the future in creating furnishings and products for the home.

Two unique projects of the postwar era did
not address the pressure for low-cost housing; however, they did explore concepts that
would later prove to be valuable. They were
the Case Study program initiated by John
Entenza, and the Idea House II developed at
the Walker Art Center in Minneapolis. Both
were conceived on the assumption that a
postwar home should be designed as a single-
story open plan built on a concrete slab and
having a flat or nearly flat roof and floor-to-
ceiling windows. Dedicated to the idea of
indoor-outdoor living in a servantless house,
they endorsed the philosophy of architecture
as a social art. However, both were supported
by private funds, and no responsibility for low-
cost housing or prefabrication as solutions to
future housing was claimed.

*A typical Levitt house of the 1950s. Credit: Levitt Homes.*

John Entenza had purchased the magazine
*California Arts and Architecture* in 1938 and
had changed its title in 1941 to *Arts and
Architecture.* The magazine published the
work of young architects and quickly attracted
national and international attention. The de-
finitive book on Entenza and the Case Study
program praises *Arts and Architecture* as
"a slim magazine with no outside financial
backing [that] became the greatest force in
the dissemination of cultural information
about California" (27, 3). In 1945 Entenza gave
up the editorship for a more dynamic role as a
promoter of, and a major client for, postwar
domestic architecture. He acquired five acres
of valuable property on a high meadow above
Santa Monica and invited eight architects to
design individual houses to be built there. The
choicest part of the tract was to be occupied
by Entenza's own house (designed for him by
Eero Saarinen and Charles Eames) and a
house designed by Eames for himself and his
wife, Ray.

The Case Study houses were based on an
exclusive concept of what modern small
houses should be. Although the architects
used standardized elements where possible,
their primary goal was not to reduce costs but
rather to arrive at an ideal small house in
terms of modern materials, spatial organization, and contemporary good taste. The success of the program helped to make such
houses more acceptable to the public, and
also to banks (which had previously considered them poor investments with limited
resale value). The thirteen Case Study houses
that were completed by 1949 have been credited as the forerunners of the California Modern style of architecture. The most famous of
the Case Study houses, and the one that has
been kept closest to its original form, is the
Eames house. This house was honored in
1978 by the American Institute of Architects
for its "enduring significance." The use of
steel components selected from catalogs of
standard parts was considered especially
noteworthy.

The Case Study program stimulated the
growth of a number of small factories that

had been established by designers to turn out furniture, floor coverings, textiles, lamps, tablewares, kitchen utensils, and other accessories for the houses. Rita and Mat Lawrence produced a line of dramatic ceramic plant containers in a small enterprise that eventually grew into Architectural Pottery. Hendrik Van Keppel designed the tubing-and-cord patio furniture and the slat benches that were used in many of the houses, and this helped to establish him and his partner Taylor Green in business. Except for a few accessories and pieces of furniture from Germany and Scandinavia, most of the furnishings of the Case Study houses were made in California.

The director of the Walker Art Center, Daniel S. Defenbacher, was convinced that a modern museum had a social as well as a cultural role to play in the community. He had pioneered this concept in 1939 by introducing innovative concepts for modern living in a small house on the grounds of the museum. In the short time that it was open, the "Idea House" was visited by more than 50,000 people. In 1946 Defenbacher announced the establishment of the center's Everyday Art Gallery and the publication of the Everyday Art Quarterly, a journal to be devoted, like the gallery, to serving as a guide to the best in modern products. He appointed Hilde Reiss, who had studied at the Institute of Design in Chicago, to be curator of the gallery and editor of the quarterly. In another bold step, Defenbacher decided to revive the program of Idea Houses. Idea House II was to be built on the grounds of the Walker Art Center, as the original Idea House had been, and models of other proposed Idea Houses, one designed by an architecture student at the University of Minnesota and others by local architects, were to be shown in the new gallery. It was hoped that all the designs would be realized in the Minneapolis area.

The Walker Art Center intended to demonstrate that good modern homes could be built without architectural or technological innovations, rather than to compete with existing prefabrication and mass-housing activities. In effect the program, like the Case Study program, was directed at the middle and upper

classes, on the understanding that there could "be no minimum house until factory-fabricated modular building units or complete prefabricated houses are readily available" (84).

Idea House II was designed by William Friedman (assistant director of the Walker Art Center) and Hilde Reiss, with Malcolm E. Lein as associate. In the autumn 1947 issue of the Everyday Art Quarterly, which was devoted to the house, Defenbacher stated that "a man's house is his art. . . . a good house is an artistic creation in which all other factors are controlled and molded into an aesthetic entity" (85). The second Idea House was closer in spirit to the Arts and Crafts movement than to the International Style. It was built for a casual lifestyle, on an open plan, with the living, dining, and kitchen areas flowing into one another. Although the kitchen could be closed off, it was usually open so that the woman of the house would not be isolated from other family members or guests. Privacy was sacrificed to communal living; the only private spaces were a "bed-sitting room," the children's "apartment" (which had individual bed alcoves and a common playroom), and the compartmentalized bathroom. Although the form of the house and the materials used now seem rather quaint, at the time it was considered to offer the ultimate in modern living for young Americans. The house was built on a concrete slab, with an excavation at one end to provide for a utility room, storage, and a carport. The roof was a combination shed and flat structure, and the ceilings were finished in natural wood or white acoustic tile. Much of the south wall was glass, with roof overhangs to provide shade in the summer. The exterior and interior walls were made, for the most part, of vertical redwood siding finished with a clear oil preservative. Other wall materials included Donald Deskey's striated Weldtex, painted wallboard, and concrete block. The cabinets and the wall storage units were of natural birch. The floors were either natural cork, asphalt, or rubber tile, covered to some degree with straw mats or handcrafted cotton rugs with no pattern or decoration. Traditional window blinds and curtains were

The Walker Art Center's Idea House II was a split-level structure built against a sloping wooded site. Though it was as modern in a craft way as the Eames house was technologically, both appear quaint today. Credit: Ezra Stoller, Esto Photographics, Inc.

The interior of Idea House II was essentially the same as the exterior. Credit: (42).

replaced by either bamboo screens or slotted wood roll-down shades. Tweedy upholstery and nubby cotton draperies completed the decor. General lighting was provided by ceiling fixtures. Most of the lamps were flexible or adjustable in one way or other. The furniture and the furnishings had been selected from the so-called contemporary shops of the period; Scandinavian pieces by Alvar Aalto and Bruno Mathsson were combined with pieces by Eames, Nelson, and Saarinen from the Herman Miller and Knoll companies.

In retrospect, Idea House II—much as it was admired for bringing together the best examples of modern living—appears to have been an agglomeration of the fast-fading tastes of its time. It provided a series of enticing stage settings—almost-forgotten scenes of domestic culture from the first few years of peace. As an idealized home, it combined the open spaces of the International Style with familiar arts-and-crafts elements. It, and its counterparts displayed in museums and smart shops from coast to coast, played counterpoint on the themes of Scandinavian imports and innovative American furniture in combination with natural materials.

Many of the major department stores also recognized the drawing power of special exhibitions dealing with the home. Macy's, John Wanamaker's, and McCreary's exhibited models of homes of the future or set up full-scale furnished interiors. Bloomingdale's held a competition entitled Suburban Houses for New Yorkers. Rich's department store in Atlanta commissioned the nationally known architect Hugh Stubbins, Jr., to develop a house to meet the needs of a family of four with an annual income of $3,000. Altman's department store showed six models of "Homes for Today" that had been produced under contract by the staff of *Better Homes and Gardens.* Macy's exhibition of "Homes America Wants" featured rooms originally designed for *Good Housekeeping* to promote the idea that a home should have a traditional exterior and an interior that provided every modern convenience.

The attempt to find an accommodation between the International Style and an American style of casual living was given a major public test in 1949 when the Museum of Modern Art commissioned Marcel Breuer to build a single-family house at the east end of its sculpture garden. The problem presented to Breuer was to "design a moderately priced house for a man who works in a large city and commutes to a so-called 'dormitory town' on its outskirts where he lives with his family" (160). Breuer and the directors of MOMA were in agreement with John Entenza that the problems of low-cost housing would have to be solved by industry, not by museums.

The "House in the Museum Garden" was quite similar to Donald Deskey's Sportshack and the Walker Art Center's Idea House II. The "butterfly" roof was nearly flat. The exterior walls were narrow vertical cypress siding, and the interior was paneled with Weldwood. The floors were asphalt tile or stone flagging with either rush or hemp matting. Breuer, like many other émigré architects, made a concerted effort to capture what he called the "wilderness" atmosphere of America by using rough stone, hewn wood, and other natural materials.

Breuer selected all the furnishings except for a few pieces that he chose to design himself. Among the latter was a combination radio, television, and record player that was remotely controlled from a trapezoidal coffee table. Since Breuer had not found any lighting fixtures that were to his liking, he did not specify any for the house. He saw no reason why lighting fixtures should pose as sculpture. His position was and remains pertinent; lamps continue to depend on figurative elements or desecrated artifacts, and illumination is still subordinated to form.

A different approach to bringing modern design to the public was taken by Mary and Russel Wright, who had devoted their professional careers to the design and development of furnishings and tablewares for the modern

Breuer's House in the
Museum Garden was the
Museum of Modern Art's
contribution to postwar
home design. Except for
its modified butterfly roof,
it, too, was a rectangular
box with wooden walls
and white trim. Credit:
Ezra Stoller, Esto Photo-
graphics, Inc.

Mary and Russel Wright's
book suggested that
"cleanup can even be part
of the evening's pleasure,
if managed properly."
Credit: (42, 176). Drawing
by James Kingsland.

home. They collaborated in 1950 on the publication of a well-illustrated book, *Guide to Easier Living,* that gave them an opportunity to present their convictions and concerns about modern lifestyles in the United States. "Do our homes really express," they asked in the foreword, "the ideals of democracy and individualism we profess? Do they provide a place where we can relax together, or a spirit of family living can thrive? In this increasingly mechanized civilization, our homes are the only remaining place for personal expression. The place where we could really be ourselves." (42, 1) The Wrights tested and refined the ideas that were presented in the book in their penthouse studio-apartment and later in a brownstone house on 48th Street in Manhattan that they had remodeled into a home and office. Their recommendations were accepted by many design-conscious young couples. In the same year, the designer Harper Richards remodeled a nineteenth-century brick building on Superior Street in Chicago to provide offices and an apartment for himself on the upper floors and the first showroom in that city for Knoll Associates on the ground floor. In a move that was applauded by the design community of the time but would be condemned today, Richards removed some of the ornamental brickwork and modernized the facade.

It was not unusual in the late 1940s (nor is it today) for architects and designers to test their ideas by designing and furnishing their own homes and offices. The results were more often than not dramatic enough to attract the attention of the editors of trade magazines. It was expected that the exposure would enhance their reputation enough to attract clients whose interests were in harmony with those of the designer. Even more important was the designer's need to live and work in an environment of his own making. Eliot Noyes, for example, built a house for his family that demonstrated his mastery of the International Style and his gift for balancing its cool logic with an affection for nature and for natural materials. Moreover, the furnishings Noyes chose illustrated his ability to combine old and new things.

*No sign was needed to acclaim the industrial design firm housed in this building, declared the caption accompanying this photograph in* Interiors *(August 1949). Later other designers would be praised for restoring the original facades of similar transformations.*

*Florence Knoll transformed the ground floor of the Richards building into Knoll's first Chicago store, a modern showroom with minnow netting, pandanus and flat white screens, a dropped white ceiling, and a black floor. Credit:* Interiors *(August 1949). Photograph by Idaka.*

## Show and Tell

*Right from the beginning, these shows have been a big hit. The public has been fascinated with them and has also found them extremely useful as a source of ideas for Christmas shopping.*

Eliot Noyes, 1950 (69)

The idea of attracting people to a museum by focusing on artifacts as well as art was not new, despite the fresh attention devoted to it in the postwar years. Early in the century John Cotton Dana, director of the Newark Museum, had tried to disprove the notion that museums were interested only in the fine arts and to show Americans that a powerful new movement in design was gathering momentum abroad by staging a Werkbund exhibition, and through the 1920s the Metropolitan Museum of Art had held annual exhibitions of everyday products. Under the direction of Richard Bach, the museum saw itself as an important resource for the ideas and sensitivity of other times that could be drawn upon to serve present needs. In the 1930s, the locus of interest in the arts in modern living had shifted from the Metropolitan Museum to the Museum of Modern Art, which had been chartered in 1929 by the State of New York to, among other things, "encourage and develop the study of modern arts and the application of such arts to manufacture and practical life" (161). This goal was entirely in line with the conventional premise that art comes first and is then "applied" to things. However, one could also argue that the form that a manufactured product takes for reasons beyond aesthetic pleasure also provides the substance for art in the sense that art mirrors life.

MOMA had made plans in 1945, while Eliot Noyes was still director of the department of industrial design, to honor selected designers with a "seal of approval" on the basis of "how a thing looks rather than how it works," in order to "stimulate consumer demand for really good modern design in manufactured objects." Noyes's criteria for selection were to be "design quality as demonstrated by fitness for intended use, an intelligent use of materi-als, reasonable adaptation to the manufacturing process, and a contemporary aesthetic solution" (172). The museum's sixth annual Exhibition of Useful Objects, assembled by Suzanne Wasson-Tucker, curator of industrial design, between the tenures of Eliot Noyes and Edgar Kaufman, Jr., and held in the autumn of 1945, was a first step in this direction. However, the annual awards had apparently been lost somewhere along the way.

Shortly after he became director of the department of industrial design, in 1946, Kaufman wrote the following in the *MOMA Bulletin:* ". . . never before has design been so influential, its study so complex, or its evaluation more necessary." (161) He wanted the people in his department to be well informed, keeping in mind that utility and price were as important to the public as aesthetics. He expected the department to build an extensive reference file documenting modern design and a permanent collection of products. However, like other art museums, MOMA was generally unable to make a broad commitment to the study of everyday objects; its management and its financial patrons (private citizens, mostly) were unable or unwilling to support such a program. The well-respected and much-emulated British Council of Industrial Design, which maintains an exhibition center and a designers' reference file, is sponsored by the government and supported by commercial and trade interests and has had to walk a perilous path between the wishes of the financial, manufacturing, and marketing establishments and the presumably more altruistic goal of a national aesthetic. Some forty years' experience with design centers in a number of countries, and briefly in the United States as a private venture, suggests that they have been of limited value in either bringing better design to the marketplace or enriching private and federal coffers. Perhaps the raw interests of the marketplace and the volatility of the public are too strong for government agencies or private entrepreneurs to control.

The Museum of Modern Art's two 1946 exhibitions of industrial design affirmed the museum's commitment to its role as a patron of the arts of the environment. The first was an exhibition of furniture designed by Charles Eames, who in collaboration with Eero Saarinen had won first prize in the museum's 1941 Organic Design competition. By 1946, the shell-molded chairs of 1941 had evolved into "potato chip" forms of molded veneer mounted on bent-wood bases via electrically glued rubber shock mounts. The panels were adapted from the molded splints that Eames had developed for the Navy during the war, and the rubber mounts from those used in the instrument panels of airplanes. The second of MOMA's 1946 industrial design exhibitions was a showing of 25 pieces of dinnerware designed by Eva Zeisel and produced by the Castleton China company.

The Museum of Modern Art's seventh Useful Objects exhibition, held during the 1946 Christmas season, included products that ranged in price from 25 cents to 25 dollars. The approval of battery jars as flower vases and of laboratory dishes as salad bowls and ashtrays sent many young consumers into hardware stores and junk shops in search of other such objects that could be elevated to the status of "modern" household accessories. Edgar Kaufmann, Jr., was aware of the justifiable desire for public recognition expressed by the designers of the objects included in the exhibition. He observed in response that only some forty designers had been identified by the manufacturers, and that getting those names had been difficult. "Too many designers," Kaufmann was quoted as saying, "still function in modest seclusion, either by choice or more frequently by request of the manufacturers." (121) It appears that the manufacturers were afraid that the designers would demand a greater share in the profits earned by their contributions. Perhaps, also, many American designers, unlike most of their European counterparts, preferred anonymity.

In 1947 Kaufmann decided that the price range of the goods selected for the Useful Objects exhibition should be extended up to $100 in order to broaden the selection. Although many of the 100 products shown were priced below the $25 limit of the previous years, the museum drew criticism for having abandoned its commitment to practical manufactured products by including such things as a magnesium hunting bow from Abercrombie and Fitch and a silver stamp box from Cartier. In 1948 the museum put a price limit of $10 on the objects in its annual Christmas-gift show, announcing the limit as an "anti-inflationary measure" that would "serve as a guide to inexpensive as well as attractive gifts" (133).

Many other museums also scheduled exhibitions of useful objects to coincide with the Christmas buying season, thus suggesting that, although the products were presented as utilitarian, they were really intended to be purchased as gifts that would testify to the buyer's good taste and to his high regard for the taste of the recipient. And the products themselves leaned more toward art than toward function; many of them were charming knickknacks, clever gadgets, or decorative accessories. The idea of utility was being used to promote the sale by museums of things that could easily be found in local gift shops or department stores. (Even today, some museums continue to sell products in this manner—often via glossy catalogs that elevate the good taste of the museum's buyer above the experience of going to the museum.)

There was some speculation as to whether the selection and display of modern products in a museum endowed them with values commensurate with those of its older treasures. In the traditional sense of a museum, such treasures were, for the most part, either archaeological artifacts rescued from oblivion to be studied for an understanding of past cultures or else bona fide treasures in rare materials or masterpieces of outstanding artisans of the past.

Installation view of exhibition of "New Furniture Designed by Charles Eames" at the Museum of Modern Art. Craft Horizons *noted in February 1948 that the new pieces had "escaped the clichés of more superficial designers." Credit: Museum of Modern Art, New York.*

The selection of modern products for display in museum exhibitions was usually based on photographs or illustrations in magazines or promotional literature, rather than on direct experience. Popular acceptance—which the shows were intended to foster—was not a factor, nor was durability, safety, or environmental impact. The jurists, by virtue of their assigned responsibility, presumed that their taste was superior to that of the public and expected, with all good will, that their stamp of approval would ensure a product's acceptance by the public.

John Vassos, president of the American Designers Institute, expressed his concern about the drift of museums toward commercial tie-ins with business and industry. At a meeting of the ADI at the Cooper Union, he questioned the effect that such practices would have on all of the parties involved. He drew an analogy to the Williamsburg restoration: "... originally intended to keep and to preserve intact a record of the period, it has degenerated into a purely commercial venture" (132). Vassos was also concerned about the museums' connections with department stores and industries in conjunction with competitions or funded development of furniture and tableware. Aside from the possibility that the names of the museums might be misused in marketing ploys, he considered the possibility that the approbation of certain products by design juries might be out of step with the public's actual needs and practices and thus might end up inhibiting rather than advancing the evolution of contemporary design.

The optimism of the postwar era swept away most such reservations, replacing them with aspirations for a better life through better design and expectations that the best guides to a well-designed future would be museums, galleries, and similar nonprofit institutions, which were assumed to be above financial temptations.

The Walker Art Center's Everyday Art Gallery (mentioned in the preceding section of this chapter) was the first gallery of its kind to attract national attention. Curator Hilde Reiss stated that the gallery had been established "to help build a better environment for daily living." "This," she noted, "includes many things we use every day—buildings, vehicles, furniture, pens, door knobs, drinking glasses. Large or small, all affect human well-being. None need be ugly or awkward. . . . we believe anyone can learn to discriminate between good and bad design, given opportunity." (86) The gallery's first major exhibition, "Ideas for Better Living," opened in January 1946 and included both handcrafted and machine-made products—among them bowls by James Prestini, ceramics by Margerite Wildenhain, lamps by Kurt Versen, radios by Alexander Girard, and an electric iron by John Polivka. In addition, George Fred Keck provided a model of a solar house, and the design firm of Barnes and Reinecke contributed concepts for a "kitchen of tomorrow." In the inaugural issue of the *Everyday Art Quarterly* (the gallery's own periodical, which later became the *Design Quarterly*), Edgar Kaufmann, Jr., noted that machines made demands upon designers that were similar to those made by tools upon craftsmen, but that the designer was driven by a need to be of service to others whereas the artist-craftsman was motivated primarily by self-expression. From the beginning, however, although the EAG and the *EAQ* were aware of the importance of fit and function in products, they took the position that their limited resources and their focus on artistic values obliged them to advise their public to look elsewhere for other information.

Luke Lietzke, curator of industrial design at the Akron Art Institute, also believed that designers deserved recognition and professional dignity as much as artists did, and that the value of their work went beyond mere styling and appearances. In 1946 and 1947, with support from Charles Van Clear, the institute's director, she staged four exhibitions dealing with products and furniture for the home. The last of these, "Useful Objects for the Home," included 200 products for everyday use. Every effort was made to include the name of the designer of each product, as well as those of the manufacturer and the retailer. As in other shows of the late 1940s, the emphasis was on tableware, kitchenware, furniture, and home furnishings and accessories. This was understandable in light of the great attention given to acquiring and furnishing one's own home in the postwar era. Nor was it unusual that these exhibitions were biased in favor of arts-and-crafts industries; they were more in keeping with the sources of income, and the collections and courses of study, that supported art institutes, galleries, and museums.

The Albright Art Gallery of Buffalo set its sights on mounting a major exhibition on the theme "Good Design Is Your Business." The idea was that it was the public's business to support good design so that the quality of the environment would be improved. Director Andrew C. Ritchie stated that the gallery had "set itself up as a bureau of standards, so to speak, on the good appearance of objects in and around the home." It was his hope that, by the launching of the exhibition in 1947, the Albright Gallery might "arouse enough interest nationally and locally in the subject of good design of everyday objects to make possible the establishment of a permanent industrial design department" (231). Assistant curator Charles P. Parkhurst, Jr., who was placed in charge of organizing the exhibition and selecting the objects that would be shown, decided early on that the selection would be limited to products used in or around the home. He and his staff, working from photographs and other visual materials, based their selections on "visual evaluation and underlying common sense." The 200 manufactured products that were finally selected included kitchen and table wares, appliances, furniture, garden equipment, and automobiles.

By this time, it was beginning to appear that such shows were in danger of becoming dreadfully narrow. It seemed as though each gallery was selecting products from the catalogs of previous exhibitions. In fact, Parkhurst expressed his gratitude to the Museum of Modern Art and the Walker Art Center for putting "their stores of information at [his] disposal with characteristic generosity" (239). The result was an aesthetic sterility that in the end defeated the high ambitions of such well-intended enterprises.

Nonetheless, virtually every respectable museum, gallery, and academic institution in the United States had already held or was planning to hold an exhibition of art in everyday living. The Addison Gallery of American Art in Andover, Massachusetts, restaged "Good Design is Your Business." The St. Paul Gallery and School of Art held a "Design for Living" show featuring objects provided by stores in the area. The Newark Museum held an "Objects Under Ten Dollars" exhibition (aimed at Christmas shoppers) and another exhibition entitled "Decorative Arts Today." The Munson William Proctor Institute in Utica held an exhibition called "The Modern House Comes Alive." The Museum of Art of the Rhode Island School of Design held a "Furniture of Today" show in which furniture was displayed in settings where it could be sat on and handled. The San Francisco Museum of Art held four product-design exhibitions in 1949, each devoted to a different part of the house. The New York Public Library, whose picture files had long been mined for ideas by illustrators and by designers of costumes, stage settings, exhibits, packaging, and products, called attention to its services with an exhibition ("The Designer Begins Here") of books, photographs, and prints alongside the products for which well-known designers had used them as a design source.

The Brooklyn Museum of Art accepted a grant of $50,000 from the Abraham and Straus department store for the establishment of a design laboratory in its industrial section. The laboratory (named after Edward C. Bloom, one of the owners of the store) was open to designers, manufacturers, and retailers who were interested in analyzing basic forms, ancient and modern, that might be applicable to contemporary design problems. For access to the laboratory's cubicles, workrooms, and research assistants, individuals were charged $100 and associate members $500 a year.

The cap on this period of exhibitions devoted to art in everyday living was "For Modern Living," organized in the fall of 1949 by Alexander Girard. The director of the Detroit Institute of Art, E. P. Richardson, had suggested a show that would illustrate the renaissance of the American sense of design, which he felt had disappeared for a century with the rise of the machine. Detroit's J. L. Hudson department store supported this exhibition with a grant of $75,000. Girard, taking a cue from other "art in everyday living" shows, suggested that the public would flock to an exhibit that emphasized vernacular products. He proposed that the show would be even more attractive if well-known designers were to be commissioned to put it together. With the help of George Nelson and other design "stars," "For Modern Living" turned out to be a comprehensive, provocative, and popular display of modern home furnishings, combining high standards of design with promotional goals.

By the end of the 1940s, the promotion of modern design had carried over to the academic world. Schools of architecture, as well as design and art schools, were organizing exhibitions and meetings to promote the role of art in better living. At the University of Illinois, the college of architecture began a series of annual exhibitions called For Your Home to complement the work of the Small Homes Council, which had been established on the university's campus. The Yale University Art Gallery held an exhibition that was essentially based on a series of articles on design by Eliot Noyes in the magazine Consumer Reports. Noyes, who directed the show, was design consultant to the magazine and an associate professor at Yale at the time.

Eliot Noyes had played an important role in trying to fan the flame of good design. In 1940, as the young director of the Department of

Industrial Design at the Museum of Modern Art, he had organized and staged the Organic Design competition (discussed above). After serving in the military, he had joined the office of Norman Bel Geddes as design director. He had established his own office in 1947.

Noyes's articles in Consumer Reports (the series was entitled The Shape of Things) appeared between April 1947 and November 1950. His premise was that good appearance need not be sacrificed for the sake of sound construction or mechanical efficiency, and that when two competing products were equal in performance, appearance became the most important factor determining selection. In the July 1949 issue he claimed that, although it was easier to create handsome and appropriate shapes for simple items than for complex appliances, it was reasonable to expect better forms for all products. Noyes was convinced that "given the chance, a conscientious designer can usually make things more useful, cheaper, smaller, lighter, stronger, easier to clean and more pleasant to look at." "The consumer," he wrote, "has a real interest in well-designed objects, for the qualities that the good designer seeks to achieve are largely the qualities that best serve the user." (71)

As a man of culture, Noyes was able to appreciate an authentic Windsor chair as well as an Eames chair. However, he deplored historical costuming. He also frowned on products that borrowed the character of another family of products. Refrigerator doors were not, he wrote, automobile grilles, and therefore bumpers and chrome nameplates were out of place in the kitchen. He referred to toasters as "social climbers"—humble kitchen appliances dressed up to go into the dining room with pseudo-monograms and stamped curlicues that carried overtones of royal plate (66).

Consumer Reports was by no means the only publication to climb on the "art in everyday living" bandwagon. Motivated in part by a desire to contribute to better living and in part by an awareness of the appeal of design-related articles to advertisers and to the

*The great hall of the Detroit Institute of Arts was transformed into a garden for this exhibition. A raised ramp around the garden supported seven modern rooms created by top-flight designers. Credit: Detroit Institute of Arts.*

public, many other magazines published design articles addressed to their particular audiences. In 1947 the publishers of *Mademoiselle* introduced a new magazine, *Mademoiselle's Living,* designed to expand the fashion consciousness of 18-to-35-year-old women beyond clothes and cosmetics into the realm of homes, furnishings, appliances, and baby carriages.

In 1946 the Society of Industrial Designers had accepted a proposal from the Philadelphia Art Alliance to organize a traveling exhibition on industrial design, which was to open in Philadelphia in 1947 and then to tour as many as twelve other cities, including Detroit, Buffalo, Toledo, Milwaukee, and Minneapolis. The resulting exhibition, "Industrial Design—The Creative Link Between Business and the Consumer," comprised photographic panels showing the work of 32 designers (about half of the membership of the society) in six categories: transportation; domestic appliances and accessories; machines and instruments for business and professional use; commercial interiors and exteriors; recreational equipment; and toys and products for personal use. Virtually all the products shown were outside the realm of home decoration and furnishings, on which most of the museum exhibits had concentrated. The products illustrated ranged from a water-operated toothbrush by Harold Darr, a sewing machine and an ice crusher by Dave Chapman, and a utility core for a prefabricated house by Donald Deskey to trains by Brooks Stevens, ship interiors by Henry Dreyfuss, and aircraft interiors by Raymond Loewy. Egmont Arens and his associate Whitney Stuart had contributed panels tracing the evolution of familiar products (such as a meat slicer and a tape dispenser) from concept to production. Walter Dorwin Teague projected a facsimile machine that would bring the daily newspaper into the home. John Gordon Rideout showed a photo of a wheelchair, Francesco Collura one of an electric cocktail mixer.

*The new magazine* Living *spun off by* Mademoiselle *rode the crest of interest in new homes and furnishings from its introduction in 1949 until the wave subsided in 1954 and it was sold to* House and Garden. *Credit:* Interiors *(April 1949).*

An article about the SID exhibition in the January 11, 1947, issue of *Business Week* noted that for years the principle function of the industrial designer had been to satisfy the public taste for streamlined products. Now it seemed that he was emerging as an individual who combined engineering with functional styling in products that were both efficient and beautiful. *Business Week* suggested that many designers would probably find their best clients among smaller manufacturers who could not afford large staffs of engineers and designers and yet had to put attractive and efficient products on the market in order to meet the competition. In the British magazine *Design,* Dorothy Grafly made the point that "much of the beauty to be noted in these American designs could be produced only by machines under conditions of mass production" (78).

This first showing of professional work in industrial design attracted a lot of attention in both the public press and the design journals. It was widely agreed that the aesthetic quality was generally high, even though some pieces were streamlined in the fashion of the prewar period.

It is particularly important to note that this was the first time that industrial designers themselves had exhibited their own works together in friendly competition. One of the important results of this experience was the decision to periodically produce a book featuring the works of members of the SID that would "make the layman more aware of the significant role which the professional industrial designer has assumed in the shaping of today's mass-manufactured products" (122).

*Francesco Collura designed this futuristic "drink mixer" for the Waring company. Credit: (216).*

*Dave Chapman's sewing machines, included in the first exhibition of the Society of Industrial Designers, had an automobile-style grille and three chrome "speed lines." Credit: (216).*

*John Gordon Rideout's folding wheelchair, a well-organized structure of chromed tubing, was very much in the style of the time. Credit: (216).*

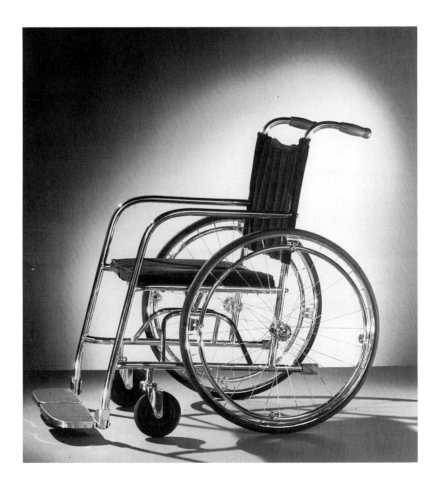

## Contemporary and Exotic Furniture

*There has probably never been a period in the history of furniture when there was so much variety in design, when so many kinds of shapes, materials and techniques were being explored. . . .*

George Nelson, 1949 (137)

By the late 1940s, increasing numbers of mobile, lower-income families were buying houses, and the average size of new houses was decreasing. The *New York Times* reported in 1949 that a "new silhouette" for living had emerged, and that luxurious living now depended on an illusion of spaciousness rather than on oversize furniture. Furniture was becoming increasingly "transparent," with leaner upholstery raised off the floor on thinner legs. It was also observed in *House and Garden* that the development of a new American look in furniture had been hastened by America's isolation from Europe during the war. The new look was seen as forthright, innovative, and "more honestly functional than any previous important collection of American Furniture, . . . with beauty not sacrificed to utility" (92). George Nelson considered modern furniture to be in the American tradition because, like historic furniture, it was the result of the materials and the technology of its own time.

Much of the modern furniture that was promoted to the general public, however, amounted to coarsened caricatures of the original style. Conscientious promoters of good design did their best, but with little lasting effect. Edgar Kaufmann, Jr., of the Museum of Modern Art, implored the public to select furniture that complemented the user rather than abused him, yet many of the chairs selected for the museum's permanent collection were chosen for their aesthetic independence (or their extravagance) rather than for their functional suitability. Eliot Noyes recommended "disposables" for low-income purchasers, suggesting rather loftily that it was better to buy things "that will not last forever instead of things that might" (174). He recommended fishnet and burlap fabrics, straw

mats, labware rather than china, flush doors for tables, concrete blocks for shelf supports, folding chairs, and photographers' lamps.

Until the Depression, virtually all American furniture manufacturers had ignored the developing modern movement; the only modern furniture in the United States had been a small number of pieces imported for a few exclusive shops or fabricated on a custom basis from the designs of architects and designers. After the stock-market crash, the majority of the producers of traditional furniture, finding themselves competing for shrinking orders, lowered the quality of their products to meet the prices that the public was willing to pay. However, the Herman Miller company of Zeeland, Michigan, with D. J. De Pree as president, refused to lower the quality of its product and decided to shift its orientation from traditional to modern design. In 1931 De Pree retained Gilbert Rohde (1894–1944), who had established a reputation designing custom-made furniture in the modern idiom, to design a line of space-saving multi-purpose furniture that his company would be able to manufacture without reducing quality or raising prices excessively. The wisdom of De Pree's decision became evident when, under the National Recovery Act of 1932, the federal government set minimum prices for products in an attempt to save destitute companies from bankruptcy. De Pree's decision (on Gilbert Rohde's recommendation) to shift to modern design that was multipurpose and architectural in character saved the Herman Miller company and established it as the leading manufacturer of contemporary furniture in the United States.

In 1933 the Herman Miller company exhibited a modern house with Rohde-designed furniture at the Century of Progress Exposition in Chicago. By 1934 the company had committed itself entirely to the production of modern furniture. "We came to believe," De Pree writes, "that faddish styles and early obsolescence were forms of design immorality, and that good design improves quality and reduces cost because it achieves long life. . . ." (7, 8)

After Gilbert Rohde's untimely death, De Pree sought a successor for two years before deciding on George Nelson. In him he found a sensitive champion of integrity and technological innovation who expanded the Herman Miller company's commitment to modern design by bringing in Charles Eames, Alexander Girard, Isamu Noguchi, and others to design furniture and textiles. Nelson also shaped the company's public image by designing its new logotype and directing its graphics and promotional programs.

By war's end the Molded Products division of the Evans company, in Venice, California, was manufacturing the first laminated-wood Eames chairs. In 1946, after George Nelson introduced Charles Eames to the president of Herman Miller, D. J. De Pree, the company contracted with Evans to distribute the Eames furniture. Shortly afterward, Herman Miller bought out the Molded Products division in order to make the Eames line of furniture under its own name.

George Nelson has been quoted as saying that without the work of the Swedes and the Finns the Eames chair would not have been possible. Even though such an analogy can be drawn between Eames and the Scandinavians, the fact is that Eames's furniture was the result of his own explorations of laminated-wood technology. His classic chair of the 1940s had shaped veneer laminates attached to a base of welded steel rods by means of rubber shock mounts. It is now acknowledged as one of the outstanding products of the postwar era.

While Herman Miller and a few other companies managed to carve out a special corner of the furniture market for themselves, it became increasingly evident toward the end of the 1940s that most Americans would continue to prefer furniture based on traditional styles for their homes, and that the future for modern furniture lay in the office-furniture market (which was more responsive to the impact of changing technology). Moreover, "the cost of producing quality furniture barred the Herman Miller Company from promoting lines of furniture priced for the mass market" (7, 14)—in other words, Herman Miller either would not or could not orient its corporate policies and facilities toward the production of high-quality, low-price modern furniture for the home.

The dearth of domestically produced modern furniture attracted imports—initially from Sweden, a country whose neutrality had permitted the continued development of modern furniture and furnishings during the war and whose price controls had encouraged the development of new products by applying only to existing ones. The term *Swedish Modern* was already familiar to Americans, having been coined by a critic at the 1939 World's Fair, and American consumers welcomed Swedish textiles, ceramics, and glassware as well as Swedish furniture. (The Swedes, surrounded by conflict, actually had turned away from the experimental and toward a folk-oriented style in modern form, in which Americans saw evidence of a sensitive, socially conscious, humanitarian culture.) The opening of the American market encouraged Swedish manufacturers to develop furniture that could be shipped in a knocked-down state and led to the formation of Swedish export companies such as Priva and Nordiska, which brought moderately priced furniture designed by Bruno Mathsson and others to American showrooms early in the postwar period.

The second Nordic country to seek out foreign markets was Finland. In 1932 Alvar Aalto had devised a technique of bending and gluing layers of Finnish birch to form the structural members of a chair, and the successful exhibition of his laminated furniture in England in 1933 had resulted in the establishment of an English import firm, Finmar. No export agency existed in Finland at the time; however, Artek was soon formed, and by 1947 it was shipping Aalto furniture to the United States. The American interest in Aalto's furniture was heightened by the construction (in 1947–48) of his Baker House at the Massachusetts Insti-

The classic Eames Chair—a complete design, technologically innovative, aesthetically pleasing, and functionally satisfying. A cultural monument. Credit: Philadelphia Museum of Art.

tute of Technology, which was fitted with furniture of his design. About half of the
furniture pieces designed by Aalto are still in
production.

Denmark established an export agency called
Portex; with the Danish Cooperative Society, it
was responsible for locating and servicing foreign markets for Danish furniture (particularly
the less expensive products designed by
Borge Mogensen and others). It was customary for Danish designers to develop the prototype for a piece of furniture and then to
work closely with a manufacturer to adapt it
for production. Incidentally, the manufacturers thought of themselves as cabinetmakers
rather than as market-oriented industrialists.

The most noted of the Danish designer-
craftsmen was Hans Wegner, whose approach
to design (it has been compared to that of a
sculptor) was tempered by an understanding
of manufacturing processes and by consideration for the comfort and convenience of the
user. Wegner had been trained as a cabinetmaker and contined to make custom pieces;
however, he really hit his stride when he was
designing and working out prototypes for
manufacture. Design for high-quantity production obligated him to reconcile the richness of
handcrafted form with machine processes and
accurate duplication by others. In addition,
since much of his work was to be sold abroad,
Wegner had to take into account the need to
facilitate knocking down, stacking, and reas-
sembly. His manufacturer through the years
was Johannes Hansen, master craftsman and
founder of the Copenhagen Cabinet Maker's
Guild. Edgar Kaufmann, Jr., referred to Wegner as "an artist" who had "completely
accepted a professional responsibility" and
who handled the needs of mass production
and mass distribution with "the same careful
freedom that [made] his designs . . . eligible
for the name 'classic' " (109). The design of
Wegner's renowned armchair, which received
the Grand Prize at the Milan Triennale in 1951,
can be traced back to the Han dynasty.

*To Hans Wegner, this was
one of his most satisfying
chairs because of its utter
simplicity and harmony of
parts in relation to the
whole. It represents a
peak in handicraft trans-
formed into contemporary
form.* Credit: Interiors
*(February 1950).*

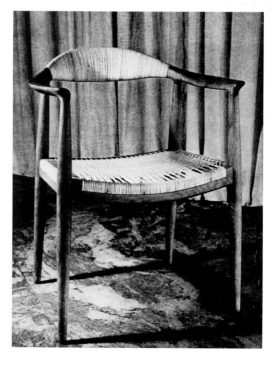

Finn Juhl's line of furniture
for the Baker company
coupled the Scandinavian
concern for shape and
structure with the Ameri-
can flair for the exotic.
Credit: Interiors (September 1950).

Borge Mogensen com-
bined oiled teak and birch
in plain, handsomely pro-
portioned furniture that
was imported at prices
Americans could afford.
The line was produced by
the Danish Cooperative
Society. Credit: Furniture
Forum (June 1952).

Finn Juhl, another Dane, had turned to furniture design from architecture during the war because of the lack of building commissions, and had established himself in his new field by winning first prize in every contest he had entered. Unlike Wegner, Juhl approached furniture design as an exercise in the creation of innovative structures and forms. His furniture, executed by the skilled cabinetmaker Niels Vodder, was more daring than Wegner's but not quite so elegant. In addition to furniture, Juhl designed lighting fixtures, porcelain dinnerware, and residential and commercial interiors. He also served as the director of a school of interior design that was supported by the Danish government. His selection by the Royal Academy of Fine Arts in Copenhagen to design the interiors of the Trusteeship Council Hall at United Nations headquarters led to an invitation from Edgar Kaufmann, Jr., to design the 1951 Good Design Exhibitions in Chicago and New York. Other commissions in the United States included the interiors of the new Georg Jensen store in Manhattan and a line of dramatic furniture for the Baker Furniture Company.

The cost of the better Danish furniture put it beyond the financial reach of most Americans. Noting this, the Danish Export Council challenged architect-designers to develop less costly furniture systems for the U.S. market. Borge Mogensen rose to the challenge by developing a line of furniture made of birch or maple and either veneered with teak or simply oiled or waxed. Furniture by Mogensen and others was marketed in New York by Swedish Modern, Inc., and on the West Coast by Pacific Overseas, Inc. It was also sold on order through the so-called contemporary shops located in major cities across the country.

For some years the Danish designers had a strong impact on contemporary interiors in the United States. Oiled teak and light wood veneers became popular not only for furniture but also for other products. Westinghouse applied the "Danish look" to air conditioners, and Hotpoint to kitchen ranges. (After some

Danish furniture importers filed suit to protect the sale of their products in the United States, the Federal Trade Commission ruled that the adjective *Danish* could not be applied to products not made in Denmark.)

Jens Risom (1915–) occupies a special place in the furniture-design community. He brought with him from his native Denmark in 1938 a Scandinavian commitment to traditional craftsmanship and an affection for natural materials. However, it was his innovative furniture that set Hans Knoll on the way to modern furniture design in 1942. If Herman Miller may be thought of as a uniquely American corporation, founded by Americans to produce designs by Americans, Knoll Associates was the opposite. That company, founded by Europeans, was to depend heavily, at least at the onset, on foreign designers. Hans Knoll (1914–1955) came to the United States in 1937 from Germany by way of England. His father, a furniture manufacturer in Weimar in the early days of the Bauhaus, knew Walter Gropius and had made some of the school's early furniture. A year after his arrival in the United States, the young Knoll had already set him-

self up as a manufacturer in New York City; his early line consisted of one good chair design that he had brought with him from Germany and a few nondescript pieces in the Grand Rapids style.

Risom worked with Dan Cooper as a textile and furniture designer before meeting Knoll and agreeing to design a line of modern furniture for him. In 1942 Knoll and Risom toured the United States for four months, visiting architects and designers referred to them by Howard Meyers, the publisher of *Architectural Forum,* who was convinced that the modern buildings that were beginning to appear on more and more drawing boards ought to have modern furnishings. He encouraged Knoll and Risom to strike out on their own and used the pages of his magazine to support their efforts.

The first product to be designed by Risom and manufactured and marketed by Knoll was a modest little straight chair that Risom had conceived to be made out of non-priority wood and surplus Army webbing. It proved to be not only modern and attractive but also durable and inexpensive to make, and it was the basis of Knoll's first line of some fifteen pieces (including a reclining chair and two- and three-seat settes) that could be produced from standardized seat and frame components and upholstered in whatever material was available—such as military webbing, leather straps, or surplus parachute cloth. This handsome seating helped to establish Knoll Associates as a quality modern furniture company.

By the time Risom went into the army in 1943, he and Knoll had collaborated on a wide variety of projects, ranging from military and transportation lounges to corporate offices and stores. They had also designed and built two interiors for the New York World's Fair: the press lounge of the General Motors pavilion and a kitchen for a modern house in the "America at Home" exhibition. Knoll and Risom were never partners, however; Risom chose to maintain his independence and to be

July 10, 1945.  J. RISOM  Des. 141,839
CHAIR
Filed Sept. 8, 1943

*Fig. 2*

*Fig. 1*

JENS RISOM
INVENTOR

BY

ATT'Y

This small chair by Jens Risom was an early mainstay of Knoll Associates. Simple wood construction requiring minimal handwork, and the use of surplus military webbing, made it and its multiple-seating version virtually the only modern furniture available during the war. Credit: U.S. Patent Office.

Eero Saarinen's "womb chair" (1946), manufactured by Knoll Associates, was an outgrowth of the furniture that he and Charles Eames had designed at Cranbrook. Florence Knoll had encouraged Saarinen to create something she could curl up in, and this was the result. Credit: Interiors (October 1948). Photograph by Herbert Matter.

paid royalties for his designs. Knoll realized that his young company was too dependent on one designer, and after Risom was drafted Knoll expanded the company's stable of designers to include pieces designed by other (primarily foreign) architects and designers. Among other products Knoll arranged to import and sell were a stacking wooden side chair by Ilmari Tapiovaara of Finland and a lightweight stacking chair with an aluminum tubing structure and cord seat and back by Andre Dupre of France. Eventually the firm also added the works of other foreigners: Alvar Aalto, Hans Wegner, Franco Albini, Hans Bellmann, Abel Sorensen, Pierre Jenneret, and Ludwig Mies van der Rohe.

By the time Risom was discharged from the army in 1945, Hans Knoll was moving away from the warmer Scandinavian character to a cooler look that was more appropriate to the International Style. Knoll's shift was due in part to the influence of Florence Schust, who he married in 1944 and with whom he formally established Knoll Associates and opened the first Knoll showroom (designed, incidentally, by Jens Risom). Florence Knoll had studied architecture and design at Cranbrook in its vintage years with Eames, Bertoia, and Saarinen, and later with Mies at the Illinois Institute of Technology.

His own reputation established, Risom severed his connection with Knoll Associates in 1947 to organize Jens Risom Design Incorporated. He not only designed his own furniture in detail but also contracted for its manufacture and distribution. Later he set up and ran his own production facility. Risom's first independent line was still Scandinavian in character, but it also had a certain American economy of means that made it welcome in the American business environment (which was not yet ready for the Bauhausian discipline). Convinced that people needed the warmth, the lively texture, and the visual security that only wooden furniture could provide, he stayed with wood (walnut, primarily) while other office-furniture designers experimented with other materials.

One of the designers Hans Knoll turned to after Risom's departure from his firm was Eero Saarinen, a friend of Florence Knoll's from their Cranbrook days. By 1950 Saarinen had designed two chairs for Knoll Associates. The first was a "relaxation chair" called the Grasshopper, made of laminated wood and resembling somewhat the bentwood chairs that Bruno Mathsson and Alvar Aalto had pioneered in the 1930s. Despite Florence Knoll's early aversion to the Scandinavian look, and despite its limited success in the marketplace, this chair remained in the Knoll catalog for over a decade. Saarinen's second chair for Knoll—the "Womb," a fiberglass shell carried in a cradle of steel rods—was a marketing success. It was developed at Florence Knoll's suggestion as an offshoot of the molded-plywood chair with which Saarinen and Eames had won first prize in the Museum of Modern Art's 1941 Organic Design competition. Its promise of opulent comfort helped to change the public's perception of modern furniture as uncompromisingly inhuman. Saarinen's observation that a chair should

look like a piece of sculpture in a room brought into the open the concept of furniture as exotic conversation pieces. In 1948 *Interiors* magazine described the "Womb" as the season's most revolutionary chair, and soon variants of Saarinen's design began to appear as its influence filtered through the furniture industry.

As the decade ended, Knoll Associates and the Herman Miller company began to turn their attention from the domestic to the business environment. These two companies drew a clear line between constructivistic forms dependent upon modern materials for offices and more familiar forms based primarily on wood for homes. This division in furnishings style also affected imports from the Nordic countries. Swedish, Danish, and Finnish modern contined to serve the home more than the office. Only Jens Risom, it seems, was able to serve the business and domestic environments successfully.

The Museum of Modern Art continued its crusade to bring modern design into the home by announcing in 1948 an expanded version of its prewar international competition for low-cost furniture "to serve the needs of the vast majority of people [for] furniture that is planned for small apartments and homes; furniture that is well designed yet moderate in price, that is comfortable but not bulky, and that can be easily moved, stored and cared for; in other words, furniture that is integrated to the needs of modern living, production and merchandising" (159). In order to prepare the market for the award winners, Nelson Rockefeller, the president of the museum, established a nonprofit organization in conjunction with a group of retail furniture stores located in more than 160 cities. (The idea for this collaboration was supported by, and may well have come from, the director of the MOMA's Department of Industrial Design, Edgar Kaufmann, Jr., who had once managed his family's department store in Pittsburgh.) It was agreed that no awards would be announced until the winning designs were in production. There

were actually two competitions: one (open to anyone) for seating and storage-unit concepts, and one involving six invited teams of prominent architects and designers working closely with prestigious research laboratories with experience in materials and processes. The open competition offered $17,500 in prize money; the team competition promised a $5,000 grant to each team and an additional grant of $2,500 to the team submitting the best report. The winners were announced in January 1949. First prize for seating was shared by Donald Knorr and George Leowald of Germany, Charles Eames and Davis Pratt shared second prize, and Alexis Brodovitch came in third. The only prize awarded for storage units was given to Robin Day and Clive Latimer of England. James Prestini and his Armour Institute of Technology research team were awarded the prize for the best report. Despite the efforts of a distinguished jury, the great hopes of the sponsors and the design community at large, and the anticipation of the general public, the results were disappointing. A year later, when the first production samples were shown at the museum, Knorr's chair proved to be a modest echo of an earlier chair by Ray Komai, Eames's chair was simply the next stage in the development of the 1941 Eames-Saarinen winner (it was now being proposed for manufacture in fiber-reinforced resin), Pratt's inflatable chair was not yet in production, and the manufactured versions of the Day-Latimer storage units did not come up to the quality promised by the design. Eliot Noyes, writing in *Consumer Reports,* commented diplomatically that, although there had not been a great deal of progress since the 1941 MOMA competition, the variety of ideas presented had enriched the design field.

Other competitions were also held during the same period, also with little impact on the development of modern furniture and furnishings. The Museum of Modern Art's 1946 Printed Fabrics competition was in keeping with a flurry of interest in contemporary fabric printing. The Swedish Modern company held a competition for furniture designs suitable for manufacture in Sweden and sale in the United States, but the illustrious jury concluded that not enough thought had been given to current needs and awarded no prizes. Competitions were also held by the San Francisco Museum of Art (for decorative arts), by the Syracuse Museum of Fine Arts (for pottery suitable for mass production), by Haeger Potteries (for vase and console sets), and by the Community Silverware Company of Oneida, New York (for flatware).

It appears that, despite the good intentions of those who promote and sponsor competitions for products to be manufactured, the results seldom come up to expectations. Rarely is a practical yet revolutionary concept stimulated into existence by the promise of instant fame and fortune; generally, a worthwhile new concept grows to maturity to meet the particular needs of its creator before being brought to public light. Perhaps the main functions of a competition are to promote its sponsors and to attract attention to unfilled needs and desires.

Wartime experience with the bending and welding of steel rods was applied to the design and production of chairs, tables, lamps, and other furnishings in the postwar period, and for a time there was a rather mad fascination with "minimal" chairs with frames of steel rods or aluminum or steel tubing and seats and backs of webbing, canvas, leather, or plastic. The frames were painted flat black, as much to hide poor craftsmanship as for the sake of style. Most of these wire or rod furnishings were pedestrian in design, merely duplicating in metal what might just as easily have been made in wood. In the case of the Hardoy chair, however, metal was appropriate because of its strength and resilience. American rights to manufacture the Hardoy chair before the war had been held by Clifford Pascoe. After the war Hans Knoll signed an agreement with the designers to manufacture and sell the Hardoy chair in the United States. The chair had been designed in the mid 1940s by three Argentinian architects after an earlier

wooden chair from England. In 1950 the design was ruled to be in the public domain, despite Knoll's attempts to retain exclusive rights to its manufacture. Some thought the Hardoy chair too difficult to get out of, but Eliot Noyes praised it as a "first-rate example of imaginative design that adapted the flexibility of a hammock to the requirements of the informal easy chair" (68).

The Barwa chair of 1947 was named after its designers, Edgar Bartolucci and Jack Waldheim, who described themselves as socioindustrial designers who dealt first with people's wants and wishes and after that with design and means. Jay Doblin has called the chair "an ingenious piece of whatizit" that "allows a person of any level to rest as nature intended" (9, 69). Harold Cohen and Davis Pratt, who like Waldheim and Bartolucci had been associated with the Institute of Design in Chicago, developed a chair made of steel rods and a nylon sleeve. Their company, Designers in Production, later expanded to a variety of other furniture pieces.

Probably the most important of the rod-frame chairs was the "40/4" chair, designed by David Rowland (who had also been affiliated with the Institute of Design). This chair found its expression beyond function as a ubiquitous product that has yet to be surpassed for economy of manufacture and seating, storing, and ganging effectiveness. Like the others of its kind, it was not the result of market surveys, consumer research, product planning, or any other quasi-scientific methodology, nor was it the result of an artistic approach. Rather, it was the result of three-dimensional design development over an eight-year period. Like many similar products of the period (including chairs, lamps, cabinetry, and a wide variety of other products), it was developed as a piece of sculpture in small scale out of plier-bent wire, bits of paper, and sheet materials. In a way, like Calder's sculptures, it was the result of a three-dimensional medium popular at the time. Since 1964, when it won the grand prize for a manufactured product at the Milan Trien-

This "Allegro" furniture by the Woodward company was chosen by a design jury for Furniture Forum, a trade publication. These skeletal pieces were essentially line drawings executed in steel rod. Credit: Furniture Forum (September 1952).

The Hardoy chair caught the fancy of the design establishment in the 1950s and eventually turned up in the Sears Roebuck catalog. Its simple construction made it easy to copy. Credit: Knoll International, Inc.

Another example of the
possibilities of steel and
plastic was this lounge
chair, designed and
manufactured by Cohen-
Pratt. It and its companion
straight chair were structurally more than lines
reproduced in metal.
Credit: Harold Cohen.

David Rowland's 40/4
chair was the last of 24
prototypes that he made
by hand over an eight
year period. Its first production run went to the
Museum of Modern Art's
new galleries. Credit: (43,
105).

The Barwa chair was
sometimes described as
the best sitting/lounging
chair since the Morris
chair. Whether one sat or
lounged depended on the
exact location of the center of gravity of the base.
Credit: Furniture Forum
(June 1952).

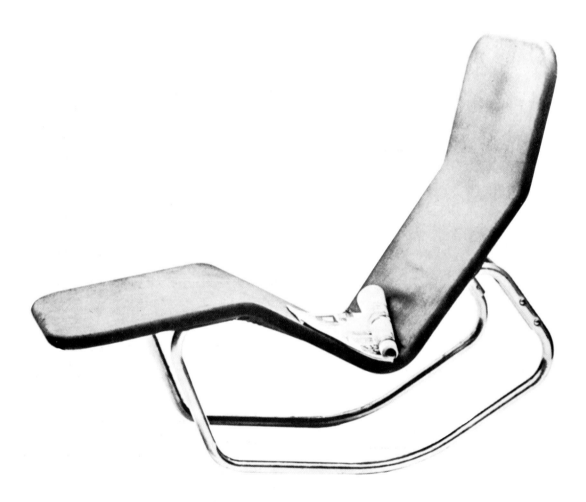

nale, the 40/4 chair has been manufactured under license by the General Fireproofing company.

There were conflicting opinions about the effect that wire and rod frames would have on the visual environment. George Nelson praised the metal-legged furniture for having opened up the "subscape" and thus increased the sense of interior space, but Eero Saarinen (a onetime steel enthusiast who had used steel rods to make the cradle for his "womb" chair) condemned what he called the "slum of legs" and abandoned rod frames for cast aluminum pedestals.

By 1950 most of the classics of modern European furniture had reappeared in the United States. These designs, many of which had been manufactured briefly in the 1920s and the 1930s, found a new lease on life despite the fact that many of the specifications, agreements, drawings, models, and prototypes had been lost during the war. Thus, important designs by modern design pioneers became fair game for anyone who had an early manufactured example and was financially able to manufacture and market the furniture.

Many of these pieces of furniture can properly be classed as exotics—that is, expressive works whose primary value is aesthetic rather than functional. They were not intended to meet human needs at reasonable prices, and they dominated the spaces they occupied rather than fitting into them.

Much of the exotic furniture designed in the 1950s was the work of architects who were exploring new materials and forms as an outlet for their imaginations at a time when architecture was dominated by the unrelenting formalism of the International Style. Although use, production, and economics had to be considered, form and expression took precedence. In effect, the results ended up as centerpieces in the living environment, standing proudly away from the walls and other furnishings to be admired from all sides while life went on around them. In business offices, chairs and other pieces of furniture joined the reception desk as barometers of the up-to-the-minute good taste of management. In the lobbies of prestigious buildings and resorts, chairs and other seating units were used to command respect and awe. Above all, they aspired to be placed on a pedestal or behind a barrier or glass in a museum as "stars" of the best in modern aesthetics. In a way they may be parallel to the baroque automobiles of this intriguing era.

Exotic furniture pieces seemed to be metaphors of functional contemporary furniture. George Nelson's 4658 desk was stripped of superfluous elements. The Nelson office's "sling" sofa (conceived with assistance from Ronald Beckman) was essentially an example of innovative structural design. George Nelson and Charles Pollock developed the "swaged" leg as the basis for a group of chairs, desks, and tables (which were less useful than they were elegant). Nelson's "marshmallow" sofa and "coconut" chair offered whimsical evidence to support his earlier conviction that a human being can sit on anything. In response to contemporary criticism that modern furniture was very limited in expression or even dull, Nelson commented forcefully: "There has probably never been a period in the history of furniture when there was so much variety in design, when so many kinds of shapes, materials and techniques were being explored. . . . many blind alleys will have to be explored before the main directions are established." (137)

Charles Eames's most exotic piece of furniture was the lounge chair he is said to have designed as a gift for the film director William Wilder. The chair, of laminated rosewood with thick cushions upholstered in black leather, was intended to provide the ultimate in comfort. When the prototype, built by Eames with the assistance of Don Albinson and others, was shown to Herman Miller, Miller arranged for his company to put it into production. The chair was an instant success and can now be found in hundreds of studies and private

Eero Saarinen's answer to
the "slum of legs" was this
pedestal chair (1956)
manufactured by Knoll.
Although the seat and the
base were of different
materials, the chair came
across as one aesthetic
form. Credit: Philadelphia
Museum of Art. Photo-
graph by Will Brown.

George Nelson's 4658
desk for Herman Miller
retained the functions of a
desk but eliminated the
furniture. It was, Nelson
noted, not very different
from some eighteenth-
century writing tables.
Credit: Herman Miller, Inc.

The Nelson group's
"sling" sofa for Herman
Miller was designed for
heavy use as well as to
dominate lobbies. The
steel parts were joined by
epoxy resin; the pillows
were supported by neo-
prene back straps and a
seat platform. Credit: (43,
32).

*Nelson and Company's playful sofa for Herman Miller (appropriately named the "Marshmallow") consisted of bar-stool seats mounted on a frame. Credit: Herman Miller, Inc.*

This Alan Dunn cartoon, captioned "A chair, they say, is to sit," accompanied George Nelson's article "Chairs" in Holiday magazine. Dunn was particularly interested in the world of design. His sharp perception brought the mad race to design into focus. Credit: Holiday (November 1957).

The "swaged-leg" group of furniture designed by George Nelson and Company for Herman Miller began with a search for a beautiful sculptured leg, which the remainder of the design was then developed to match. Credit: Industrial Design (December 1958).

Charles Eames's master-
piece is this lounge chair.
Herman Miller has been
manufacturing it since
1956, and more than
100,000 have been sold.
Credit: Philadelphia
Museum of Art.

offices. R. Craig Miller claims it has "achieved a mythological aura afforded few objects in modern design, although in this instance an extremely comfortable status symbol" (29, 127).

Harry Bertoia (1915–1978), a colleague and associate of Eames at Cranbrook and in California, applied his early experience with silversmithing to the development of exotic furniture with welded-wire shells after he joined the Knoll company's development group. "The urge for good design," he wrote, "is the same as the urge to go on living. The assumption is that somewhere, hidden, is a better way of doing things." (20, 66) Warren Platner's exotic wire furniture was an extension of Bertoia's pioneering work.

Much as chairs were now being referred to ("scientifically") as *seating units,* cabinets were now labeled *storage units.* Whereas cabinets had been thought of as secure vaults for treasures, storage units were often meant to display their contents. It was a short step from the term *storage units* to a system of structural components that could be purchased separately and assembled into a variety of configurations. Purchasers liked the flexibility and mobility that such systems provided, and retailers were happy to be able to meet a wide range of storage needs with a limited number of parts.

Charles Eames designed a storage system for Herman Miller that was constructivistic in character, exposing and even flaunting its structural elements and cross bracing. The panels, doors, shelves, and drawers were emphasized by the use of colors, textures, and both transparent and opaque materials. This was, in effect, a domestic interpretation of standard warehouse storage structures, and thus a forerunner of the short-lived "high-tech" style. The Eames system was followed by a number of similar storage systems that also tried, without lasting success, to break with the traditional use of natural or natural-appearing materials in the home.

Wharton Esherick, George Nakashima, and Sam Maloof were among the designer-craftsmen who specialized in making furniture one piece at a time, primarily by hand. They were less interested in the bizarre than in forms that were in the craft tradition of modern furniture. To the extent that this attitude resembled that of the Shakers, these men had something in common with the Scandinavian designer-craftsmen, who were respectful admirers of the Shakers' work.

T. H. Robesjohn-Gibbings, Edward J. Wormley, and other prominent furniture designers worked with respected manufacturers such as Widdicomb and Dunbar to develop more sedate furniture that was modern in spirit and was meant for upper-class homes.

Paul McCobb (1917–1969), called by *Business Week* the "creator of the contemporary look for young moderns," had come to furniture design from the field of marketing. He had been selling furniture in stores and designing store layouts and displays on the side when he had realized that the furniture industry was paying little attention to the needs of young couples who were trying to furnish small apartments and had to make do with hand-

Wire sculpture was Harry
Bertoia's preferred
medium. His "Diamond"
chair for Knoll Associates
uses wire for the seating
shell and rod for the base.
Bertoia claimed that his
chairs were mostly air,
and that "space passes
right through them."
Credit: Philadelphia
Museum of Art.

Warren Platner's furniture
for Knoll Associates was
made of wire joined by
resistance welding to
create shaped planar sur-
faces. Credit: (44, 3).

Charles Eames's storage
system for Herman Miller
was an answer to the
basic need for a com-
prehensive but modestly
priced storage system of
shelves and cabinets.
Credit: Herman Miller, Inc.
Photograph by Charles
Eames.

The designer-craftsman
Sam Maloof believed that
design permeated every
step in the creation of his
work. Maloof used an
electric band saw as
freely as an eighteenth-
century craftsman used
his chisel. Credit: Sam
Maloof. Photograph by
Schenck & Schenck.

*T. H. Robsjohn-
Gibbings's furniture for
the Widdicomb company
had a clarity of form that
made modern ideas palat-
able to those with more
conservative tastes. Even
his "wobble"-shaped side
table seemed to have an
air of respectability.
Credit:* Interiors *(February 1948).*

*Edward J. Wormley's
furniture, such as this
handsome cabinet
manufactured by the
Dunbar company, was
refined from the best in
the modern spirit and was
eminently suitable for
upper-class environments.
Credit: Dunbar. Photo-
graph by Frank Willming.*

Paul McCobb's Planner Group brought modern furniture design within the financial reach of young consumers. Its fresh, rather neutral style and its flexibility suited the needs of a younger, more mobile generation. Credit: "Planner Group Designs by Paul McCobb" (catalog).

Gilbert Watrous was awarded a special prize in the Heifetz competition for this delicately balanced floor lamp, which was selected for manufacture by the company. However logical, the concept was apparently too advanced for its time. Credit: Interiors (May 1951).

me-downs or cheap copies of traditional furniture and heavy overstuffed chairs and sofas. In 1945, after military service, he established his own firm to develop a line of reasonably priced modular furniture for this market. McCobb's experience and his sensitivity to the times helped him to create forms that were modern without being bizarre and folksy without being rustic and that conveyed an awareness of Windsor and Shaker furniture and an affection for Scandinavian furniture without requiring handwork. After completing his first line (the Planner Group) in 1947, McCobb formed an organization in 1950 with B. G. Mesberg to find factories and to handle distribution and sales; they were fortunate to locate and tie in with the Winchendon Company in Massachusetts, which was looking for products to manufacture after the war. The McCobb-Mesberg organization offered its first line, the low-priced Planner Group. Later they added Directional (a higher-price line sold only through showrooms by decorators and designers) and Linear (priced to sell between the other two lines). McCobb also designed the Predictor line for the O'Hearn company. Of all the designers of his generation, McCobb came closest to meeting the aspirations of design-conscious young couples—without playing down to them. In the late 1950s McCobb developed a mass-produced system of modular cabinet and counter components for the Mutschler company. Based on a framework of aluminum extrusions and panels of hardwood veneers, the system made it possible for homeowners to plan and install arrangements to suit their own needs. George Nelson and Company developed a similar line for the Omni company. Both lines, however, proved too complex to compete with ready-made cabinet systems.

The Museum of Modern Art was persistent in its determination to bring designers and manufacturers together in the interest of good modern design. In the wake of the spirited controversy that grew out of Marcel Breuer's comment in 1949 that he had not found any lamps in the marketplace that were suitable for his House in the Museum Garden, MOMA decided to sponsor a competition in 1950 to encourage the design of modern incandescent lamps for the home. (In the office environment, lamps had given way to fluorescent fixtures concealed by translucent plastic panels or metal "egg crates.")

The Heifetz company agreed to sponsor the competition and to manufacture several of the award winners for sale through 24 department stores across the country. The competition drew some 3,000 entries, from which the jury (consisting of the architect Marcel Breuer; the hopeful manufacturer, Yasha Heifetz; and some representatives of the museum) selected fifteen winners. All the winning designs were interesting space structures made primarily of sheet metal or plastic baffles or reflectors with rod or wire supports. They were objects that could be made in any small shop. Like the lamps they were intended to replace, they were conceived more for the interplay of light and form than for function. A few Italian designers were also creating lamps in unusual forms and selling them (often to collectors) through shops such as Arteluce in Milan.

Despite Breuer's complaint, there were some modern lamps of good design being made in the United States. Walter Von Nessen and Kurt Versen had designed some for their own companies. John Vassos had developed a lamp for the Egli company that provided what he called a "periphery of darkness," which provided a reader with a pool of light in a darkened room without disturbing others who might be watching television. Jean Reinecke's Dazor lamp (still in production today) was described as an "all-purpose floor lamp" with "a rather jaunty air" (83). These men with others were designing lighting products that met all the criteria for good modern design and that were unpretentious and suitable for the domestic environment.

Only a few of the modern lamps of the postwar period were commercially successful. One was Isamu Noguchi's 1948 table lamp, a translucent plastic cylinder standing on three legs.

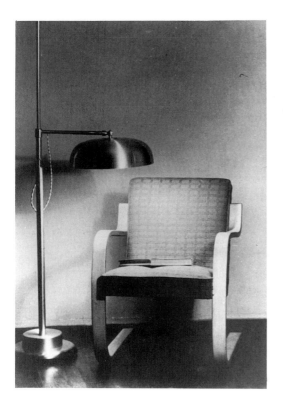

*John Vassos designed a series of lamps for the Egli company that combined an incandescent bulb with GE's Circline fluorescent tube. The lamps had a technological appearance that was to become high style. Credit: John Vassos papers, George Arents Research Library, Syracuse University.*

(Noguchi went on to design the Akari series of more dramatic hanging and standing paper lamps, which were made in Japan for export.) Also successful were the "bubble lamps" developed by George Nelson and William Renwick for the Howard Miller company. The bubble lamps were produced by a method—developed during the war for protecting materiel stored on the decks of transport ships—that involved spraying plastic over a wire frame. For a while they were popular, especially in shops and restaurants; however, the white translucent plastic shades yellowed with time and trapped dust on their fuzzy internal surfaces.

Danish lighting products, such as the folded paper lanterns of Kaare Klint, were widely admired but found a limited market in the United States; they may have been too decorative and too playful. The Finnish designer Paavo Tynell became best known in the United States for a series of hanging fixtures consisting primarily of pierced brass reflectors shaped like leaves and flowers. Introduced to the United States at Finland House and its adjacent restaurant in New York, they were popular for a time in American shops and restaurants as a foil to Scandinavian furniture and textiles.

Despite the postwar efforts of American designers and manufacturers, few of the modern lamps of the era stood the test of time. Like their Italian and Nordic counterparts, they provided interesting conversation pieces but tended to transform a utilitarian product into a short-lived fashion commodity. Whatever merit they may have had was drowned in a sea of imitations. So lamps continued to depend on more traditional forms and styles. The lamp area, no matter how brightly lit, is still the dreariest part of a furniture or department store.

Other products besides furniture and lamps also offered challenging opportunities. Simpler products, such as clocks, calendars, and desk sets, came within the technological range of simpler manufacturing processes

Isamu Noguchi, taken with the lanterns used by cormorant fishermen in Japan, brought two lamps made to his own designs to New York in 1951. They were successful enough to make them an enterprise of the whole town of Gifu. Credit: Fifty-50 Gallery, New York.

"Bubble lamps," produced by spraying plastic and vinyl over wire frames. Credit: (43, 34).

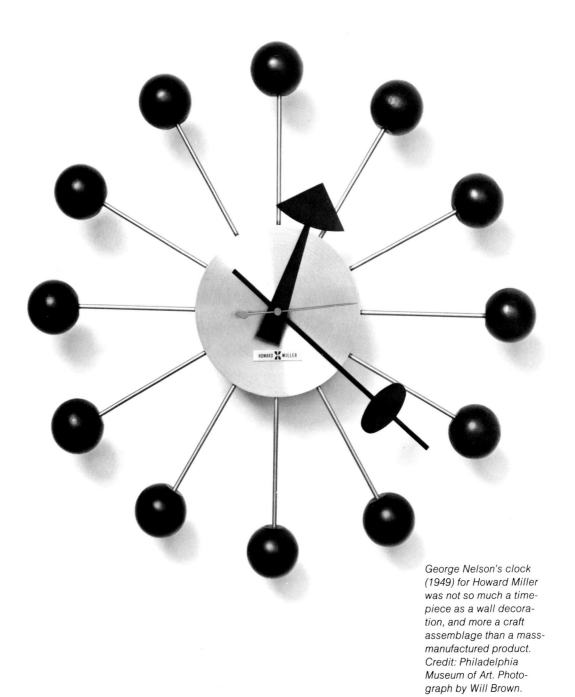

George Nelson's clock (1949) for Howard Miller was not so much a time-piece as a wall decoration, and more a craft assemblage than a mass-manufactured product. Credit: Philadelphia Museum of Art. Photograph by Will Brown.

The first models for architectural pottery that came out of La Garde Tackett's class assignments in 1949. Credit: Industrial Design (October 1957).

and could be constructed and tested without the sophistication demanded by complex mechanical and electronic products. Designers could easily carry their ideas through the prototype stage in their own shops. Furthermore, educators found such products to be good exercises for designers in training. In one notable case, La Garde Tackett, a teacher at the California School of Art in Los Angeles, assigned his class to develop monumental pottery planters that would harmonize with modern architecture. When the results were exhibited at the Evans and Reeves nursery in Los Angeles, they aroused so much interest that the nursery ordered duplicates for sale. Architectural Pottery, the firm that was formed to meet the orders that soon came in from architects and interior designers, later branched out to produce plastic benches, shelters, and lamps.

## The "Good Design" Syndrome

*The Good Design exhibitions mean different things to a great many people. . . . When its meaning is clear, and generally accepted, . . . it will be time to put an end to the Good Design program.*

Edgar Kaufmann, Jr., 1951 (141)

The Museum of Modern Art's exhibitions of useful objects available on the open market at modest prices had been held prior to the war over the Christmas shopping period in order to introduce a gift-buying public to modern design. During World War II, one Useful Objects exhibition had been staged that was especially directed to the needs of men and women in the service. Then in 1950, with Edgar Kaufmann, Jr., as director of the Department of Industrial Design, a different program was launched with a similar philosophy in mind: to bring good modern design to the attention of the public. The Good Design program, as it was named by Kaufmann, was conceived as a collaborative effort between the museum and the Merchandise Mart of Chicago. It was initiated by a request from the Mart for assistance in attracting manufacturers of modern furnishings to display and market their products to dealers in its exhibition area.

René D'Harnoncourt, representing the museum, and W. G. Ollman, general manager of the Merchandise Mart, signed an agreement providing for a series of exhibitions of products to be selected from among the wares offered at the Mart on the basis of "eye appeal, function, construction and price, with emphasis on the first" (118). "It is," declared a joint statement, "the first time an art museum and [a] wholesale merchandising center have cooperated to present the best examples of modern design in home furnishings. . . . These two national institutions, whose very different careers began just 20 years ago, believe and hope that in combining their resources they will stimulate the appreciation and creation of the best design among manufacturers, designers and retailers. . . . The attention of all America will be focused on the good things being created by the home furnishings indus-

try." (145) The plan was that a three-person selection committee—consisting of a permanent chairman (Edgar Kaufmann, Jr.) and a designer and a retailer appointed for each show—would be charged with selecting items from the showrooms maintained by various manufacturers at the Mart. The selections would then be installed in a special exhibition on the seventeenth floor. During the winter market the exhibition would be open only to wholesale buyers; afterward it would be open to the public, with a guided tour offered for a fee.

The two judges appointed for the first Good Design exhibition were Meyric C. Rogers, curator of decorative arts at the Art Institute of Chicago, and Alexander Girard, a designer and architect from Detroit. With Kaufmann, they selected some 250 products, primarily American but a few from Scandinavia. The installation, designed by Charles and Ray Eames, used showmanship and humor to ease the minds of visitors, most of whom were experiencing modern design for the first time. An introductory section displayed both old and new products in a manner intended to suggest to the wary visitor an analogy between classics of the past and classics of the present. The exhibition opened in January of 1950.

According to plan, the exhibition was refreshed and expanded for the summer market with some 150 new products. The members of the second selection committee—Kaufmann, Serge Chermayeff (an architect and the director of the Institute of Design in Chicago), and Berthold Strauss (the president of the Moss Rose company)—were urged by the sponsors to consider usefulness, methods, materials, and the progressive taste of the moment. (Polls taken during the summer show reveal that the wholesale buyers who were surveyed agreed with the consumers in only one instance. In retrospect it can be presumed that the buyers who took time out from their dealings in the market to visit the exhibition were more accustomed to safe, traditional styles, whereas many of the consumers who were

*The goal of the first Good Design show was to convince wary visitors that modern design was friendly and had roots in the past. Perhaps this installation, with a thirteenth-century Madonna and an eighteenth-century fork, helped. Credit:* Interiors *(March 1950). Photograph by Carl Ullrich, Inc.*

interested enough to visit the show and to pay the admission fee were people with a personal interest in modern design.) After the summer exhibition, selected items were shipped to New York to be shown in a similar Eames installation at the Museum of Modern Art during the pre-Christmas season. At the private preview of the show, John Jay Whitney, the chairman of MOMA's board of trustees, acknowledged the major role of manufacturers and distributors of everyday objects in the creation of public taste and commended the Merchandise Mart for its pioneering venture in cooperation between art and industry. He also called attention to Kaufmann's discriminating taste and his knowledge of industry, merchandising, and art.

Good Design began its second year at the Merchandise Mart with a fresh collection of items selected by Kaufmann, William Friedman (an architect associated with the Walker Art Center in Minneapolis), and Hugh Lawson of the Carson, Pirie and Scott department store in Chicago. Kaufman used the occasion to respond to some misconceptions about the program that had surfaced during the previous year. The jury's selections, he said, did not necessarily represent the best work designers could do. Rather, they were the best of the designs that had made their way through the processes of development and manufacture and had been able to survive in the marketplace. Furthermore, they were not truly representative of public taste, because they had been chosen by buyers. Kaufman insisted that the restriction to products actually available on the market kept Good Design from being an "ivory tower" program, and he suggested that the shows be measured not in terms of ultimate cultural value but in terms of their value as presentations of the current state of the art. They should, he asked, be taken as a buying guide by consumers, as a lead to new markets by retailers, and as an index of achievement by designers, teachers, and students.

The Danish architect and designer Finn Juhl designed the 1951 installation at the Merchandise Mart, an elegant and reserved sequence of living spaces. In a commentary on the planning of this installation, Juhl called attention to a fundamental difference between craft-based and mass-manufactured products. Contrary to conventional wisdom, he pointed out that older products had been conceived as parts of a larger whole and thus had been obligated to respect their intended environment and find a logical place in it. On the other hand, products designed in the modern idiom were intended to stand apart and to compete for attention in the modern environment.

The year 1951 brought the introduction of Morton Goldshall's graphic symbol for the Good Design program. With it came a publicity program conceived by Robert Johnson, promotional director for the Merchandise Mart. For a fee his office provided manufacturers of products selected for exhibition with a kit of promotional literature complete with tags, labels, suggested window displays, and other materials.

During the 1951 summer market, another 150 items were added by the new committee, which included Philip Johnson (director of the department of architecture at the Museum of Modern Art) and the architect-designer Eero Saarinen. The additions included a large number of foreign products from Italy, India, England, France, Germany, Sweden, and Finland and several new pieces of furniture designed by Finn Juhl for the Baker Furniture Company of Holland, Michigan.

As in 1950, selections from the show at the Merchandise Mart were displayed during the pre-Christmas period at the Museum of Modern Art. The higher quality of this second MOMA show was taken as proof that more attention was being given to the appearance, the efficiency, and the pricing of contemporary furnishings. In conjunction with this showing, the museum held a conference (entitled "How Good is Good Design?") in

*Finn Juhl's installation was a careful grouping of ensembles of related products. In the foreground are Franco Albini's glass-topped desk (from Italy) and Ernest Race's cast-iron chair (from England), both of which were on sale in the United States. Credit:* Interiors *(March 1951). Photograph by Carl Ullrich, Inc.*

*Morton Goldsholl of Chicago designed this symbol, whose use was reserved to products selected for Good Design exhibitions. Credit:* Industrial Design *(October 1954).*

which a panel of designers and design editors discussed the results of a poll in which visitors had been asked to name their most liked and their most disliked item in the show. The general conclusion that consumers and designers were not as far apart in taste and preference as might have been supposed seems to support the inference that wholesale buyers were blocking the popular acceptance of well-designed contemporary products.

Paul Rudolf's installation for the 1952 Good Design show at the Merchandise Mart was theatrical, with screens of various materials and dramatic lighting drawing attention to the products. The selection committee for the January show included Harry Weese (an architect-planner from Chicago) and Charles Zadok (the head of Gimbels' department store in Milwaukee). With Edgar Kaufmann, Jr., they selected 250 items, to which a few were added that had been held over from 1951. Despite the spectacular installation, or perhaps because of it, the products were not judged to be as interesting as those of previous years. It is also possible that the shock of the new had worn off, and that buyers at the Mart had become more complacent about modern design. The judges noted that an unusual number of wrought-iron and wire furniture pieces and lamps had been submitted, and prided themselves on having rejected many such items and having balanced those they accepted with the more fluid sculptural forms of the Scandinavians. The selection committee for the 1952 summer market—Edgar Kaufmann, Jr., F. Carlton Ball (a potter and designer from Southern Illinois University), and Gordon Fraser (a merchandiser of modern products from California)—also resisted the black-iron mania. The more than 300 new products they selected reflected their own interest in tableware.

Alexander Girard's installation for the Good Design shows of 1953 was even more dramatic than the white environment Paul Rudolf had created for the late-1952 show at the Museum of Modern Art. Girard placed products on white surfaces in pools of bright light in completely black surroundings. The

The "centerpiece" of Alexander Girard's installation was a double wall of illuminated styrofoam. It dramatized the small tablewares contained even as it made it difficult for the observer to see and evaluate them. Credit: Interiors *(February 1953).* Photograph by Carl Ullrich, Inc.

*Alexander Girard
dramatized other objects
in the 1953 show by spot-
lighting them in an otherwise black environment.
They were thus once
removed, like museum
exhibits, from the public.
Credit: Arts and Architecture (March 1953).*

thematic center of the show was a lighted white styrofoam wall against which shelved glasswares and other small products were silhouetted. The installation had seemingly become as important as the products. The members of the selection committee for the January show—D. J. De Pree (president of the Herman Miller company), Russel Wright (listed as a designer of home furnishings), and Kaufmann—had agreed to look for products that met the needs of sensible buyers rather than for things that would shock them. This jury also refused to yield to the avalanche of black iron. They selected a good range of small products (such as flatware, kitchen utensils, and other metal, wood, and glass items) as well as new patterns in printed textiles. For the summer show, the architect and designer Florence Knoll and Harry Jackson (vice-president of the Jackson Furniture Company) worked with Kaufmann to select some 200 items from the 6,000 submitted. The inclusion of wire chairs designed by Harry Bertoia and some chrome-and-leather furniture designed for Laverne, Inc., by William Katavolos, Ross Littell, and Douglas Kelley made this one of the most modern of the Good Design exhibitions. *Interiors* magazine decided to publish photographs of all the products selected for the 1953 Good Design exhibitions, and devoted most of its February, March, and September issues to the task. *Time* and several other publications also took note. *Time* referred to these exhibitions in terms of the museum's having been showered with thousands of new items through the Merchandise Mart and then having selected a few hundred for Good Design awards.

The 1954 Good Design exhibition included (in another dramatic installation by Alexander Girard) some 350 items culled from 2,500 submissions by Lasette Van Houten (a former home-furnishings editor for *Retailing Daily*), Edward Wormley, and Edgar Kaufmann, Jr. The committee noted two different trends that were evident in the selections: a formal modern style that favored clear-cut shapes, precise details, smooth surfaces, and black and white and primary colors; and a softer, friendlier

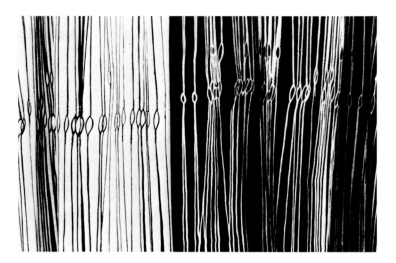

*Eszter Haraszty's silk-screened linen textile "Fibra" was based on the hettle loops once used as thread guides in weaving. Displayed in the 1953 Good Design show, it was one of the classic fabric designs produced by Knoll Associates. Credit:* Interiors *(September 1953).*

*Paul McCobb's two silk-screened patterns on cotton, Space Flowers (above) and Cross Wedge (below), manufactured by the Riverdale company, were in the 1953 Good Design show and were very much in fashion. Credit:* Interiors *(September 1953).*

*This "T" chair in chrome, black steel and cowhide, by William Katavolos, Ross Littell, and Douglas Kelley for the Laverne company, was in the 1953 Good Design show. Its handsome, classic form reflected the architectonic character of the International Style. Credit: Douglas F. Kelley.*

look that involved flowing forms, natural materials, and muted colors. In a report published in *Arts and Architecture* they also called attention to the new cabinet systems of Norman Cherner and George Nelson, which they described as mature versions of Charles Eames's earlier storage units. Also included in this show were Isamu Noguchi's Akari paper lanterns and the innovative sheath-and-tube furniture of Davis Pratt and Harold Cohen.

Since 1954 happened to be not only the fifth year of the Good Design program but also the twenty-fifth anniversary of the founding of the Museum of Modern Art, the sponsors decided to offer three special retrospective exhibitions in a new, larger space in the Merchandise Mart. The first of these included 100 products selected for excellence of design from previous shows by a committee that included MOMA director René d'Harnoncourt, Alfred H. Barr, Jr., Philip Johnson, Porter McCray (MOMA's director of circulating exhibitions), and Edgar Kaufmann, Jr. The second exhibition consisted of photographs and textile swatches of 100 popular sellers, selected through a survey taken by *Retailing Daily* of manufacturers who had had two or more of their products in Good Design shows. Thirteen of these products had also appeared on the MOMA jurors' list: three Eames chairs, three simple metal or enameled bowls (one by Ernst Lichblau, one by Gross and Esther Wood, and one by Ronald Pearson), two plastic dinnerware sets (one by George Nelson and one by Russel Wright), a Cohen-Pratt chair, a Katavolos-Littell-Kelley chair, Tom Lamb's handles for a set of Cutco kitchen tools, Paul Rand's Abacuş print, and a Plas-Tex wastebasket. The third section consisted of special exhibitions from several schools of design that were invited to present their own impressions of what developments they believed would affect Americans' way of life and their homes in the decade to come.

However, by 1954 it was evident in the field of home furnishings that the modern design movement was beginning to slow down. Indeed, during that year's winter market the

*These simple yet elegant
perforated metal bowls
(black enamel on steel) by
Gross and Esther Wood
were selected by both the
jury and the manufactur-
ers for the special 1954
Good Design exhibition.
Credit: (45, 64).*

Merchandise Mart staged—in addition to the Good Design exhibition—an exhibition called Today in Tradition, which showed "what the manufacturers of traditional furniture, fabrics and lamps are providing for the homes of today" (146).

There was one last gasp of life left in the Good Design program. The jury for the 1955 winter-market show at the Merchandise Mart, Edgar Kaufmann, Jr., Arthur BecVar of General Electric, and Just Lunning of Georg Jensen's New York store, selected 400 products for presentation. The installation was done by the young architects Daniel Brennan and A. James Speyer, who had also designed the 1954 retrospective exhibition. *Interiors* noted with some editorial surprise that this final Good Design show included a number of "industrial designs that hardly qualify as home furnishings" (such as a camera, some telephones, and a folding play-yard), but acknowledged the inclusion of kitchen equipment and household appliances as an "indication of the broadening scope of Good Design" (147).

Edgar Kaufmann, Jr., resigned from the Museum of Modern Art in 1955, in part because he felt that his exhibition program had accomplished its original goal of making consumers and manufacturers aware of good design. Others contended that the museum had been attempting to force manufacturers and designers to subscribe to a rather narrow theory of what constituted good modern design.

The Good Design program had come into existence because manufacturers and consumers had needed guidance about modern design. The exhibitions had provided the public with an opportunity to experience modern design that it might not have otherwise had, and manufacturers with access to potentially useful new design ideas. In the final analysis, the Good Design program, though it was not without its failings, provided positive evidence that a modern movement in design did in fact exist.

As Herwin Schaefer notes in his book *Nineteenth Century Modern,* during the 1950s the exhibitions and publications dealing with "good design" and "everyday art" came almost to a complete stop. "The exhibitions phase of the modern style," Schaefer writes, "was in a sense an aftermath of its creative phase in the postwar decades." (36, 199)

## Better Design for Better Living

*A new kind of Elegance emerges for a middle-class classless society. As a trend it . . . [reflects] a healthy self-indulgence, a new interest in simple routines and humble objects, a belief in the ceremonial enjoyment to be found in everyday occasions.*

Industrial Design, 1955 (94)

After World War II it was natural that, as long as shortages existed, any shelter that could pass as a house or any appliance that would run when it was plugged in would be tolerated. But what of the extravagant wartime promises by designers and advertisers that their clients had dramatic new products ready to be rolled out at war's end?

The promises disappeared into thin air. Some manufacturers merely cleaned up prewar tooling and put it back into service on production lines. Even those manufacturers who had found time to work on postwar products needed more time to convert to new tooling.

W. A. Dodge, the new-products editor of *Business Week,* expressed the impatience of the public when he complained to a meeting of the American Designers Institute in November 1945 that "no overall trend in design [was] perceptible in the new products released by manufacturers since VJ Day" (171). Dodge allowed that there might be new products on designers' drawing boards, but regretted they had not yet been brought to the consumer. But the editors of *Interiors*, in their first annual survey of postwar products, noted with satisfaction that "the period of Post-War Promise as represented by the super-deluxe, super-streamlined designer's concept of the gadget-of-the-future-not-yet-in-production seems to be dead" (128).

The editors of *Interiors* had more products to choose from when the time came for the 1948 Annual Design Review. They noted that the number of candidate products had increased substantially because manufacturers, now that the magazine was increasing its attention to designers, were less reluctant to let them be identified with their efforts. The editors were also careful to point out that their selections were not necessarily the best that might have been available, but expressed their concern over the increase in gimmickry and excessive styling. As particular markets became saturated, some makers felt obliged to resort to such extremes in order to attract and hold consumers' attention. The editors suggested that industrial designers should police their own ranks and should influence manufacturers to make, and consumers to insist on, better-designed products.

Among the products in the 1948 review that deserve special attention was the vacuum cleaner designed by Raymond Loewy Associates for the Singer Sewing Machine Company. It represented a complete rethinking about the product, based on functional improvements. With all its advantages, it is difficult to understand why the product did not succeed in the marketplace. Perhaps it was not given the advertising and marketing support that it deserved.

Peter Blake, curator of architecture and industrial design at the Museum of Modern Art, reacted to the 1948 Annual Design Review with a caustic letter to the editors of *Interiors* in which he complained about the fact that square corners were out of favor among industrial designers. In a sense his comments reflect postwar architecture's immersion in the International Style. Architects judged everything in terms of the flat surfaces and square corners that were dictated by their instruments and by building materials and were not generally familiar with industrial processes that favored die casting and injection molding. In fact, forms that are to be cast or stamped are much more logically conceived in non-rectilinear shapes.

Blake also criticized the fins and grilles on automobiles, perhaps neglecting the fact that Americans associated these motifs with the airplanes and armored vehicles that had brought victory to the Allies. (This is not to condone the senseless transference of sym-

*Jane Fiske Mitarachi,
editor of* Industrial Design,
*promoted formal dining in
an informal environment.
Credit:* Industrial Design
*(December 1955). Photo-
graph by Frances Foote.*

*Raymond Loewy's vacuum cleaner for Singer (1946) was a new concept for an old product. Credit: (39, 33).*

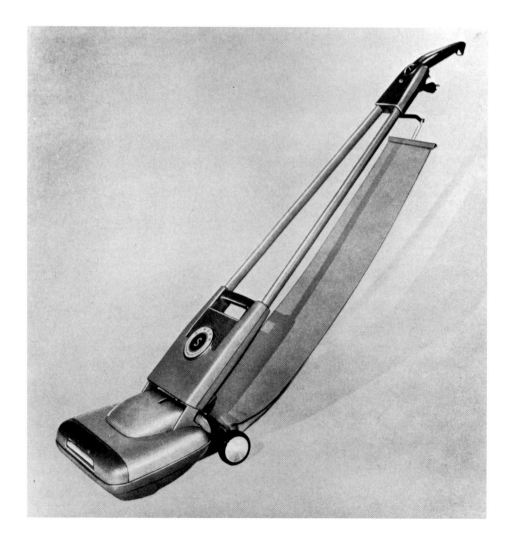

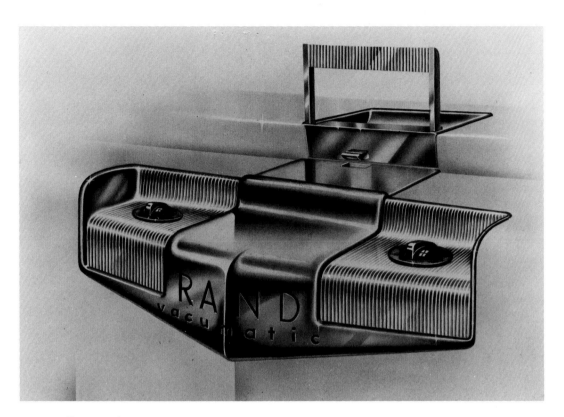

*An armor-like escutcheon (1947) designed by Raymond Spilman for the Rand Washing Machine Company. This airbrush rendering emphasizes the attempt to combine rectangular shapes with the softer forms necessitated by die-casting technology. Credit: (216).*

This bold chrome-plated
freezer latch (1953) was
designed by J. M. Little
for the Bendix company.
Its form echoes the high-
lights of an airbrush rendering. Credit: (216).
Photograph by Toledo
Photographic Service.

Bendix Duomatic washer-
dryers (1954) on the
production line. The
designer, Mel H. Boldt,
had picked up the circular
theme of the company's
original "porthole" dryer
and added a chrome "pro-
peller" handle. Credit:
(216).

This electric range (1958),
designed by J. M. Little,
combines the Bendix
company's circular theme
with suggestions of an aircraft control panel. Four of
the "dials" are actually
circles of push buttons.
Credit: (216). Photograph
by Toledo Photographic
Services.

The XR-10 experimental refrigerator was developed by Arthur BecVar and the Advanced Appliance Design Section of General Electric in 1953 to test the potential of a horizontal unit. Consumer enthusiasm led to production; however, sales were disappointing because existing home layouts could not accommodate the new form. Credit: (216).

Exploring potential markets for refrigerators, Servel developed the Wonderbar in 1953. Credit: (216).

bols and shapes, but simply to acknowledge that at any period in history the products and the art of a people reflect their experience.)

By 1955, production of some appliances had caught up with and surpassed demand. The annual production of refrigerators had gone from 2.5 million in 1940 to 6.2 million in 1950 to 4.2 million units in 1955. A similar rise and fall was evident in the production and sales of electric and gas cooking ranges. Appliance manufacturers were aware that an increasing percentage of sales in the near future would have to be in a replacement market. Since major appliances did not normally wear out as quickly as other products, consumers would have to be induced to replace their still-usable ranges, refrigerators, and washing machines through the introduction of new features and dramatic new designs.

General Electric had been experimenting with alternative configurations for refrigerators since the early 1950s. One proposal was the XR-10 horizontal refrigerator, which took advantage of a new insulating material that reduced the bulk and weight of a refrigerator to the point that it could be hung like a cabinet above a kitchen counter or installed as a divider between kitchen and dining room. Even those refrigerators that retained the conventional form had their interiors reorganized to provide specialized compartments to meet different temperature and humidity requirements. A major change was the development of a separate freezer compartment to store the increasingly popular quick-frozen foods. One smaller company, Crosley, had survived into the 1950s on the strength of a patent granted in 1933 for shelving on the inside of a refrigerator door. In 1950 the patent ran out, and door shelving soon became common. The 1950s also brought self-defrosting refrigerators and automatic ice-makers. Servel (the company that introduced ice-makers) also offered small refrigerators, patterned after those used in hotel rooms and cabins, for offices and dens.

*This Servel icemaker (1953), with an appearance design by Donald Dailey in collaboration with Reinecke and Associates, was adaptable to standard refrigerators. Credit: (216).*

The modern cooking stove, too, was becoming a more flexible appliance. As its source of energy had changed from wood to coal to oil to gas to electricity, its placement in the home had become more and more a matter of function and preference. When the Thermador company had begun (in 1946) to offer separate ovens and stovetops, the stove had begun to lose its place of honor in the kitchen. In 1954 the microwave oven was invented. Design efforts for the moment, however, were primarily devoted to relocating the fundamental components of the traditional stove and to applying veneers and trim. One arrangement that received a great deal of attention in the mid-1950s had the oven and its controls above the stovetop, at eye level.

A number of more practicable appliance concepts were explored by Raymond C. Sandin, manager of the Hotpoint company's Visual Design Department. Sandin, born in Sweden, had been educated as an architect at the Massachusetts Institute of Technology before joining Hotpoint in 1935. During the war he had organized a service within the company to help people plan the modernization of their kitchens—for a small fee his staff (at one time consisting of twenty young women) would recommend solutions to various problems. This program provided Sandin and Hotpoint with a wealth of information that proved valuable when they designed appliances in the postwar period.

Between 1954 and 1959 Sandin and his staff and design consultants developed an original approach to predictive product design, which they called the "Custom Trend" approach. They designed and built full-scale prototypes of new appliance configurations and displayed them at markets and shows across the country in order to gauge the reactions of prospective customers. "The 'Custom Trend' idea," Sandin writes, "gave us designers a chance to stretch our wings and soar a little higher in the clouds. I believe that out of this experiment the company also gained new respect from our dealers and the consumer who were perhaps made to realize that we were in there swinging." (202)

The great interest in the kitchen reflected a general feeling that the saturated appliance market, the promises of new product configurations, and the recent technological breakthroughs called for not only a new approach to appliances but also a new approach to the layout of the kitchen. The prewar concept of the kitchen as a white porcelain laboratory was not consistent with the casual lifestyle of the postwar era, nor did it seem as important as it once had to treat the home as a place to display capital goods.

The trend in kitchen layout and styling was toward a combination of modern efficiency with more comfortable finishes and materials. The preference for natural materials (or at least a semblance thereof) was evidence of a growing interest in the "honest" and "rural" rather than the sophisticated and urbane. Cabinets of white woods, such as maple, birch, and oak, were favored over those of dark woods. Scandinavian design had popularized teak, and stoneware had achieved a modest respectability. Despite the visions of the kitchen of tomorrow as a technological miracle, kitchen decor was working its way back to the past. Although many of the materials were synthetic imitations, the nostalgia was real.

Even before the war, the trend in kitchens had been toward built-in cabinets and continuous counters. Built-in cabinets were a natural outgrowth of the "Hoosier cabinets" of the 1920s and also a response to the need for more storage capacity that accompanied the general shift from daily shopping in local grocery stores to the once-a-week trip to the supermarket.

It was entirely reasonable that major appliances should be made dimensionally compatible with kitchen cabinetry. In practice, however, "built-ins" often consumed space rather than conserving it. As walls were extended to conceal the sides of refrigerators, ranges, dishwashers, cabinets, and counters, ceilings and floors shrank and kitchens became rather galley-like. Another conse-

*The Thermador com-*
*pany's first separate oven*
*and burner units were*
*custom-built before World*
*War II. In 1946, recogniz-*
*ing the growing potential*
*for their use in modern*
*kitchens, the company,*
*with Norman Rae as staff*
*designer, developed*
*these elegant stainless-*
*steel units. Credit:* Industrial Design *(October*
*1957).*

Raymond Sandin with a
Hotpoint pull-down cook
top at the Merchandise
Mart in 1959. Hotpoint
was bucking the trend
toward built-ins. Credit:
Raymond C. Sandin.

The Hotpoint company's
High Oven Range, devel-
oped in 1957 by Raymond
Sandin, moved away from
old antiseptic white look.
Credit: Raymond C.
Sandin.

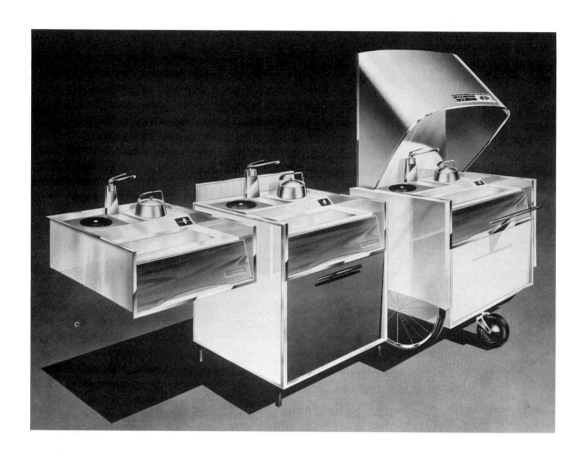

An airbrush rendering by design consultant Brooks Stevens for Hotpoint's Custom Trend program, showing three applications of a cook-top. Credit: Raymond C. Sandin.

Mock-up of Gourmet Center (1959) developed as part of the Custom Trend program by Raymond Sandin with Brooks Stevens and displayed for comment at the Merchandise Mart. Credit: Raymond C. Sandin.

quence of the fashion for "built-ins" was that cabinets and major appliances, which had once been thought of as property that came and went with the residents, now were seen as part of the house and left behind with it.

Appliances once offered only in white finishes began to show up in colors—turquoise one year, copper the next, then avocado, then harvest gold. The introduction of color and fashion in the kitchen influenced the design of other appliances, such as irons, vacuum cleaners, sewing machines, washers, and dryers. General Electric introduced a "Roll-Easy" vacuum cleaner with a turquoise and copper color scheme.

The counterpoint to fashion in appliances was "human engineering," which had proved valuable during the war. (The British preferred the term *ergonomics*.) Human engineering blended static and dynamic anthropometry with a consideration of the physical and psychological relationship between human beings and the man-made environment. There was nothing really new about human-factors studies in the home. In a way, this was an extension of an academic stirring that began in the 1850s with the Domestic Science courses that the Beecher sisters proposed as the feminine equivalents of the science courses that young men took. Even before World War II the program had expanded from nutrition and health to home economics, which covered all aspects of domestic life. In 1952 a research publication, *The Cornell Kitchen,* presented a detailed study of various kitchen tasks. It became a bible for architects and others concerned with domestic planning, and it may have stimulated the development of the task-oriented small appliances that later flooded the market.

In the 1950s there was renewed interest in futurism in kitchen and appliance design as several companies decided that circumstances justified another foray into the world of tomorrow. There appears to be a correlation between the state of the economy and a

decline in sales that periodically justifies such excursions. Management may also feel the need to overcome whatever complacency may have crept into the company's design and development areas by providing a field day for imagination. There is always the possibility that a nebulous concept may take form that will, in fact, direct the future of kitchen and appliance design. At the very least, such projects serve as market-oriented propaganda. By promoting promises, they refresh the name of the company in the public mind and may lead to subsequent purchases.

In 1954, the Frigidaire division of General Motors unveiled (at the Waldorf-Astoria Hotel in New York) a "Kitchen of Tomorrow" with stainless-steel appliances that retracted into cabinets. Developed by Frigidaire designers with the consultation of Alexander and Rowena Kostellow, it also featured a refrigerator that dispensed cubed and crushed ice and ice water. Two years later Frigidaire displayed the "Kitchen of Tomorrow III," designed and built in Leroy Kiefer's Product and Exhibit Studio with George Pollard as project head. All the appliances (except the ultrasonic dishwasher) had been designed to fit into counters. One counter had a marble cooking surface and a glass-domed oven. A revolving under-counter storage unit had separate compartments for dry and frozen foods. There was also a "communication and monitoring center." Despite its obvious showmanship, this kitchen demonstrated many rational ideas. After being displayed at the Waldorf-Astoria, it toured the country as part of GM's Motorama.

Not to be undone, other companies introduced their own dream kitchens and futuristic appliances. Westinghouse experimented with a countertop microwave oven with a lamp-like metal hood. RCA/Whirlpool's "Miracle Kitchen," developed in 1957–58 with assistance from the Detroit consulting firm of Sundberg-Ferar at a cost of $250,000, had a central command post from which a seated housewife could control a variety of appliances, including a robot vacuum cleaner.

By the late 1950s it was evident that the trend in the design of major appliances was away from the softer shapes of the streamline era and toward sharp rectilinear forms. Where once the use of high-temperature glass enamels had necessitated rounded corners for proper flow and fusion, now the introduction of thinner insulation made it possible to use lighter-gauge, prepainted sheet metal, which could be formed into sharp rectangular boxes on new continuous roller machines without stamping and crowning. Moreover, rectangular boxes were in harmony with the International Style of architecture and suitable as "built-ins."

Frigidaire captured the public's attention with an inspired advertising campaign (conceived by the Kudner agency) that promoted the "Sheer Look" of its new appliances. Other companies had taken slow, hesitant steps toward the new look, but Frigidaire boldly redesigned its entire line in the style of the 1956 Kitchen of Tomorrow. No one seemed to regret the elimination of the armorial escutcheons and chrome hardware that had characterized appliance design for a decade. The Kudner agency's advertisements for the new line in magazines and newspapers showed models in Oleg Cassini "Sheer Look" gowns performing the "Sheer Look" gesture with elbow-length gloves. In a further effort to fix the line's association with high style in the public mind, Frigidaire staged a well-publicized fashion show to which other prominent fashion designers were invited to contribute costumes inspired by the "Sheer Look." Thus one word, *sheer,* was used to identify a line of products with high fashion, and with runaway success.

It must be said, however, that the very plainness of flat, unadorned surfaces invited color, textures, and meaningless and even frivolous decorations that, in their own way, may be criticized as being as senseless as their predecessors' "fat" baroque forms had been. The wisdom of tying the appearance of major appliances to high fashion in women's clothes is also questionable, but the new look was actually generated by technological advances

*The ingenious General Electric Roll-Easy Vacuum Cleaner, designed by R. H. Koepf and J. C. Shalvoy in 1955. Credit: Industrial Design (December 1955).*

General Motors' Kitchen of Tomorrow III was a popular feature of the 1956 Motorama. From this experimental project (developed for research purposes as well as for show) came the "Sheer Look," which set the pace for the appliance industry. Credit: General Motors Corporation.

The "Sheer Look" discarded the clutter of applied baroque decoration on appliances and virtually eliminated the use of metal stampings and glass enamel. Credit: Ladies' Home Journal (April 1958).

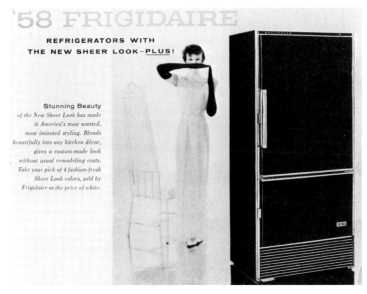

**'58 FRIGIDAIRE**

REFRIGERATORS WITH
THE NEW SHEER LOOK—PLUS!

**Stunning Beauty**
of the New Sheer Look has made
it America's most wanted,
most imitated styling. Blends
beautifully into any kitchen décor,
gives a custom-made look
without usual remodeling costs.
Take your pick of 4 fashion-fresh
Sheer Look colors, sold by
Frigidaire at the price of white.

Although the Disposall
would be installed out of
sight, it was seen and purchased in view. In 1950
Arthur BecVar and his
staff, the Appearance
Design Section of GE,
transformed the clumsy
device into a clean-look-
ing one to increase its
consumer appeal. Credit:
(37, 41).

rather than by fashion—it was associated with fashion in order to make it more palatable to the public.

The public had accepted the displacement of heavy porcelain-enameled steel sinks with lighter ones made of stainless steel, and more and more kitchen sinks were being equipped with a strange contraption that ate garbage. General Electric had introduced its Disposall before the war and had sold few—perhaps because of the device's clumsy appearance. Though it was meant to be installed out of sight, the Disposall began to sell well after it was given a new housing that made it look more like other appliances. Another postwar innovation in kitchen sinks was the Moen faucet that mixed hot and cold water and controlled the flow with one lever.

The Revere company was the first manufacturer to ship out a carload of stainless-steel pots and pans after the war. In 1946 the Ekco company introduced a set of stainless-steel kitchen tools, the Flint Line. Developed by Ekco engineers Jack Zimmer and Walter Luneberg, with James Hvale as a staff designer, the Flint Line set a no-nonsense style that became the typeform for such products. Sold in sets, with the packaging designed by the firm of Latham, Tyler, and Jensen, the Flint Line was a marketing success (owing largely to its popularity as a gift to new brides). The Flint Line and the Revere Ware line are among the few postwar designs to have achieved classic status.

A particularly innovative development of the early 1950s was the wedge-lock handle developed by Thomas Lamb as a result of his extensive studies of the dynamics of the human hand. This revolutionary handle, which made use of the hand's tension to lessen fatigue and improve grip, was used extensively in cutlery, hairbrushes, luggage, and crutches.

*The "Flint" line of kitchen tools, designed in 1948. Credit: Jay Doblin.*

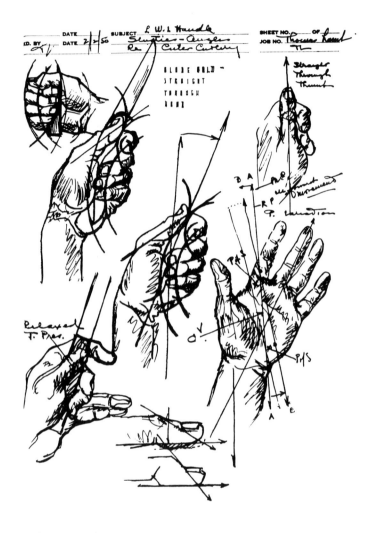

*Some of the sketches in which Thomas Lamb refined the design of his Wedge Lock handle. Credit: Thomas Lamb.*

*Two of Thomas Lamb's handles. Credit: (216).*

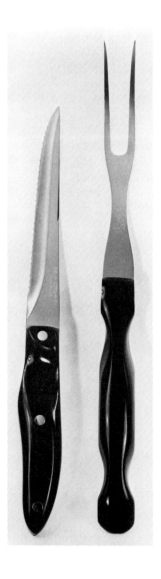

C. F. Graser, who worked with Arthur BecVar at General Electric during the 1950s, credits the president of GE, Ralph Cordiner, with the introduction of Product Planning, the technique that stimulated the invention of many new portable appliances (such as electric skillets, saucepans, can openers, Toast-R-Ovens, and spray irons). "Products that once appeared as gimmicks," writes Graser, "are considered staple items in almost every home today." (196)

A great amount of the design activity centered on small appliances, whose portability suited them to the new spirit of mobility and whose size and price suited them to gift-giving. Many of these appliances were related to the new methods of processing and packaging foods, and most of them were technologically simple (which encouraged entrepreneurs to enter this lucrative market).

The electric toaster had already been around for a while. In 1938 the McGraw Electric Company had contracted with Jean Reinecke to cut the cost and upgrade the appearance of a toaster designed earlier by Joseph Sinel. The result, Toastmaster 19B—the most popular electrical appliance ever produced—served for years as the typeform for other toasters.

Most of the new appliances were aimed at the American passion for labor-saving devices. With names like Broil-Quick, Redi-Baker, Fry-ryte, they promised to help the amateur prepare food correctly with minimal skill, time, or energy. And for those consumers who thought they had everything, there was always another miraculous device—an egg poacher or a corn popper—to make life even easier.

For others who wanted electrical conveniences that combined practicality with traditional elegance, there were coffee makers in which sterling silver was replaced with chrome-plated or bright anodized aluminum on forms adapted for volume production. Peter Müller-Munk went the other way; his Cafex percolator declared its function directly, without pretending to be an aristocratic treasure. Automatic saucepans, skillets, griddles,

and grills also searched for acceptable forms, and Salton's warming Hotray depended upon printed circuitry to simulate the engraved pattern of a serving tray. Dave Chapman was hired by the Club Aluminum company to design a line of "cooking vessels with a dinner-table air" (130).

The blender, introduced in 1937 by the Waring Mixer Corporation, reappeared in 1945 in a new version (designed by Francesco Collura) that looked rather like an Art Deco rocket launcher. Peter Müller-Munk's simpler 1948 version, with its "waterfall" base, was more economical to produce. (The latter design was put back into production in the mid 1980s.)

Americans prefer individually powered products in the kitchen, although a single power source with attachments could perform as well. Attempts to provide a single power source are applauded as rational but seldom universally accepted. This is due both to the consumer's impatience with the time it takes to change the attachments and to an affection for things that leads to the proliferation of appliances and tools.

Peter Schlumbohm, who had come to the United States from Germany in 1935 with a doctorate in chemistry, invented a number of unconventional products. Best known for the Chemex coffeemaker, a successful domestic adaptation of the laboratory practice of filtering, he obtained over 300 patents—each of them representing an effective understanding of scientific principles and a unique use of forms. His best-known products other than the Chemex coffeemaker were the Filterjet fan and a blown-glass water kettle with a cork ball for a stopper.

In 1942 the Castleton China Company asked the Museum of Modern Art to recommend a designer to develop a high-quality line of modern dinnerware. Eliot Noyes suggested Eva Zeisel, a well-known European ceramic designer who was teaching at the Pratt Institute, and she was given the commission. An agreement was reached by which the museum

This cast-aluminum cook-and-serve ware, designed in 1947 by Dave Chapman for the Club Aluminum company, had a simulated hammered finish that hid flaws, broke up the mechanical look, and suggested the planished surface of hand-wrought holloware. It was said to be reminiscent of Georgian silver. Credit: (39, 16).

This electric knife sharpener, designed by Joseph Palma, Jr., in 1947 for the Cory company, was described as "deluxe styled" and was intended to compete at a higher price with an existing sharpener. Credit: (39, 44). Photograph by Allen, Gordon, Schroeppel and Redlich, Inc.

Jean Reinecke's Toast-
master (1943) introduced
a distinctive three-loop
decoration, which was
intended to distract attention from minor surface
distortions and imperfec-
tions. The decoration
became the company's
symbol and was emulated
in various forms by other
companies. Credit: Jean
Otis Reinecke.

The General Mills toaster,
designed by John Polivka
in 1949, picked up the
Toastmaster's styling and
carried it to a baroque
extreme. Credit: General
Mills.

John Polivka carried the
Toastmaster styling
approach—complete with
embossed decoration—
over to this General Mills
Electric Waffle Maker
(1946). In form and details
it was suggestive of silver
tableware. Credit: (216).

A similar approach was used by Polivka in this squat coffeemaker for the M. K. Graham company (sold under the private label of Duncan Hines). Credit: (216).

The "Cafex" percolator, designed by Peter Müller-Munk for the Hartford Products Company, was a straightforward modern design suitable for kitchen or table use. In proportions and detailing it reflects the designer's experience with silverwares. It achieves elegance without aristocratic pretense. Credit: (216). Photograph by Newman-Schmidt Studios.

A coffeemaker designed in 1964 by A. M. Felske and M. C. Havenstein for O. E. Haggstrom, manager of industrial design at General Electric. Credit: (216).

Peter Schlumbohm, who
invented the Chemex
coffeemaker in 1941,
believed that design
should be a by-product of
the inventive process. He
claimed that the hourglass
form of the coffeemaker
was dictated by function.
Credit: Chemex Corpo-
ration.

A water kettle designed
by Peter Schlumbohm in
1949. "The boundary line
for product design,"
Schlumbohm declared,
"is the borderline between
the virility of invention and
the femininity of fashion."
(115a) Credit: Philadel-
phia Museum of Art. Pho-
tograph by Eric C.
Mitchell.

This lightweight GE portable mixer was designed in 1949 by Rudolph Koepf and his staff, but production was delayed by material shortages until 1952. An injection-molded plastic shell replaced the die-cast metal one used on the previous model. Credit: (216).

Peter Müller-Munk's 1948 design for the Waring electric mixer has maintained its popularity and is in production again. Credit: (216). Photograph by Newman-Schmidt Studios.

In 1953 GE replaced a
well-established iron that
had been in production
since the war. It was felt
that a "new and better
appearance would ensure
its continued acceptance"
(220). Chrome details
brightened the form and
increased the focus on the
controls. Credit: (216).

This open-handle dry iron
developed for GE in 1956
by John Salvoy with
Rudolph Koepf, manager
of industrial design, is an
example of form as the
purest expression of function. Credit: (216).

The Hotray electric food-warming tray was developed by Lewis Salton, with appearance design by Peter Quay Yang, in 1957. Salton used printed circuitry to simulate traditional engraving and teak handles and an extruded-aluminum frame to maintain a modern look. Credit: "Design U.S.A." exhibition catalog, 1965.

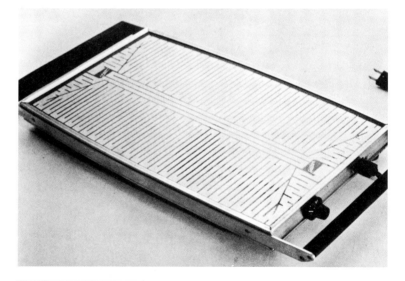

The GE Toast-R-Oven had its origins in 1957 in a search for a new appliance that would serve a range of functions, from toasting and warming food to baking. Designers Roger Funk and Paul Rawson, working under Ollie Haggstrom, contributed to this 1967 model. Credit: (43, 21).

Eva Zeisel's fine china-
ware achieved modern
elegance with recogniz-
able traditional forms.
Credit: Eva Zeisel.

The Coors company's
porcelain labware was
"discovered" by the
design establishment and
promoted for use in the
home. Though these
wares were not conceived
as aesthetic objects, their
simplicity and their technical perfection were in
harmony with modern
design. Credit: Coors
Porcelain Co.

would promote the line if it came up to expectations. However, final development and production were delayed by the war. In 1946 the line, now called Museum Modern, was finally introduced. Despite the quality of the chinaware and the prestige of the Museum of Modern Art, the line did not survive.

The market for fine American china was on the decline. Except for one or two companies that had established solid reputations with traditional designs, the American china manufacturers fell before an onslaught of imports from Europe and Asia. (The Castleton company was eventually bought out by a Japanese firm and used as a cover for exports to the United States of so-called English ironstone with names such as Independence Hall.) One of the problems besetting the American china industry was a trade agreement that permitted imports of fine china while it restricted imports of hotel and commercial china. Another factor working against the success of the Museum Modern line was the apparent unwillingness of American consumers to accept modern china for formal dining and entertaining. However, modern china was accepted for everyday purposes, and the design establishment "discovered" the fine porcelain laboratory ware produced by the Coors Porcelain Company of Golden, Colorado, and promoted its use in the home.

Fine modern porcelain that could be sold at fair prices was being imported from Germany. In 1950, after having been shown in the Detroit show "For Modern Living" and at the Museum of Modern Art, the cleanly shaped products of the Arzberg porcelain factory in Bavaria were imported for sale in the United States. The line had been designed in 1931 by Hermann Gretsch, an architect who had been working for Arzberg, and had won gold medals at exhibitions in Milan (1936) and Paris (1937). At $5.50 a place setting, this was the only fine china that Americans with modern tastes and moderate means could afford.

In 1952 Philip Rosenthal, Jr., son of the founder of the century-old Rosenthal porcelain factory in Bavaria, put together a four-man "international design team," each member of which was to develop a basic shape. Other designers were commissioned to provide decorations. Raymond Loewy and his associate Richard Latham were responsible for the "2000" design, which won the Grand Prix in the Brussels World's Fair of 1958. The Rosenthal company established its own displays in major American department stores. In addition, special shops were opened by Rosenthal in the United States and other countries to sell the company's products in association with other products of comparable quality. Rosenthal's fine contemporary porcelain products, known as the Studio Line, found a good, albeit exclusive, market in the United States but made little impression on those Americans who insisted on traditional styles.

The American market for "casual" china was well served by American companies. Eva Zeisel designed two successful lines (Tomorrow's Classic and Century) for Hall China and one (Town and Country) for Redwing. Frederick Read designed Fiesta for Homer Laughlin, and Viktor Schreckengost designed the Manhattan line for American Limoges. Russel Wright, after the success of the American Modern line of low-cost earthenware he had designed for Steubenville Pottery, undertook the development of a new line of high-fired dinnerware for Iroquois China of Syracuse. The line, originally called Casual China, consisted of simple, thick, durable pieces that could go directly from refrigerator to oven to table. Protrusions and thin edges were eliminated to reduce breakage. The line thus had every functional advantage that Wright could imagine; however, it was heavy, somewhat clumsy, and perhaps too strange-looking to attract as many purchasers as the Steubenville line had. Eventually, it was shipped in boxcar lots to California, where it was marketed as California Modern.

Casual china, a line of
heavy fine china designed
by Russel Wright in 1946
for manufacture by Iro-
quois China with the goals
of maximum strength and
heat-shock resistance,
was introduced in the
1950s and sold with floral
decoration. Credit: (45).

The hourglass shape of the "2000" line of fine porcelain, designed by Raymond Loewy in association with Richard Latham, was very much in vogue in the 1950s. The decoration was by Ute Schroeder of Hamburg. Credit: Rosenthal Studio Line brochure.

Tupperware (1945) proved that lightness, translucency, and flexibility could be assets rather than faults in container design. Credit: (249).

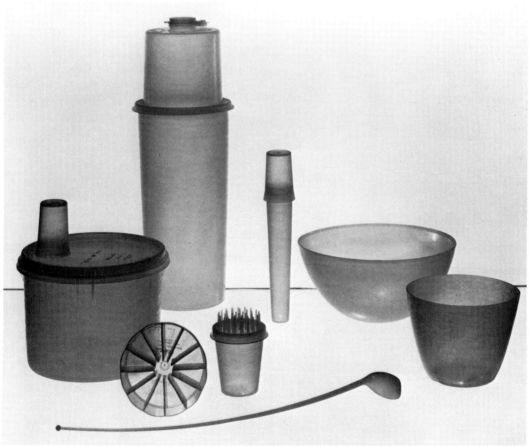

*This polyethylene refuse container was designed for the Rubbermaid company in 1958 by the consultant firm of Smith, Scherr and McDermott and company designer Clyde Breneman. Credit: F. Eugene Smith.*

In the 1930s the plastics industry was still in its infancy insofar as domestic housewares were concerned. Despite the urea formaldehyde Skippy bowls and other plastic premiums that were given away to stimulate lagging sales of cereals and other food products, the limited range of available materials did not encourage widespread application. Then a number of new thermoplastics opened the way. Acrylics, under the trade names Lucite and Plexiglas, appeared in 1935 in the form of crystal-like giftware. Their toughness and optical clarity led to their use in transparent bubbles on military aircraft. When polyamide resins (e.g. nylon) appeared in 1939, the future of the industry was still uncharted; however, no longer were plastics thought of only as cheap substitutes. The polystyrenes, introduced in 1938, had only just begun to displace the less stable cellulose acetates in housewares when Pearl Harbor was attacked.

In 1942, a new thermoplastic called polyethylene appeared. This flexible yet remarkably durable material was immediately put into war service as an insulating material. A chemist, Earl S. Tupper, sensed its greater possibilities, and in 1945 (after reformulating the material) he began to manufacture a tumbler. That application opened up new opportunities for plastics in an area previously dominated by glass, metal, and wood. By its very nature, Tupper's material was at its best in simple modern shapes that were flexible, durable, and eminently adaptable for refrigeration, storage, and table use. And, perhaps above all, the products were inexpensive. Tupper called his material Poly-T to avoid lingering doubts about anything called plastic, but later on products made of it were dubbed Tupperware. In the late 1940s, Tupperware began to be marketed through a unique system of parties that brought the product directly into people's homes. By 1951, sales had grown to the point that conventional retail sales were abandoned, and by 1958, when the Tupper Corporation was sold to the Dart Company, Earl Tupper was able to retire comfortably with an estimated 9 million dollars. Polyethylene also came to be used for much larger containers, such as the garbage can developed by the Akron firm of Smith, Scherr, and McDermott for the Rubbermaid company.

Melamine, a formaldehyde-based thermosetting compound, had been known for more than 100 years as a tough yet light material that was scratch-resistant, odorless, and tasteless. It was not, however, until the Army needed light helmet liners and the Navy light, virtually unbreakable shipboard dinnerware that manufacturers reconsidered this material. James Devine of Devine Foods was one of the first to experiment with its applications to food trays and the like.

At war's end, the American Cyanamid company saw a future for melamine in dinnerware. There was laboratory evidence that it could be manufactured in brighter colors than had previously been called for, and there was a belief that its resistance to scratching could overcome the whispering campaign—encouraged by the ceramics industry—that plastic dinnerware harbored dangerous bacteria. In 1945, American Cyanamid decided to challenge the public's resistance to plasticware by commissioning Russel Wright to develop a line of melamine dinnerware for restaurants. (The commission went to Wright because the wife of the president of American Cyanamid was an admirer of his American Modern dinnerware.) With a surface that had the appearance of glazed china, Wright's melamine was acceptable at the table. Several restaurants were furnished with sample sets to test the line under severe conditions. Within a year after the spectacularly successful introduction to the market of American Cyanamid's melamine dinnerware, more than a dozen other companies had introduced similar products. Retailers were still reluctant to display such products alongside their fine china and glasswares, but melamine found a convenient and profitable place in the housewares sections of department and specialty stores.

Joan Luntz's 1951 Desert Flower line for International Molded Plastics and Belle Kogan's 1954 Boonton Belle line for Boonton Plastics

brought the feminine sense of form to melamine, and the development of printed melamine inlays inspired a fresh approach to decoration. At first, melamine wares were designed to look as much like china as possible. However, as plastic dinnerware became more familiar to the public, the designs were changed to take advantage of the material's molding possibilities. Concern about the sanitary qualities of plastic disappeared, and today plastic wares are as common as ceramics.

Perhaps the most elegant line of melamine dinnerware was the Florence Ware line, developed in 1955 by Irving Harper of George Nelson's office for the Prolon division of the Prophylactic Brush Company. This line's dignity and elegance brought it up to the quality level and the desirability of fine china. Thus, while the American porcelain-dinnerware industry virtually disappeared because it could or would not break away from traditional styles, designers demonstrated that they could conceive new forms in new materials that the general public was ready to accept.

In 1959, Restaurant Associates commissioned Garth and Ada Louise Huxtable to design an entire range of tableware for the Four Seasons restaurant in the new Seagram Building in New York. The Huxtables described their challenging task as being, in an incredibly short time, "to translate the unusual food and service requirements of the Four Seasons into equally unusual accoutrements that would match the simplicity and elegance of the restaurant itself" (111). Philip Johnson and Ludwig Mies van der Rohe, who were responsible for the building's design integrity, and the interior designer, William Pahlmann, insisted that no expense be spared in developing or locating a harmonious grouping of china, glassware, and holloware that would contribute to the elegance and the high style of the novel modern restaurant. The result was an elegantly severe set of tableware that complemented the rich menu. Eighteen of the pieces designed by the Huxtables were subsequently selected by the Museum of Modern Art for its permanent collection. For once, the judgment

"Florence," an elegant
line of melamine din-
nerware, was designed in
1955 by George Nelson
and Irving Harper. The
pieces were as delicate
as fine porcelain yet
strong and durable.
Credit: George Nelson.

Serving pots designed by
Garth and Ada Louise
Huxtable in 1959 for the
Four Seasons restaurant in
the Seagram Building.
Credit: (43, 15).

Russel Wright's "Highlight" flatware pattern for John Hull Cutlers was designed in 1952. Because the technology for forging stainless steel was still developing, the line was stamped from heavy-gauge sheet metal. The pieces, however, were organic in form, shaped to fit the hand and to suit their functions. Credit: (41, 171).

Don Wallance's flatware pattern "Design 2" for the H. E. Lauffer company (manufactured abroad in 1957) forged stainless steel into solid sculptural forms. Deep forging resulted in eloquent modern shapes that were free of superficial styling and decoration. Credit: (216).

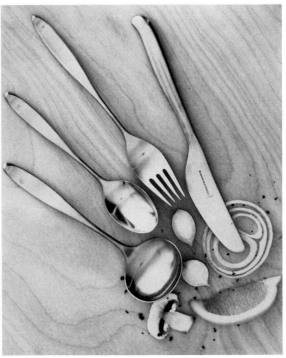

of designers had prevailed rather than that of marketing experts and buyers. The fact that the Four Seasons and its furnishings and accessories have become modern American landmarks suggests the potential quality of the American environment if designers had more to say about it.

While the Huxtables were silver-plating alloys for the Four Seasons, stainless steel was making its way to the dinner table. In the home, stainless-steel flatware had been accepted as a stand-in for sterling silver that either was being saved for special occasions or had not yet been acquired. Now, having evolved simple and elegant forms through the difficulty of stamping and embossing, stainless-steel flatware became fully acceptable for home use. Russel Wright and Don Wallance pioneered the use of satin-finished high-quality stainless steel for modern flatware. Their designs stand as classic expressions of the medium.

In the past it was customary to expect that women would make their entry into industrial design by way of the design of products for the domestic environment. Joan Lutz and Belle Kogan have already been mentioned as designers of melamine dinner wares, as has Ada Louise Huxtable for her work with her husband on appointments for the Four Seasons restaurant. However, they and others, including Freda Diamond, Dale Hansen Beck, and Ellen Manderfield worked across a broad spectrum of products. Ellen Manderfield, who was the first woman to become a member of the ASID, had designed decalcomanias and radio and television cabinetry before she went to work for the Oneida company. One of her stainless-steel flatware patterns, Omni, was selected for the study collections of the Museum of Modern Art.

American silverware manufacturers fought a valiant but losing battle. Reed and Barton and International Silver organized competitions for the design of new silver flatware. The entries ranged from the austere to the exotic; how-ever, only one (by Ronald Pearson) ever made it to production. The industry was, and remains, trapped in the past—a victim of its own blind allegiance to dead styles.

For years the Sterling Silversmiths Guild of America conducted annual student design competitions for holloware. Some of the entries were bold, exciting, and harmonious with the exotic modern furniture of the time; however, these competitions, too, were intended primarily to attract attention to the silver industry. The Museum of Contemporary Craft in New York City, as one of the driving forces behind these competitions, hoped and prayed in vain that these ventures would break the hold of the past on the popular taste in ceremonial tableware. However, it seems that most Americans consider the home a sacred colonial haven from the modern world.

## Setting the Course

*To me architecture is a tailor-made job—it still has a lot of handicraft. Industrial design is based on the machine and what the machine can do.*

Donald Dohner, 1940 (48)

Within a decade after the United States refused to participate in the 1925 Paris Exposition of Modern Decorative and Industrial Arts because American manufacturers claimed they had nothing new to show, industrial design had come into prominence in the United States. The "first generation" of designers was credited with breathing new life into industry and offering Americans hope for the future in the midst of the Depression. The rapid growth of the field created a demand for specially trained industrial designers.

Although none of the practitioners of industrial design had been educated in the field, many of them gave freely of their spare time to help direct or shape the industrial design programs that were beginning to take form. A number of teachers of art, commercial art, and arts and crafts moved into industrial design education.

Other academic assistance came from abroad. In the period between the two world wars there was a substantial migration to the United States of artists, architects, and designers, mostly from countries where aesthetic and intellectual freedoms were threatened by the rise of National Socialism or Communism. With very few exceptions, the émigrés gained a professional foothold not as practicing architects or designers, but rather as teachers in the new schools of industrial design. Will Burtin (1908–1972), who had taught graphics and design in Cologne, took a similar position in 1938 at Pratt Institute. Walter Landor had been educated in Switzerland and had come to the United States from London, where he had been a co-founder of the Industrial Design Partnership; after working on the British Pavilion at the New York World's Fair, he opened an office in San Francisco and became an associate professor of industrial design at the California College of

Arts and Crafts in Oakland. Henry Glass had come to the United States from Vienna with a master's degree in architecture from the Wiener Technische Hochschule and had designed furniture for Thonet and for Russel Wright's American Way project while taking courses at the Institute of Design in Chicago; in 1945 he initiated the Chicago Art Institute's first industrial design program.

In 1935 the Works Progress Administration (WPA), recognizing the opportunities for employment in industrial design and the need to provide schooling for young people who could not afford private schools, allocated funds for the establishment of a special school in New York City to be called the Design Laboratory. Gilbert Rohde, who agreed to serve as director, announced that the curriculum would be based on that of the Bauhaus and supplemented with practical experience in manufacturing processes and merchandising. Its emphasis, however, would be empirical rather than theoretical, with a commitment to training students to fill existing needs. In 1936 the Design Laboratory, about to close owing to a withdrawal of WPA support, was given a new lease on life by the Federation of Architects, Engineers, Chemists and Technicians and renamed the Laboratory School of Industrial Design. John McAndrews, curator of architecture at the Museum of Modern Art, claimed that the Laboratory School was the "first school in the United States to devote its entire curriculum to training for the various fields of industrial design—namely, product, textile, interior, advertising, and display design" (183). The school closed in December 1940.

In 1941, in a paper published by the Society for the Study of Education, Gilbert Rohde commented on the aptitudes of prospective industrial designers. He stated that 30 percent of a student's capacity for industrial design lay in an ability to see where products could be improved combined with an instinctual ingenuity in thinking of ways to effect the improvements, 30 percent in an ability to sense what most people will like, 20 percent in scientific-mindedness (a feeling for materials and construction, manifested at an early age), and 20 percent in a sensitivity to aesthetic form. He rated aesthetic sensitivity last because with it alone one could be an artist or a craftsman, but not a successful industrial designer.

Donald R. Dohner (d. 1943) was a graphic artist and a member of the faculty of the Carnegie Institute of Technology (now Carnegie-Mellon University) in Pittsburgh in 1930 when he was commissioned by the Westinghouse Electric Company of East Pittsburgh to try, according to Sidney Warner, "to redesign and improve any manufactured article and develop new ones within the whole company" (207). Dohner and Warner (the latter had just graduated from Carnegie Tech) went to work in Westinghouse's "Art-Engineering" department, trying their hands at redesigning everything from small appliances to locomotives. At one point they experimented with Micarta, a new laminated phenolic formaldehyde that was available in a remarkable range of colors. They designed colorful inlaid murals combining Micarta and anodized aluminum, and they also found other applications for the material: bathtub enclosures, furniture, lighting fixtures, instrument panels, and signs.

It is not surprising that Dohner, a professional design educator who also had experience as a designer with Westinghouse, conceived the idea of establishing a program in industrial design education at Carnegie Tech. With support from Alexander Kostellow (1896–1954), who had joined the Carnegie faculty in the late 1920s as an instructor in painting and design, Dohner proposed that the institute establish a degree-granting undergraduate program in industrial design. The program—the first of its kind in an American institution of higher learning—was approved and made a part of the curriculum in 1935. It is fair to say that it was at Carnegie Tech that the unique strain of American industrial design philosophy (combining aesthetic principles with empirical exploration and practical experience), which has permeated industrial design education in the United States, was identified.

Alexander Kostellow (1896–1954) is considered by many to have been the father of American industrial design education. A practicing artist and designer, he developed a philosophy of form that brought the rational into balance with the aesthetic. Credit: Industrial Design (October 1954).

Alexander Kostellow had come to the United States after World War I by way of schools in France and Germany. After studying and teaching design and painting at the Art Students' League, the New York School of Fine and Applied Arts, and the National Academy of Design, he had begun his formal teaching career at the Kansas City Art Institute. From there he had moved (with his wife and colleague Rowena Reed Kostellow) to Pittsburgh, where (despite his growing reputation as a painter) he elected to concentrate his energies on the development of the new program in industrial design at Carnegie. In addition, he expanded his understanding of the growing field of industrial design as consultant designer to companies in the Pittsburgh area. Peter Müller-Munk, who taught at Carnegie with Kostellow, calls him "one of the most brilliant people that I have ever met" and notes that "his influence on everybody he came in contact with, his magnetic enthusiasm, and his almost hypnotic effect on academic and industrial authorities have no equal" (198).

In 1936, after the Carnegie degree program had been launched, Donald Dohner accepted an invitation from James Boudreau, dean of Pratt Institute's art school, to organize a similar industrial design program there. His position at Carnegie Tech was taken by Peter Müller-Munk, who had come to the United States from Germany in 1926 with a degree in the humanities from the University of Berlin and a diploma in silversmithing.

Müller-Munk had worked at Tiffany's in New York for three years as a metalworker before establishing his own silver studio. Then, after being asked by a New York department store to design a line of chinaware, he had branched out to design other products, from compacts to electrical appliances. At Carnegie Tech, he helped Kostellow organize and teach the pioneering program in industrial design. He was a member of the faculty from 1935 until 1944, when he resigned to devote his attention to his independent practice and to promote the international develop-

ment and recognition of industrial design as a profession. Müller-Munk brought to industrial design education a spirit of worldly scholarship and a conviction that it was essential to the quality and success of industrial design to develop a body of special knowledge that could be shared and passed on.

In 1938 Donald Dohner invited Alexander Kostellow and Rowena Reed Kostellow to join him at Pratt Institute, where—with Alexander Kostellow representing the philosophical, Rowena Reed Kostellow the aesthetic, and Dohner the practical—they laid the triangular foundation for Pratt's program in industrial design. Dohner's pragmatic approach to design is expressed in the school's catalog for 1936–1937: "Industrial Design, like advertising, grew out of mass production. The limitations of mass production have focused attention on the futility and weakness of handicraft design when applied to machine-made products. Alert manufacturers and merchandisers are realizing, to an ever-increasing extent, the part good design plays in sales; that utility alone is not sufficient. Today there is a recognized need for well-trained designers who can work within the requirements of trade and industry." (241)

Alexander Kostellow was responsible for the "foundation year" curriculum, which in his wife's view was the heart and soul of the program. He held that design was a "creative interest expressed graphically or plastically in terms of materials and manipulative processes . . . even when purely aesthetic in its nature" (124), and that industrial designers should develop the power of abstract conception and visualization and should emphasize aesthetics while bearing in mind that it is not their function to exercise personal expression or to please a limited number of people.

According to Rowena Reed Kostellow, whose mastery of three-dimensional form brought elegance to her teaching and to the work of her students at Pratt Institute, the quality of the program lay in the fact that the introductory courses were based on abstract formal relationships. She taught that two- and three-dimensional design were essentially the same; that the principles of form—from line to plane to volume, from the simple to the complex—shaped the aesthetic quality of all design solutions and, with color and texture, constituted the palette of the industrial designer. She has said that the goal of "[bringing] order and logic where there was none" was fundamental to all design education and not unique to any school, even the transplanted Bauhaus (190).

When Donald Dohner left Pratt Institute to open a design office with one of his students, J. Gordon Lippincott, Alexander Kostellow was appointed a full professor and the head of the industrial design program. Under Kostellow, Pratt Institute's influence on American industrial design education (and, in turn, on professional practice) became great—at least as great as that of any other school. Pratt graduates, including Robert Kolli and (later) Yasuhiko Okuda, Giles Aureli, and Joseph Parriott, continued the work of the Kostellows at Pratt. Others carried their philosophy, at least in part, to other schools: Marc Harrison to the Rhode Island School of Design, Robert Redman to the University of Bridgeport, Jay Doblin to the Institute of Design in Chicago, James Pirkl and Lawrence Feer to Syracuse University, and Robert McKim to Stanford University.

The first signs of formal education in industrial design on the West Coast appeared in 1937 when a group of Pasadena citizens organized the California Graduate School of Design with advice from Richard F. Bach (of the Metropolitan Museum of Art), Royal Bailey Farnum (of the Rhode Island School of Design), Peter Müller-Munk (of the Carnegie Institute of Technology), and George Howe (an architect with offices in New York and Philadelphia). The goal of the California Graduate School of Design was to supplement the undergraduate design courses of other schools with a two-year graduate program concerned with technological, social, and economic factors in industrial design. Hunt Lewis, an architecture graduate of Princeton University, was named director of the school, and he invited Kem Weber and Karl With, who shared his humanistic approach to design, to join the faculty.

When the war called most of the male students into service, the California Graduate School of Design was absorbed by the California Institute of Technology (Caltech) and renamed the California School of Design. Walter Baermann (1903–1972), who was appointed the new director, had emigrated to the United States from Munich with a diploma in architecture from the Technische Hochschule and another in engineering from the University of Munich. He had worked from 1929 to 1932 as a designer in New York. Between 1932 and 1937 he had served as educational director of the Springfield (Massachusetts) Art Museum and as a consultant to other museums while also operating a private design practice.

The first-year program at the California School of Design was devoted to exploratory design projects and workshops in industrial materials and processes and to lectures and seminars on economics, sociology, and technology. In the second year, the assigned problems were on a larger scale and an independent design thesis was required.

In 1942 Walter Baermann left the California School of Design to take a position as head of the design program at the Cranbrook Academy of Art in Bloomfield Hills, Michigan. He was replaced by Antonin Heythum (1902–1952), who had come to the United States from Czechoslovakia to work on his government's exhibitions at the 1939 San Francisco Fair and the New York World's Fair. Heythum had received a certificate in architectural engineering in 1922 and worked as a designer for theaters and the National Opera before receiving an engineering-architecture diploma from the Prague Institute of Technology in 1934. His professional activities in Czechoslovakia, in collaboration with his wife Carlotta,

*Antonin Heythum (1902–1954) made his mark in industrial design education by emphasizing the importance of human factors in product design and development. Credit:* Industrial Design at Syracuse University *(catalog).*

*This model of a small radio by Lawrence Roberts, a student under Heythum at the California Graduate School of Design in 1940, illustrates the persistence of form. The teardrop shape was described as "functionally logical, practical and economical." Credit: 1940–41 California Graduate School of Design catalog.*

*Laszlo Moholy-Nagy (1895–1946). Credit: (47, 139).*

had included the design of furniture and exhibitions. After completing his work at the New York World's Fair, he had stayed on for a year in New York as an associate professor at the New School for Social Research, teaching display and exhibit technology.

Heythum saw the position in California as offering an opportunity to organize and direct an experimental program in industrial design based on what he called Design Analysis. "The need for technologically trained designers," he wrote, "makes the technological institute a more adequate place for industrial design training than an art school can ever be." (50) Heythum and his students had access to Caltech's research in time and motion and in human factors. But whereas the goal of such studies in wartime was the use of machines with maximum efficiency by human beings (in other words, putting the machine before the human), Heythum's goal was the inverse—putting human interest before the machine.

In 1944 Heythum decided to move back to New York to introduce and teach his Design Analysis course at Columbia University. His place at the California School of Design was taken by two of his former students, Sal Merendino and Harry Greene, who went on to train many of the first postwar generation of California industrial designers. In 1949, when the new administration at Caltech decided to concentrate on pure scientific research and closed the School of Design, Merendino and Greene joined the faculty of the University of Southern California's school of architecture.

Walter Baermann's decision to leave the California Graduate School of Design was in harmony with his conviction that an independent art school was a better place for design education than an institute of technology, where the atmosphere was more constrained. The invitation to join the faculty of Cranbrook—a school that was attracting national and international attention—was an opportunity not to be missed.

Charles Eames, Ray Kaiser, Harry Weese, Harry Bertoia, and Eero Saarinen had all been at Cranbrook in the late 1930s (which Eames called "the vintage years"), and they had planted the seeds for changes in design that would come to fruition in the postwar era. During the war, Cranbrook—with Baermann as head of design—shifted to more orthodox educational methods, offering specific courses leading to formal academic degrees in order to qualify veterans for financial support under the G.I. Bill. However, the school retained its reputation as a place for independent design exploration at the graduate level.

In 1937, after the Bauhaus had been closed by the Nazis, Walter Gropius (who had emigrated to the United States) asked the Chicago-based Association for Arts and Industry to support the establishment of a New Bauhaus. On his recommendation, the association contracted with Laszlo Moholy-Nagy, who had been in charge of the foundation course at the Bauhaus, to organize and direct the new school. The New Bauhaus opened in Chicago in 1937 with a faculty consisting of three émigrés from Europe—Hin Bredendieck (who had studied at the Bauhaus in Dessau), Gyorgy Kepes, and Alexander Archipenko—and a number of visiting professors from the University of Chicago. There were 25 students in the first class.

Differences between the faculty and the sponsors led E. H. Powell, president of the Association for Arts and Industry, to inform Moholy-Nagy over the summer of 1938 that, owing to financial difficulties, the school would not be able to open for a second year. In a letter to the art editor of the *New York Times,* Moholy-Nagy sought to dispel the rumors about the inappropriateness of the Bauhaus approach to American design needs. He quoted from a declaration by faculty members, seven of them Americans, supporting the New Bauhaus and calling it "congenial to the best educational leadership and the deepest educational needs of the country" (162).

After surviving for a while in temporary facilities, the school reopened in the fall of 1939 as the School of Design, with Moholy-Nagy continuing as director. Its new home was the former quarters of the Chicago Historical Society, and its new benefactors included Walter J. Paepke of the Container Corporation of America.

However, after Laszlo Moholy-Nagy's death in 1946 and the appointment of Serge Chermayeff to replace him, it became increasingly difficult for the School of Design to attract sufficient funds to continue as an independent institution. In 1949 the Illinois Institute of Technology agreed to provide an academic home for the School of Design, changing its name in the process to the Institute of Design. In 1955, after Serge Chermayeff resigned, Jay Doblin was selected to head the school. Under his intelligent and inspired leadership, the Institute of Design made its own important impact on industrial design education.

During the war, many of the assignments given to students in the design schools addressed wartime needs. Some dealt with exploring substitutes for priority materials, others with problems related to housing and furnishings, and others with survival under attack.

When the war ended, those art schools that had design programs in place expanded quickly to handle the rush of new students—most of them veterans attracted by design's glamor and its promise of opportunities. Those art schools that had paid scant attention to design before the war now moved to take advantage of the increased enrollment of veterans (whose education was being subsidized by the Federal Aid Program to Education, popularly known as the G.I. Bill).

The presence of disabled veterans on the campuses had brought a new recognition of the value of the arts in treating the physically and the mentally ill. The Rehabilitation Program at Dartmouth College, sponsored by the College Student Workshop and supported by the American Craftsmen's Educational Council (ACEC), was inspired in December 1944 by the arrival at Dartmouth of a Marine who had been discharged from service with combat wounds. The ACEC, which comprised some thirty craft organizations and which was dedicated to perpetuation of the Arts and Crafts tradition, found a new purpose in helping disabled veterans find their way back to civilian life. Before the end of the 1944–45 academic year, the program had changed its name to the School of American Craftsmen. To its first goal (to keep alive the Arts and Crafts movement of the last century), the ACEC had added a humanitarian one, concerned with mental well-being and physical health. Over the next few years this and other similar programs evolved into occupational therapy programs, which attracted financial support from public and private sources.

In 1946 it was decided to move the School of American Craftsmen to Alfred University, a liberal-arts institution in south central New York that had an interest in the crafts and a well-established and respected school of ceramics. This was a move away from the philosophy of crafts as therapy. Mention was made of "the dependence of industry and its machines on the hands of skillful craftsmen, who work not only as designers, model makers, foremen and artisans, but also as setters of fashion and styles and as experimenters in the use of materials and methods" (134). In June 1950, the School of American Craftsmen, with Harold Brennan as its director, made a second move, this time to become a full academic program at the Rochester Institute of Technology. At this point it came under the control of RIT, although the ACEC maintained its advisory role. (The school as well as the ACEC existed because of the beneficence of Aileen Vanderbilt Webb.)

In 1949, James Plaut, the director of the Institute of Contemporary Art in Boston, established a department of "Design in Industry" at the ICA. Theodore S. Jones, a former dean of Hamilton College, was selected to head the program, and Serge Chermayeff, Edgar Kaufmann, Jr., and Gyorgy Kepes were among the advisors. The purpose of this program was to address the misalignment between craftsmen and craft-based industries. The experience gained through exploratory programs involving the Corning and Steuben companies seemed to herald a bright future for on-the-job training courses in a variety of craft-based industries; however, the ICA's well-intended venture did not succeed, largely because of the general decline of such industries in the United States.

It is interesting to speculate on the Bauhaus's failure to take root in the United States. Certainly, despite problems with its original benefactors, it had found fertile ground. In 1940 the School of Architecture at the University of Michigan held a conference to explore the academic relationship of architecture and industrial design. The participants were the deans of architecture at Harvard, Columbia, Princeton, Cranbrook, and Michigan and three industrial design educators. Two of the latter, Peter Müller-Munk of Carnegie Tech and Walter Baermann of the Graduate School of Design, questioned whether industrial design should be associated with architectural education unless introductory courses were to be shared, with the two disciplines going their separate ways in the upper years. Donald Dohner of Pratt Institute was not convinced that industrial design belonged with architecture. "To me," he was quoted as saying, "architecture is a tailor-made job—it still has a lot of handicraft. Industrial design is based on the machine and what the machine can do." (48)

The architects found it difficult to accept the idea that there was a philosophical difference between the two professions. Walter Gropius of Harvard referred to industrial design as one of the "optical arts" and, therefore, as in the same academic frame as architecture. Architecture deans Leopold Arnaud of Columbia, Joseph Hudnut of Harvard, and Eliel Saarinen of Cranbrook acceded that architectural education could be improved by an increased emphasis on direct experience with materials and processes but concluded that design was design, suggesting that the only difference was in the area of specialization.

Understandably, art schools believed that industrial design fell into their academic domain rather than that of the architects. After all, the first generation of designers had been artists rather than engineers or architects.

*We have created a profession and some of them are delighted to teach it with only the vaguest idea of what it is all about.*

Walter Dorwin Teague, 1946 (206)

During the war, the two professional societies, the Society of Industrial Designers and the American Designers Institute, were well aware that the postwar rush to manufacture new products would create a demand for more designers. In anticipation, they stepped up their involvement in design education. After the ADI moved its national office to New York, in 1944, one of its first projects was the development of a prototype of a program for the education of industrial designers. The education committee, headed by Alexander Kostellow with Laszlo Moholy-Nagy and Donald Dohner, came up with an idealized program that was based on a survey of the ADI's members and on the contributions of John Vassos, Ben Nash, and George Kosmak. The ADI's prototype curriculum was so comprehensive that it could not have been covered in a four-year or even a five-year program, but its mix of courses in the arts, the natural sciences, the behavioral and social sciences, and the humanities became the model for most of the curricula that followed.

John Vassos insisted that designers should be concerned with the legal status of their profession. In 1944, Vassos, Kostellow, and others proposed an amendment to the New York State Education Law (Article 84-A) that would have established educational requirements and licensing regulations for industrial designers. They made several trips to Albany in order to promote their amendment, and in April 1945 Kostellow optimistically reported its progress to the annual meeting of the New York chapter of the ADI. "From the moment the bill is passed," he stated, ". . . every future industrial designer will have to go through school, work six months in a factory, and a year or more in a designer's school or office, before he is licensed to practice industrial design." (210)

# THE INDUSTRIAL DESIGNER

| FIRST YEAR | | |
|---|---|---|
| 1. **Structural representation** | Analysis and reconstruction of forms, natural and man made. | 1. **Delinea represe** |
| 2. **The human figure** | Mechanics of articulation. Structures. Human figure, animals. | 2. **Design, dimensi** |
| 3. **Nature study** | An organized approach to the observation and study of natural forms. | 3. **Design, dimensi** |
| 4. **Design, 2 dimensional** | Graphic and plastic elements, line, plane, volume (positive and negative), value, color, texture | 4. **Industri design** |
| 5. **Design, 3 dimensional** | Architectonics & techtonics. Design elements and typical organizations. Forces and mechanics. | 5. **Materia structur** |
| 6. **Color experience** | Physical and physiological factors. Measurements. Theory of organization and control. (Munsell, Ostwald, Helmholtz). Psychological factors. | 6. **Ceramic** |
| 7. **Art history** | The advance of civilization through architecture and sculpture. | 7. **Product methods** |
| 8. **Mathematics** | Plane and solid geometry, algebra, trigonometry. Descriptive geometry. Use of slide rule. | 8. **Art hist** |
| 9. **Physics** | College level. Special stress on general mechanics. Light, acoustics and electricity. | 9. **Aesthe** |
| 10. **Communications** | Practice in oral communication and study of techniques in composition. Interpersonal relations. Presentation of ideas. | 10. **Social instituti** |

# Educational Program for Industrial Design

| ...EAR | THIRD YEAR | | FOURTH YEAR | |
|---|---|---|---|---|
| ng, perspective, technique entation. | 1. **Industrial design** | Product development in metal, glass, plastics and wood; packaging. Steps in developing design ideas for production. | 1. **Product development** | Further study of consumer needs for the development of new items. Designing for specific industries. |
| structure, advanced study lements of design. | 2. **Drafting** | Instrumental drafting. Making and reading blue-prints for shop use. Structural plans and projections. | 2. **Industrial design** | Three-dimensional, interiors, re design. |
| oncave, convex, amor- constructivistic, techtonic, onic, compounded. | 3. **Production methods** | Further study of production engineering in its relationship to industrial designing. | 3. **Production methods** | Strength of materials. Testing methods and devices. Industrial management. |
| ationship of forms to func- d materials. Style analysis. | 4. **Anthropology (history of forms)** | Survey of contemporary architecture in terms of traditional styles and existing materials. Economic and social factors. | 4. **Market research analysis and merchandising** | Case studies of consumer reaction. Pricing problems. Cost analysis. Production planning and marketing. |
| entation in different mate- functional and aesthetic | 5. **Aesthetics** | The theory of aesthetics through history, and its application as guide and measure for mass acceptance of specific designs. | 5. **Business procedures** | Fundamentals of organization and management. Contract writing. Copyrights. Patents. Royalties. |
| introducing ceramics in the year because it demon- ell the complete cycle from to a finished article ex- n most advanced methods. | 6. **Design, 3 dimensional** | Advanced study of construction techniques. Application of abstract design principles in expressing function. | 6. **Presentation** | Rendering techniques. |
| ools and machines versus ols. The meaning of con- ry technology. Mathematics ndustrial designer. | 7. **Experimental design** | Design problems presented by industry as cooperative projects. Shop procedures. Use of jigs and fixtures for specific problems. | 7. **Contemporary civilization** | Present-day national and international society: American economic and political problems, competing politico-economic systems, and the problem of world organization. |
| ance of civilization as ex- in painting. | 8. **Design, 2 dimensional** | Packaging, study of color, etc. | 8. **Principles of photography** | Elements of photographic presentation. Study of light. Color in photography. Laboratory techniques. |
| and theories of art judg- | 9. **Human relations** | The adjustment of the individual to family, professional and community relationships. | 9. **Advanced graphics** | Successive steps in developing simple and complex structures and ultimate presentation. |
| and development of social ns. Main principles of col- ehavior. Various types of rganizations. The role of gy and art in society. | 10. **Impact of science** | The nature of science; the relationships between social conditions and knowledge. | 10. **Great books** | Investigation of the major ideas in the *Iliad*, three Greek dramas, Plato, the Old Testament, Lucretius, Dante, Machiavelli, Montaigne, Cervantes, Goethe and Flaubert. |

*The educational program developed by the Industrial Designers' Institute called for a four-year course combining design training with technological and business subjects and academic courses in personal, social, and cultural affairs. Credit:* Interiors *(April 1953).*

The proposed amendment, written by Benjamin Nash with the help of two attorneys, defined "the practice of industrial designing" as "a science and art whereby a person educated and trained in the humanities, in the industrial techniques and in the principles of aesthetics, applied his knowledge and skill to modern technology in the designing for mass production of commodities which are functional, safe and possess inherent aesthetic qualities," and called for an applicant to be questioned by a five-member board of industrial design examiners before being licensed to practice (209).

The amendment came before the state legislature in 1947 and 1948, but was not passed. The designers who lobbied against it seem to have been jealous of their independence, unwilling to submit to the scrutiny of their peers, and suspicious of the growing academic design establishment. Raymond Spilman speculates that designers opposed the amendment "because the majority of them practiced . . . in many different states and felt that if licensing were done on a national basis they would have to be licensed in every state they worked in" (203).

Interest in licensing (or at least certification) in New York State was revived in 1966 when Henry Dreyfuss, the first president of the Industrial Designers Society of America (the product of a merger of the ASID, the IDI, and the IDEA), asked John Vassos to head a committee to review the possibility once more. The ensuing discussions raised the same issues that had doomed the idea twenty years earlier. Again the biggest stumbling block was whether or how to license a designer who might design a product in one state that would be manufactured in a second state and sold in a third state to a consumer from a fourth state.

The Society of Industrial Designers published its first Educational Bulletin in March of 1946. The subject was the guidance of veterans and others seeking professional education in industrial design. The information had been obtained from available school catalogs and, therefore, was not necessarily complete. Without implying endorsement, the society listed the following schools and courses: Alabama Polytechnic Institute (a four-year course), California Institute of Technology (a two-year graduate course), Carnegie Institute of Technology (a four-year course), Chicago Art Institute (four years), Chicago Academy of Fine Arts (two years), University of Cincinnati (four years), Cooper Union Art School (a three-year day course and a four-year night course), Georgia School of Technology (four years), University of Illinois (four years), Institute of Design (four years), Kansas City Art Institute (four years), University of Michigan (four years), Minneapolis School of Art (a three-year day course and a four-year night course), Newark Public School of Fine and Industrial Art (four years), Philadelphia Museum School of Industrial Art (four years), Rhode Island School of Design (four years), University of Southern California (four years), Stanford University (four years), and Syracuse University (four years). New programs in industrial design were also in development at the Art Center, in Los Angeles; at Alabama Polytechnic Institute, in Auburn; at North Carolina State College, in Raleigh; and at the University of Bridgeport.

The second Education Bulletin, issued in 1946, expanded on what the SID considered to be an appropriate "professional education for industrial design." It defined the profession and explained how industrial designers work both as employees of industry and as consultants to it. Paul McConnell, executive secretary of the society and former consultant to the Board of Design of the New York World's Fair, acknowledged in the bulletin that industrial design education was in the midst of development, and suggested that future programs might combine elements of architecture, engineering, and business. The bulletin also reflected the concern of the professional members of the society that existing educational programs were too narrow (representing, it was suggested, only a third of the techniques and the knowledge needed for full service in industrial design).

In 1944, Richard F. Bach, dean of education at the Metropolitan Museum and since 1917 the motivating force behind a long series of exhibitions in the industrial arts and design at the museum, offered to host a conference of the administrators of schools of design at which the state of industrial design education would be examined.

The first session of the conference (moderated by John E. Alcott, a designer and the acting dean of the Rhode Island School of Design) was concerned with the industrial designer, his field, his profession, and his place after the war. Antonin Heythum was a member of the panel. The panel for the second session (presided over by Edward Warwick, principal of the Philadelphia Museum School) included Alexander Kostellow of Pratt Institute. It reviewed academic requirements for the profession of industrial design; general, special, cooperative, and graduate training; and research. Most of the talk was about art, but some consideration was given to mass production, economics, advertising, and sales. It was suggested that adding courses in the latter subjects would require a five-year program of study. James C. Boudreau, dean of the art school at Pratt Institute, chaired the third session, which surveyed the present situation in schools, comparing course requirements, facilities, faculties, admission policies, and requirements for graduation. The final session (presided over by Dana Vaughan, director of the School of Industrial Arts in Trenton and president of the Eastern Arts Association) was devoted to the possibility of establishing a formal organization of administrators of schools of design. This prospect appears to have been closer to the hearts of the administrators than whether or how industrial design programs should be organized or taught.

A summary of this conference, published in preparation for a second one, states that "the conference carefully avoided definition of the term 'industrial design,' fearful that the effort to arrive at a definition might constrain discussion" (230). There were, it seems, two reasons for this fear: First, most schools' design programs were rather broad in scope (that is, they were not strictly *industrial* design programs). Second, recognizing industrial design as a unique entity might separate it from existing curricula and lead to pressure for the establishment of independent schools of industrial design.

The second conference, held in June of 1946, brought together the administrative heads of some 45 art schools. Bach's letter of invitation emphasized the idea that schools of design should make a contribution to the postwar environment and stressed the place of design in international relations as well as in industry and commerce. Although the formal list of participants contained no industrial designers or design educators, several attended at least some of the sessions. The title Conference of Schools of Design was misleading. This was actually a meeting of administrators of art schools and colleges of art. Of the 45 invited schools, only 15 were listed by the Society of Industrial Designers as offering courses in industrial design. Among the schools excluded were the California Institute of Technology, the Georgia Institute of Technology, the Carnegie Institute of Technology, and the Institute of Design.

Dana Vaughan, now head of the Cooper Union Art School, reported the results of a questionnaire that had been circulated to all schools that offered industrial design courses. His presentation was essentially a mechanical comparison of entrance requirements, credit hours, courses, and facilities. Although it was acknowledged that those teaching many of the courses had no academic or professional experience in industrial design, the conference took no action to rectify the situation. Nor was an attempt made to set intellectual or philosophical goals for industrial design.

The second so-called Conference of Schools of Design seems to have provided the stimulus for the establishment of the National Association of Schools of Design, which was organized formally two years later by 22 leading art schools, institutions, and colleges. The objectives of this association were to raise standards in art curricula and to establish an accrediting body for art schools in order to improve professional standards and educational practices. In general, the association has succeeded in these areas; however, it is still essentially an organization of administrators of art schools and not an association of schools of design.

Just after the 1946 Conference of Schools of Design, Walter Dorwin Teague summarized his impressions of the seminar and of the academic world bluntly in a letter to Richard Bach: "It was a great pleasure for us to meet the educators and exhibit ourselves to them. I hope the meeting was in some measure enlightening. I think, however, that none of us gives a damn about whether or not they 'liked the group picture.' We feel that they need us a lot more than we need them. We have created a profession, and some of them are delighted to teach it, with only the vaguest idea of what it is all about. If nothing more, I hope it gave them some idea of the difficulty of an adequate academic training for industrial design. By our practice we will create a definition of industrial design and I trust the conference committee will be acute enough to discern it." (206) (Despite his cynicism, Teague had not hesitated, five years earlier, to call attention to existing academic industrial design programs in support of his own claim to be a professional. In a case heard by the New York Supreme Court, he had succeeded in being exempted from paying taxes levied on nonprofessionals.)

Very little has changed since the conferences at the Metropolitan Museum. The philosophical arguments about the proper relationship of the design professions, and about whether humanistic, technological, or aesthetic values should dominate design education, continue, and industrial design education is still largely held in academic chains by the administrators of art schools.

After the 1946 Conference of Schools of Design, the Society of Industrial Designers and the American Designers Institute held independent meetings on design education. At the SID meeting, concern was expressed that industrial design education was still inadequate, especially in the area of science and technology. George Sakier, Harold Van Doren, Egmont Arens, and Walter Dorwin Teague—prominent SID members who had attended Bach's conference—concurred that industrial design education had a long way to go before it would meet the needs of the profession. Paul McConnell commented on the difficulty of convincing art school administrators that it was necessary to expand traditional art-based programs to include courses in the physical and the behavioral sciences. The ADI devoted its meeting to a discussion of the copyrighted "educational program for industrial design" that had been developed over a two-year period by the organization's Education Committee under the chairmanship of Alexander Kostellow.

James R. Shipley's wise evaluation of the ADI's educational program was shared by most other design educators. Shipley, who was in charge of the industrial design program at the University of Illinois, had three years' experience as a practicing designer at General Motors behind him. He acknowledged that technical courses might drive away some artistic students, but he felt that in the long run such courses would raise the standards of design education and the competence of the schools' graduates. This position reflected the growing realization that the art studies appropriate for an industrial designer were not identical with those appropriate for an artist. It was evident that universities' programs in industrial design would have to be brought up to the level of the programs offered by institutes of technology through the addition of workshop and laboratory courses.

Later in 1946, the Museum of Modern Art, at the suggestion of the SID, organized a meeting entitled Conference on Industrial Design: A New Profession. Edgar Kaufmann, Jr., director of the museum's department of industrial design, invited members of the SID, representatives from the ADI, design educators, and other interested professionals (including architects and lawyers) to a three-day meeting to consider the emergence of industrial design as a profession. Kaufmann called particular attention to the importance of education, because so far the efforts to create a curriculum for the education of designers had not reached consensus. In his introductory comments, he mentioned MOMA's long-standing view of design as "the result of the laws of development and appearance inherent in every object—laws which produce forms often beautiful and sensible" (227). had already stated his own position in the fall issue of the *MOMA Bulletin:*

Modern design is the aesthetic shaping of objects according to principles developed during the last century by leading modern designers and writers on design. Many of these designers were practicing architects, and the writers were often influenced by painting, sculpture, and music in their ideas about the practical arts. . . . These minds have shared and developed clear ideas which continue to prevail wherever modern design is practiced. . . . Modern designers do not wish to overcome conditions, they wish to meet them. . . . Sales are episodes in the careers of designed objects. Use is the first consideration, production and distribution second. (158)

The MOMA conference (chaired by Joseph Hudnut, dean of the school of architecture at Harvard) ranged over the entire spectrum of industrial design, from education and practice to industrial, commercial, and social implications. At one point the attendees seem to have been preoccupied with the role of the designer as an artist. George Nelson was certain that the industrial designer was a creative artist, functioning to please himself. Edgar Kaufmann, Jr., supported Nelson but lamented that artists were no longer integrated with society. Russel Wright observed that designers had become fascinated with functionalism and had forgotten that they were artists. J. Gordon Lippincott conceded that while the industrial designer was primarily an artist, he was also a merchandiser with his finger on the pulse of consumer tastes. Relatively little was said about the designer's responsibility for the consumer's welfare or about the impact of products on the environment. The predominant view seems to have been that manufactures were the medium through which the designer sought expression.

However, Laszlo Moholy-Nagy claimed that after coming to the United States he had had to change his ideas about design. In contrast to Europeans, he noted, American designers were often instruments of American manufacturers' policies of artificial obsolescence, by which products were discarded when a factory decided the time was appropriate for replacement even though the products may still have been useful. James Boudreau of Pratt Institute responded that a European philosophy of what was good should not be imposed on Americans. The U.S. economy, he said, was based not on artificial obsolescence but on accelerated obsolescence. Many products, he suggested, were discarded when their owners had rejected them.

In response to a question about the objectives of the Institute of Design, Moholy-Nagy observed that they were consistent with the original Bauhaus's goal of enabling its students to integrate intellect with sensitivity. On this point, it seems, the educational philosophies of Moholy-Nagy and Kostellow had much in common. Both men hoped for an integration of art and science. Both acknowledged that, in the end, students must face the practical problems of earning a living. And both, it must be added, insisted that a designer's early training should emphasize imagination, fantasy, and invention as basic conditioning for dealing with a constantly changing social, economic, and technological scene.

Kostellow believed that the industrial design student needed more than the intuitive and repetitious exercises that were common to the well-established art programs. The essence of the foundation program he had introduced at Pratt Institute was that it taught the student to create organic entities by transposing forces analogous to those in nature into expressive symbols, using dynamic balance, tension, form integration, opposition, and rhythm as design tools. The program was, therefore, conceived to move from nature to formalism and then to functionalism. Kostellow acknowledged the Bauhaus program's clarification of functional design; however, he warned that "it lacked compactness and basic integration, it possessed some contradictory elements; and in many instances, indulged in too lengthy and pragmatic experiments for experimentation's sake" (123). Kostellow did not agree with the premise that function gave birth to aesthetic expression. To him, function was the expression of a time, and man-made forms were influenced by aesthetic reactions. "The aesthetic concept," he claimed, "is inseparable from its embodiment" (125). Thus, problems of line, plane, volume, value, texture, and color were to be solved in terms of materials and processes. Students were made familiar with power tools and machinery so that they might "avoid the somewhat therapeutic quality of handicraft." In the advanced courses, Kostellow introduced "functional aesthetics," a concept intended to teach "the background of human endeavors in creating beautiful objects for everyday living" (126).

Beginning in February 1947, the Society of Industrial Designers announced, a program of evening courses for designers and nondesigners would be held in collaboration with New York University. Over the next three semesters, these courses—each consisting of fifteen lectures—were conducted by Philip McConnell, Benjamin Webster, Egmont Arens, and various guest lecturers. The subjects ranged from the philosophical ("Socio-Aesthetic Aspects of Machine Civilization") and the pro-

fessional ("Management of the Industrial Design Enterprise") to the applied ("The Anatomy of Eye Appeal and Product Design, Packaging and Distribution").

New York University announced the establishment of an experimental center for industrial design education. The executive secretary of the SID was responsible for the curriculum and the faculty, and the program was intended to appeal to novice industrial designers and to artists in related fields. Four courses of fifteen lectures each were scheduled for each semester of the 1948–49 academic year. The subjects ranged from the philosophical to the practical.

"How Industrial Designers Should be Trained" was the subject of the SID's third Education Bulletin, published in 1948. In it the society accepted its share of the responsibility for proper education in industrial design. It acknowledged that most design educators were struggling against academic institutions whose interests were not in tune with the needs of industrial design. Most of the existing programs were art-oriented and thus lacked courses in psychology and merchandising that would help design students understand marketing issues. Moreover, the SID was concerned about the absence of science and technology from most of the curricula. The bulletin acknowledged the importance of art and design courses; however, it suggested that industrial design should not be taught as the application of design to industrial products. It went on to outline how a curriculum could be built that would serve the purposes of industrial design education.

Raymond Spilman's lifelong commitment to industrial design education began when, as a student at Kansas State University, he put together his own program before the school had established a degree program in that field. In the 1930s he worked as a designer for General Motors and Walter Dorwin Teague, and during the war he worked on priority projects with the firm of Cushing, Johnson, and Neville. He established his own practice in

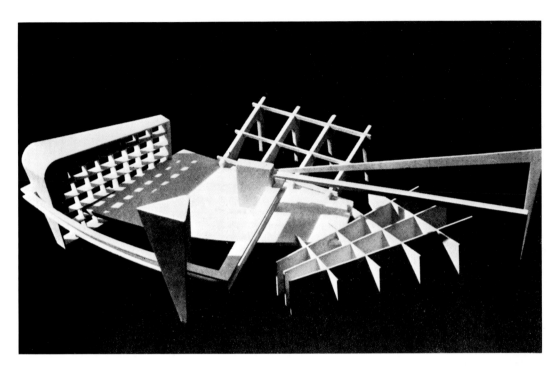

*An exercise (described as "an architectonic arrangement with spatial tension) by a first-year student at Pratt Institute in 1947. Credit: Interiors (July 1947).*

*As a student at the Institute of Design in 1941, Angelo Testa was assigned to develop springs of wood rather than metal. Credit: (30, 79).*

1946. His experiences as a lecturer and as an educational advisor to schools developing programs in industrial design led him to propose (in 1947) a course that he believed would come closer to meeting the needs of the profession. His recommended curriculum, which the ADI suspected he had plagiarized from its copyrighted program, was well considered in terms of a balance of the disciplines and in terms of a balance between lectures and workshops.

The SID's position on education was that it would not propose a model program, as the ADI had, but that it would offer advice and support to those who asked for it. In 1947 George Sakier, head of the society's education committee when Henry Dreyfuss was president, stressed the importance of education as a responsibility of the society. Henry Dreyfuss went further by suggesting that the society should also enlighten industry and the public about design.

At its annual meeting in October 1948, the SID considered a request from the engineering school of Lehigh University for assistance in conducting a summer seminar on product design. The members welcomed and approved the idea. Raymond Spilman was named co-director of the program for 1949. The first seminar resulted in a financial deficit, but the university was willing to try a second (a four-week rather than a six-week program). The second Lehigh seminar, held in June 1950, was directed at representatives of leading American companies who were interested in becoming familiar with industrial design and designers. The participants (most of them engineers) listened to Dave Chapman, Walter Dorwin Teague, and other consultant designers and talked over their own design problems in discussion groups. Aesthetic and functional considerations served as the background for discussions on how consumer appeal could be increased through design.

Thus, the SID reached out to familiarize managers and engineers with the practice and the values of industrial design, while the ADI concentrated its educational activities on curricular recommendations and on attempts to bring legal status to the profession through licensing. Members of both societies visited and lectured at design schools and opened their offices and studios to organized student field trips. Educators were not, however, accepted as full voting members by either organization unless they could prove that they were, or had been, practicing designers.

## Finding Common Cause

*Industrial design teachers are a curious lot—
they hold meetings at which they actually discuss what they do and how they might do it
better. . . . In a culture that exaggerates the
distinction between teaching and doing, the
teacher of design is in trouble.*

Ralph Caplan, 1962 (117)

There was, unfortunately, very little useful collaboration on educational matters between
the American Society of Industrial Designers
and the Industrial Designers Institute. Moreover, design educators, who often found
themselves caught in the competition between
the two organizations, had not been able to
establish an academic dialogue on a national
basis. In 1955 the editors of the new magazine
*Industrial Design* brought the need for a
national dialogue on education to the surface
by devoting a major part of the June issue to
educational issues. They acknowledged that
schools were in flux, and they urged educators to consider which philosophical approach
was most appropriate: a rational approach
favoring technical proficiency over imagination, or a "blue-sky" approach stressing
creativity.

With *Industrial Design*'s support, Joseph Carriero (1920–1978), head of the industrial
design program at the Philadelphia Museum
School of Art, invited representatives of
schools of industrial design and representatives of the two design societies to a meeting
in Philadelphia, and in November of 1955
some 25 educators, academic administrators,
and designers convened at the Museum
School to establish a dialogue on design
education.

The major speakers at the Philadelphia meeting touched on the main philosophical questions that had concerned educators over the
two decades since the first degree courses in
industrial design had been offered. One of
these questions was whether industrial design
was to be taught as an art or as a science.
Were designers primarily artists applying their
aesthetic judgment to the products of industry
(their very presence in schools of art seemed

to support this position), or were they tech-
nologists who solved product problems affecting public safety, comfort, and convenience?
Another question was whether designers
should try to guide industry and the public
to higher levels of cultural expression, or
whether they should gauge the needs and
desires of the public so that industry could
meet them. A third question was whether
design was to be a means to an end or an end
in itself. These questions, of course, were not
resolved at the meeting; indeed they have not
been resolved yet.

The Philadelphia meeting revealed a certain
defensiveness among the educators present.
They had developed their own programs, with
a good deal of independence, and they were
reluctant to abandon or even to dilute their
convictions about the purpose and the content of design education. However, they
agreed to continue the dialogue in 1956. Most
of them attended the second symposium, held
at the Institute of Design of the Illinois Institute of Technology, in Chicago, and hosted by
Jay Doblin. Again they were joined by practicing industrial designers. Dave Chapman
brought up for discussion the parallels and
conflicts between the teaching of design and
its actual practice, and suggested that educators pay more attention to the needs of practicing designers and less to esoteric academic
issues. However, more attention was paid to
curricula, course structures, and academic
credits. There was also a discussion about the
advisability of allowing students to participate
in competitions that were outside the normal
course of their academic studies.

Despite the inexorable movement toward a
more formal organization of design educators,
a fear was expressed by the educators at the
Chicago symposium that such an organization
would threaten their freedom. Moreover, it
was suggested that such an organization
would become preoccupied with the mechanics of industrial design education rather than
the substance. It was felt that the mechanics
might best be left to the administrators, who

had recently organized themselves as the National Association of Schools of Art. The symposium closed with the acceptance of an invitation extended by E. A. Adams, head of the Art Center School in Los Angeles, to continue discussions at that school in 1957.

At the Los Angeles meeting, the educators went back on their original intention to remain an informal assembly by deciding to organize formally. They elected Joseph Carriero as president pro tempore, charging him with responsibility for preparing a financial and organizational plan for the new organization.

More than thirty educators met in October 1957 at Syracuse University, with Arthur J. Pulos as host, to review and approve a constitution and by-laws establishing the Industrial Design Education Association (IDEA) as a third national design group—a link, as it were, between the IDI and the ASID.

IDEA was said to be "dedicated to the development of industrial design education through strengthening the lines of communication between individuals, educational institutions and professional organizations" (102). To this end, the education chairmen of the professional design societies were invited to serve as ex officio members. Joseph Carriero was formally installed as president, with James Shipley of the University of Illinois as vice-president and Arthur J. Pulos as secretary-treasurer. The guest speaker—George Beck, national president of the Industrial Designers Institute—said: "We are setting out to make IDEA a link between active members of the profession and the young men and women studying industrial design in schools and colleges. Success in this effort will be a major contribution to the growth and health of industrial design as a profession. . . . " (59)

One result of the establishment of IDEA was the creation of a network of design educators, many of whom had not known their colleagues. Another was the organization of a number of regional conferences that helped

clarify the particular academic focus of each school so that applicants could be better advised as to which school could better suit their interest.

The second meeting of IDEA, held at the Georgia Institute of Technology in 1958, with Hin Bredendieck as host, was devoted largely to comparisons of the curricula and the statistics of degree-granting schools of industrial design and to discussions of the broad goals of design education. Underlying the meeting was a general concern that design educators, by and large, were not considered by practicing designers to have professional status. In fact, the only educators who were members of one professional society or the other at the time were those who had gone into education from field practice. In a way this was the reverse of the situation in Europe, where it was customary for an individual to establish his reputation in education before being given the opportunity to practice.

By 1960, when the annual meeting was held at the University of Cincinnati with James Alexander as host, IDEA had grown to some fifty members representing some twenty degree-granting schools across the country. At that meeting, the minimum acceptable qualifications for industrial design graduates were debated by practicing designers and design educators. Practicing designers insisted that schools should train students for the practice of design as it existed; educators, on the other hand, insisted that the role of the schools was to educate students for the profession as it should be.

The featured speakers at IDEA's 1961 meeting at the Carnegie Institute of Technology were Ray Spilman and Edgar Kaufmann, Jr. The theme of the meeting—"Why Teach Industrial Design"—attracted some forty design educators from across the country plus representatives from General Motors, IBM, Westinghouse, U.S. Steel, and Alcoa. (Alcoa cohosted the meeting.) Ray Spilman, president of the American Society of Industrial Designers, made a controversial speech announcing that the society had introduced a School Approval

Program intended to "help teachers sincerely attempting to teach industrial design as a fully balanced professional approach . . . as opposed to those teachers who are happily wallowing around in the belief that because there are no standards there are no means of calling them to task for their approach" (116). The heart of the School Approval Program was a questionnaire to be sent to educators asking for information about the objectives of their school's program and about how the curriculum and the faculty were organized to accomplish those goals. It was carefully pointed out that this was not an "accreditation" program.

Despite the controversy the School Approval Program generated, its establishment was evidence that at last both educators and practicing designers were facing their mutual responsibility to ensure that graduates entering practice would be qualified. The name of the program was changed to "ASID Scholarship Guidance Program" to go along with the society's new plans to award scholarships. In 1965, the ASID's successor, the Industrial Designers Society of America, established a program of annual merit awards to schools.

The controversy over whether to educate or to train design graduates continued to heat up, with designers and design educators (most of whom, it must be noted, had not been formally educated in industrial design) searching for academic minimums that would satisfy both groups. At the 1962 meeting of IDEA at the University of Illinois (hosted by Edward

*The panel at the 1962 meeting of IDEA included Joseph Carriero (seated left) and William Goldsmith and Jay Doblin (standing); Serge Chermayeff (seated right) was the moderator. Credit: Industrial Design (April 1962). Photograph by Edward Zagorski.*

Zagorski), a balance was found: art courses in the first year, courses in two- and three-dimensional design and familiarization with materials and industrial processes in the second year, theoretical and practical design problems in the third year, and courses in economics and professional practice along with deeper design challenges in the fourth year. Ralph Caplan, editor of *Industrial Design* magazine, in reporting on the 1962 meeting, observed that design educators were a curious lot in that they held meetings at which they actually discussed what they did and how to do it better. "In a culture that exaggerates the distinction between teaching and doing," he noted, "the teacher of design is in trouble. His colleagues regard him as suspect, engaged in preparing students for industry, rather than, like themselves, preparing students to receive grants from the Ford Foundation." (117)

Caplan might also have noted that beneath their cover of providing an employment pool for design practice, educators were creating a theoretical basis for setting up industrial design as the aesthetic and humane conscience of industry. This aspiration was supported by Sibyl Moholy-Nagy, who keynoted the 1962 IDEA meeting by advocating a radical reorganization of the schools that would distinguish between design technicians and the builders of a designed environment.

The American industrial design profession was building an academic foundation. At the 1963 IDEA meeting (held at Pratt Institute), ten chairmen of established degree programs presented their own curricular structures and philosophies. Robert McKim of Stanford University regretted the lack of documentation of industrial design and the fact that there was as yet no clear definition of the field or of its objectives. William Katavolos of the Parsons School of Design recommended that older design educators put their ideas into writings upon which younger members could build their own structures. Others suggested that there were many roads to Rome and that both practice and education should continue on

their own paths. The respected practicing designer Raymond Spilman suggested that academic programs might be based on case histories leavened with research into the relations between people and their environment.

The American design educators' exploration of academic minimums continued at the seminars held by the International Council of Societies of Industrial Design (ICSID). After being refined and simplified for global use, the minimums they established were put into effect in the United States as well as in other countries.

During the 1950s, the demand for industrial designers and the attention that the field was getting in the mass media attracted the attention of professionals outside the fields of art and design who believed that intuition, imagination, and talent could be rationalized, measured, and dispensed to the uncreative. Some saw no need to entrust the design of products to designers. Market analysts and planners suggested that the process of design be turned over to those who had developed quasi-scientific methods for gauging what forms of a product would be acceptable to a particular market segment or what technological features could be added to make a product irresistible to the public. In a way, the reliance on planners and analysts showed that markets were becoming saturated and that management was becoming less confident of its own judgment. Businessmen had become more and more distant from the products or services for which they were responsible, and thus they were receptive to specialists who promised to help them share that burden. There seemed to be a general conviction that the economic welfare of the nation was dependent upon consumption, and that products must have shorter lifespans so that new models could be introduced every year.

On the technical side of the design process, John Arnold recognized the need to shake engineers out of the complacency that had been brought on by postwar professional security, and introduced problems in "creative engineering" to his students at the Massachusetts Institute of Technology. Arnold's approach was to assign problems in product design to a class and to have the results judged by a guest jury on the basis of presentation, originality, and the level of engineering that was used to solve the problem.

The popularity of his course convinced Arnold that it would also be of value to practicing engineers. Accordingly, he organized a series of short courses in creative engineering for engineers and product designers, which were offered for several summers in the 1950s. The classes consisted of engineers from manufacturing industries, military personnel involved in research projects, and a few industrial designers. In the beginning, the goal was to explore and demonstrate factors contributing to the human creative potential; however, by the summer of 1955 increasing emphasis was being placed on the management of creative personnel, the testing and measuring of creative ability, and the psychology of creative thinking and imagination. The 1956 program addressed techniques for organizing "inspired" creative activity and the selection and training of creative individuals. With some perspective, it seems that Arnold was trying to help engineers and engineering managers break out of petrified modes of education and experience.

The 1956 summer program at MIT was a particularly important one in that Arnold, who did not subscribe to a clearly defined method of stimulating creativity, invited other champions of this unique area to present their methods to an audience of some 150 attendees. In one of the presentations, R. Buckminster Fuller expounded on his theme of the comprehensive designer, using himself and his contributions as the best example, and called for the establishment of a society of Leonardos. Charles H. Clark of the Ethyl Corporation demonstrated the popular method of "brainstorming," invented by Alex F. Osborn of the advertising agency of Batten, Barton, Durstine and Osborn. It was a method of stimulating a

John Arnold of MIT, director of the annual seminars on "creative engineering" that began in 1953, stressed three kinds of thinking—analytical, judicial, and creative—that are combined into an end result that is greater than the sum of its parts. Credit: Industrial Design (January 1957). Photograph by Thomas Sheridan.

group to pour out ideas by free association on the premise that the free flow of ideas will, at some point, hit upon the logical solution to a problem. Arnold's position was that brainstorming's chief value was as a form of cathartic mental therapy. The last major presentation was made by William J. J. Gordon, who had conceived a methodology called Operational Creativity while working for the pioneering industrial-research firm of Arthur D. Little, Inc. Whereas brainstorming was intended primarily to be done at the outset of a project, a group practicing Operational Creativity was expected to tackle a problem as an organic unit and to stay with it until a wholly new concept could be developed.

Arnold also brought in other lecturers to stimulate his class. Psychologists, psychoanalysts, and other scholars of human behavior were represented at each session. Arnold's own position was that the creative process consisted of more than simply having an idea. He saw research and planning as equally important.

John Arnold was said to feel that, although industrial designers had a certain special talent that equipped them to apply art to industry, engineers were the real designers in industry. A visiting mission of European product-design specialists reported that he thought American industrial designers were undereducated in technical matters and too businesslike in attitude. He hoped to turn out creative engineers who would be both analytical and imaginative and who would be equipped to perform a real service to society. His pioneering work at MIT inspired similar seminars and courses elsewhere in academia. Later he went to Stanford University to start a similar program for postgraduate engineering students.

The Institute of Contemporary Art, in Boston, had been cultivating a position between industrial design and industry. In 1957 the ICA, encouraged by the activities of John Arnold and W. J. J. Gordon and by the growing interest in product planning and manage-

ment, initiated a series of programs intended to bring designers and representatives of industry together. That summer, a short course entitled Processes for Design Problem Solving was offered. The content of this course was based on recommendations made by the two professional design societies. There were presentations by Arnold, Gordon, and Fuller. Joseph Carriero served as academic director for the course.

Earlier in the summer of 1957, Carriero, in cooperation with *Industrial Design* magazine, had conducted a seminar at the Philadelphia Museum School of Art that had brought a number of practicing industrial designers and design educators together to discuss the role and the responsibilities of designers as managers. One of the questions Carriero raised was: "What is the highest level to which a designer can aspire" without becoming primarily a manager? It was pointed out that a manager's primary obligation is to the stockholders, whereas a designer's is to his colleagues. Another view expressed was that design is only one stage in the development of a product, and that research, analysis, and planning demand just as much creativity. It was also asserted that it takes as much creativity to manage the entire process as to work on any one phase. The most telling point raised at this meeting was that designers were generally expected to rely on their own aesthetic judgment, but that logic and rationality also had a place in their bag of tricks.

In October of 1958 the Institute of Contemporary Art hald (at Arden House, in Harriman, New York) a four-day conference, entitled The Evolution of Products, that took a different approach to the issue of design management. Six teams were assigned to address six different phases of product development. The various teams were led by experts in the evolution of a product from six different viewpoints: industrial design, engineering, invention, patenting, production, and marketing. In February 1958 the ICA began a fifteen-week evening course in Boston exploring the practices and strategies of industrial design. That program was under the direction of John E. Alcott, professor of industrial design at the Rhode Island School of Design.

These courses, plus others dealing with creativity and the management of new ideas at NYU, Columbia, Yale, and other universities, reflected a recession in the economy and a general concern in the broader product-development community that industry was running out of new things to manufacture and that, as a result, existing markets were stagnating. The auto industry's frantic preoccupation with extravagant styling and the appliance industry's vigorous search for new functional as well as stylistic exaggerations of their products offered ample evidence of the dilemma of affluence (i.e., the use of design to support overproduction) in the late 1950s.

Industrial designers were being called upon once more to get America's industries rolling. The last time had been during the Depression, when the people had been reluctant (if not unable) to buy anything. Now, it seemed, people had bought too much and needed something new to rekindle their interest. *Newsweek* called upon industrial designers, who had done more than any other group of men to change the face of industry in the past, to do it again. *Business Week* observed that industrial designers "search out uses for new materials for basic suppliers" and "develop products for companies that know only that they want to get into new fields," and that "the designer is beginning to take on the importance as a managerial prop that advertising and public relations have held" (104).

The recommendations of *Business Week* and other magazines had already been anticipated by a number of companies that had increased their public-relations activities in an attempt to convince the public that they were conscious of the importance of design. Some companies established design competitions, awards, and service programs directed at designers and design schools in order to stimulate new ideas for their products and materials—and in order to be able to proclaim their interest in design in promotional advertising in business and professional magazines. Metal and plastic companies were particularly active in this area.

Alcoa took a step toward bringing industry, design education, and design practice together in 1959 when it established a new program for industrial design students. The program consisted of a series of annual collaborative programs. Selected schools were to be supplied with complete technical libraries on aluminum, and with aluminum materials in a variety of forms, for approved classroom projects and seminars in which new forms and finishes for aluminum were to be discussed. The first schools selected for this program were the Philadelphia Museum School, Syracuse University, the Institute of Design, Pratt Institute, the Rhode Island School of Design, and the University of Illinois. It was agreed that after two or three years the program would move on to other schools. The obvious objective of Alcoa's program was to make direct experience with aluminum a part of design education, but its deeper value was that it helped develop a bond between industry, design education, and design practice. The program was so successful that the idea was picked up by other corporations (including Armco, Dow, and St. Regis) and perpetuated for many years.

In 1967 the board of the Industrial Designers Society of America asked an ad hoc committee of practicing designers and design educators to explore the relationship between practice and education of industrial design and, if possible, to recommend a procedure for selecting those schools that would appear on the IDSA's list of recommended programs. Dave Chapman, as coordinator, called a meeting, held in April at the Plaza Hotel in New York, at which ten prominent designers and three educators agreed that a set of criteria and a recommended set of minimums would have to be established first. The members of this ad hoc group also agreed that each of them would prepare his own set of minimums

This standing wheelchair
was conceived and devel-
oped in 1968 by Peter
Bressler, a student at the
Rhode Island School of
Design. Credit: "Alcoa
Student Design Merit
Awards for 1968"
(brochure).

This "ski-horse" was designed and built in 1960 by S. Jack Magri, a student at Syracuse University. Credit: "Alcoa Student Design Awards for 1960." Photograph by Louis Ouzer.

and circulate it among the other members prior to a second meeting, scheduled for July.

For a number of reasons, the second meeting was canceled, and thus the question of recommending a list of schools to be recognized by the IDSA remained unresolved. Apparently some of the members of the committee either could not or would not submit recommendations, and those that were circulated did not promise an easy procedure. Furthermore, some felt that the ad hoc committee was preempting the area of responsibility of IDSA's standing education committee.

The subject was then passed on to IDSA's Education Committee, whose chairman, James Alexander, called for a meeting on industrial design education to be held at the University of Illinois in March of 1968. In addition to considering the criteria and minimums for IDSA recognition, the Education Committee (made up of the educators James Shipley and William Katavolos and the designers Dave Chapman, Paul Rawson, and Carl Clement) suggested that the society recognize those schools considered to be "effective" by IDSA's members.

At the meeting, Chapman stated that IDSA had been asked to extend formal approval to recommended schools but had realized that, despite the collective experience of its members, it was unable to act on this request. He admitted that they could not "survive out there in this jungle . . . on the basis of selling good design. Congress and industry are not interested—all they want is profit. We smuggle in virtue . . . we give these clients good things in spite of them." (243) Jay Doblin of the Institute of Design carried on the point: "We've got to reconstruct this profession. We have welded together in this country a technology. . . . Now the question is, what shall we do with it, to make it human so we aren't victimized by it?" (244) James Shipley suggested that "most professionals are aware that historically American education has been vocationally oriented" (245). The general conclusion

was that minimums, properly determined and enforced, would provide a much-needed foundation for the profession.

Arthur Pulos reported on the minimums that had been recommended by ICSID's international working group. As a member, he had attended the three meetings of the working group held since 1964 (one at Bruges, Belgium, one at Ulm, West Germany, and one at Syracuse, New York). He reported that ICSID's minimums were built around Information (the acquisition of knowledge), "Formation" (the solution of problems related to products and product systems), and Communication (the development of skills for exploring, storing, and transmitting ideas). In percentages, referring to number of courses and hours of required study, 50 percent was to be devoted to Formation and the other 50 percent was to be divided between Information and Communication according to the interests of each school.

James Shipley mailed a proposal for educational minimums and for IDSA recognition of schools to all design educators in late 1967. His proposal stated minimums in general terms and tested whether IDSA recognition of schools would be considered "effective." The educators accepted Shipley's proposal. Favoring the establishment of minimums, they agreed to circulate them by mail and, upon approval, to submit them to the ICSID board (which subsequently approved the recommendations and provided the funds to publish and distribute them).

Since then, each school had built its own concept of industrial design education on the minimums and on the particular school's idea as to what the industrial design graduate's capabilities should be. In the main, those schools philosophically closer to the immediate market for graduates tended to *train* students to meet the day-by-day needs of that market; other schools tended to see themselves as *educating* their students for a loftier position, often one once removed from the immediate needs of the employment market.

Industrial design education in the United States has never depended on federal agencies for direction or funding. Rather, as is the case with all education in this country, it was the responsibility of those citizens at local or state levels who were involved to determine the nature and the quality of the academic programs. In this sense the original philosophical conflict between the ASID and the IDI now joined in the IDSA and among the various emerging curricula in industrial design was entirely in line with the American system. Thus, face-to-face confrontations over theory, goals, and methodologies led to a common ground upon which all individual programs could be built. Each school conformed to a set of agreed-upon minimums then went off in its own direction—some to focus on theory, some on practice, and others on personal or social expression.

American design educators were aware of developments in design education in other major countries and, by correspondence and conferences, managed to share experiences. The reorganization of the Royal College of Art in London in 1958 to include a full program in industrial design (engineering) was of particular interest. Misha Black, a partner in the Design Research Unit, was appointed in 1960 to head the program, which quickly became a model for American educators. Gordon Russell and Paul Reilly (successive directors of the British Council of Industrial Design) and Black were in close contact with their American colleagues.

The establishment of the Hochschule für Gestaltung at Ulm, West Germany, in 1953 was in large measure due to a grant of $250,000 from the American High Commission for Germany, which was matched by the Germans. Its purpose was to encourage creativity in young people and to regenerate a war-ravaged Germany. The school was internationally acclaimed from the very beginning as a reincarnation of the Bauhaus with principles and goals adjusted to the circumstances of the postwar world. Its students were primarily foreigners (some of them Americans) who were attracted to its philosophy that the social functions of the artist and the designer were different and that design was a global rather than a national force. Reyner Banham observed that "Ulm was the first school to withdraw completely and programmatically from the earlier dispensation dominated by architecture and the fine arts. . . . It has become a cool training ground for a technocratic elite." (2, 107) There was considerable exchange between American designers and educators and the Ulm school—both as students and members of the faculty. However, despite the school's high resolve and commitment, it became estranged from German authorities, and in 1968 the faculty and students elected to close the school so that it would "not suffer the same fate as the Bauhaus, i.e., to be rendered harmless and put on show as an exhibit in the museum of cultural objects" (187).

Industrial design was relatively little known in the Orient until 1949, when the Japan Trade Exhibition in Yokohama included a foreign pavilion in which, with the consent of American authorities, everyday American products were exhibited. Japanese industrialists were particularly impressed by the role of industrial design in the development and marketing of American manufactures. After the president of the Matsushita appliance company visited the United States, he returned to set up an industrial design section in his own company. It was soon emulated by other Japanese manufacturers.

In 1951, when the San Francisco Peace Treaty was signed, the Japanese began to look to their own renaissance. First of all, on the basis of the American example, the national polytechnic schools and the Academy were reformed into university-level institutions. However, until such time as graduates from these schools could take their place in Japanese industry, American designers (among them Raymond Loewy, who left behind his book *Never Leave Well Enough Alone* to be translated into Japanese) were invited

ジェイ・ダブリン、デイブ・チャプマン　デザイン講習会報告（I）

# デザインの発想とその展開

産業工芸試験所は，その34年度事業の一つとして米国からジェイ・ダブリン，デイブ・チャプマンの両氏を招き，昨年10月12日〜31日の間，同東京本所においてデザイン講習会を開催した。本誌では3回にわたってその報告を連続掲載することにしたが，今回はその第1回であり，ダブリン氏担当の講習の前段をまとめたものである。なお，両氏については本誌昨年，9月号，10月号に，それぞれくわしく紹介してある。

手前はチャプマン夫妻
後方はダブリン夫妻

*Dave Chapman and Jay Doblin, with their wives, arriving in Japan to teach a special class on design concepts and development at the request of the Industrial Arts Institute. Credit: Industrial Art News (January 1960).*

to Japan to design products and packages. Others who came were Russel Wright, George Nelson, Freda Diamond, Jean Reinecke, Alfred P. Girardy, LaGarde Tackett, and Walter Sobotka. In addition, Japanese government subsidies sent about seventy young designers from Japan to study in the United States and Europe.

A group of faculty members from the Art Center School in California was invited in 1956 by the Japanese External Trade Recovery Organization to acquaint Japanese industry with industrial design practice and education. The school's founder and director, E. A. Adams, and John Coleman, the head of product design, visited 86 factories throughout the country to meet with management in order to evaluate their product designs and marketing practices. George Jergensen, head of the school's industrial design department, stayed in Tokyo to conduct a special course for designers and engineers from industry who gathered at the Industrial Arts Institute to learn "how modern design methods can be applied to Japanese products for the betterment of that country's export business" (97). This team of Americans was followed in 1959 by Jay Doblin and Dave Chapman, who taught a special class at the Institute on concept development. That same year, and again in 1961, groups of Japanese industrialists, designers, and teachers visited the United States on study tours co-sponsored by the Japan Productivity Center in Tokyo and the International Cooporation Administration in Washington. Their research reports were helpful to the Japanese in understanding American design and marketing practices.

Since its founding in 1957, the International Council of Societies of Industrial Design had been aware of the importance of education to the practice of industrial design. Concerned statements had been presented at ICSID congresses about the need for a study of education on a worldwide basis for the purpose of arriving at a consensus that would serve as a guide to developing nations. As a result, the board of ICSID established a working group of educators under the chairmanship of Misha Black. The group (including three Americans, William Katavolos, Arthur Pulos, and Nathan Shapira) agreed that an international seminar should be held to bring together experts to establish an international basis for industrial design education. It was also suggested that an international survey of existing programs be made, that consideration be given to recommended curricula for schools of industrial design, and that objective criteria be developed by which the status and competence of such schools could be evaluated. To this end, UNESCO authorized funding for the first seminar, held in Bruges, Belgium, in 1964. Subsequent seminars were held in 1965 at the Hochschule für Gestaltung in Ulm and in 1967 at Syracuse University. From those discussions there emerged a framework of recommendations and a set of academic minimums upon which industrial design curricula could be built upon a global basis, acknowledging the inevitable rapprochement between democratic and socialistic design philosophies.

# National Convergence

*We had to contend with a group of 20 to 30 crackpot commercial artists, decorators, etc., without experience, talent, taste or integrity, who called themselves industrial designers.*

Raymond Loewy, 1951 (24, 128–129)

The American Designers' Institute, senior forerunner of today's Industrial Designers Society of America, had its beginnings in the early 1920s, when scattered American furniture manufacturers were coalescing into a trade association. The American Furniture Mart in Chicago had been opened to provide manufacturers with a common building for biannual exhibitions.

From the start, the American Furniture Mart was closely guarded to keep out designers, who were presumed to have no other interest in visiting the Mart other than to plagiarize the designs of others. Some designers managed to gain entry to the exhibition hall through individual memberships in the Furniture Club, a part of the Mart from which they were not excluded; nevertheless, the furniture manufacturers continued to look upon designers as invaders. Even those manufacturers who employed designers did not quite trust them.

In 1933, the accusations of design piracy brought representatives of the furniture industry together with a number of designers, and the National Furniture Designers' Council (NFDC) was founded. That organization's main purpose seems to have been to draw up and submit to the National Recovery Administration a code enjoining copying. Though design protection of a sort was available under existing patent and copyright regulations, the members of the NFDC felt that more effective protection was necessary. At a time when the furniture manufacturers should have been stimulating open competition in design, they were instead trying to protect the limited number of design ideas they had been passing back and forth. The proposed code did not, however, have the support of the furniture industry, and so the NRA committee that was trying to formulate a code for the furniture

manufacturers discounted it. In 1934—the year in which the NRA was declared unconstitutional by the U.S. Supreme Court—the NFDC disintegrated.

But the NFDC had planted the seed for a design organization. Undaunted by the NFDC's demise, Lawrence H. Whiting, the director of the American Furniture Mart, took it upon himself (with help from Rosalie Flank, his director of public relations) to call a special meeting of designers—including some members of the defunct NFDC—to discuss designers' problems. The speakers at this meeting, held in July 1935, included Richard Bach, director of industrial relations at the Metropolitan Museum of Art, and Alfred Auerbach, editor of *Retailing* magazine. When the discussion turned once again to the negativism of providing protection against design piracy, John Root, a prominent Chicago architect, offered a more positive suggestion: that a committee of architects and designers be appointed to stage an exhibition of designs related to the furnishings of homes and institutions at the Furniture Mart's winter market.

During the American Furniture Mart's January 1936 market, Whiting invited a group of leading furniture designers to a luncheon at the Furniture Club, and they agreed to form a new organization: the Designers' Institute of the American Furniture Mart. (The designers who spoke at the luncheon included Kem Weber, Donald Deskey, Gilbert Rohde, and Leo Jiranek.) It was decided that at each market, designers and manufacturers would hold individual meetings and then a joint session.

When the above-mentioned group (now calling itself the American Furniture Mart Designers Institute) met during the AFM's July 1938 market, the principal speaker was John Vassos, an artist, an author, and a consultant designer for RCA Victor. In his talk—the theme of which was "Have designers missed a bet?"—Vassos encouraged his colleagues to sever their connection with the American Furniture Mart and to expand their area of interest beyond the focus on furniture. The name of the group was changed to American Designers' Institute, and John Vassos, who had not even been a member of the group before the July meeting, was elected to head the new organization.

The first closed meeting of the ADI was held in 1939 at the American Furniture Mart. John Vassos writes that the group decided to move out of the Furniture Mart because of a feeling that "the patronage limited the freedom of design of the members" (223).

The ADI, which had been operating unofficially, decided to apply for legal recognition in the state of Illinois. In the incorporation statement (filed by Lawrence Whiting, Rosalie Flank, and John Vassos), the organization was described as "a society for the promotion, education, and dissemination of information and good will with reference to the art of designing; to bring to the public information concerning the standards and ethics of designers" (213). On July 10, 1940, the American Designers' institute was approved as a corporation in the state of Illinois.

That the ADI was conceived as an organization of designers, not as one of *industrial* designers, may have reflected the fact that most of its members were rather closely tied to craft-based industries. Furthermore, the early members tended to specialize in a single area, such as furniture, fabrics, or ceramics.

In October 1941, with the war underway in Europe and with the United States entering a state of military preparedness, the ADI organized a national conference on the subject of "Design in the National Emergency." At this conference (held in New York) the ADI formally promised that the talents of its members would be made available to the U.S. government and to manufacturers who needed help to meet the difficulties imposed by shortages of materials, labor, and manufacturing equipment. A National Emergency Committee, with Leo Jiranek as chairman, was asked to submit a report to the National War Production Board and the Office of Price Administration outlin-

John Vassos was not only elected the first president of the ADI; in 1939 he also won the competition held for the organization's symbol with this stylized depiction of a hand holding a stylus. Credit: Industrial Design, May 1958, p. 60.

ing how designers could best serve the country. The *New York Times,* referring to this meeting, commented that "the period of defense emergency and its aftermath should serve as a spur to industrial design in its broadest sense" (165).

By 1942, when Edward J. Wormley was elected chairman, the ADI's center of activity was shifting to New York. The New York chapter questioned whether the group should continue as a corporation under Illinois law. Owing to the unsettled conditions of wartime, no action was taken. However, in 1943 the Illinois Secretary of the State dissolved the corporation for failure to file the annual report required by state law. This break in continuity gave the ADI its final impetus to move its legal base to the East Coast. On May 13, 1944, on the basis of an application filed by Alfons Bach, Ben Nash, and George Kosmak, the American Designers Institute (now with the apostrophe omitted) was granted a new charter of incorporation by the state of Delaware.

New York was the home base of a group of first-generation industrial designers, most of whom had been in practice since the late 1920s. They had come from different disciplines—engineering, illustration, advertising, stage design, and display design, among others. While not formally organized, they knew one another and had competed or collaborated on various occasions. Their growing reputation had been capped by their outstanding contributions to the planning and the design of the New York World's Fair.

The price of the public recognition these designers received was that they attracted the attention of New York State's tax authorities, always on the alert for new sources of revenue, who decided that industrial design earnings were taxable under the unincorporated-business tax statute. The designers protested that their earnings, like those of architects, were derived from services rendered rather than from the sale of goods. Henry Dreyfuss, in an interview, summarized the circum-

stances: ". . . we believed that as professionals we were exempt from the unincorporated business tax. Therefore, we were astounded to be billed for half a million in back taxes [for the years 1935, 1936, 1937] by the state of New York. . . . two problems existed, a. to accept the accusation and the legal and technical loss of our professional standing for which we had worked so hard, and b. I question whether any one of us could have met the payment of the bill if we had to. . . . The common danger brought us together and the three of us [Dreyfuss, Raymond Loewy, and Walter Dorwin Teague] shared the cost of engaging an outstanding attorney to represent us. Walter Dorwin Teague, who looked the most professional, was to stand trial. Fortunately, we won the case and remained both professional and solvent." (189) In the hearing *Teague* v. *Graves et al.* (New York State Supreme Court, Appellate Division, third department, April 30, 1941), attorneys representing Teague petitioned for exemption of his income from the unincorporated-business tax on the point that "the vocation of industrial design is a 'profession,' " rather than a 'trade' or 'business,' within provision of the Tax Law exempting professions from unincorporated business tax" (247). It was also stated that industrial design was a separate field of endeavor, and that many institutions of learning—including Pratt Institute, the Carnegie Institute of Technology, the Universities of Illinois and Michigan, and New York University—now offered courses leading to the degree of Bachelor of Arts in Industrial Design. Despite the fact that neither Teague nor any of the other early industrial designers had a formal education in the field, they claimed credit for having established it and for having creating the body of knowledge on which the new academic programs were based. Teague's defense also referred to the scholarly character of his recent book *Design This Day* and the recognized quality of his professional service to clients. The successful petition for dismissal was based on the portion of section 386 of the statute that "excludes the practice of law, medicine, dentistry, [and] architecture[,] which under existing law cannot be conducted under corporate structure, and in any other case in which more than eighty percent of the gross income is derived from personal services actually rendered by the individual" (248). Since that time, despite repeated attempts to tax industrial designers under the unincorporated-business tax law, they have always been found exempt. This is taken as prima facie evidence that industrial design is a profession. (Since the establishment of "professional corporation" status for those in the traditional professions, the issue has become academic; even incorporation does not excuse them from liability.)

The establishment of architecture as a profession had followed a roughly similar course. Some ninety years before the SID came into existence, the American Institute of Architects had been organized after a judge had ruled that an architect was entitled to be paid for his design services as a professional.

For a while after the settlement of the tax issue, Dreyfuss, Loewy, and Teague discussed the possibility of organizing a professional society that would promote high standards and would protect designers' professional status should that again become necessary. They invited other designers to join them in exploring the possibility further. "There were giants around the table," Dreyfuss said. "I recall Normal Bel Geddes, Don Deskey, Egmont Arens, Russel Wright, and others who were to take their place in the fraternity." (189)

On February 7, 1944, three months before the ADI was chartered anew in Delaware, fifteen practicing industrial designers met in Teague's office to lay the groundwork for a new professional society. They agreed that the society should include those who were "successfully engaged in industrial design" and the heads of the academic programs. (In point of fact, it was years before the organization accepted as members educators who were not also practitioners.) For the moment, they defined an industrial designer as "one who

*This stylized pattern of the letters SID was adopted by the board of the Society of Industrial Designers as its symbol in 1946. Credit: Society of Industrial Designers.*

has successfully designed a *diversity* of products for machine and mass production" (222). It was on this last condition that much of the conflict between the two organizations developed.

On August 20, 1944, at its first annual meeting, the group elected Teague president, Dreyfuss vice-president, Loewy chairman of the executive committee, Harold Van Doren treasurer, and Egmont Arens secretary. Philip McConnell, formerly with the U.S. Treasury Department and former secretary to the New York World's Fair Design Commission, was appointed executive secretary of the new organization. The by-laws and the constitution were drafted and endorsed, and on August 29, 1944, the organization was chartered by the State of New York under the name Society of Industrial Designers. Aside from the above-mentioned officers, the founding members were Donald Deskey, Norman Bel Geddes, Lurelle Guild, Ray Patten, Joseph Platt, John Gordon Rideout, George Sakier, Joseph Sinel, Brooks Stevens, and Russel Wright. Wright recalled that George Nelson, Charles Eames, and several members of the ADI were considered for membership but were not thought acceptable at the time (possibly because their work was limited to furniture design). Brooks Stevens recalls: "I remember vividly the feeling of pride I had in being invited to join the gods on Mount Olympus at the first meeting in New York. It was a strange gathering with guarded conversation on the part of the people who were meeting for the first time and who were, in a sense, to become competitive or already were." (204)

Under Philip McConnell's direction, the rules and procedures of the SID were clarified. A 1945 flyer states the qualifications for membership as follows: "Membership in the Society shall be limited to practicing Industrial Designers, and members of Industrial Design departments in institutions of higher learning. . . . To be acceptable a candidate must have practiced Industrial Design for several years and in the course of his practice must have had three or more of his products manufactured and offered for sale in the usual mar-keting channels. He must have honorably and satisfactorily served three or more manufacturers. . . . The term Industrial Designer is defined to include persons who are professionally engaged in designing a diversity of products for machine and mass production." (235, 5–6) These rules specifically excluded businessmen, specialists, handicraft designers, and engineers.

Over the years, the SID was occasionally criticized for being an exclusive club. After all, Dreyfuss had referred to it as a fraternity, and each candidate for admission was required to submit a portfolio to the board of directors, where one dissenting vote was enough for disqualification. However, the assessment of dues was unusually considerate. It was agreed at the 1946 annual meeting that dues would be levied according to each member's income. Furthermore, for a number of years, lecture income was by gentlemen's agreement contributed to a common pool to be used for scholarships and other similar assistance.

In 1947, at the request of the SID, the American Management Association (AMA) conducted a survey of its own members on the subject of "American Business and Industrial Design." Of 400 members, 133 responded. The report stated that there had been a 50% rise in the reliance of business on professional designers to give their products consumer appeal from the standpoint of art, engineering, and merchandising. Those companies using industrial designers included 90% of the companies making consumer goods, 80% of those making packaging, and 50% of the manufacturers of industrial products. The majority felt that industrial design was a function of top management and that senior officers should be responsible for selecting the industrial designer. The summary of the AMA report noted that the hiring of persons to perform industrial design work had begun shortly after the 1925 Paris Exposition. Hiring had grown steadily through the 1930s until the war, then had leveled off. However, in 1943, the numbers had begun to climb again, reflecting preparations for peace. The report concluded with comments that were both laudatory and critical of industrial design. One respondent had praised American businessmen and manufacturers and said that they had "learned through experience that design makes a difference which can be measured in terms of dollars and cents and that design is the province of a specialist" (225). Another had complained that "industrial designers are fugitives from mental labor," that designers "sell themselves to gullible management and impose themselves on engineering to put their ideas . . . across," and that "brass is notoriously lacking in aesthetic sense and is willing to pay high prices to hide that deficiency." (225) It would seem that at this point industrial design had entered the level of other professional services that expand the capabilities of top management.

In September 1945, without editorial fanfare, "+ industrial design" appeared as a subtitle on the title page of *Interiors* magazine for the first time. In the October issue, also without editorial comment, an advertisement announced that *Interiors* had opened its pages to industrial designers. The ad quoted an item in the trade paper *Retailing Home Furnishings:* "Industrial designers are having a field day these days. Their advice is being sought as never before. . . . in short, they have come into their own and are frantically being outbid for on every side by manufacturers who want a designer's name attached to their products. . . ." (119) Four years later the editor, Francis de N. Schroeder, made the following announcement: "In November, 1949, *Interiors* became the first magazine in the field to establish a department of industrial design which was a recognition of the fact that the various designs which are part of the modern home and commercial interiors are quite as much a part of interior design as the paper on the wall. Ever since we have been breathlessly trying to keep apace with industrial design, the most rapidly expanding of all design fields." (138) At first, *Interiors* concentrated on small products and domestic furnishings. But then, as the magazine began to cover the

practice of industrial design and to illustrate a broader spectrum of manufactured products, it became evident that there was a market for a separate publication on industrial design. In 1955, Whitney Publications was able to spin off *Industrial Design* as a vigorous brother to *Interiors.* The first editor was Jane Fiske Mitarachi, who proved an inspired choice.

Publicity attending the work of industrial designers and the activities of the two new organizations in the New York area attracted the attention of representatives of the New York State Department of Commerce, who in May 1944 "suggested that a Design Section be established as part of the department." This section "would become responsible for the encouragement of well-designed products, thereby making the goods manufactured in the state of New York more readily sold at home and abroad" (221). The recommendation called attention to similar programs that had been established with success in England, Austria, and other countries, and noted that trade associations and industries had ignored design, had failed to impress the public with the importance of good design, and had made no effort to help in the education of designers. The plan stated (under the head "The Importance of Good Design in Industry") that "if the United States is to hold a foremost place in the world's commerce after the war, her manufactures must equal or excel those of other countries in beauty of design and in quality of material and workmanship" (221). It called for a Design Section to be run by an advisory board with a staff of specialists in various functions and product areas. It also suggested that 111 trade associations collaborate on traveling exhibitions, competitions, awards, designer registration, research, and reports. Unfortunately for the cause of design (and, perhaps, for the national economy), the New York proposal failed to go any further than discussions with members of the board of the American Designers Institute.

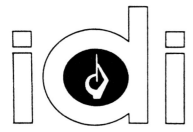

The symbol of the Package Designers Council, like that of the SID, followed the then-current style of interlocking lowercase letters to form a recognizable, if not always readable, graphic mark. Credit: Package Designers Council.

The American Designers Institute decided in 1951 to change its name to the Industrial Designers Institute. Vassos's hand-with-stylus was preserved inside the pattern of the letters "idi." Credit: Industrial Designers Institute.

In 1948 Frank Gianninoto, chairman of the board of trustees of the ADI, noting that package design was a valid form of industrial design bridging the gap between product design and graphic design, suggested that the ADI open its membership to package designers. The trustees supported his proposal, but the package designers, fearing that their identity would be lost, decided to form their own organization—the Package Designers Council. Thus, the opportunity to establish an umbrella organization of designers was lost for the moment.

In 1949 Gianninoto presented to the board legal counsel's recommendation that the name of the organization, American Designers Institute, should be changed to Industrial Designers Institute because it was in the interest of the members "to identify themselves particularly with the developing and emerging profession of industrial design" (211). The trustees agreed with the recommendation and proposed the idea to the membership. In 1951, with the approval of the members, an amendment to change the name to Industrial Designers Institute was approved by the Secretary of State of Delaware.

By 1955 the Industrial Designers Institute, now headquartered in New York City, had over 200 active members. Its attorneys recommended that, in order to strengthen its quest for legal recognition, the group amend its definition of industrial design to make it conform to the requirements of New York State's Education Law while avoiding the precincts of architecture and engineering. The new definition—written by the IDI's president, Benjamin Nash, and approved by the board and subsequently by the membership—sweepingly described an industrial designer as "a person practicing Industrial Designing . . . who is able to perform, or who does perform, professional service such as consultation, evaluation, planning, design including structural design, or reasonable supervision of construction or operation, in connection with any machine-made, mass-produced commodity for consumer use or accessory thereto, wherein the

safeguarding of life, property or human benefits are concerned, or involved, when such
service requires the application of Art, Science of design, and construction based upon
the principles of aesthetics, humanities and
industrial techniques" (217).

In 1955 the SID changed its name to *American
Society of Industrial Designers* in order to
emphasize the national affiliation of those
members who were doing more and more
work for foreign clients. Raymond Loewy had
established offices abroad, and other members (e.g. Donald Deskey) had formed working
alliances, often on a reciprocal basis, with foreign designers.

The expanding international commitment of
the ASID was evident in 1956 when it co-
sponsored, with the Museum of Modern Art, a
seminar on "Industrial Design in Europe
Today" with speakers from England, France,
and Germany. And the American designers
who had connections with European colleagues were exploring the possibility of forming an international organization.

All this international activity was inevitable.
Industrial design was destined to become an
international profession. Unlike buildings and
interiors, manufactured products were en-
countering competition from foreign-made
counterparts. Some countries were establishing design centers and organizing export-
promotion projects. The U.S. government
organized two export-promotion programs
that involved industrial designers in the 1950s:
one (under the aegis of the Department of
Commerce) that involved participation in
international trade fairs, and one (run by the
State Department's International Cooperation
Administration) that sent teams of American
designers around the world to serve as
advisors in the areas of crafts, product manufactures, and export. At the 1956 annual
meeting of ASID, federal representatives outlined these programs to the members and
invited their participation.

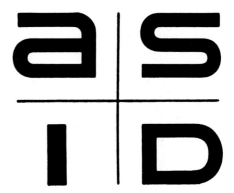

*When the Society of
Industrial Designers
decided to precede its
name with the word Amer-
ican, another new graphic
mark was in order. Credit:
American Society of
Industrial Designers.*

Good evidence that the IDI and the ASID were beginning to cooperate came out of Chicago in 1955. James Hvale of the IDI and William Goldsmith of the ASID worked together to organize an exhibition of members' work at the Illinois Institute of Technology. This exhibition, entitled Industrial Design—Today and Tomorrow, was held in conjunction with the opening of Crown Hall, the academic home of the Institute of Design.

Soon the ASID and the IDI were collaborating across the entire range of their common interests. The staging of the international exhibition in Brussels (1958), the Milan Triennales (1954 and 1957), and the American National Exhibition in Moscow (1958) depended upon joint action. Seminars conducted by both societies on such themes as "New Conflicts in U.S. Design," "Design for Survival," and "International Aspects of Industrial Design" brought American and foreign industrial designers together with government representatives who were interested in the global role of industrial design.

In 1958, a the end of his tenure as president of the ASID, William Goldsmith reported to Robert Redmann, then president of the IDI, that the ASID board was aware that the IDI had called for a joint effort toward a merger of the two societies. Goldsmith informed Redmann that, with the approval of the board, he had set up a review committee, with Richard Latham as chairman.

One difference that had to be addressed was the wide discrepancy in dues. Whereas the IDI had a fixed annual fee of $40, ASID dues ranged from $50 to $540, depending upon the size of one's office or corporation. But the largest stumbling block was the question of membership requirements. The IDI accepted as evidence of professional practice products manufactured by a single company, but the ASID insisted on at least three products made by companies in different industries. The latter requirement was eventually accepted as evidence of the fact that industrial design was a generalist rather than a specialized profession.

In 1959 the officers of the IDI (George Beck was chairman of the board and Robert Redmann was president) addressed the following resolution to ASID president Donald McFarland: "The officers of the Industrial Designers Institute believe that the profession should be represented by one national organization and are confident that a vast majority of members are of the same belief." (215) There were, however, to be six more years of wary meetings and careful collaborations between the two organizations before the embers of conflict would cool and the merger could be made.

As a preliminary step, the two societies agreed to demonstrate their common purpose by holding a joint annual meeting in Philadelphia in 1964. The occasion was used to make the annual IDI awards as well as to continue the ASID series of annual meetings on special subjects. The major guest speaker, Misha Black of England, explored the dichotomy between art/design and science. His conclusion was that the task of the designer was to sift research and analysis for those facts that could be used as the basis for a creative design decision. The designer's importance, Black suggested, dependent upon his ability to spring forward to new solutions, to create new forms and a new unity in order to produce something that had never existed before. By early 1965 there were no longer any obstacles in the way of a merger. The elder statesmen of both societies had stepped aside to let younger men sort out the details. Robert Hose of the ASID and Joseph Parriott of the IDI concluded the merger, which was followed immediately by the absorption of the Industrial Design Education Association to create a single voice for industrial design in the United States. Members of the boards of the two societies met in New York on January 25 to sign the legal documents that created the Industrial Designers Society of America. Henry Dreyfuss was elected president; John Vassos chairman of the board; Robert Hose, Joseph Parriott, Donald Dailey, and Tucker Madawick vice-presidents; and George Payne treasurer.

The new board of directors was drawn from the two parent organizations, and the IDSA settled into new headquarters on West 55th Street in New York.

IDSA agreed to continue to public programs that had already established themselves. These included the Design Awards program (honoring outstanding work by members), the Student Merit Awards (by which each school with a student chapter of the society was empowered to select and honor its outstanding graduate in the name of the society), and the Walter Dorwin Teague Scholarships for qualified students of industrial design.

The times proved to be auspicious ones for the merger. Business was good, with more than enough work to go around. The number of design offices was increasing rapidly as experienced designers split away from major companies and offices to establish offices of their own. A growing number of industrial design schools were graduating more and more students to fill the need for entry-level designers. Experienced designers found themselves pulled up management ladders to administrative responsibilities unheard of in the past. Arnold Wolf, who had been a consultant to the J. B. Lansing loudspeaker company, joined that company as its president in the late 1950s and served in that capacity until 1969. Tucker Madawick of RCA, Eugene Bordinat of Ford, and C. Joshua Abend of SCM, and others were made vice-presidents of their companies. And perhaps even more significant was the fact that many offices that had not been incorporated, despite their size, because of implications that they would thereby have traded their professional status for that of businessmen, broke ranks in that direction. Industrial design in most companies and several of the major consulting offices had, in fact, become a business. To some it was disturbing evidence that a number of designers had happily traded the clerical collar of human service and the artist's smock for the pinstripe suit and profit.

Opportunity came knocking on designers' doors, bringing assignments from the aircraft

*The mark of the Industrial Designers Society of America was designed by James Fulton and Partners. Credit: Industrial Designers Society of America.*

When the IDSA moved its office from New York to the Washington area in 1973, a new mark seemed in order. Breaking with the past, Barry Deutsch of the firm of Tepper and Steinhilber designed this ribbon-like identity, which was still in use in the 1980s. Credit: Industrial Designers Society of America.

industry, from manufacturers of motorboats, cabin cruisers, recreational vehicles, gardening machinery, and tools for the home workshop, from makers of high-fidelity sound systems and other electronic equipment, from producers of industrial equipment, from makers of heavy road-building and construction machinery, and from the nation's schools. In this atmosphere of challenge and opportunity, new ideas about forms and materials were welcomed and even demanded. Some worried that prosperity and runaway production would result in pollution and irresponsibility, but few listened.

By the end of the 1950s, the practice of industrial design had settled into a recognizable pattern. Though the variety of problems and the number of industries that could benefit from industrial design seemed to be infinite, designers were called upon more and more to help their clients keep up with fast-moving technology. Professional practice was divided between those who maintained private offices that served various clients and those who were fully employed by one company as staff designers. For a while there was some contention between the two camps. However, eventually the name-calling stopped; the "freelancers" came to be known as consultant designers, and the "captives" as corporate designers.

Although large industries would seem to be better able to meet the needs of a large middle class, about half of the country's gross national product came from small industries. As might be expected, small manufacturers (those employing fewer than 500 workers, according to the U.S. Census of Manufacturers) generally made a single product or a limited family of products and did not normally employ in-house or corporate designers. If they turned to outside or consultant designers at all, it was most likely on a project-by-project basis or on a limited retainer contract that reserved a portion of a designer's time for periodic service. Consultant design offices were thus able to serve several such clients whose products were not in competition with

one another. Furthermore, the broader experience of the consultant brought new ideas and technology into a somewhat cloistered small company. Most often the designer in this case reported directly to the principal officer or officers of the company.

Some middle-sized companies also depended upon outside consultants. However, as pressures developed for them to keep up with market changes, they were likely to have at least one industrial designer on their organization chart. These companies generally covered a broader spectrum of products. Corporate designers working for such companies were not expected to stand out like "star" consultants who were sought out for their unique talent, expression, or personality. Rather, a corporate designer was given assignments that were appropriate to the department for which he worked. If it was engineering, he might expect to be concerned with the appearance and human factors of a product under development. If it was marketing, he would normally be concerned with the position of a product with respect to its competition. Some corporate employees became hourly rather than salaried employees, concentrating on the workaday processes of product development, such as drafting or modelmaking. Companies also sought outside design assistance when workloads become excessive.

Major manufacturers were the most likely to have fully staffed corporate design departments, the heads of which reported to top management and were on the same level as the heads of engineering and marketing. In some companies (General Electric at one time, for example), the industrial design group operated, in effect, as a company within the company, "selling" its services to the various manufacturing divisions and depending upon them for its budget. Within the large auto companies, each "studio" (as management called the styling group assigned to work on a particular automobile brand) was directed by a studio head, who was responsible to a corporate vice-president of styling, who, in turn, with his own staff, set themes and directions for the studios. Most large merchandisers, such as Montgomery Ward and Sears Roebuck, had internal design staffs that worked with the buyers to direct the design of products manufactured by various suppliers. In this capacity, designers tended to be dominated by the buyers, who were responsible for gauging the market and directing the styling of products to fit the merchandiser's marketing program. Designers were usually assigned to different classes of products, and changes in styling were controlled by weekly sales reports rather than by the taste or judgment of the designer.

It was not unusual for the larger companies to also use consultant designers to provide overview, direction, and stimulus for the internal group and to support its position with respect to other corporate interests affecting product development. Consultants were also often asked to take on special assignments, such as exploring future product areas for the company. Toward the end of the 1950s, some industrial designers began to cross the line from the practice of industrial design into the field of product planning.

In the keynote speech at the 1959 annual meeting of the ASID, Raymond Loewy took issue with the notion that, since this was the "age of specialization," designers should specialize. He felt that designers who limited themselves to one product area were no longer industrial designers, whatever else they might call themselves. Loewy believed that designers working within a system tended to be absorbed by it and thus lose their basic value to the company. He warned them that "if designers get reabsorbed, ingested, digested, mutated, or reoriented by the action on them of non-designing forces or executive enzymes, there will be no industrial design profession and . . . it is important that there be an industrial design profession" (112).

More than once a respected industrial designer rose above oversimplified classifications to be retained by a corporation as consultant design director, charged with establishing standards of excellence and providing overall philosophical and cultural guidance for the company. Eliot Noyes, for example, became Consultant Director of Design of IBM in 1956 and organized and directed a comprehensive program directed toward achieving a consistent design character that controlled every aspect of the company's image, from buildings and signs down to the smallest product and its packaging. Later, Noyes served Westinghouse and Mobil in a similar capacity.

Even when the work of Eliot Noyes and others like him broadened out to include assignments in product packaging and graphics or in the design of stores and offices, they continued to maintain their professional affiliation with other industrial designers. Although the term *industrial designer* (or even *designer*) did not always appear in the literature and the correspondence of designers, they continued to invoke its glamor and popularity. The term *designer* was developing an identity of its own, much as *architect, artist,* and *engineer* had.

## A Global Network

*The only hope for world peace is a growing understanding of nation by nation, of people by people. Professional bodies are able to engender this essential sympathy which eludes politicians.*

Misha Black, 1975 (226)

In England the transformation from the artist-craftsman to the industrial designer had been underway ever since the early decades of the nineteenth century. Even though the Design and Industries Association had omitted the word *art* at its founding in 1915, in 1930 a Society of Industrial Artists was established. The word *design* did not get its due until 1944, when the Council of Industrial Design (CoID) was founded as a grant-aided body by the Board of Trade to improve design in the products of British industry. Owing to the dominance of graphic artists and illustrators in England at the time, it still took more than another decade for the Society of Industrial Artists to add the word *design* to its name.

The purpose of the CoID, it was claimed, was not to control or direct design but rather to promote good design. By implication this meant modern design, although some insisted that good design should be applicable to traditional styles as well. Sir Stafford Cripps, president of the Board of Trade in 1945, was particularly interested in quality in design. "It would be a tragic contradiction of our war effort," he warned, "if the products of our reviving civilian industries were to pass into world markets unworthy in appearance of those who made them." (89) He called on the CoID to stage, as one of its first activities, a major exhibition of British goods that would arouse the interest of industry and the public in industrial design, encourage British designers, and advertise British design to the world.

The title selected for the CoID's exhibition, "Britain Can Make It," was adapted from the wartime slogan "Britain Can Take It." In the spirit of the moment, and since time was short, the planners elected to "stress light-hearted, gay decor and display so that if the worst came to the worst, and in some sections it should prove impossible to find more than a handful of exhibits, the show would not be a flop" (35, 232). *Design* magazine reported that gaiety, although it may have been forced, flourished at the exhibition. Held at the Victoria and Albert Museum in the last quarter of 1946, it turned into a postwar celebration that gave the nearly 1.5 million visitors a taste of products to come. It also attracted buyers from 67 countries to view products offered for export. One of the most striking displays, designed by Misha Black of the Design Research Unit, explained the process of industrial design and showed the importance of good design to daily living and the national economy. (The DRU, formed during the war by Herbert Read to provide liaison between designers and manufacturers, was one of the first firms in England to provide a total design service, including engineering, architecture, interiors, exhibits, graphics, packaging, and product design and development.)

In retrospect it appears that the austerity brought on by Britain's war effort was carrying over into peacetime products. Despite the celebratory state of mind that prevailed, the products themselves were characterized by a rather cloistered aesthetic that did not, except to Anglophiles, make the country's products particularly attractive in overseas markets. British designers apparently had a more difficult time breaking out of their traditional character than their colleagues in other countries. British industry still had to be convinced of the importance of industrial design. Nor was government edict a substitute for personal motivation and sensitivity. Moreover, gaiety and frivolous ornament, no matter how determined, were not enough.

Gordon Russell, director of the CoID, was Master of the Faculty of the Royal Designers for Industry in 1948 when the RDI staged its first exhibition, "Design at Work," at the Royal Academy in London. The purpose of the show was to demonstrate the contribution designers were making to industry. It consisted of a series of case histories showing the work of its members, each telling the story of how everyday articles were conceived and developed through manufacture to the market. Raymond Loewy, an honorary member of the RDI since 1937, displayed case histories of the Eversharp Fountain Pen, the Studebaker automobile, and the Pennsylvania Railroad locomotive. Loewy had already established an industrial design office in London, thus bringing American industrial design practices to the attention of his English colleagues.

In 1945, in an open letter addressed to Sir Stafford Cripps, the editor of the *News Chronicle* had urged that "a great trade and cultural exhibition . . . be held in London during the centennial year of the Great Exhibition of 1851" (236). At the time, a movement for such an exhibition—conceived as a follow-up to the "Britain Can Make It" event—was already underway. The goal was to stage, on the south bank of the Thames, a Festival of Britain that would rehabilitate that section of the city and leave behind a permanent festival hall.

Whereas the 1851 exhibition had been open to any exhibit, the products to be exhibited at the 1951 festival were to be screened by the CoID to keep out anything that did not emphasize the high standards of British industry. Gordon Russel declared that Britain was "stating her belief that design must be taken much more seriously in the future." "Our customers abroad," he noted, "are often more conscious of design than we are. How can we expect to produce a high standard for export unless we have a high standard at home?" (6, 11)

One of the most important outcomes of the 1951 Festival of Britain for industrial design and for British postwar commerce was the decision to establish a Design Centre in central London to house the stock list that had been developed by the CoID from which all products used and exhibited at the Festival were selected. The index of products, manufacturers, and designers compiled for this task

became the reference file for the Design Centre, which opened on Haymarket near Picadilly in 1956.

The Design Centre, co-sponsored by government and industry, quickly became a major public attraction in the center of London as a showcase for the best in British design and as a window on the world of design for local visitors. In time it was to be emulated in virtually every other country—from Argentina to the Soviet Union—that could lay claim to being industrialized. Only the United States somehow never caught the fever, despite several strong attempts by government and by the private sector.

*Design,* the magazine of the Council of Industrial Design, observed in 1970 that before the Second World War the English had managed somehow to stay outside the mainstream of modern design. The British, "having gone through a period of austerity worse than that endured during the war . . . latched on to the idea of gaiety. It was, without doubt, forced gaiety, but it flourished at the Britain Can Make It exhibition. It served the Festival of Britain well, and . . . blended smoothly with a brand of revived pomp for the Coronation which was to herald in the New Elizabethan Age. . . . [D]esign in Britain, unlike the United States, was surprisingly little influenced by the Bauhaus. . . . Gropius, Mies and others passed through England . . . but left no real marks at that time. . . . The resulting home grown style, decorative in a light-hearted and modest way, had an acceptable affinity to the unassuming housing of post-war Britain." (76)

In 1949, the Council of Industrial Design had circulated a letter seeking advice as to what agencies and what individuals should be invited to an international design congress proposed for 1951 as an official event of the Festival of Britain. With no precedent for such a conference, the CoID found it difficult to determine what such a congress should cover and who should be invited to participate. Should representatives of government and industry meet with persons directly involved in design practice and education? Should art and technology be represented equally? Should all of the design professions, architecture, graphics, and the crafts play equal parts? In the end, it was decided that "instead of dealing with the question of Industrial Design from an academic point of view, it is now intended to be strictly practical and to aim at hard-headed businessmen, by arranging for the speakers to be high executives in British and foreign firms, who are known to have operated a consistent design policy for some time" (201). Accordingly, the meeting (held at the Royal College of Art) was limited to industrialists and senior executives of business firms from Britain, the Netherlands, Sweden, Italy, and the United States, with only token representation of designers and educators.

Twenty-three case histories were read and discussed. The United States was represented by Arthur Houghton, vice-president of Corning and president of the Steuben companies, and Arthur BecVar, director of design at General Electric. Although English management could point to a successful integration of design and commerce, one English manufacturer at the congress urged that the "ideas and instincts" of the designer not be "probed too closely by too many insensitive minds" lest spontaneity be lost. A Danish furniture manufacturer supported him: "There are two kinds of logic—the designer's and the machine's—and we simply cannot limit the designer's logic to the machine's capacity." The opposite view was expressed by another English engineer: "The dictator-designer, however brilliant or however lucky, can never achieve more than a limited success and has no place in the modern set-up." (144) Paul Reilly, information officer for the CoID, wrapped up the meeting by observing that there was "unanimous support for the contention that design policy must come from the top" and that it should be tackled as a whole (73). Interest in industrial design had, it seems, worked its way up from the designer's drawing board to the boardroom, and was now acknowledged as essential to corporate survival.

Even before the Festival of Britain, Walter Paepke, the culturally enlightened president of the Container Corporation of America, had been a staunch supporter of the rebirth of the Bauhaus in Chicago. In 1946 the CCA had invited Herbert Bayer, of the original Bauhaus, to serve as a consultant in graphic design and as the principal contributor to the company's growing reputation as a leader in corporate culture. Paepke and his wife Elizabeth, who had been "looking for somewhere to create 'an American Salzburg,' " had found Aspen, a virtually abandoned mining town in Colorado, and they conceived the idea of starting a center for intellectual and physical renewal there. The Aspen Institute of Humanistic Studies was the result. (3, 12) In 1950 Herbert Bayer and Egbert Jacobsen (CCA's director of design) conceived the idea of a conference on design that would bring the heads of major corporations together with outstanding designers, museum directors, educators, and philosophers in Aspen. Walter Paepke approved the idea, and the first Aspen conference ("Design as a Function of Management") was held in the summer of 1951.

In November of 1951, Paepke called a meeting in Chicago to review the first Aspen conference and assess the prospects for more such meetings. The attendees included major Chicago-area businessmen and designers. It was agreed that there should be another conference in 1952. The main concern was whether the mix of business leaders (those who were receptive to design and, even more importantly, those that needed to be convinced) could be sustained. This issue, it was concluded, would only be resolved by conferences to come.

The second Aspen conference, held in 1952 and also entitled "Design as a Function of Management," was built around major presentations by the comprehensive designer R. Buckminster Fuller, the industrial designer Walter Dorwin Teague, the editor and publisher Alfred A. Knopf, and the San Francisco merchandiser Richard Gump. It attracted an enthusiastic audience—mostly from the design world.

By 1953, the annual Aspen conference had developed a format. The program chairman (in 1953 it was Leo Lionni, art editor of *Fortune* magazine) and the principal speakers discussed issues of interest at roundtables before an audience. Though the title of the conference was again listed as "Design as a Function of Management," the conferees and the speakers also explored other, more specifically design-related matters—for example, whether an artist and a designer could exist in the same person, and how design (the application of artistic talent to everyday objects and needs) fared in comparison with free artistic self-expression.

"Planning: Basis of Design," the theme of the 1954 Aspen conference, was developed by a program team of graphic designers that included Will Burtin, Saul Bass, Alvin Lustig, and Gyorgy Kepes. Members of the audience came from the fields of newspapers, radio, television, film, sociology, museums, and education. The consensus seems to have been that the public's taste was fickle and that its indifference to design was more difficult to combat than downright bad taste.

After the 1954 conference it was decided that a permanent organization called the International Design Conference at Aspen (IDCA) would be created, with an administrative board and a paying membership of designers, manufacturers, educators, and consumers. An executive committee and regional chairmen were selected.

In 1955 the focus of the Aspen conferences began to shift away from the relation of design and management to the arts and human values. The fifth IDCA ("Crossroads: What are the Directions of the Arts?") and the sixth ("Ideas on the Future of Man and Design," 1956) brought an increasing number of internationally distinguished thinkers in many fields together with their American

*Walter Paepke introducing the panel at the June 1954 design conference in Aspen. Credit: Industrial Design (August 1954). Photograph by Max Yavna.*

*One of the panels of the
1956 International Design
Conference at Aspen
faces its audience. Credit:*
Industrial Design *(October
1956).*

*Asaba*      *Flanagan*      *Vienot*      *Hal*

*incott*　　　*Black*　　　　*Lane*

counterparts. By this time, the participation of foreign experts was probably being subsidized by European or American industries, or by American firms with European offices (such as IBM). Attendance by higher-level managers declined substantially, and the 1956 conference turned its sights further inward to discuss design education and practice.

The 1957 IDCA seems to have been the strongest of the 1950s. It attracted an audience of some 700 to hear papers on "Design and Human Values" read by a group that included twelve foreigners. The underlying concern of the conferees seems to have been the emerging conflict between the liberal and the service arts. Another issue that commanded attention was the "vulgarization of American taste" evident in automobile styling. The stylists, it was pointed out, emboldened by what they believed to be a captive market, had run amok and were showing little or no regard for human beings. Moreover, the automotive styling circle was closed, with selected schools heavily subsidized to support the styling establishment.

In 1958 the scope of the IDCA was broadened to include a consideration of the urban environment. At this conference, Hin Bredendieck suggested that mistakes, many of them made by designers, had created many of the problems in the man-made environment. Most present-day designers, he observed, were busily and perhaps superficially attempting to correct the mistakes of the past. In 1959 the IDCA returned to the subject of communications.

In 1953, L'Institut d'Esthetique Industrielle, headed by Jacques Vienot and supported by several government agencies, held an International Congress on Industrial Design in Paris. The meeting recognized the importance of the first step that had been taken by the Council of Industrial Design in 1951 in staging an international Design Congress during the Festival of Britain and agreed to organize a more formal international meeting, again in Paris, in 1955.

Before that, however, a special conference on the subject of industrial design as the meeting point of art and industry was called in Milan in 1954, coincidental with the tenth Triennale. The participants included Walter Dorwin Teague, Paul Reilly, and Max Bill, who were struggling with the same issue in their own countries. Their views, while not as abstract as those of the Italians who had organized the conference, would be carried on into subsequent international meetings on industrial design.

The Paris meeting, delayed until April of 1956, brought together representatives from American, British, French, West German, Belgian, and Italian design organizations, with India and the Netherlands represented by proxy, for what was then called the International Coordinating Committee of Industrial Design. The group intended to serve as a clearing house for exhibitions, information, and personnel as well as to organize conferences and encourage the participation of industrial design organizations in all countries. The meeting elected a provisional executive board, with Peter Müller-Munk as president, Misha Black as vice-president, Pierre Vago as secretary, and Robert Delevoy as treasurer, to lay plans for the next meeting. They were charged with developing a constitution for an International Council of Societies of Industrial Designers. The title was approved and registered in Paris in June 1957. It was also agreed that the next meeting would be held in London that same year.

The CoID convened a second meeting of its own in 1956 on the business of design management and methodology under the title The Management of Design. The issue in question, again, was one of trying to bring business and industrial design onto common ground. R. D. Russell, brother of Gordon Russell, faulted designers for wishing to develop their own ideas in their own time in their own way. In this Russell was reflecting a certain myopia, not unique to the British by any means, that placed other considerations ahead of the personal intuition and sensitivity of designers. Its

result was that the imaginative courage and sensitivity that characterized some designers were suppressed in favor of timidity and compliance with the wishes of others.

The danger of refusing to recognize the importance and the potential impact of freer industrial design was acknowledged by *Design* magazine some years later: "In the mid-fifties Eames chairs and Saarinen pedestal chairs and tables burst on the English design scene. The stronger, richer look, already well established in the United States since the late forties, had arrived in Britain. The effect was traumatic—industrial design was never quite the same again. . . . The transatlantic mainstream for modern took root while most people had their backs turned." (77)

The International Council of Societies of Industrial Designers, a provisional organization, was founded at London in June of 1957 by designers representing professional organizations from Denmark, France, West Germany, Italy, Norway, Sweden, the United Kingdom, and the United States. Peter Müller-Munk was elected president, Misha Black executive vice-president, Enrico Peressutti vice-president, and Pierre Vago secretary-treasurer. For its goals ICSID set itself the tasks of establishing international standards for professional performance and business conduct as well as reviewing applications for membership from other societies. It was agreed that control of the organization would be vested in an assembly made up of six delegates from each country, with all of a given country's professional societies represented equally.

The new organization pledged to address itself not only to the education of design students but also to informing the general public and industries about the value of industrial design, and to serve as a source of global information about significant trends, ideas, and activities in the field. Peter Müller-Munk referred to this move as the beginning of a transatlantic community of interest and professional cooperation.

Müller-Munk's 1958 survey of industrial design organizations found that there were as many as 33 such organizations in the world. The 21 societies that responded to his questionnaire represented some 6,500 individual members. Many of the societies had mixed memberships that included architects, engineers, craftsmen, and decorators. Only nine organizations (two of them American) were exclusively for professional industrial designers.

By 1959, ICSID had attracted a membership of sufficient size—23 constituent societies from 17 countries—to be economically viable. In June of that year, representatives of the design societies were welcomed to Stockholm by Count Sigvard Bernadotte of Sweden and Peter Müller-Munk, president of ICSID. As its first order of business, the meeting ratified a constitution and a set of by-laws. The United States was represented by Jack Collins, George Labalme, Jr., and Raymond Sandin of ASID and George Beck, Leon Gordon Miller, and Theodore Clement of the IDI. Paul Reilly, director of England's Council of Industrial Design, led an open debate that resulted in the official definition of an industrial designer as one who is "qualified by training, technical knowledge, experience and visual sensibility to determine the materials, construction mechanism, shape and color, surface finishes and decoration of objects which are reproduced in quantity by industrial processes" and who "may, at different times, be concerned with all or only some of these aspects of an industrially produced object" (80). There was also extensive discussion as to whether the use of the term *industrial design* implied that the newly defined profession was the particular intellectual property of English-speaking countries. The general conclusion was that the term should be kept, since no other term had gained as much currency. Since then, the cognates of the term *industrial design* have been formally adopted by many other countries, the most recent one being the USSR in 1985.

In a special issue of *The Designer,* the journal of the Societies of Industrial Artists and Designers, Misha Black outlined the practical reasons for ICSID: the stature that each member society gained from belonging to an international association; collaboration in establishing international codes for practice, professional conduct, and competitions; the development of an international consensus on industrial design education; public recognition of design excellence. Even more important was Black's conviction that "the only hope for world peace is a growing understanding of nation by nation, of people by people." "Without understanding and tolerance," Black wrote, "a third world war is inevitable. Professional bodies are able to engender this essential sympathy and cooperation which eludes politicians." (79)

The 1961 Congress and Assembly of ICSID were held in Venice. Polly Miller reported in *Industrial Design* that a businesslike attitude prevailed at the conference. Misha Black, the second president, stated that the organization had overcome the perils of its infancy and was ready to meet the challenges of its adolescence. He was convinced that designers wanted an international representative body and had proved they could work together for common goals. The American societies again demonstrated their ability to work together by forming a jury to select fifteen products from the almost 300 submitted to represent the United States in an exhibition that was to tour Europe.

An unexpected issue was raised at the ICSID Assembly in Venice that was to have an important impact on the organization in the years to come: whether the word *Design* should be substituted for *Designers* in the name. When this change was approved, ICSID developed a split personality that has since been, at best, inhibiting. It now strives to hold a tenuous position between those organizations whose members practice industrial design and those who promote it for their government.

The American delegation
to the second congress
and assembly of ICSID
(Stockholm, 1959)
included, from the left,
Leon Gordon Miller, Jack
Collins, George Beck,
George LaBalme, Ray-
mond Sandin, Peter
Müller-Munk (the first
president of ICSID), and
Theodore Clement. Credit:
Industrial Design (October
1959). Photograph by
Polly Miller.

Sigvard Bernadotte, Peter
Müller-Munk, and Misha
Black presiding at the
opening of the ICSID
Assembly at Venice.
Credit: Esthetique Indus-
trielle (November-
December 1961).

ICSID has managed to walk a path between political and economic ideologies. It has a Memorandum of Understanding as a Non-Government Organization with both UNESCO and UNIDO. Now grown to represent some sixty design organizations in forty countries, it has continued to seek the goals that it set for itself some thirty years ago. It has provided support for older societies and encouragement for new ones in emerging industrialized countries. It has also worked closely with international agencies to provide expertise and guidance in design on a global level. Some countries that had a record of significant achievements in art and design and were devastated by events of World War II found in ICSID support for a renaissance of their own cultural commitment to design (e.g., East and West Germany, Poland, Japan, Italy, Austria).

The third meeting of ICSID was held in the UNESCO Building in Paris in 1963. It was devoted to two subjects that were of universal concern. The first—plagiarism—brought to the surface the problems that faced designers and their clients as products began to compete in international markets. The consideration of the second subject—education— focused on the search for a common international base by comparing the philosophies and methodologies of England, Italy, West Germany, Sweden, and Japan. Rowena Kostellow of Pratt Institute, who with Jay Doblin of the Institute of Design represented American industrial design education, suggested that any common foundation would have to take into account the "precision and directness of the Germans," the "exquisite sensitivity of the Scandinavians," the "creative genius of the Italians," the "taste and style of the French," and the "integrity of material and the fine detail of the English" (232). As an outcome of this session, an international working group was charged with developing an academic base for industrial design.

Although its meetings have occasionally witnessed criticism of one country by a representative of another (as at the 1965 Congress and Assembly in Vienna, where the British editor

John Blake complained that in the United States all awareness of the arts had "been killed by a total preoccupation with material affluence"), ICSID has, ever since its founding, fostered the development of a global web of relationships among designers and of an interlocking philosophy of design (75).

In Canada, industrial design was recognized at the federal level in 1947 when Donald W. Buchanan of the National Gallery received a grant from Parliament to explore the government's role in this area. His recommendations included a register of Canadian designers, an exhibit and service center for design, academic programs in industrial design, and a national design advisory committee. At his instigation the National Gallery organized, with support from the National Research Agency of Canada and the National Film Board, the first Canadian design exhibition: "Design in Industry," which toured Canadian galleries and department stores in 1947. The following year, Buchanan convened a meeting in Ottawa of manufacturers, retailers, designers, educators, and representatives from several government agencies that resulted in the formation of the National Industrial Design Committee (NIDC). As one of its first actions, the NIDC recommended that until such time as professional training for industrial designers on a university level was established, it would offer scholarships for postgraduate studies in that field in other countries. It also assisted the Ontario College of Art in establishing a course in industrial design. The NIDC approved the building of a permanent "Design Centre" display at the Canadian National Exhibition. Coincidentally, designers met in Toronto to found the Association of Canadian Industrial Designers and elect a representative to the NIDC.

Twenty years later the Canadians, riding on a crest of design awareness and national enthusiasm, decided to stage an international exposition in Montreal celebrating the centennial of their country. Expo '67 turned out to be

one of the most impressive events of its kind
in the postwar era. Industrial designers contributed as much to its success as they had to
that of the 1939 New York World's Fair. The
organizers of Expo '67 set up an international
committee on industrial design to plan the
role that product design should take in the exposition. The committee, with Jacques Besner
as chairman and with Misha Black, Tomas
Maldonado, Eliot Noyes, and Arthur Pulos
among the members, overviewed street furnishings, the script for a film on industrial
design, and the organization of an exhibition
of the work of fourteen industrial design
schools around the world. Expo '67 also
served as the venue for the biennial ICSID
Congress and Assembly.

A view of the interior of
the American pavilion at
Expo 67. Exhibits de-
signed by Chermayeff and
Geismar ranged from
Raggedy Anns and
Andys and Indian head-
dresses to a full-scale
model of the Lunar Lander
and Claes Oldenburg's
soft sculptures. Credit:
author's collection.

R. Buckminster Fuller's
American pavilion—a
shimmering globe with
light-sensitive blinds that
kept out direct sunlight
—was one of the out-
standing experiences of
Expo 67. Credit: (216).

## The Open Door

*If one considers how to transfer to European countries what the Mission saw and learnt in the United States concerning Industrial Design in firms making consumer goods, it could perhaps be said that the European producer has more to learn from the philosophy of the Industrial Designer than his American counterpart.*

OEEC Mission to the United States, 1959 (234)

In comparison with many other countries, the United States had come through World War II relatively unscarred politically, physically, and financially. It was understandable that this country should be targeted as a rich market for foreign products. Whether the products came from allies or from enemies was considered relatively immaterial; it was expected that commerce would help stabilize political elements in favor of American democracy. General and trade magazines saw the promotion of foreign products as a duty (and as a circulation builder). And it was still presumed that American design could not grow without being fertilized by foreign aesthetics.

Within a year after the end of the war, the flow of products from Northern Europe to the United States was underway again. Although the selection was small, the quality was high. These shipments included the best those countries had to offer: furniture by Aalto and Matthson, glasswares from Orrefors and Ittala, folded paper lamps by Klint, and stainless steel by Herlow.

In 1948 Scandinavian imports acquired a second handsome showcase in New York City (the first being the Georg Jensen store) when Bonniers, a 150-year-old Swedish and Danish publishing company, opened a store offering furniture, furnishings, fabrics, tableware, and kitchenwares as well as Bonniers' own products. The shop, designed by Warner-Leed, an American team of architects, provided a bright two-story glass display case that was wholly modern yet unpretentious and natural.

Warner-Leed also designed the store's trademark, the packaging, and many of the display fixtures. The products shown were generally selected for their portability and stowability, in keeping with the interest in smaller, more open, more flexible living spaces. In fact, the shop itself was conceived as a living space, and it set the theme for many of the "good design" shops that were to follow.

Swedish Modern, Incorporated, an American import firm organized with Arthur Schlossman as president in 1950, brought in a variety of products from some fifteen Swedish manufacturers and distributed them from warehouses in New York, Dallas, and San Francisco. In some cases, American designers were apparently contracted to adapt Swedish products to American needs and desires.

In 1950, Swedish Modern, Inc., announced a furniture-design competition. The winning designs—by Americans—were to be put into production in Sweden, in an effort "to promote international understanding through a direct exchange of ideas and to combine American plans with Swedish craftsmanship" (139). The jury included, among others, Richard Bach of the Metropolitan Museum, Edgar Kaufmann, Jr., of the Museum of Modern Art, and Alexander Kostellow of Pratt Institute. Despite hopes that the competition would bring out new ideas suitable for informal living in America, the jury found nothing worthy of a prize. Even though promises were made to repeat the competition, there is no evidence that it was done. In effect, this was a cheap attempt (considering the size of the awards that were offered) to pick up new ideas.

The following year, a Swedish timber-industry group decided that the path of least resistance into American markets would be to tune products to American tastes. Accordingly, an American design firm, Edmond J. Spence, was contracted by a group of sixteen Swedish manufacturers to design a line of furniture that would appeal to Americans. The resulting products were neither Swedish nor American; rather, they were what each thought the other would like. The respected Swedish magazine *Form* lamented the association and deplored the result. While not dismissing the possibility of an American-Swedish alliance in design and manufacture, *Form* considered the employment of American designers to give Swedish goods an American character not only an economic error but also a cultural disappointment.

By 1960, British companies were exhibiting their products in the New York Coliseum for the purpose of familiarizing the American market with British names and "bridging the psychological gulf of the Atlantic" (115). One of the exhibits was a selection of modern consumer products; however, a majority of the exhibits emphasized traditional and already familiar aspects of British industry. A few years later, the British transferred their space in Rockefeller Center from the British Chamber of Commerce to the Board of Trade, hoping to increase their volume of exports to the United States by providing display space for British companies there.

The tide ran the other way as well, but without the vigor of its westward thrust. American consumer-product manufacturers at the time, it seems, were too preoccupied with filling their domestic markets to take the challenge of foreign sales seriously. In the area of packaging, the situation was quite different. Supermarketing, packaging, and promotion were on the rise in Europe and searching for assistance at every level. In 1965, Design USA—the first U.S. trade show devoted to industrial design—was held at the U.S. Trade Center in London.

Although many foreign companies were eager to export products for sale to the United States, they were concerned that their most saleable designs might be pirated by American manufacturers. Design piracy was of particular concern in the areas of fashion and the decorative arts. The American Council on Style and Design acknowledged that it was

facing stiff opposition in its battle against "certain retailers who apparently considered it their right to 'borrow' foreign designs as they had been doing for years" (173). Francois Hepp, a French design expert, expressed his country's concern about design piracy and noted that UNESCO was trying to find a way to protect works of industrial design.

Despite their concern about design piracy, the French were determined to expand their exports to the United States. In 1949 they installed a permanent exhibition called "Formes Francaises" at Rockefeller Center. Pierre Clavel, director of the magazine *Art et industrie* as well as the New York exhibition, stated that neo-traditional as well as more strictly modern furniture would be shown.

The Scandinavians, the French, and the English were not the only foreigners seeking outlets for their products in the United States. In 1949—the same year in which the French opened their showroom in Rockefeller Center—Czechoslovakian industries staged an exhibition titled "Let's Do Business" in the Museum of Science and Industry, also at Rockefeller Center.

Less than a decade after World War II, all three of America's onetime enemies—Germany, Japan, and Italy—had staged exhibitions or established showrooms in the United States. It appeared that they were becoming economic allies of the United States in the political realignments of the Cold War era.

In April of 1949, more than 1,500 tons of products from the American-occupied zone of Germany, representing about 350 manufacturers, were sent to New York to be displayed in the Museum of Science and Industry. This show was authorized by the Joint Export/Import Agency in order to increase German exports to the United States. According to *Interiors,* "the exhibition had the full support of the Economic Cooperation Administration, the State Department and the Army, and the participating manufacturers were guaranteed

In connection with the
opening of a Japan Trade
Center in New York, a traditional Japanese house
was erected in the garden
of the Museum of Modern
Art. It was brought in
finished pieces and
assembled on the spot.
*Credit:* Industrial
Design *(August 1954).*
*Photograph by Betty
Rosensweig.*

to be de-Nazified and de-cartelized" (135). The United States government had a strong interest in this show, *Interiors* noted, because "by some means or other, German exports must be brought to the level of imports if that foreign nation is to become self-supporting." Interiors mentioned that the German products ("which no one even dreams will compete with our mass-produced articles") included "hand-carved furniture, textiles, china from Rosenthal in Bavaria, and a rear-engined Volkswagen said to run 50 miles on a gallon of gas and 1500 on a quart of oil" (136).

Coincidental with the opening of the Japan Trade Center in New York in 1954, a traditional Japanese house was erected in the garden of the Museum of Modern Art. The Center, and the branch of Tokyo's Takashimaya department store that opened on Fifth Avenue in 1958, displayed, along with examples of Japan's rich arts and crafts, modern manufactures such as cameras, binoculars, and watches. (Though well engineered and well crafted, they were derivative in design.) In 1955, Design Research—a Cambridge, Massachusetts, shop founded in 1951 by Benjamin Thompson— exhibited a collection of some 200 Japanese household accessories and tools that had been selected by leading Japanese designers and architects. It was in shops such as Bonniers and Design Research—shops that catered to sophisticated buyers willing to pay a premium for vernacular products if they were elegant and above touristic taste—that the better products from around the world found a cultural meeting ground.

In 1960 the Japan Export Trade Organization in collaboration with the Walker Art Center and the Smithsonian Institution, staged an exhibition entitled "Japan: Design Today." This show (assembled by Meg Torbert, curator of design at the Walker) subsequently toured fourteen American museums and art centers. Meg Torbert stated in the *Design Quarterly* that she had limited the show to craft objects because she had "felt that some of the industrial products, especially cameras and optical

equipment, radios, television sets and other electronic equipment, were excellent as products but not outstanding as original contributions to design" (82). Nevertheless, such Japanese products were already becoming familiar to Americans. (Japanese automobiles were introduced to Americans in 1957.)

In the years to come, Japan and other countries would send designers and other specialists to the United States to gather information for their companies to use in tailoring products to the American market. Designers were being conditioned to think of design as a global commodity.

After the war many Americans felt that the Italians had been dupes of Hitler, and some turned their attention to Italy's plight. Max Ascoli, a professor of political philosophy at the New School for Social Research in New York, and his friends began collecting raw materials and tools for handicrafts and shipping them to Italy. By 1947 Ascoli's nonprofit organization, Handicraft Development Incorporated in America (HDIA), had opened the House of Italian Handicrafts in New York. A parallel organization in Florence, the Committee for Assistance and Distribution of Materials to Artisans (CADMA), had set up branches in Milan, Venice, and Naples through which Italian designers and craftsmen were funneling products for foreign markets. By 1948 the House of Italian Handicrafts was well enough established to mail some 4,000 questionnaires to stores across the United States in order to determine which products were most wanted. The New York showroom served as an American outlet for Italian products and a means of communication between Italian craftsmen and American distributors. Its main objective was to determine what American raw materials should be sent to Italy. The presumption was that Italian craftsmen could be induced to make those products that could be sold profitably to the Americans, rather than that markets could be found for the things they could make best. In 1948 the Export-Import Bank extended some $4.5 million in credit for this

*Italian craftsman Enrico
Bernardi showing his
cabinets to members of
the American selection
committee for the Italy at
Work exhibition. Left to
right: W. D. Teague,
C. Nagel, M. Rogers,
R. Alexander. Credit:
(34, 8).*

purpose. CADMA was merged into the larger Comagna Nazionale Artiginia (CNA), which also took over the House of Italian Handicrafts. In other words, the importation of Italian handicrafts was subsidized. Furthermore, the project provided income to architects as well as artisans. Ernesto N. Rogers seems to have been the Italian spark behind the entire enterprise. He, with the assistance of others, designed many of the objects for production by artisans.

In 1949 the Art Institute of Chicago, as a result of its contacts with the House of Italian Handicrafts, authorized a field survey of Italian crafts and industrial arts to see if enough work of quality could be assembled for an exhibition to be held in the United States. Ramy Alexander, vice-president of the CNA, and Meyric Rogers, curator of decorative arts at the Art Institute, who made the survey together, were convinced that a strong renaissance in Italian crafts and design was underway that would be of interest to Americans. When the prospectus for such an exhibition was circulated, eleven other major museums agreed to take part in its projected three-year tour.

Accordingly, Ramy Alexander, Meyric Rogers, Charles Nagel (director of the Brooklyn Museum), and Walter Dorwin Teague toured Italy for three months in 1950, visiting artisans and designers and selecting some 2,500 items for the exhibition. The products were collected in the cellars of the Uffizi Galleries in Florence, cataloged, photographed, and prepared for shipment to the United States. As might be expected, the products were largely craft-based and unique or else available in limited quantities. They included ceramics, glass, wood, textiles, jewelry, and metalware. Of particular interest were a number of innovative prototypes for furniture, lighting fixtures, and other furnishings—some utilitarian but the majority decorative—that showed the emerging dynamism of Italian design. Also included were a few mass-manufactured products— expresso machines, office machines, and the Lambretta motor scooter. The designers Gio

Ponti, Fabrizio Clerici, Luigi Cosenza, Roberto Menghi, and Carlo Mollino were sought out to design special room settings for the exhibition. And finally, the work of artisanal shops such as Arteluce and Fontana Arte were included, along with products from manufacturers such as Olivetti, Venini, and Innocenti.

Walter Dorwin Teague, in his foreword to Meyric Rogers's handbook for the exhibition, *Italy at Work,* reflected on the "upsurge of the Italian vitality that [had] stored itself up during the long, grey Fascist interim" (34, 11). "The whole purpose for the project," Teague wrote, "was to stimulate, through the twelve museum exhibits, the importation of Italian craft works into America, and so assist the craftsmen and improve the dollar position without competing with American industry. . . . I'm no traitor to mass production, which enables Americans as a whole to enjoy far better and better-designed products and many more of them than are available to the mass of Italians, but a designer could not help but be delighted and stimulated by the daring *tours de force* his Italian colleagues could indulge in at will." (140)

The above-mentioned exhibition was only the beginning of an American interest in the postwar Italian design. While in Italy on a Fulbright Fellowship, Ada Louis Huxtable organized a traveling exhibition entitled "The Modern Movement in Italy: Architecture and Design" for the Museum of Modern Art. Like Teague, sh recognized that the repression of the Fascist era had been succeeded by an outburst of creative expression that had impelled Italian design to the forefront of contemporary design. She also complimented the ability of the Italians to maintain their personal expressive identity within the restraints of industrial processes.

Thus, by 1950 Italy was in the midst of an amazing cultural resurgence that released the distinctive Italian sense of form and imagination. Its architects and designers absorbed rationalist philosophy but humanized it with their free spirit and their sense of fantasy.

The cover of the Italy at Work exhibition handbook. Credit: (34).

Guido Gamboni's polychrome faience pieces for "Italy at Work" recalled the "vigor and fantasy" of Etruscan ceramics but were contemporary in form and expression. Credit: Interiors (November 1950).

*In this dining room, designed in 1950 for the "Italy at Work" exhibition, Gio Ponti combined rich Italian decoration with his own modern furniture. His goal was to demonstrate the range of the Italian imagination in various fields. Credit: (34, 61).*

*Dining table and chairs by Carlo Mollino for the "Italy at Work" exhibition. Credit: (34, 69).*

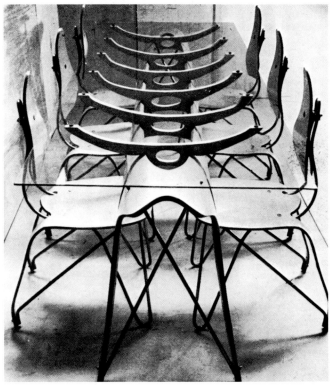

Theodore Clement (third
from left), Kodak's head
of industrial design,
describes Kodak products
to visitors from the Netherlands team. Wim Gilles
(fifth from left) later emigrated to Canada to head
the industrial design
department at Carleton
University, and Jaap Pen-
raat (sixth from left) came
to the United States to
practice design. Credit:
(46, 4).

The practice of industrial design in the United States was closely monitored by design, economic, and industrial interests in Europe. Some of the reactions were critical, with a touch of envy and more than a little concern about the impact abroad of American practice. Arthur Hald of Sweden described it as "a hyphen between what is out-of-date and what is glittering on the horizon of the future" (81).

In 1950 the Anglo-American Council on Productivity, in recognition of the postwar strength of American industry and marketing, sent a team of thirteen specialists to the United States to investigate American package design. The team was drawn from representative technical and business sections of the packaging industry; however, it did not include anyone qualified to report on the appearance and general effectiveness of packaging in the marketplace. The report acknowledged that designers in the United States influenced not only the appearance and utility of the product but also the whole policy of marketing it. One respondent to the report pointed out that it was essential that British products be designed and packaged to appeal to Americans in order to earn the dollars that Britain so badly needed. "The American consultant," observed Michael Farr in his 1955 book *Design in British Industry,* "is a species of advertising agent who tells his client that good design will mean good business. . . . Faced with a buyer's market . . . British manufacturers may well demand similar service." (15, 150–151). Again, it was in this atmosphere of economic need, perhaps more than admiration, that the Americans and their design practices were targeted by other countries.

In 1953 a group of six industrial designers from the Netherlands visited the United States. Their report, *Industriele Vormgeving in Amerika,* shows that they were given a thorough introduction to American industrial design by designers and educators in the northeastern sector of the United States. The report makes a particular point of the philosophical conflict in the United States between the idea that the designer should aim to find his own best solution to a problem on the basis of function and construction and the idea that the designer should be guided by the requirements of the manufacturer and the wishes of consumers. With respect to the attention that American designers gave to the consumer, the report observed that "American industry often compels the designer to concessions tending to what, not without reason, we habitually call 'bad taste' " (46, 87). The Dutch study group was left with the impression that American industrial design was a matter of dollars, with sales considered to be the best test of the quality of a design. Willem Gilles, one of the industrial designers in the group, mentioned in an interview with the author that he and his colleagues were amused by the impression that Americans at the time expected them to be wearing wooden shoes, if not complete native costumes. Even so, their American hosts (including Henry Dreyfuss, Francesco Collura, Carl Otto, and Ray Spilman; the design offices of Walter Dorwin Teague, Raymond Loewy, and Jean Reinecke; design executives with General Electric, Westinghouse, Kodak, and Corning; and the Massachusetts and Illinois Institutes of Technology) were open and frank with their visitors from the Netherlands. Gilles reported to his countrymen that industrial designers in America had the same aim as industry—to make a profit—and that industrial design was a form of commercial, almost scientific methodology that, in the right atmosphere and at the right management level, was indispensable to modern industry.

In the same year in which the Dutch study group came to the United States, the German Industries Association revived its special exhibition of well-designed manufactures at the German Industries Fair in Hanover. Then, in 1955, a study group of West German designers, educators, and historians visited the United States following an itinerary similar to that of their colleagues from the Netherlands.

Also in 1955, a group of 26 European executives of industrial firms, directors of product development, engineers, and educators, representing ten countries, was sent on a fact-finding mission to the United States under the auspices of the Organization for European Economic Cooperation and the American International Co-operation Administration. Although the objective of this team was to study the function, organization, and methods of industrial design in the engineering industries, only two of the members were industrial designers. The rest were not fully aware of the special meaning that the term *industrial design* had in the United States and were, therefore, not prepared to study industrial design in the American sense. Nevertheless, with the assistance of Peter Müller-Munk (president of the American Society of Industrial Designers at the time) and others, visits were arranged to four schools and to six independent and ten corporate industrial design offices. As a result, the initial misunderstanding did not detract from the success of the mission and the value of its study. In fact, it may have helped advance the introduction of industrial design to Europe because of the management-level positions of most of the mission's members.

The final report of the European mission contained an excellent summary of the state and practice of industrial design in the United States at the time. However, the report placed undue weight on the impact of the Bauhaus on industrial design. None of the academic institutions, companies, and offices visited were in fact under the influence of the Bauhaus émigrés, and the report acknowledged that design theory and American business had combined to "form a modern Industrial Design Philosophy, a typical American product, where idealism and business live side by side" (233).

The European mission observed that in the United States the industrial designer's contributions included

appearance design or "styling" (giving a manufactured product an attractive and "convincing air of quality"),

introducing special features into a product in order to "capture the customer's interest, imagination and favor,"

designing for obsolescence in order to stimulate the public's desire to look for new models every year—a concept that was difficult for the European engineers to understand,

simplifying a line of products to reduce production costs and to allow variants to be offered for sale at different price levels,

applying the war-born discipline of human engineering to adapt products to human requirements, and

exploiting the use of color as a functional component as well as a fashion and marketing component in product design.

Corporate identification, packaging, and exhibit design were also identified as being essential to marketing success. Industrial design, it was concluded, had proved most effective in the United States in mass-production industries—especially in increasing sales and maintaining consumption habits. The mission suggested that American industrial design practices could be adapted with success by European countries providing they took into account that, although individual countries might not be able to justify high-volume production of consumer goods, the impending removal of customs barriers and other trade restrictions between European countries promised to turn the whole of Europe into a common market on a scale greater than that of the United States.

Within the United States, the federal government offered assistance in industrial design and product development to small industries that were anxious to share in the seller's market that existed. In 1955 the Small Business Administration, aware of the need for assistance in supplying ideas, facts, and sound procedures for developing and marketing new products, joined with the Department of Commerce to publish a second edition of its 1949 Guidebook for Manufacturers, *Developing and*

*Selling New Products.* Two years earlier, the SBA had recognized industrial design with another booklet, *Design is Your Business,* which contained this bluntly worded thesis: "For nearly every business there are two kinds of design problems: design for selling, and design for making. For some business one kind of design is the main problem and it is vice versa for others. In general, design for selling is growing fastest in importance." (242, 2)

The United States, with its unscarred cities, its intact industries, and its affluent citizenry, was in an enviable position in the first two decades after the war. It had become a mecca for subsidized foreign students and for foreign experts on funded research missions. The tide, however, also ran the other way, as American designers looked to other countries for fresh opportunities. In 1953 Raymond Loewy (who had maintained an office in London between 1938 and 1945) established the Compagnie de l'Esthetique Industrielle (CEI) in Paris. Harold Barnett, who was brought over from the United States to serve as the managing director, helped build the CEI staff from three to seventeen designers by 1960, when he left to organize his own office, Groupe Harold Barnett. His replacement, James Fulton, had been working with the Harley Earl office in Detroit when Raymond Loewy asked him to take a position with CEI in 1958 as director of design. When Fulton left CEI in 1959 to join the Loewy/Snaith office in New York, Raymond Loewy turned to Douglas Kelley, who was in business for himself in New York after having studied at the Ulm school on a Fulbright scholarship. Kelley worked as managing director of CEI from 1960 to 1966, when he resigned to head the newly established design office of Lippincott and Margulies in London. This flow of talent through the Loewy office and up supported Loewy's private opinion that he ran the best school in the business.

The ebb and flow of international design alliances in the late 1950s and the early 1960s reflects the international activity that was generated by in 1957 the establishment of the European Economic Community and the launching of Sputnik I. Within a year, more than 1,600 American corporations had opened new operations on the Continent. In most cases, their corporate and consultant designers added foreign design responsibilities to stateside duties. In some instances they were asked to adapt American products for foreign distribution; in others they reprocessed foreign products to meet American demands. In either event, the assignments had both technical and aesthetic aspects. In some cases designers had to be careful not to dilute a product's national character; in others they were asked to mask it in order to ensure transborder sales.

By 1963, sixteen American design firms had established offices abroad and more than thirty were serving foreign clients from the United States. Manufacturers in twenty-two European and Latin American countries and in Japan had contracts with American designers for projects almost equally divided between packaging and product development. It is true that most of their activity was devoted to bridging the differences between Americans and foreigners, with the primary sales target at that time being the richer Americans. Even so, it must be recognized that manufactures, and with them the practice of industrial design, have become increasingly global since World War II. National identity is not being exploited or suppressed so much as it is evaporating in an atmosphere of globalization of product development, manufacture, and consumption. Ethnic, social, and regional characteristics once considered essential to success are being neutralized. The United States, as the world's first common market, has been providing an international example for everyone.

## Foreign Service

In the developing nations, designers, educators, and government officials must first overcome the basic inertia of economic systems at a comparative standstill. . . . Designers must help these craft nations develop improved economies built on the countries' own terms.

William Goldsmith, 1958 (72)

The Marshall Plan to provide financial aid to Western Europe had been approved by the U.S. Congress in 1947. In 1955, a Hoover Commission proposed that one-tenth of the almost $4 billion dollars that had been earmarked for the Mutual Security Program of the United States be set aside to support a similar program for the developing countries around the world. The new program, administered by the International Cooperation Administration (ICA), was instituted in 1955 to help unstable countries maintain their political independence by developing a secure and promising economy.

The Marshall Plan had been relatively easy to implement, because in Europe the knowledge and the experience needed to serve the needs of a more sophisticated society already existed. Such was not the case in the developing countries. Moreover, it was believed that political circumstances did not allow for a careful, gradual buildup of intellectual, natural, and technological resources. It was decided, therefore, to implement a short-term program of assistance that would, at the very least, demonstrate the good will of the United States.

American industrial designers' professional interests had already expanded beyond the borders of the United States. They were active in bringing exhibitions of foreign products to the United States and in working to display American products abroad in exhibitions such as Italy's Triennales. Raymond Loewy, Walter Dorwin Teague, Henry Dreyfuss, and Peter Müller-Munk were already well known abroad and had been honored for their achievements in England, France, and Italy.

After the Society of Industrial Designers changed its name in 1951 to the American Society of Industrial Designers, Müller-Munk was appointed to head its Foreign Affairs Committee. As Müller-Munk was a founding member and the first president of the International Council of Societies of Industrial Design, it was natural that the ICA should seek his advice on creating its program of assistance in product development to emerging nations. The general conclusion was that any assistance that was offered should go beyond the product itself to include advice on seeking out foreign outlets—primarily in the United States—that promised an immediate financial return.

In 1955 the ICA decided to offer contracts to several prominent industrial design organizations that had experience in seeing products through the entire process from design through manufacture to market and consumption. Their assignment was to survey the craft-based activities in assigned countries and recommend action that would increase the quality, quantity, and dependability of such products to make them competitive in the open marketplace—especially that of the United States. In addition, the designers were expected to open markets for the products and advise their makers on presentation and other marketing principles. They were not expected to introduce new designs that would interfere with long-established traditions. The underlying philosophy of this approach was that the resulting product should be carefully adjusted to appeal to Western tastes. This last point was undoubtedly based on a State Department opinion that political allegiance would be more likely to arise if the United States did not appear to threaten the native culture. By way of contrast, the USSR simply bought products, without attempting to induce changes presumed to be essential to competitive success in an open marketplace.

Each of the five design organizations selected by the ICA was assigned to a different set of developing countries. Russel Wright Associates went to five Southeast Asian nations: Hong Kong, Taiwan (then called Formosa), Thailand, Cambodia, and Vietnam. Walter Dorwin Teague Associates went to Greece, Jordan, and Lebanon. Design Research Incorporated went to Pakistan, Afghanistan, Mexico, Surinam, El Salvador, Jamaica, and Costa Rica. Peter Müller-Munk Associates went to Israel, Turkey, and India. Smith, Scherr and McDermott went to South Korea.

Russel Wright approached his Southeast Asia assignment primarily as a marketing program. His first step was to survey some 150 American firms on their interest in marketing products from Southeast Asia. Then, in the winter of 1955–56, he toured the countries with Ramy Alexander (the craft specialist who had served a similar purpose in the "Italy at Work" project) and Josette Walker (an expert on women's clothing and accessories). Working, in effect, from a shopping list matched to Wright's original American survey, they returned with examples of craft-based products, motion pictures of craftsmen at work, detailed information about the craftsmen and their capabilities, and information on peripheral considerations affecting packing, shipping, and regulations. Back in the United States, Wright organized an exhibition at the New York Coliseum in June 1956, coincidental with the International Housewares Trade Show. The exhibition attracted a great deal of publicity and a respectable number of trade inquiries.

Wright was enthusiastic about the opportunities for design and trade in Southeast Asia, both for the entrepreneurial developer and for the imaginative designer, although he wondered whether native culture might not be irretrievably lost as a result of this well-meaning attempt to help these countries find an economic and political accommodation with the West. Yet, in contrast to Walter Dorwin Teague's strict policy of not interfering with indigenous design, Wright undertook to provide design assistance as well as marketing assistance to the countries he visited. Wright's

position was that, since each country's needs were different, training centers should be set up to train local workers in modern methodologies and processes. Taiwan in particular, he believed, was sufficiently developed to sustain a national promotional center for the handicrafts. Though Cambodia was technologically far behind the other countries to which he had been assigned, Wright noted that its traditional design was so strong and of such a high quality that Cambodian products should be marketed through exclusive shops. He found Hong Kong and Vietnam to be well along the road to mass production and saw little need for technological assistance to these two countries; rather, he suggested that they be given specific leads to commercial outlets in the United States that were receptive to their unique products. His comments about Thailand were full of praise for the American James Thompson, who had revitalized the Thai silk-weaving industry.

Dave Chapman's Design Research group, despite the distance separating Pakistan and Afghanistan from the Caribbean nations, found that craftsmen in all these countries shared a belief that only by producing low-quality products with cheap labor could they hope to compete in Western markets. Chapman concluded that by setting up training institutes and introducing better methodologies they would improve quality and thus increase their sales. Unfortunately, this view was not in concert with that of the marketing establishment. Merchants, both native exporters and foreign importers, stood to gain more under the conditions that prevailed. Their position was embedded in the colonial mentality that equated profit and production control with cheap labor. Chapman's solution was to suggest that designers-in-residence be stationed in each country to help direct the development of products that would appeal to American markets. While this was in contradiction with his original assignment, it did promise that diversification and the exploration of more exotic concepts might do more for the economy of developing nations than defending the status quo.

# The designer as economic diplomat

*The government applies the designer's approach to problems of international trade.*

*Russel Wright, far-flung designer, disembarking on the banks of the Mekong (Vietnam).*

*Russel Wright disembarking in Vietnam during his 1956 visit to Southeast Asia for the International Cooperation Administration. Credit: Industrial Design (August 1956). Photograph by Louis Reens.*

*Vietnam's largest pottery—owned by Chinese émigrés—was commended by Russel Wright to the ICA in 1956 as efficient with excellent promise of exporting fine ceramic wares to the United States. Credit: Interiors (August 1956). Photograph by Henri Gilles.*

Russel Wright, under contract with the ICA, examining sample baskets and other examples of weaving handicrafts for possible export to the United States. Credit: Industrial Design (April 1957).

William Goldsmith and Dave Chapman evaluating handicrafts collected in 1956–57 from Middle Eastern and Central American countries for export to the United States. Credit: Industrial Design (April 1957).

Peter Müller-Munk's recommendations were similar to Chapman's. He suggested that India establish a long-term technical assistance program through which American designers, working in government industrial design training centers in New Delhi, Bombay, Calcutta, and Madras, would train Indian teachers, who would then assist industries and work in the field to assist village craftsmen. His plan for Turkey was similar. Müller-Munk went even further in an apparently independent action to establish an industrial design office in Haifa with funds provided by the American and Israeli governments. The office was staffed with designers from both countries to work on projects for manufacture outside the craft orientation of the ICA assignments. It was expected that the office would become self-sustaining, and that within two years it would be run entirely by Israelis.

Other, similar projects were set in motion at the same time. One was a contract—roughly parallel to Peter Müller-Munk's—that was written by the International Cooperation Administration for work between the Institute of Contemporary Art in Boston and the Technion Institute of Technology in Haifa. The ICA-Technion project, under a special grant from the "Point Four" technical-assistance program, called for the development of a full-scale curriculum in industrial design and the Technion and for the establishment of a National Design Center in Israel and a consumer-research project in the United States to provide guidelines for both product and packaging design.

The International Cooperation Administration's South Korea project, under the guidance of the Akron firm of Smith, Scherr and McDermott, came to a conclusion that broke with the pattern of the other ICA program countries. The principals in the firm recognized and included in their exhibition examples of the Korean preference for Western ideas and aesthetics in the design of technological products. The Koreans had come through decades of occupation by Japan, and were less interested in recapturing the past than in catching up with the future.

After the Korean project, the Smith, Scherr and McDermott office reorganized, with Scherr and McDermott going on to organize a program of trade in association with the Cooperative League of the U.S.A. and, later, with the Agency for International Development's Alliance for Progress. The project was designed to bring to American markets the products of artisans from Bolivia, Colombia, Ecuador, and Peru. An office was set up in the Empire State Building, and with its first market exhibit (at the National Design Center in New York) the group managed to import and sell a million dollars' worth of goods in the United States. The success of the project was aided considerably by Peace Corps workers.

The majority of the short-term ICA projects did not enjoy the success that had been predicted for them. The premise that the political allegiance of uncommitted developing countries could be gained by playing on their emotional attachment to traditional craft industries did not pan out. Some thirty years later, many of the countries involved were little closer to democracy than they had been in the mid 1950s. However, Taiwan, South Korea, Israel, and Japan exchanged students, educators, and practicing designers with the United States and grew close to the U.S. not only in technology but also in political and economic ideology.

The fact that American industrial designers were willing to undertake assignments from the ICA was evidence that their professional horizons were expanding beyond the borders of the United States. Both of the American design organizations had committees on foreign affairs that responded to requests for assistance from abroad.

Henry Dreyfuss had been invited by the government of the Netherlands to visit the Utrecht Fair in 1950 and, at the request of the Netherlands Ministry of Economics, had met with government officials, financiers, industrialists, and businessmen to discuss the role of American design in merchandising.

Peter Müller-Munk had served as an advisor to the U.S. government on the ICA program, and his office had taken on field assignments in the Near East. In 1960 he served as consultant to the European Productivity Agency, which had been set up in 1953 by the Organization for European Economic Co-operation to stimulate productivity and thereby to raise European standards of living. Müller-Munk and his partner Paul Karlen spent fourteen months in seventeen OEEC countries conducting seminars and workshops on the relationship between industrial design and management, engineering, and marketing. In response to implications that planned obsolescence was a uniquely American phenomenon, Müller-Munk responded that perhaps Europeans were mistaken in their opinion of the importance of durability. Europe, he pointed out, was shifting from a seller's to a buyer's market, and as consumers in an emerging Common Market were offered choices between products from competing manufacturers, marketing would become increasingly important to industrialists.

C. F. Graser, manager of product planning for the portable-appliance division of General Electric, was given a six-month leave by his company at the request of the ICA to give seminars on product planning and industrial design in Europe. In 1957 he visited and lectured to groups in ten OEEC countries, and in 1959 his final report, *Product Planning and Development,* was published and distributed to the OEEC countries.

Austria's design-related postwar contacts with the United States, according to Charlotte Blauensteiner of the Austrian Design Institute, "started with envious admiration: there was a rich, even affluent society, and of course everybody wanted to have things looking as those from the States." "It was realized," she continues, "that there was a lot to be learned by the experience of American designers. Our Institute organized lectures by Peter Müller-Munk, and Raymond Loewy was very much 'in' with the first generation of design students in Vienna." (192)

The experience of Austria was representative of the postwar period in countries that had been the battleground of World War II. Charlotte Blauensteiner writes: "Industrial design in a modern sense only started after the second world war. In the first years, however, resources were scarce and production in many fields nonexistent due to destruction. . . . Therefore the first aim was to build up again the factories and produce *anything.* Only in the fifties with economic stabilization and increasing saturation of the market the demands for quality, function, and aesthetics developed." (192)

The first courses in industrial design in Austria were offered in the 1950s at the Vienna Academy of Applied Arts under Franz Hoffmann. With the stimulus of international exhibitions in Italy and Belgium and the example set by councils of industrial design in Great Britain and West Germany, the Austrian Design Council was established in 1958 under the leadership of Karl Schwanzer. However, design in Austria, as in most countries, was still identified with individual objects, much in the tradition of each product as an individual work of art. Not until the 1960s did products come to be viewed as elements of larger systems, with all the economic, social, and environmental implications that entailed.

In the 1950s, American industrial designers were drawn into a plan to bring the message of everyday life in the United States to other countries through participation in international trade fairs. Underlying the federal government's interest was the realization that capitalism and communism were now facing each other along a frontier of developing countries that were, as yet, politically as well as economically uncommitted. After it was realized that the USSR had participated in more than 130 international trade fairs since 1950, not so much to display export products as to promote communism, the United States decided to enter the trade-fair circuit. In 1955 an Office of International Trade Fairs was established, with funding authorized by President Eisenhower from his discretionary budget. (The fact that the United States did not have an ongoing international fair program was, in large measure, due to the fact that it did not depend as much on foreign exports as other countries did.) It was considered essential that those countries that were already on the side of capitalism should have their own faith reinforced by the American presence abroad, and that the propaganda arena not be conceded to the USSR by default. It was also recognized that any foreign trade that did come America's way would strengthen American industry's support for the Eisenhower administration.

Beginning with a trade fair in Bangkok, American exhibits were visited by some 12 million people in fifteen countries in 1954, the first year of this program. At first, such exhibitions were designed by the Office of Design and Production the OTIF had established in Paris under Peter Harnden. However, the fairs were criticized as being too similar and for concentrating too much on the good life in the United States and too little on the particular conditions of the country in which they were staged or the state of mind of the audience. The OITF decided that contracts for future trade shows should be put out for competitive bids to designers, and the Paris design office was closed.

In 1956 the U.S. Congress, confirming the importance of American participation in international trade fairs, gave permanent status to the OITF with an appropriation of $3.5 million. In the process, as Jane Fiske Mitarachi wrote in *Industrial Design,* the OITF provided designers with ''a new kind of responsibility for presenting, and in some cases formulating, America's approach to other nations. Designers were asked to be propagandists; design became a tool of communication and the visual composition of an exhibition a secondary problem.'' (99)

In retrospect, it appears that industrial designers were uniquely suited to the task of design-

ing international trade fairs. They knew their trade, they were patient and competent in overseeing the setting up of exhibits, and their political innocence made their displays more palatable to foreign visitors. They took on these contracts in the spirit of service to their country rather than in the hope of financial return. Henry Dreyfuss observed that if there was anything wrong with the work of industrial designers on such trade fairs, it was that they tried too hard.

A partial list of the cities that received American exhibitions in the late 1950s includes Salonika, Bari, Verona, Milan, Izmir, Damascus, Casablanca, Kabul, Karachi, Bangkok, Djakarta, Barcelona, Bombay, Osaka, Tokyo, Stockholm, Vienna, Paris, Poznan, and Zagreb. Toward the end of the program, the OITF opened up access to its trade fairs to private manufacturers in order to free funds so that more countries could be visited.

Participation in trade fairs opened up to the world a profession that had been bound closely to domestic clients and consumers. According to William Barton, a former senator and Assistant Secretary of State, the experience made industrial designers ''not merely front-line soldiers, but generals in the design for survival.'' ''Good design,'' wrote Barton, ''reaches whole foreign populations and often becomes the image of their aspiration.'' (106) It was inevitable that American designers should, in many cases, form and set the standards for products in other countries.

Trade fairs were not the only means by which American products and design philosophy became known abroad. In 1951 Edgar Kaufmann, Jr., assembled a traveling exhibition for the Museum of Modern Art to be sent to Stuttgart on the invitation of the West German government. This exhibition, ''Design for Use, USA,'' concentrated on the interest of Americans in gadgets and material comfort. It was not intended to display the highest achievements of American culture, but rather to illustrate American ingenuity and open-

Pavilion and sign
designed by Raymond
Spilman in 1963 for U.S.
exhibit at Poznan Inter-
national Trade Fair.
Credit: (216).

Surgical exhibit in U.S.
pavilion at 1956 Salonika
fair. Bernard Phreim was
the designer. Credit:
Industrial Design (Febru-
ary 1957).

mindedness. The products included fabrics made of glass and plastic, a rug made of paper, and a transparent plastic bassinette.

Several years later, MOMA was asked by the American embassy in Paris to send a selection of small manufactured products from its permanent collection to represent American industrial design at the Musee d'Art Moderne as part of a festival of cultural events, the "Salute to France," to be presented in the spring of 1955. MOMA sent unpretentious products—including kettles designed by W. Archbald Welden and Peter Schlumbohm and polyethylene containers by Earl Tupper —and they were presented as classics of American mass production.

Another project, similar in a way to one of Peter Müller-Munk's earlier recommendations for India, was an exhibition entitled "Design Today in America and Europe" that opened in 1959 in New Delhi. This project, also produced under the direction of the Museum of Modern Art, was assembled at the request of India's National Small Business Corporation with financial support from the Ford Foundation. The exhibition, comprising primarily duplicates of objects in MOMA's permanent collection, was designed by Gordon Chadwick of the George Nelson office.

The U.S. government was also involved in a unique project intended to share American philosophy and methodology in industrial design education with teachers and students in other countries. In 1957 Jack Masey, director of exhibitions of the United States Information Service, contracted the Institute of Design of the Illinois Institute of Technology to organize a traveling exhibition, to be called "Industrial Design Education, U.S.A." This project, which brought together eight students from eight prominent industrial design schools to design and build the exhibition, was itself a demonstration of the American approach to design. Under the direction of Jay Doblin and Warren Fitzgerald, the team assembled and built a 3,000-square-foot exhibition in twelve weeks over the summer of 1957. The exhibi-

WALTER
ERLEBACHER
Pratt Institute

DON McINTYRE
Univ. of
Bridgeport

DAVE
WORKMAN
U.C.L.A.

JOHN
DALTON
R.I.S.D.

JOAN
BLOUNT
Syracuse U.

JIM MAH
Philadelp
Museum

These eight students from
various schools designed
a display system,
selected the products to
be shown, and built an
exhibition of "American
Design Education" to be
shown abroad by the U.S.
government. Credit:
Industrial Design (Novem-
ber 1957). Photograph by
Ray Metzker.

JL
ESTLY
itute of Design, IIT

WILLIAM
BARON
Univ. of Illinois

tion illustrated, with over 200 designs and models created by students, the three program philosophies that characterized industrial design education in the United States: design as a humanistic activity, design as the transformation of aesthetics into utilitarian products, and design as a merchandising tool. The schools represented were Pratt Institute, the University of Bridgeport, the University of California at Los Angeles, the Philadelphia Museum School of Art, the University of Illinois, the Rhode Island School of Design, Syracuse University, and the Institute of Design.

In 1958 the United States authorized two foreign exhibitions that illustrated opposite ends of the design spectrum. The "Atoms for Peace" display, designed by Walter Dorwin Teague Associates under the direction of Walter Dorwin Teague, Jr., for the second United Nations Atoms for Peace Conference in Geneva, was complex and scientific in its content; the other was a traveling exhibition, designed by Edgar Kaufmann, Jr., of the work of fourteen American designer-craftsmen. The show was based on case studies done by Don Wallance as part of a "Study of Design and Craftsmanship in Today's Products" sponsored by the Walker Art Center and the American Craftsmen's Council. The research also resulted in Wallance's book *Shaping America's Products.*

## The Design Olympics

*What makes the Triennale so important is that it pioneers new ideas and discovers new talents. The opportunity to compare the creative talents of different nations focused on the same subject is an extremely valuable lesson to your own national pride and professional self-esteem.*

Peter Müller-Munk, 1960 (64)

The Triennale exhibitions were established in 1923 in Monza, Italy, as periodic exhibitions devoted to architecture and the decorative and industrial arts. In 1933 the site of the exhibition was changed to the new Palazzo dell' Arte in Milan. In 1947 the Triennales, which had ceased in 1940, were revived. The eighth edition observed postwar priorities by concentrating on the rehabilitation of shattered buildings and the potential of prefabricated housing. A smaller amount of space was set aside for innovative furniture. Manufactured products were not included.

Although the Triennales were known in the United States, Americans had never participated. One reason for this was that American products in the decorative and industrial arts were still considered to be so dependent upon European sources that no one dared present them as original, and originality was one of the requirements for admission. A second reason was there was no organization in the United States—private or public—that was sufficiently interested in international design competitions.

When the Italians began planning for the ninth (1951) Triennale, they expected to demonstrate their country's recovery from the traumas of Fascism and war. To the surprise of many, they decided to expand the exhibitions to include objects that were within reach of the general public and yet faultless in taste, execution, and functionality—in other words, to admit manufactured products in addition to the furnishings and accessories of previous years.

Franco Albini, a member of the executive board for the Ninth Triennale, was authorized to invite the Society of Industrial Designers to send an exhibition of American products. Albini explained that he had approached the SID directly because "there is not, in the States, a Body of the Government, which could take upon itself the initiative and to which our Foreign Office could address the official invitation." This gave the Italians, Albini noted, an opportunity to make a direct approach to those Americans who were "working in the most vivid artistic currents" (208).

Walter Dorwin Teague (a member of the Italian-American Council) knew about the invitation to the SID and wrote to the society supporting the idea. He pointed out, however, that it would have to be an exhibition of photographs. Although he did not believe that such an exhibition would have much commercial value, he felt that it could be justified on the grounds of prestige and as a gesture of good will toward Italy.

Subsequently the organizers of the Triennale sent the SID a list of the American products that they had in mind. They had apparently selected them from the catalogs of recent product exhibitions in the United States. When this turned out to be unrealistic in terms of available time and resources, the SID selected and sent some seventy photographs of representative work from its members. Peter Müller-Munk noted that he hung the photographs at the show.

In addition to the photographs sent by the SID, a traveling exhibition that had been prepared by the Museum of Modern Art for the United States Information Agency was redirected to Milan for display at the Triennale in a small pavilion designed especially for it by the Italian architectural firm of Belgiojoso, Peressutti, and Rogers. It appears that some of the products were selected from the 1950 "Good Design" exhibitions at the Museum of Modern Art. Walter Dorwin Teague resented the inclusion of this other American exhibit in the Triennale. In a flurry of letters to *Interiors,* Teague criticized MOMA's preoccupation with what he termed the "Functionalist" school of design, which he saw as just another elitist style imposed upon the public by the museum. Teague hoped to see mass-manufactured products recognized by the Triennales as an important part of contemporary cultural life, and he did not consider MOMA's selections typical of the "original characteristic achievements in mass-produced designs for living that fascinate the European public" (142).

The Italians were aware of the conflict that their dual invitation to the Ninth Triennale had generated in the American design community, and they decided to try to avoid creating a similar situation next time. They designated a neutral observer—Olga Gueft, the editor of *Interiors*—to be the official American agent for the 1954 Tenth Triennale. After Congress refused to authorize an appropriation for a pavilion, Peter Müller-Munk assured Olga Gueft that the SID would provide exhibit materials. She responded to him that "since the State Department has forfeited its priority by lack of decisive action, I can offer you the space provided that the Society of Industrial Designers can mobilize to do the project" (214). Under this agreement, Müller-Munk, with the assistance of his colleagues and the SID's national office, collected, packed, and shipped to Milan some forty products, most of them about to be shown to Europeans for the first time. Included were an outboard motor by Brooks Stevens, a hand drill by L. Garth Huxtable, an electric plane by Peter Müller-Munk, an electric typewriter by Eliot Noyes, a blender by Francesco Collura, plastic dinnerware by Russel Wright, a dictating machine by Carl Otto, and a bathroom scale by Raymond Loewy.

As a justification for the inclusion of utilitarian products, the central theme of the 1954 Triennale was identified as Industrial Aesthetics. The catalog for the exhibition spoke of industrial design ("an American term that has now come into general use") as "the interpolation of the concept of 'form' into the industrial pro-

*The symbol of the Tenth Triennale, held at Milan in 1954. Credit:* Industrial Design *(May 1954).*

The Italian-designed U.S.
exhibition at the Tenth
Triennale was introduced
by a collage of photo-
graphs of subjects rang-
ing from "a spoon to a
city"—a favorite Italian
design slogan. Credit:
(216).

*The forty products that the SID sent to the Tenth Triennale were exhibited in a lower gallery. They were shown in isolated cages or lined up along the wall with little regard to their complex and meaningful relationship in the real world. Credit: (216).*

cess, or into the formal aspect of technology, the essential meeting-point between art and industry" (1, 323).

Despite its awkward beginnings, the shortage of time, and the paucity of resources, this first full participation of Americans in the Tenth Triennale was considered a success. Some visitors complained because the American products were non-juried and lacked government approval; however, this demonstration of the ability of Americans to operate independently if necessary was not lost on anyone. Walter Dorwin Teague represented the United States in the international conference on industrial design that was held in conjunction with this Triennale.

The American industrial design community had been trying for the better part of a decade to convince the federal government of the contribution that formal participation in the Triennales would make to the global stature of the nation. Somehow, however, the suggestion that cultural prestige had a bearing on the acceptance of American ideas and products had not gotten through to government officials. But at last the two government agencies that had withheld assistance in the past—the United States Information Agency and the Trade Fair Division of the Department of Commerce—each made a $25,000 grant to the American Society of Industrial Designers to support an American exhibit at the Eleventh (1957) Triennale. Walter Dorwin Teague was appointed chairman of the selection committee, which included Jane Fiske Mitarachi (the editor of *Industrial Design*), Jack Masey of the USIA, and representatives of the Industrial Designers' Institute as well as ASID members. Paul McCobb, selected to design the exhibit, created colorful tent islands and cylinders in which 115 products (from 58 manufacturers, by 56 designers) were displayed in a plastic-and-aluminum geodesic dome provided by the USIA. The committee chose "Communication at Home and at Work" as the theme of the exhibit and agreed that it would be made available to the U.S. Department of Commerce for use in trade fairs throughout Europe in 1958.

The organizers of the Triennale also invited 25 designers from 10 countries to make individual case-study presentations in a special exhibit that would illustrate the practice of industrial design in their countries. The six Americans who were involved in this exhibit were Arthur BecVar, Henry Dreyfuss, Walter Dorwin Teague, Raymond Loewy, Herbert Bayer, and Peter Müller-Munk. BecVar presented a General Electric refrigerator, Dreyfuss a number of Bell telephones, Teague a Ritter x-ray machine, Loewy an Atwater outboard motor, Bayer his corporate graphics program for the Container Corporation of America, and Müller-Munk a Westinghouse refrigerator-freezer.

With some 22 countries now participating, the Triennales had become a cultural Olympics.

In a vote taken among visitors to the 1957 Triennale, the American pavilion was voted second only to the Swedish exhibit. The international jury also selected several American products for recognition. Charles Eames received one of the 25 grand prizes for his Herman Miller lounge chair and ottoman. Gold medals were awarded to Walter Dorwin Teague (for a Kodak movie camera) and to Alfred Zuckerman (for a Bogen amplifier). Silver medals went to Carl Otto (for an Edison dictating machine), to RCA (for a portable television), and to L. Garth Huxtable (for hand tools for the Millers Falls company).

This series of Triennale exhibitions brought American industrial designers into the international design community as full participants and forceful competitors. Since 1957 was also the year that the European Economic Community was established, European designers and manufacturers were now obliged to consider the challenges of global marketing. This fact attracted particular attention to the design case histories from the United States as examples of the practice of designers who had been serving precisely such a common market for many years.

*The America committee for the Eleventh Triennale (1957) included (left to right) Frank Jacoby, Sally Swing, Peter Müller-Munk, Jay Doblin, Walter Dorwin Teague (the chairman), Paul McCobb, Jack Masey, Jane Fiske Mitarachi, Robert Gruen, and Jacqueline Griffith. Credit:* Industrial Design *(May 1957).*

At the Eleventh Triennale, visitors were able to see American exhibit design at its imaginative best. Although the pavilion tended to overwhelm the products, it came closest to responding to the Triennale's challenge. Credit: Industrial Design *(November 1957). Photograph by Sergio Bersani.*

In an editorial in *Industrial Design* magazine, Jane Fiske McCullough applauded the event and expressed the hope that this experience would force the design profession to put its house in order. However, while there have been some consolidations since then, they have been within rather than between the design specializations. It seems that while designers in other countries and on an international level are moving toward a common center, Americans are still repairing the fences that keep them apart. Only occasionally, on such matters of a shared national interest as the Triennales, do they attempt to join forces—and then only on a temporary basis.

Later Triennales dropped the product-oriented approach for themes such as Home and School (1960) and Leisure (1964). In 1960 the show-stopper was Casa Americana, an innovative home of the future designed for Alcoa by John Matthias and Samuel Fahnestock with furnishings selected by Walter Dorwin Teague. The 1964 medal winner was a tent-like stretched nylon structure designed by Charles Forberg to house a selection of avant-garde furnishings. The committee included Olga Gueft, Mildred Constantine, Edgar Kaufmann, Jr., and Jack Lenor Larsen (who called the result "white, brilliant, clean, ordered, full of things to look at, delightful").

When the United States received an invitation in 1954 to participate in the 1958 Brussels World's Fair, the question was raised whether such fairs were not obsolete. Some recalled the blissful innocence with which Americans had staged the New York World's Fair of 1939–40 under the gathering clouds of World War II. Yet a global celebration seemed to be in order, not so much in the interest of commerce as out of a psychological need for all nations to stand in the same cultural space for a moment. There was a yearning for a kind of absolution from the sins and cruel alliances of the past and a sharing of hopes for the future. The United States and the USSR were assigned adjoining spaces. While the USSR

used most of its site for an impressive structure displaying its advances in utilities, resource management, transportation, and space exploration, the American planners decided to allot most of their space to an open plaza. Edward Durrell Stone designed a structurally innovative, visually idyllic circular pavilion and two smaller buildings—one for films and a second for live theatrical and musical performances.

Other countries had governmental mechanisms in place for handling and financing such enterprises. The United States, however, had no budget line for international cultural affairs. Congressional approval and funding had to be acquired for each event. By the time that this was done, the opening of the Brussels fair was less than 18 months away. Stone was contracted to design the pavilion, and James Plaut, the former director of Boston's Institute for Contemporary Art, was assigned responsibility for acquiring and organizing the exhibits. Peter Harnden and Bernard Rudofsky were contracted to design the exhibits.

Plaut organized one of the first pan-society committees in the United States—including representatives from the societies of industrial design, interior design, and crafts—to plan the theme and content of the exhibits. Joseph Carriero served as the administrative director under Plaut; he was responsible for the selection and procurement of the craft objects and manufactured products to be shown. The selections were exhibited at the Institute of Contemporary Art before being shipped to Brussels.

The American presentations were planned by a group of some 90 business and professional people who met with educators and government representatives at the Massachusetts Institute of Technology. They agreed that the exhibits should be low-key, elegant, and non-political. A large part of the main pavilion was reserved for special public events, such as a daily fashion show and continuing exhibitions of modern architecture, painting, and sculpture. The remainder was devoted to exhibits of everyday products and exhibits explaining

The planners of the Amer-
ican pavilion at the 1958
Brussels World's Fair
wanted an elegant pavil-
ion, and Edward Durell
Stone gave them one.
*Credit:* Industrial Design
*(July 1958).*

The fashion show orga-
nized by Vogue was the
unexpected hit of the
American pavilion at
Brussels. *Credit:* Industrial
Design *(July 1958).*

Visitors to the American
pavilion could look down
into various living levels
of an abstracted home,
each dedicated to a different aspect of American
life. Most of the products
were modern, with an
occasional traditional
object included for reference. Credit: Interiors
(September 1958).

These exotic modern
American furniture
pieces—architectonic in
spirit—were on display at
Brussels. Credit: Industrial
Design (July 1958).

the aspirations and talent of Americans for enhancing the spaces they lived in. The exhibits were arranged as islands depicting various aspects of daily life, such as dining, recreation, and children. There was also an abstracted version of an American home, which was equipped with the best modern American furniture and other furnishings.

In the interest of frankness, Leo Lionni created an exhibit entitled "Unfinished Business," which was placed behind the main pavilion. It acknowledged the problems of race relations, urbanization, and the depletion of natural resources, and the progress that was being made toward their resolution. This presentation was a daring shift from the sweet and boastful propaganda that is normally associated with World's Fairs. It was in the form of three linked sections, each the size of a railroad boxcar. The first consisted of disorganized triangular panels papered with newspaper accounts of the problems. The second was a more ordered crystalline structure that reported on the studies made and steps taken toward resolving the problems. The third was a structure of white rectangular panels and photographs of solutions achieved.

Not surprisingly, the presentation in the main pavilion was less believable than Lionni's exhibit—particularly, it seems, to self-conscious Americans and critics of the United States. *Industrial Design*, however, understood. It found "the designers' deviation from the standard viewpoint . . . not only valid but vital." At previous fairs, *Industrial Design* noted, "Uncle Sam had been less casual, more serious, more preachy, more powerful. He has seldom been more winning." (105)

To some of the visitors to the Brussels World's Fair, it must have appeared that the USSR had gotten the best of the United States. While the Americans were admitting their weaknesses, the Soviets were promoting their strengths. The Sputnik hanging in the Russian pavilion was, after all, difficult to ignore. Later, however, Armstrong's footprint on the moon brought the Americans up to par again.

*Leo Lionni's "Unfinished Business" exhibit at Brussels, which admitted of problems in the United States, was criticized by self-conscious Americans and praised by European intellectuals. Credit:* Industrial Design *(July 1958).*

In the atmosphere of warming international relations provided by the fair in Brussels, the two superpowers agreed in September 1958 to exchange exhibitions on science, culture, and technology in the summer of 1959. In line with the agreement that was signed in January 1958, it was decided that the cultural events would be free of political propaganda. This eased reservations about giving aid to the enemy and wasting money, and the U.S. Congress voted to allocate between $2 million and $3 million for the American exhibition and to invite private industry to contribute displays. The American National Exhibition, designed by George Nelson and Company and installed in Moscow's Sokolniki Park, consisted of two major structures and several smaller specialized structures. A large Fuller dome served as an information center. There were graphic exhibitions on education, health, and agriculture. A computer had been prepared to respond to 4,000 questions with answers flashed on a screen for all to see. The most impressive and memorable displays were the two 12-minute presentations of 2,000 slides of American life, one designed by Charles and Ray Eames and the second by Billy Wilder. The Eameses' show dealt with the American work week, Wilder's with the weekend. (The final scene in the Eameses' show consisted of a field of flowers displayed simultaneously on all seven screens. Every time these slides were shown, Ray Eames noticed a wave of warm empathy in the audience. Later she learned that the name for the flowers meant the same in Russian as it did in English: forget-me-not.)

The second major building was a glass pavilion housing a "jungle gym" structure that displayed 5,000 American products at various levels in a bazaar of abundance that presented indisputable proof of the fruits of technology that were available to Americans. Several American companies provided special exhibits—RCA a color television studio, Grand Union a supermarket, and RCA/Whirlpool a kitchen (the site of the famous debate between Nikita Khrushchev and Richard Nixon). Outside the major buildings were three clusters of large umbrella-like shapes contributed by the plastics industry to exhibit photographs of modern American architecture and photos from the "Family of Man" series and to serve as an open arena for fashion shows. There was also a movie theater, called the Circarama. This exhibition was intended to present proof that shared technology could provide a higher standard of living for the citizens of a democracy. Ralph Caplan observed in *Industrial Design* that the burden of trying "to communicate the most elementary facts of American life to a people whose experience is such that they may not be expected to believe them" had led to "an almost wearying emphasis on credibility, on avoiding the air of propaganda" (110).

The United States Information Agency was responsible for three exhibitions that were sent to the USSR in the 1960s. "Graphic Arts USA" (1963) was devoted to advertising, signs, trademarks, and other forms of visual communication. The selections were made by the American Institute of Graphic Arts, and the exhibition was designed by Ivan Chermayeff and Thomas Geismar. "Hand Tools USA" (1966), designed by George Nelson and Company, was an exhibition of machines, power tools, and other devices used in factories, on farms, in other workplaces, in the home, and in recreation. "Industrial Design USA" (1967), also designed by George Nelson and Company, included a broad range of American products, such as Teflon-coated frying pans, paper dresses, television sets, refrigerators, sailboats, and automobiles. Each product area was represented by both old and new examples, showing how industrial design and technological advances had made functional, handsome products available to average people. A film depicted the daily lives of Americans. This exhibition, which traveled to Moscow, Leningrad, and Kiev (and later to Brasov, Romania), was accompanied by professional designers who lectured, conducted seminars, and answered the questions of visitors. The visitors (in Moscow, some 10,000 per day) came away with a handsome picture book containing photos of the products and of scenes of the United States and an essay about American life.

The pioneering multi-screen projection technique developed by Charles and Ray Eames for an exhibition in the USSR in 1959 was particularly effective in crowding the rich American lifestyle and environment into a 12-minute show. *Credit:* Industrial Design *(April 1959).*

One of the cluster of umbrella-like forms at the U.S. exhibition was devoted to photographs of major American architecture. All the photographs had been taken from eye level, in order to give visitors the illusion of seeing them in person. *Credit:* Industrial Design *(September 1959). Photograph by Robert Lautman.*

# ПРОМЫШЛЕННАЯ ЭСТЕТИКА США

The symbol for "Industrial Design, U.S.A.," designed by George Nelson and Company for the U.S. Information Agency. Credit: George Nelson and Company.

A visitor to the exhibition "Industrial Design, U.S.A." contemplates old and new versions of American household appliances. Credit: Product Engineering (May 22, 1967).

In a way, the real "Olympics" of industrial design were neither the Triennales (where the emphasis was on product aesthetics) nor the international trade shows and cultural exchanges (where political posturing and persuasion were the goals). Rather, they were to be found in the competitions between companies seeking to score in alien markets at the same time as they tried to protect their own goals at home. They were also to be found in the increasing professional forays of designers into one another's territory.

The European Economic Community established a single market where before there had been many independent smaller national markets whose variety and volume had precluded the need for industrial design service, at least on the American model of the profession. In short order, more than 1,500 American companies had established European offices, bringing industrial designers with them. By 1962, sixteen American design firms had opened satellite offices in Europe. Raymond Loewy's Paris office, with a staff of more than forty, provided graphic-design and product-design services to European companies; some of the other satellite offices had only a single employee, who was there to provide liaison between American designers and European clients.

Despite the fact that the European scale of compensation was not as high as that in the United States, American designers liked the prestige attached to such foreign service and were not averse to subsidizing it in return for the entry it provided into Europe. A number of Americans took leave from their own employers in the United States to gain experience abroad in anticipation that the flow of products across national borders would continue to increase, thus adding to their own value in the marketplace. Some European companies established offices in the United States in order to adjust their products to appeal to American consumers, employing American designers on occasion to help them.

Foreign and American designers had much to learn from one another. Europeans generally manufactured products in smaller quantities to serve a more homogeneous national market. Their products were developed with less dependence upon marketing and consumer studies, with smaller production volumes that could be achieved with simpler tooling and higher labor costs. American products, on the other hand, had to appeal to a diverse consumer base; therefore, they were more dependent upon marketing analysis and promotional planning and on high-volume production, which demanded more complex tooling and lower labor costs. As international competition increased, industries and their designers shifted to global goals and values, with both manufacturing and marketing moving from one part of the world to another as opportunity beckoned.

# The Marketplace

## Design and the Consumer

*The urgency of wants does not diminish appreciably as more of them are satisfied. . . . Wants originate in the personality of the consumer.*

John Kenneth Galbraith, 1958 (16, 143)

During the 1930s, industrial designers, in collaboration with marketing experts, had developed a methodology for attracting attention and holding it long enough to make a sale. At one level it involved door-to-door salesmen (in some cases including designers) who brought the product to the home of the consumer and flattered her with attention and the promise of a product that would make domestic chores endurable if not pleasant. One designer, Lurelle Guild, recalls driving a truck full of competing refrigerators along neighborhood streets inviting curious residents to tell him which one they preferred and why. Industrial designers such as Guild did not see themselves as directors of public taste and as guides to the world of tomorrow; they saw themselves as following the public rather than leading it.

Harold Van Doren placed his faith in market surveys and other marketing techniques as means of determining consumer preferences and needs and of pre-testing public response. During World War II Van Doren's Philadelphia office tested models made up from designs for new clocks against competitors and a variety of alternative shapes by surveying consumers in a major department store in Philadelphia and in New York's Central Park.

Market surveys, competitions, and other marketing-oriented projects that were based on public participation had several effects. First of all, they flattered consumers by asking for their opinions. Moreover, such surveys had obvious public-relations value—they caught the public's eye, and they fixed the company's name in the public's mind. They also attracted attention to the store and provided material for newspaper and magazine articles.

The design community was generally divided on the merit and the reliability of surveys. George Nelson believed that they had a "degenerating influence on design" because they discouraged innovation. Laszlo Moholy-Nagy declared that the "so-called market survey and consumer study" was "mainly an unnecessary evil, mainly an excuse for the negative design" (228). Those on this side of the argument were convinced that surveys were used by both designers and their clients as a method of avoiding personal responsibility for a product by shifting that obligation to the consumer.

Designers who advocated consumer surveys took the position that they did not have the right to impose their aesthetic judgment on the consumer. They supported an approach to design based on surveys that claimed to have made a practical science out of the art of marketing. Harold Van Doren called industrial design "a science of precasting mass-produced articles, machines, and equipment into forms which will ensure acceptance before expensive capital investment has been made" (149).

Ernest Dichter, who was in many ways the high priest of psychoanalytical marketing, preached that the mass media had provided the means by which people could be reached with cues that "could bring about changes in human response and behavior." In his book *The Strategy of Desire* he recognized that some people considered "any kind of interference with human nature wrong and immoral" and objected to the goals for which persuasive techniques were used (8, 4).

It was claimed that the designer had much to gain from becoming a scholar of the sociological and behavioral characteristics of the public. He thus became aware of the cultural ladder that was climbed by people on one side and descended by their products on the other. It was pointed out that products began as curios, then were elevated to luxuries for the few, then became necessities for everyone.

The layering of products by price and features, known in marketing as the "line," took into account the fact that some people can and will pay more to get a new product whereas others will wait until it comes within their financial reach. An automobile that was sold for a higher price to its first owner was expected to reach its fifth owner at a price no higher than one-fourth the original price. Each level extended the life of the product, thus helping support the purchase of the level above it. This same ladder principle could be applied just as readily to clothing, furnishings, accessories, appliances, and other manufactured products.

There was, however, a negative side to the "practical science" of basing design decisions on research. If studies were directed toward giving the public what it wanted without judgment or empathy on the part of the designer or his client, they might be accused of having pandered to public cupidity with no regard for its well-being. In the end, the professional designer was expected to be aware of the impact of his designs and the degree to which they protected or threatened public psychological as well as physical well-being. Style was singled out as a negative element in product design without an acknowledgment that it was the inevitable component of the personal and social environment. What was reprehensible was "*styling*"—endowing a product with superficial and misleading forms and details that abused the consumer's faith.

Industrial designers, identified generally as wizards of change, were expected to sustain public demand by means of product innovation and attractiveness. The fact that postwar production had not caught up with demand did not dim the interest of manufacturers in preparing for the scramble for consumers that lay ahead. Some designers were pleased to be identified as agents of the marketing side of the manufacturing equation. "There is only one reason for hiring an industrial designer," advised J. Gordon Lippincott, "and that is to increase the sales of a product." (22, 19)

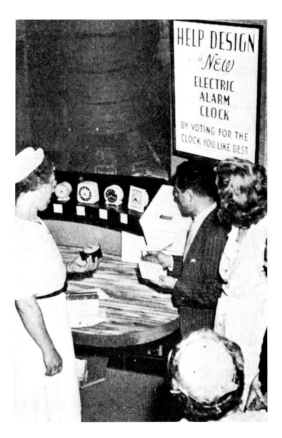

Harold Van Doren preferred on-the-spot surveys as a means of gauging the public's design preferences. The quasi-scientific conditions under which they were conducted relieved the designer and the manufacturer of concern about the success or failure of a product. Credit: (41, 275).

Edgar Kaufmann, Jr., director of the Department of Industrial Design at the Museum of Modern Art, recognized that although designers had become stars, their appeal to businessmen was based primarily on their ability to increase sales. Despite the fact that Kaufmann tagged sales as being only episodes in the life of products, they were the fulcrum across which action balanced. It was expected that the designer would rise above the product to consider the climate in which the product would be sold. Moreover, he carried part of the burden of contributing to a favorable impression of his client company in its respective market. In the postwar years this became as much of an obligation for the designer as the design and development of the product.

The practice of industrial design in the United States was changing. The profession that had been established in the 1930s by talented artist-designers was now falling under the control of marketing men who saw design primarily as a means of ensuring profits in an increasingly competitive market. The package was becoming as important as the product. In fact, products were often marketed in sealed cartons, with the consumer being preconditioned by print and television advertising to respond to the package.

Some designers, corporate and consultant, were moving up the management ladder to positions where the appearance, the performance, and the dependability of the product were only part of a broad spectrum of concerns that included price planning, programming, line control, and market analysis. Product planning had been defined as a discipline at General Electric earlier in the 1940s, and by the end of that decade other major corporations had given it a major role. The actual product was being reduced to a "price point." Richard Latham, once associated with Raymond Loewy but now a planning consultant to General Electric, was typical of those who crossed the line. "Most designers today," he was quoted, "concentrate on styling, merchandising, selling. These are the tail of the dog; the body is planning." (100)

Some designers responded to the changing focus of design by striking out on their own into the wilderness of market research and motivation. J. Gordon Lippincott and Walter Margulies organized the Market Research Institute, which published a house journal, *Design Sense,* that provided information on consumer buying and which promised to use "new scientific wizardry" to "[give] manufacturers, faced with the terrifying unknowns of impulse buying, the confidence to make a move when nobody really knows which way to go" (74). Dave Chapman's well-respected industrial design firm established a separate organization—Design Research, Inc.—in order to analyze factors affecting buyer motivation for the benefit of companies facing the need to invest in new or expanded plant facilities.

The unique character of the independent designer in the United States was in danger of being transformed into an impersonal abstraction. Showmen like Brooks Stevens, H. Creston Doner, and Raymond Loewy, down-to-earth designers like Carl Sundberg and Montgomery Ferar, European sophisticates like Peter Müller-Munk, and artist-scholars like Alexander Kostellow seemed about to be replaced by organization men, operational diagrams, statistical analyses, and other substitutes for human instinct and concern. So-called scientific planning posed a genuine threat to imagination, creativity, and a maturing aesthetic. When products began to lose their personality and designers their identity, design became a game that anyone could play. In 1949 Seymour Freedgood warned in the pages of *Fortune* that industrial design—only a generation earlier a hotbed of entrepreneurship—was in danger of becoming "just a part of corporate structure" (88).

## Trademarks and Corporate Images

*. . . a delicate matter that may be of great value but that is easily destroyed and therefore should be protected with corresponding care.*

Chief Justice Oliver Wendell Holmes, 1922 (250)

The patent laws of the United States encourage competition by offering a limited monopoly to inventors and designers for public disclosure of ideas or designs. The law anticipates that others will eventually push a new concept to higher levels of quality and utility, but it provides for penalties to those who infringe on a patent during the period (up to seventeen years) before it expires and the design enters the public domain.

A trademark protects the provider or manufacturer of a service or a product by guaranteeing his right to be identified with his work. Unlike a patent, a trademark can be renewed indefinitely at periodic intervals. Of course, the holder of a valuable trademark must remember to renew it. Chief Justice Oliver Wendell Holmes spoke of a trademark as "a delicate matter that may be of great value but that is easily destroyed and therefore should be protected with corresponding care" (250). In 1941, Justice Felix Frankfurter, speaking for the majority in a Supreme Court ruling on a case supporting the marketing value of a trademark, noted that

The protection of trade-marks is the law's recognition of the psychological function of symbols. If it is true that we live by symbols, it is no less true that we purchase goods by them. A trademark is a merchandising shortcut which induces a purchaser to select what he wants, or what he has been led to believe he wants. The owner of a mark exploits this human propensity by making every effort to impregnate the atmosphere of the product with the drawing power of a congenial symbol. Whatever the means employed, the end is the same—to convey through the mark, in the minds of potential customers, the desirability of the commodity upon which it appears. Once this is attained, the owner has something of value. (251)

The passage of the Lanham Act of 1946, an important step toward the clarification of the purpose of trademarks, was a response to questions raised by increasing competition among products and services in the marketplace. The dramatic shift from person-to-person selling to impersonal marketing through radio, television, and print media made it inevitable that things would have to sell themselves and that salesclerks would be transformed into cashiers. The Lanham Act acknowledged two traditional purposes of a trademark (to indicate the origin of the product and to ensure consistent quality by tying the product to the integrity and pride of its maker) and added a third purpose: to create demand for the product. National distribution of products, and advertisements in magazines, on radio, and particularly on television, made the trademark even more important than it had been earlier. However, at the same time as it served the manufacturer's interest, the trademark was also perceived by law as protecting the consumer by informing him of who was ultimately responsible for the product.

Trademarks often capture the temper and cultural spirit of their times. For example, marks conceived at the turn of the century tended to be cursive in character and bold or romantic. Marks conceived after World War I often incorporated the wreath of victory or its derivatives. In the 1920s, some trademarks included the zigzag of lightning to show that the company's products were electrified. The 1930s popularized the comet or teardrop shape. In the post–World War II era, the tension of the times and the globalization of industry and commerce did not encourage political symbolism. The United Nations symbol, conceived by Edward J. Stettinius, U.S. Secretary of State and chairman of the first meeting of the UN in San Francisco, was an elemental pictogram that seemed to take the heat out of national identification.

Another inevitable extension of global communication was the development of symbols and pictographs for products entering world

Raymond Loewy's Coca-Cola dispenser was bold in form and easy to clean. Coca-Cola's cursive trademark was retained. Credit: (23, 134).

This trademark from the 1920s combined the laurel branches of victory with an old typeface in a well-proportioned bullseye focusing on the modern lower-case letter r. Credit: Rockwell International.

Trademarks with "lightning bolts" were fashionable in the 1920s, when electricity was being brought into homes across the country. The bold, rounded letter forms of this mark suggested power. Credit: Radio Corporation of America.

Edward Stettinius sketched the original concept for the symbol used at the first U.N. conference, in 1945. Credit: United Nations.

The international symbol of access for the handicapped, designed in 1968 by Susane Koefoed of the Scandinavian Students Association for Rehabilitation International, is now in use in more than seventy countries. Credit: Rehabilitation International.

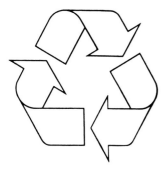

This symbol, designed in 1970 by student Gary Anderson of the University of Southern California, was chosen in a national competition sponsored by the Container Corporation of America to identify paperbound containers made of recycled materials. Credit: Container Corporation of America.

markets and for the convenience and safety of travelers. A most interesting development was the universal acceptance of public-service pictograms, such as those indicating access for the handicapped and recycling.

In the creation of trademarks for manufactured products entering international markets, there was less concern with expressing political ideology than with making a comprehensible statement about the quality of the product. Furthermore, this statement had to be made in a form that took into consideration the demands placed upon it by various applications and the nature of the media through which the product was to be promoted. It is no accident that the better marks arrived at forms that balanced positive against negative graphic elements so that shifts in scale, color, material, or process would not cause distortion. Marks had to be suitable for printed, cast, or stamped logotypes, for packages and signs, for buildings and delivery vehicles, for stationery, and for publications. They also showed up on neckties and draperies, on plaques and souvenirs, and on corporate flags. A trademark became a near-sacred symbol that brought members of an organization together to form an entity in the public eye.

In response to widespread interest in the total image of a company, a new design specialization emerged: corporate identity. Graphic designers, package designers, industrial designers, and advertising artists all found opportunities here. Their efforts ranged from quickly dashed-off freelance sketches to exhaustive field studies resulting in detailed, ponderous corporate identity manuals costing thousands of dollars.

To some in the corporate world, identity programs were a graphic prison that inhibited further growth. To others they represented liberation from vendors and suppliers who volunteered free design advice in return for patronage. In any case, the corporate identity programs resulted in a flowering of eloquent trademarks that were intelligently conceived to make a psychological statement about the

corporation (and, by association, about its products) that could be understood internationally while skirting ethnic and religious sensitivities and fostering a unique and consistent corporate character.

For all this, a trademark was, after all, only a little piece of graphic design—a simple visual device conceived to be as direct as possible, yet imbued with distinct meaning that would set it and its owners apart from competitors. it was the flag, the seal, the emblem of what John Kenneth Galbraith called the "new industrial state." Its goal was to hold its share of public good will in the area that it served.

During this period of dynamic growth, every company—new or old—scrambled to establish its position in markets that were of interest to it. Young corporations, encouraged by their wartime accomplishments, moved quickly to consolidate their public images. Older corporations faced the possibility of having to shed their prewar identities in order to keep up with the impudent young challengers.

An older corporation had to gauge the value of its old image against the presumed advantages of a new or refreshed one. General Electric elected to keep its familiar trademark (friendly, the company called it), which went back to the turn of the century. However, two of GE's closest competitors, the Radio Corporation of America and Westinghouse, saw less value in their electricity-based trademarks of the 1920s and decided to replace them.

The Columbia Broadcasting Company contracted with the architect-designer William Lescaze between 1934 and 1945 to design its buildings, interiors, equipment, and signs. The logotype that he designed in 1935 was in the then-fashionable International Style of geometric lettering favored by designers who were dependent upon drafting instruments. Still in use in 1948, it was not in keeping with the demands of the television screen for graphics that had high impact and were easily recognized and remembered. William Golden,

Saul Bass upgraded Bell Telephone's old illustrative mark to produce a powerful symbol that was universally applicable. Credit: Yasaburo Kuwayama, Trade Marks and Symbols, *volume 2 (Van Nostrand Reinhold, 1973)*.

The General Electric trademark was designed in the decorative style of the turn of the century. Credit: General Electric.

Consultants Lippincott and Margulies recommended that RCA abandon all connotations of radio. This concept, selected from three presentations, was applied to 12,000 products and services. Credit: Radio Corporation of America.

Westinghouse's trademark was designed in 1960 by Paul Rand in collaboration with Eliot Noyes, consultant design director of the company. Derived from an earlier mark, it suggests printed circuitry and electronic devices. Credit: (18, 72).

art director of CBS, had developed a unique video device in 1955 that used a camera shutter for the pupil of an eye filmed against a cloud background. Out of this evolved the trademark that, despite the fact that it did not include the company's name, became the most effective mark in the television industry.

Industries and their designers who were searching for a new mark often found it in the form of a product or process that was unique to each. Other competing companies based on the same product often used alternative forms for their trademark. In other industries, small producers scattered around the world gathered global strength by supplementing their own trademarks with common symbols such as the Woolmark, designed in 1964 by Francesco Saroglio of Milan for the International Wool Secretariat. The Woolmark, a handsome abstraction of a skein of wool, was pushed into the world's consciousness at a shared cost of some $150 million. The 700 American companies belonging to the IWS found it an effective banner in their battle against manufacturers of synthetic yarns. Later, Walter Landor Associates developed a similar mark for the cotton industry. It, too, is an effective graphic device; however, its dependence on the English word *cotton* precludes its use in non-English-speaking countries.

In the 1950s, realizing that steel was not perceived as modern or associated with good styling, the U.S. Steel company assigned the firm of Lippicott and Margulies the task of modifying its trademark to a configuration that would change that image. Lippincott and Margulies also developed the Steelmark, which was recommended for adoption in the industry by the American Iron and Steel Institute.

Until conglomerates and multinational financial organizations invaded the precincts of material- and product-oriented companies, each company concentrated on its own identity and products, and consumers saw the trademark as a symbol of responsibility. How-

*William Golden's CBS trademark has become virtually a generic symbol for television. In its abstraction of the human eye and the camera lens, it captures the visual essence of the medium. Credit: Columbia Broadcasting System.*

*William Lescaze's old trademark for CBS, designed in 1935, was still in use in 1948 when Lescaze designed his first mobile broadcasting unit for CBS. Credit: William Lescaze papers, George Arents Research Library, Syracuse University.*

The Rohm and Haas company contracted with Lester Beall in the mid 1960s to develop a new mark that would express the company's interest in chemistry and its dynamic spirit. This strong abstraction of a flask combined with an arrow does the job well. Credit: (43, 146).

## CELANESE

One of the few successful contemporary trademarks that was not based on geometry was the Celanese company's mark, designed by Saul Bass in 1965. Credit: (18, 102).

Lester Beall's corporate symbol for the International Paper Company, designed in 1960, retained some of the characteristics of its predecessor. As with other good modern marks, its boldness and uniformity assured reproduction by any method without loss of recognition. Credit: (43, 149).

The trademark of the Weyerhauser company was designed in 1958 by Lippincott and Margulies. Credit: Industrial Design (December 1959).

The "Woolmark,"
launched in 1964, is one
of the masterpieces of
contemporary graphic
design. Credit: Packaging
Design (November-
December 1968).

The National Cotton Coun-
cil contracted with Walter
Landor and Associates in
1973 to develop a trade-
mark; this was the result.
Credit: Walter Landor and
Associates.

Lippincott and Margulies
designed the "Steelmark"
in 1958 for the U.S. Steel
company. In 1960 the
American Iron and Steel
Institute was authorized to
use the mark for industry-
wide promotion. Credit:
Iron and Steel Institute.

ever, as large as well as small corporations began to dissolve into one another, their trademarks were themselves traded and sometimes trampled in the process. Though many corporations did not survive, many products did. If a product met a particular need and had a clear and unique identity and a brand name protected by the trademark law, it would develop a loyal body of followers who would use it no matter which corporate giant owned it. Names such as Jello, Ritz Crackers, Cheerios, Wheaties, Gleem, Polident, Kleenex, Pampers, Chris-Craft, Piper, and Jeep developed value that could be marketed like any other commodity. The only danger to such a popular trade name was that it would become generic.

It was estimated in the mid 1960s that the average shopper was exposed to as many as 3,000 trade names in a single day. Ralph Caplan observed in 1958 that a supermarket was "a giant cafeteria at which, for a price, the consumer may help herself to as many as 15,000 items, brands, and sizes" (103). It was also estimated that a person could retain only some 10,000 such identities in memory. The assumption, therefore, in the marketing and advertising community, was that a new name or mark could be added to the consumer's memory only by market saturation and persistence sufficient to knock off a weaker identifier. It was also presumed that, in a free economy, between 2,000 and 4,000 new products would enter the market in the course of a year, of which less than 1 percent would survive.

# The Package and the Public

*Here was a new way of democratizing objects,*
*of leveling and assimilating their appearance*
*. . . a good product was not enough: success*
*required a package that would stimulate*
*desire.*

Daniel Boorstin, 1974 (4, 434 and 436)


Packages, boxes, and bottles were once
created as special containers for jewelry,
perfume, sweets, liquor, tobacco, and other
products considered to have special value or
meaning. They were often conceived to be
treasured after the contents were gone and
perhaps put to some secondary personal use.
On occasion they matched and even exceeded
the quality of their original contents. However,
even though some special containers were
made for extraordinary giving, they had little,
if anything, to do with modern packaging as
art for its own sake. If modern packaging had
aesthetic value, it was the residue of meeting
other objectives first.

A number of factors contributed to the revolution in packaging that occurred in the United
States in the 1920s. Perhaps the most important was the dramatic increase in mass
advertising made possible by radio, color
illustrations in nationally distributed magazines, and the establishment of major news
agencies, all of which helped bring Americans
into a homogeneous common market. In addition, a dependable network of railways and
roads made it possible to bring a new product
to market while the desire created by its announcement still glowed.

At the marketing level there was a dramatic
shift from dependence on neighborhood
groceries, meat markets, bakeries, and drug
stores to chain stores, and then, in the 1930s,
to supermarkets. The modern package came
at its task from a different direction. It had of
necessity to properly transport and protect its
contents, as it had in the past. But now it was
conceived primarily as an instrument for marketing the product.

A younger designer, Ben Nash, approached
the challenge of the marketing environment
from this new direction. Rather than exclusiv-
ity at high cost, he looked for broader appeal
at a lower cost. Nash promoted the use of
research into the marketing environment and
into consumers' buying habits to transform
the package from an artistic expression into a
means of communication. He did more than
any other designer of his time to turn package
design into a profession by fusing technological and merchandising practicalities with
aesthetic and psychological values. Nash,
respected by his colleagues and his clients as
the "voice" of the profession, insisted that the
first principle of package design was to
approach the assignment from the consumer's
point of view rather than the manufacturer's.
On the subject of food packaging, he wrote
that "the chief consideration was not of the
various food products that had to be packaged, distributed, and sold, but of the family
dinner table, the pantry and kitchen, and particularly of women's shopping habits" (31,
170). By 1935 Nash had an office in New York
with a staff of thirty designers. The office was
equipped with a full-scale simulation of part of
a supermarket so that designers could test
their ideas.

It was also in 1935 that Walter Paepke established a design department at the Container
Corporation of America, with Egbert Jacobsen as manager. Jacobsen set up six design
studios, one of them a testing room in which a
package's message value and its impact on
consumers could be evaluated. Over a period
of time, this facility turned package design
into a near-science in an attempt to meet the
needs of those who had to be assured of the
market appeal of a package before investing
in its development and distribution. Albert
Kner, the director of CCA's Design Laboratory, established a museum of historical packages. Walter Granville, another key member of
the CCA department of design, developed a
Color Harmony Manual that proved to be
invaluable to graphics and product designers.
CCA, with Herbert Bayer as its major design
consultant, employed over 100 first-rate
designers and artists over the years. Because

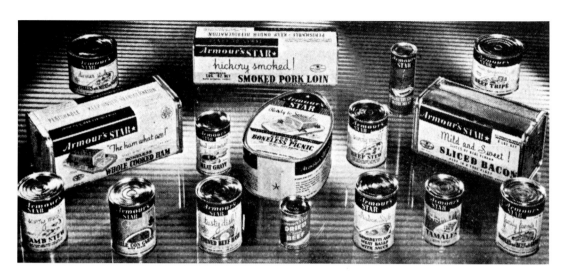

One of Ben Nash's earliest major assignments was to organize the products of the Armour company into a cohesive family while also giving each product a "self-selling individualism." Credit: (31, 170).

Raymond Loewy's office was contracted in 1944 to upgrade Armour's packaging program for postwar markets. This was done by increasing the emphasis on the company trademark. Loewy saved the company the cost of redesigning by reducing the number of colors used. Credit: (39, 138).

*Albert Kner established a Printing and Packaging Museum for CCA as a useful supplement to the Design Laboratory's service. Credit:* Packaging Design.

*This "Creative Marketing Center" was developed by Nathan Becker with Fred Leigh and Eugene Klumb of Becker and Becker Associates for the International Paper Company. Credit: (216).*

of Walter Paepke's commitment to the arts, the company's designers and consultants were given an opportunity to achieve a high level of aesthetic quality.

By 1950 package design was becoming indispensable to the American economy. Major companies had established design development and testing facilities. In addition, independent package-design offices had been opened across the United States, including those of Walter Landor (in San Francisco), Robert Sidney Dickens (in Chicago), and Lippincott and Margulies (in New York). Other design offices, such as that of Becker and Becker (in New York), assisted clients in setting up their own design departments. And advertising agencies and industrial design offices also included package design among their specialties, some of them with facilities for testing the relative effectiveness of packaging concepts. Lippincott and Margulies established a Package Research Institute, with Myron Helfgott as director.

In earlier days, faith in the product had been based upon eye contact and hand-to-hand exchange between the seller and the buyer. Then, during a transitional period, the package had become a surrogate for the manufacturer—his portrait, and/or a picture of his factory, was printed on the package, along with a list of awards and honors bestowed on the product in competitions and expositions and testimonials from satisfied customers.

Now, in the postwar era, the appearance of a package was expected to attract the prospective purchaser's attention and hold it long enough to convey a message that had an appropriate psychological appeal. Many a product was given a name intended to trigger the emotion that the manufacturer wanted the consumer to associate with the product. Other packages carried graphic designs that suggested that royalty, bold adventurers, or romantic maidens used the product. Testimonials and other space-consuming copy became obsolete as a new generation, raised on media promotion, learned to read forms

and graphic symbols as its ancient forebears had read pictograms. Free exploration of shapes introduced the language of form, whereby containers could be shaped for meaning and aesthetic quality. A family of related products could be packaged in a way that emphasized their corporate source at the same time as they announced and promoted the product within. Other products and their packages could be combined into an entity that could be displayed effectively at its point of use.

Walter Margulies became disturbed in 1952 that the packaging industry was awarding prizes for the best packages without giving credit to the designers involved. His protests to the industry representatives had been in vain. "It then occurred to me," he writes, "that I should organize a group to fight for its rights of recognition in the unique area of professional contributions that package designers made in the American economy." (237) Margulies wrote to some 200 people who were listed in the New York telephone book as being involved in package design, plus a few others outside the city that he knew to be package designers. Only four persons responded: Egmont Arens, James Nash, Frank Gianninoto, and Gerald Stahl. After several preliminary discussions among the five men, the Package Designers Council was founded in 1952. Nash was elected president. The other members were Alan Berni, Karl Fink, Robert Goldberg, Robert Gruen, Benjamin Koodin, Harry Lapow, and Robert Neubauer. The stated purpose of the PDC was to give independent professional package designers a sense of cohesion and common purpose. Like other design groups, the PDC vowed to establish and maintain professional standards of ethics and performance, to emphasize moral and cultural responsibility, and to augment the prestige and dignity of the profession of design. The requirements for joining included the submission of photographs of at least six different package designs that had been put into production and on the market. In addition, the candidate had

In 1953 a Japanese firm hired Raymond Loewy Associates to design the Peace cigarette package. After the new package was put on the market, sales multiplied fourfold. Credit: (38, 82).

These cigarette packages, one by Frank Gianninoto and Associates (left) and the other by Jay Doblin with Leedia Vitale and Ray Grove, suggest health and freshness. Credit: Industrial Design (December 1959).

This Joy detergent bottle, designed by Deskey Associates in 1950, had a non-slip surface. The carton tried to create an impression of greater size. The name was an attempt to dispel thoughts of drudgery. Credit: (37, 147).

This carton, designed by Deskey Associates in 1951 for Procter and Gamble, sought psychological advantage with a clear, fresh look and a bold, multicolored design. The three shapes on the front were intended to suggest clothes blowing in the wind. Credit: (37, 147).

This photo appeared in Design Sense, *Lippincott and Margulies's house publication. "Viewed together,"* it was said, *"[these packages] emerge as a concrete symbol of the U.S. marketing revolution which is summed up in the single phrase, 'self-service.' " Credit: (229, 2–3).*

The packaging of Yardley's line of men's toiletries was designed by Donald Deskey Associates in 1964 to suggest a beribboned athlete or member of the royalty. *Credit:* Design USA *(catalog, London, 1965).*

This packaging, by Francis Blod Associates, also suggested ribbons. *Credit:* Design USA *(catalog, London, 1965).*

This bottle, designed in 1962 by Walter Landor Associates, suggests by its form a bubble of fresh water. Its "tiltability" adds functional interest. The objective was to get into a market where there was no product difference. Credit: (43, 170).

Experiments in transparent containers by Pratt Institute students. Credit: Pratt Institute.

to pay $100 and affirm that he had at least three clients or was employed as a package designer by a company.

In the absence of full academic programs in package design, the majority of those who were practicing package design had come into the field from other areas. Walter Margulies and Walter Landor had been educated as architects, Robert Sidney Dickens and Will Burtin in advertising design and typography, and Saul Bass and Paul Rand in the fine arts.

In 1959 the Package Designers Council organized a seminar, involving PDC members and members of the Industrial Design Educators Association, at which the existing package-design courses and the lack of cooperation between the profession and the academic world were reviewed. Frank Gianninoto expressed doubt about the prospects of any effective curriculum in the field. He believed that the mix of disciplines demanded of the package designer made an effective academic program difficult, if not impossible, to organize. Seventy percent of the time in practice, he stated, was devoted to determining the what, where, when, and why of the package; 15 percent was spent at the drawing board, giving form to ideas; and 15 percent was spent selling good ideas to management.

Much of Gianninoto's concern was justified; package design continued to be taught primarily as an art rather than as a marketing discipline. E. A. Adams, head of the Art Center School, took a pragmatic position. "We want to know," he stated, "how to teach the professional youngster the responsibility he has, after leaving school, to make money for his firm." (108) Joseph Carriero, president of the IDEA, said that the role of education was to educate the students, who then had to become professionals and leaders on their own. Other educators present also resisted the proposition that the first obligation of education was to prepare students for employment, insisting that this had to be balanced with efforts to make them aware of their own abilities and of their obligations to the quality of the man-made environment. Leo Lionni, art

*The bottles for the mouthwash Micrin, designed in 1962 by Donald Deskey Associates, identify closely with traditional apothecary jars. Credit: Design USA (catalog, London, 1965).*

These containers, designed by Francis Blod Design Associates in 1968 for products directed at girls and young women, were distinctly feminine in form. Credit: (43, 171).

Lester Beall's packages designed in the mid 1960s for the Stanley tool company were informative, attractive, and masculine in character. Credit: (43, 161).

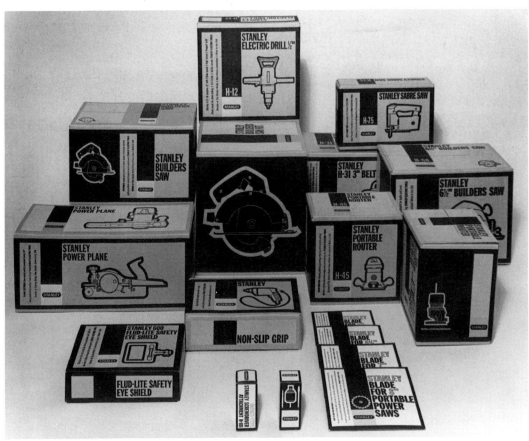

editor of *Fortune* magazine, called package design an unimaginative system that had not found a way to be successful and civilized at the same time, and complained that packages conceived only as selling devices had invaded his home with the vulgarization of the marketplace. Walter Landor searched for an accommodation by criticizing "overpackaging" and suggesting that packages that the consumer could reuse in other ways might be more socially responsible.

At a 1968 PDC seminar on package-design practice and design education, it was still evident that the designers and the educators were nowhere near an agreement. David Osler, Vice-President of Packaging, Graphics, and Corporate Identity at the office of Raymond Loewy and William Snaith, suggested that package designers might someday be forced to use the tools of "scientific" research. He wondered whether "optical measuring devices such as the Tachistoscope, the Ocular and Pupil Dilation cameras, etc." were not all "primitive efforts to bring some measure of scientific validation to a visual phenomenon which, although artistic in concept, is commercially oriented" (179).

Francis Blod, a past president of the PDC and since 1966 the director of a unique graduate program in package design at Pratt Institute, expressed the educators' frustration: "Frankly, we must admit that we do not know what packaging education is or should be." (177) Blod was concerned about the fact that the field needed a continuing supply of young talent but did not seem to know what to do with it. The heart of the conflict was the fact that, whereas the profession needed only thoroughly trained employees, the educators were trying to instill a higher level of responsibility. Irv Koons, the moderator, wrapped up the seminar in a statement that continues to reflect the complexity of the package-design field:

Packaging has become an important element in the development of society and civilization. Package design has become one of the most important folk arts of all time. Our society sees

*Lester Beall and Clifford Stead, Jr., designed the "House of Herbs" in 1964. The exotic-looking containers were sold individually or in sets of six with a plastic wall rack. Credit: (43, 168).*

and handles more of this art form and is more dependent on it than any other visual tool. . . . Because of the sociological involvements of packaging, the potential designer cannot be trained for technique alone. He should also have a good background in the humanities, culture, history, and sociology if he is to relate to the world around him. . . . He must know something about marketing, merchandising, advertising, and business practices. His designs must sell, inform, and please. (178)

Despite the broader vision of Irv Koons and a few of his colleagues who hoped that designers would be educated to a higher level of social and cultural awareness, most package designers saw themselves as agents of their clients rather than as servants of the public. Their job was to use every available means, artistic or quasi-scientific, to sell their clients' products. They were locked in a struggle for survival in which the consumer was often the victim rather than the beneficiary. The size, shape, and graphics of a package were designed to promise more than the competitors' products. In the process, the facts were stretched to the point that consumers began to lose faith in the messages that were being shot at them from all sides in the battle of the marketplace. And, in that no-man's-land where clerks had disappeared and managers were often safe in their own dugouts, someone had to come to the consumers' rescue.

The champion of the consumers turned out to be Senator Philip A. Hart, who had been crusading for five years in Congress for legislation that would ban deceptive illustrations of the contents of a package and that would set performance standards and serving sizes. Finally, the crescendo of public dissatisfaction became loud enough to be heard in Congress. Hart's bill was passed and signed by President Lyndon Johnson in 1966 as the Fair Packaging and Labeling Act. The government's Declaration of Policy for the new law stated that "informed consumers are essential to the fair and efficient functioning of a free market economy," and that "packages and their contents should enable consumers to obtain accurate information as to the quantity of the contents and should facilitate value comparisons" (70).

The Fair Packaging and Labeling Act was a qualified success. Although it made net-quantity disclosure mandatory, set controls over type sizes and placement, established standard volume and weight indications, and banned such words as *giant* and *jumbo,* it did not establish unit pricing (which allows direct price comparisons irrespective of the size and shape of the package). Moreover, it made the Secretary of Commerce the administrator of the law, despite the fact that the Department of Commerce generally represented the interests of business rather than those of consumers. The packaging industry claimed that the costs of compliance would have to be passed on to the consumer but made no move to acknowledge the conditions that had made the bill necessary.

In the spring of 1967, before the Fair Packaging and Labeling Act went into effect, the Package Designers Council was invited to demonstrate its expertise to the government. After several preliminary sessions, a special meeting was held in April at the Food and Drug Administration's headquarters. PDC representatives Sidney Dickens, Roy Parcels, and Karl Fink showed sample packages to illustrate what designers considered to be workable solutions that were consistent with the new regulations. As a result, the final regulations as published in the *Federal Register* followed the PDC's recommendations to a great degree.

Manufacturers would now turn to other ways of capturing the consumers' attention and inducing them to purchase one product rather than another. Designers could now begin to give more attention to making products more convenient to use and more adaptable to the home environment. In some cases the marketing wrapper was designed to be removable, so that a package could shout its virtues in the market and then display them discreetly in the home. For the package designer this was good business—he now had two jobs to do for one package.

There was a general feeling among packaging designers that, although the idea of truth in packaging had interfered with design freedom, it had provided an ethical base for the package-design profession. Designers, faced with the higher challenge of making a product attractive on its own merits rather than on the basis of promises it could not fulfill, found a receptive market for ideas that were more inventive, introduced new materials and technology, and offered consumers a broader choice of packages that were more reflective of their needs as well as more attractive.

The Fair Packaging and Labeling Act did not make it any easier for the consumer to compare prices between competing products. Attempts were made to pass a federal law that would set the cost of products at fixed units to be displayed by merchandisers, but in the end the matter was left to individual states. In New York, for example, a truth-in-pricing law was passed (effective March 31, 1971) as part of Administrative Code Title 20, Chapter 5, Section 707. Later unit pricing was made part of New York State Law Article 17, Section 214-H, to become effective January 18, 1978. Now, irrespective of the size or shape of the package or container, the cost per established volume or weight unit was to be posted on the shelf containing the product. For the first time the shopper could easily compare products on a price-per-amount basis irrespective of the appeal projected by the package or the advertising.

Now another problem began to face the package designers: Their handsomely persuasive packages were polluting the environment, it was said. Forty percent of America's waste products consisted of packaging materials. "What hurts," Walter Landor wrote in *Packaging Design* in 1969, ". . . is that packaging shows; apparently, Americans judge the entire disposal problem by the number of cans and bottles they see along the highways, and by the packages stuffing garbage cans coast to coast." To Walter Margulies it was "a fast game of musical chairs as the material sup-

pliers compete for new markets; as food technology changes; as the public becomes more enamored with packaging convenience; and as affluence influences a throw-away mode of living" (180). The real problem had economic, cultural, and psychological aspects that were as important as the technological ones. Margulies proposed that any company that marketed packaged products had a responsibility to consider the waste that resulted. He suggested that it was the responsibility of the designer to educate his clients on this subject.

In a 1971 forum ("Enterprise—How Free?") sponsored by the PDC, William Capitman, a sociologist and the president of the Center for Research in Marketing, said: "Designers today are at a point of making a series of choices. You can continue to design packaging until the public and the government begin to attack you directly as being instrumental in the destruction of the environment along with your corporate clients, or you can direct yourselves both as a professional group and as individuals to a search for standards and ways to make every new package an improvement on the visual, ecological, and social environment." (238) Capitman suggested that the PDC could, as other organizations had done, organize for the purpose of making the man-made environment more humane. Another speaker stated that the PDC should develop its own seal of approval to honor ecologically "good" packages. The seminar also acknowledged that package design was no longer the private domain of its designers or manufacturers but that it had a public to answer to. In a follow-up to this seminar, William Gunn, president of the PDC, issued a call to arms to his colleagues: "As you all know, 'packaging' is under attack. Whether it's called excess packaging, or consumerism, or if it's labeling untruths, legislative taxation and regulations, or excessive materials, or non-biodegradables, . . . those involved in packaging are directly affected by these issues. . . . Now, more than ever, the PDC . . . must make its convictions and professionalism known to industry and the public." (197)

## Sound and Image

*The medium is the massage. . . . Any understanding of social and cultural change is impossible without a knowledge of the way media work as environments.*

Marshall McLuhan, 1967 (28)

The variety and quality of products included in the annual Design Reviews of *Interiors* and its subsequent 1954 spinoff publication, *Industrial Design,* had an important impact on the design community. The products illustrated represented the consensus of the editors based on the appearance and promise of products determined largely from photographs and statements submitted by designers on their own behalf. Even so, for most designers, having work published in the magazine was taken as recognition and at least a touch of fame—however fleeting.

The mix of products submitted to the review also offered a barometer of the area in which design activity was concentrated at the moment. For example, early reviews contained a good percentage of radios and other audio equipment. The war had transformed the radio, a prewar luxury, into a necessity. By 1947 there were radios in 93 percent of American homes. The editors of *Interiors* found some hope for better design in the observation that radio cabinets were "beginning to reflect the glimmer of recognition by radio manufacturers and the public that radios should be permitted their own identity, and not be disguised to look like something else" (129).

There were at least three discernible classes of radios. At one end of the scale were the large floor models (often combined with record players), which insisted on being treated as important pieces of furniture. At the other end were the small plastic boxes that were at home in the kitchen, in a bedroom, or on a patio. Then there were radios for "serious" listeners. The Hallicrafters radio represented the pinnacle of advanced technology and dependable performance. The company had acquired a reputation during the war for

communications equipment that it provided for the armed forces. For a time it was possible for an enthusiast to purchase a chrome-plated Hallicrafters chassis and build a cabinet for it. Then the company asked Raymond Loewy Associates to modify the military version for the civilian market. Richard Latham (1920–), as director of the assignment for Loewy, rearranged the controls (except for the large, circular six-band dial) and fitted it with a metal bezel and a more attractive case. This radio came closer than other radios on the market to suggesting that a radio should be accepted frankly as a technological treasure.

Few inventions in this century had as much of an impact on the man-made environment as the transistor (invented in 1947 by William Shockley, Walter Brattain, and John Bardeen), which made microelectronics possible. In one sweeping move, the machine age—a world of mechanical devices, wires, and vacuum tubes—was changed into one of miniaturization and microscopic printed circuits. Roomfuls of hot, humming cabinets were reduced to cool, quiet table-top consoles. Electronics made it possible for human engineering, whose task had once been to fit people to products, now to fit products to people.

The introduction of the transistor brought new life to the radio industry. Ursula McHugh wrote in 1959 that radios were "perhaps at that time of life when, past the freshness and invention of youth, they have not yet arrived at the stability and poise of objects that know why they are and what they are for" (107). With its traditional place increasingly taken over by the television, the radio was obliged to search for another place or places in the man-made environment.

In December 1954, the first miniature transistor radio appeared in the marketplace. Manufactured by I.D.E.A. (Regency Electronics) of Indianapolis using silicon transistors produced by Texas Instruments, the TR-1 radio could fit comfortably into a hand or a pocket. Twice as expensive at $50.00 as available table radios, it would play for more than 100 hours on one small flashlight battery. The industrial designers Painter, Teague and Petertil had done their best to make the Regency radio look like a precious instrument. Within weeks, many of the major manufacturers, who had been aware of the transistor but who had been guarding their investments in existing technology, jumped into the game with their own small transistor radios.

The introduction of the transistor radio awakened the entire radio industry, which began to produce a wide variety of radios for different purposes and rooms. There were radios for travelers, for sportsmen, for children, and for teenagers, with appropriate features and styling. There were radios for the kitchen, and clock radios for the bedroom. And there were "serious"-looking FM receivers for those who preferred classical music.

Progress in the evolution of products is not always the result of competitors' vying with one another for shares of the market. In many cases it is stimulated by individuals who have a special interest and competence in a particular product area and who are unsatisfied with the quality or capabilities of the available products and perhaps even suspicious that progress is being impeded by the manufacturers in order to increase their profits from existing manufactures. In the area of high-fidelity sound, those with knowledge about electronics found that they were able to put together their own sound systems by purchasing components (speakers, tuners, amplifiers, and turntables) "off the shelf" at the same discounted prices available to radio repairmen. Thus they avoided the extra expense and extravagance of conventional cabinetry and the promotion that went with it. It was considered a mark of status to stack an assembly of components on an open shelf as evidence that one was knowledgeable about "hi-fi" equipment and committed to "good music." The disavowal of commercial cabinetry in traditional styles in favor of showing off components (which persists in the "electronic" faces or control panels that are still popular on

audio equipment and other high-technology products) resulted in an emphasis on what a product was made of rather than on what it was or did. This conflict between meaning and substance presented a challenge to designers, who were (and still are) pressed to give "honest" forms to products.

Stereophonic sound had been in use since the 1930s in conjunction with Cinerama (a process that surrounded a movie audience with sound as well as images). It was not, however, until 1957 that Westrex, a subsidiary of the Western Electric company, demonstrated the first home "stereo" system. Public response was so dramatic that within a year stereo equipment had virtually taken over both the record industry and the audio-equipment industry. The audio industry grew from a $12 million industry in 1950 to a $250 million industry in 1958.

By the end of the 1950s, 78-rpm shellac records were being replaced by vinyl disks with playback speeds of 45 and 33⅓ rpm. At the same time, magnetic-tape recording appeared, first in the reel-to-reel format and then in the cassette format. The advent of tape opened up opportunities for the design of a new generation of audio and eventually audio-visual products. Every change in the technology of manufactured products offered new opportunities for designers to develop products that were more convenient for and attractive to consumers.

However, as audio technology became more exotic, the boxes in which components were packaged became increasingly standardized and dull. Most amplifiers and tuners were flat rectangular boxes measuring about 5 inches high and 15 inches wide and deep. The materials were for the most part either black metal or walnut (real or simulated). Control faces were normally satin-finished metal with tastefully distributed knobs. Dials were either circular or lineal, and legends were microscopic. There was usually a "picture frame" bezel around the control face. The only options left to the designer often were the locations of the manufacturer's name and the model number.

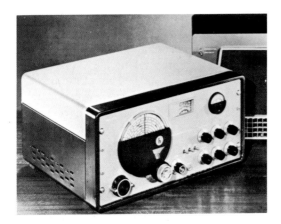

Texas Instruments marketed this tiny radio as a "giant step in electronic growth." Though Consumer Reports *questioned its sound quality, the TR-1 opened the door to miniaturization in consumer products. Credit: (216).*

This Bulova radio was designed by Jay Doblin to appeal to women. It was available in ebony, turquoise, or ivory plastic. Credit: (216).

Doblin's "man's model" of the Bulova transistor radio had a seal-brown leatherette case. This radio and the "woman's model" shown in the preceding figure were displayed at the 1957 Triennale. Credit: (216).

The Hallicrafters SX-42 radio receiver, adapted for consumer use from a military product, had a technological character that still persists in this family of products. Its case was also used for an early television. Credit: (23, 113).

Raymond Spilman designed this tone arm—counterpoised like a Calder mobile—for the Pickering company. Credit: (216).

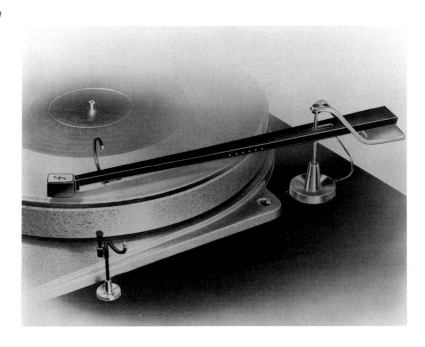

However, more than whim and incidental logic controlled the form. The size and location of the transformer and the size and shape of the printed circuit boards dictated the three dimensions of the box. The low rectangular face of the box and human-engineering considerations dictated the number and the arrangement of the controls.

RCA began manufacturing television receivers in 1939. The TT-5, designed by John Vassos, was a tabletop unit with a walnut cabinet. It had a 5-inch picture tube, and it delivered its sound by being plugged into the "Victrola" jack of an RCA radio. The TRK-5 combined video and sound in a floor cabinet. The TRK-9 had a 9-inch screen. The TRK-12 had a 12-inch screen mounted inside a cover that used a mirror to reflect the image when it was raised. This unit used 36 tubes for the video and 12 tubes for the audio, and all the circuitry was wired and soldered by hand. Its selling price was over $700—more than the price of some automobiles at the time. Such prices called for impressive cabinets.

At war's end some 5,000 American homes had television sets. Then, when mass production of TVs began in 1945, sales took off. At first, most of the sets went into taverns and other public viewing places. By 1950 some 7.5 million sets had found their way into American homes, and programs were being broadcast from over 100 stations in 70 cities.

The television set dominated the living room in most homes. Unlike the radio and other sound equipment, which could be located inconspicuously, the TV had to be located centrally at a distance and a height that was convenient for viewing. In many cases the warm flicker of the fireplace was preempted by the television's electronic glow. The shape of the TV tube burned itself into the subconscious, and soon it was reflected in automobile grilles, the windows of buildings, appliances, furniture, and decorative patterns. More than one trademark was redesigned to fill advertising space on the tube.

John Vassos designed the cabinet for RCA's TRK-12 television. Credit: Radio Corporation of America.

This first "small" portable television set, manufactured by General Electric, broke new design ground by discarding any pretense of being a piece of furniture. Credit: Industrial Design (December 1955).

RCA was quick to upstage GE with this smaller "personal" television. Perched on metal legs, it had a space-age character that earned it honors at the Eleventh Triennale in Milan. Credit: Industrial Design (January 1957).

The biggest problem in designing a TV was what to do with the depth of the tube. One approach was to give the cabinet a rather shallow form, with the tube cover sticking out the back as inconspicuously as possible. Another approach was to permit the face of the tube to thrust itself forward, with the cabinet set back against the wall. The only design approach that met the problem was that used in Philco's "Predicta" model: the electronic components were put in a flat rectangular box upon which the tube was mounted like a searchlight on a stand. Designed by Herbert Gosweiler in 1958, this more "honest" treatment of the television receiver—treated as a freak in its day—is now increasingly sought out as a special typeform of the period.

In the mid 1950s, a new market for smaller televisions opened up. After several attempts by manufacturers to find a size, a shape, and a weight that would be acceptable for a portable unit, General Electric hit the middle of the target in 1955 with a 26-pound TV that had a 14-inch screen (measured diagonally). The design staff at GE's Electronics Park, under George Beck, had prevailed over the company's market researchers and had convinced management that there was an untouched market for small television sets.

In many homes, a portable was used as a second set. As such, it did not have to pretend to be a piece of furniture. Portables, with their light metal cases painted in various colors and with their plastic knobs and die-cast handles, were described as having dropped their pretensions and taken on a pleasantly prosaic character. General Electric sold 250,000 units the first year, and a year later every other maker had joined the market for portables. Portable televisions helped break the association between quality and bigness in manufactured products.

Until the mid 1950s, American manufacturers had the domestic audio and television markets pretty much to themselves. Then European and Japanese products began to appear in volume in American stores. Herbert Zeller, the former director of industrial design for the Motorola company and for its subsequent owner, Matsushita of Japan, attributed the easy entry of Japanese products to the Americans themselves:

We brought design to Japan, [and] had the designs executed and some of them . . . manufactured in Japan. . . . Those designers . . . brought to Japan the concepts of the needs [of] the American consumer [and] gave the Japanese the start that eventually launched them into the position of dominance that they now have in consumer electronics. I think that since that time they've done a superb job, probably in some cases . . . a better job than has been done by the American designers. I think much of this was largely due to the . . . manufacturing capability that [was] developed in Japan at the urging of the American designers. (191)

In addition, the American marketing and advertising establishments welcomed foreign products. It made little difference to them what the source of a product was so long as deliveries were certain, quality assured, and profit margins guaranteed. American electronics manufacturers, rather than improving their own capabilities, tried to ride the crest of the wave by importing components and even complete units to be sold under their names.

A similar situation developed in the area of photographic equipment. For a few years after World War II, American camera manufacturers had the market virtually to themselves. The first postwar products manufactured by Eastman Kodak were cameras aimed at consumer markets. This was in line, apparently, with the company's philosophy that better service to the public and greater profits lay in appealing to amateur rather than professional photographers. Kodak's Super 620 had been one of the most advanced cameras to come onto the market before World War II, but now the company decided to concentrate on high-volume production of low-cost cameras (as well as high-quality film and photographic materials).

The average consumer was not expected to understand the physical and chemical principles upon which photography was based, but only to follow George Eastman's invitation: "You snap the shutter, we do the rest." On this point Eastman Kodak represents one of the best examples of an American manufacturer with a long history of innovation and expertise in a particular field that dedicated itself to serving the general rather than the specialized public. Its engineering and design goals were to reduce a precision instrument to a form that anyone could own and use with ease and satisfaction.

Theodore Clement was put in charge of styling at Kodak in 1945, with Walter Dorwin Teague continuing as a consultant. In the next few years the styling group, with the addition of Arthur Crapsey, Fred Knowles, and Kenneth Van Dyck, designed the Tourist camera (1947), the Brownie Hawkeye box camera (1948), the Pony (a budget camera for color slides; 1949), and the first in a line of Signet 35-millimeter cameras (1950). During the 1950s Kodak expanded its product line to include motion-picture cameras. The Brownie 8-millimeter camera, introduced in 1951, was given a multilens turret in 1955. The K100, a 16-millimeter movie camera, was awarded a gold medal at the 1957 Triennale in Milan.

The Argus, Bell and Howell, Ansco, and Revere companies competed in the burgeoning market, whose growth was due in no small part to the baby boom. Each company tended to specialize within an area. Argus appeared to be most interested in lower-cost still cameras. Bell and Howell, on the other hand, concentrated on motion-picture cameras. The company used both corporate and consultant designers. As consultant designers, Peter Müller-Munk Associates developed the 16-millimeter Model 240EE movie camera, selected as one of the 100 best designs by designers themselves in a project conceived and directed by Jay Doblin.

Toward the end of the 1950s, all the camera companies introduced automatic cameras, with built-in photoelectric exposure meters

The Brownie 8-millimeter movie camera, designed by Fred Knowles, was introduced by Kodak in 1951. Credit: (38, 67).

Walter Dorwin Teague's Kodak K-100 16-millimeter movie camera had a strong professional character, even though it was conceived primarily for the amateur. Credit: Industrial Design (August 1957).

A compact 8-millimeter movie camera designed for Bell and Howell by Peter Müller-Munk. All operating elements were clearly and simply identified. Credit: Bell and Howell.

Peter Müller-Munk's 16-millimeter movie camera for Bell and Howell. Like many similar products, it had a die-cast aluminum case with wrinkle-finish paint that suggested leather. Credit: (216).

Müller-Munk's 8-millimeter projector for Bell and Howell had the wide-band segmented styling that was popular at the time. It had the effect of suggesting weight and strength. Credit: Bell and Howell.

and rangefinders that virtually eliminated guesswork. Also, new cameras were designed for 127 roll film. The designers' challenge was to create forms that would suit these functional and operational changes while making the cameras look easy to use.

Neither slide photography nor movie photography could survive without the corollary development of projectors. Every company was obliged to include such products in its line. Even though the film itself was standardized so that it could be used with another company's equipment, the general feeling was that brand loyalty would lead the consumer to purchase the projector that visually matched the camera with which the pictures had been taken.

By the end of the 1950s, slide projectors had been lowered considerably by the development of a new type of light bulb. Moreover, the industry had apparently settled upon a slide tray that held forty slides and could be tracked horizontally alongside the machine, with each slide pushed across the projector lens. The trays were convenient to store, but they made editing a frustrating experience. Every manufacturer explored alternative projector-tray relationships, with little success. The search was still on for the ideal typeform for the slide projector.

One of the most dramatic photographic advances of the period was the invention of the Carousel slide projector. Its development began with Kodak engineers D. M. Harvey and W. P. Ewald, who were working on a projector called the Cavalcade, which passed the slide tray beneath the projection lens, lifted each slide into position, and then let the slide fall back into the tray by gravity. The idea of reversing the process to let the slide fall into position from above and then lift it back mechanically into the tray occurred between sketch renderings and working drawings by industrial designers A. Crapsey and D. E. Hansen, who were involved in the sketch development. Ewald built a model to test the concept, subsequently illustrated by F. Zagara in 1956

with a top-loading tray. In 1957 Hansen hit on the concept of a round tray in a sketch. (Design Patent 68025 was granted to him on December 22, 1961.) R. J. Olsen carried on the development through 1958. In 1959, final drawings for the refined idea were completed for an appearance and engineering model. The Kodak Carousel, put on the market in 1961, represents an excellent example of inspired creative collaboration between engineers and industrial designers. The first Carousel to reach the market swept away all competition. However, some of its features and styling details proved to be extraneous to its operation. The succeeding Model 800, designed to be easier to manufacture and use, established a typeform for slide projectors in which configuration and function are so closely linked as to make it difficult, if not impossible, to improve.

Professional photographers continued to depend largely on the Speed Graphic camera made by Graflex of Rochester. In 1958 the company introduced a new version called the Super Graphic. For the consultant designers, Peter Müller-Munk Associates, the challenge was to change and improve the camera in construction and materials and to simplify its controls and improve it in appearance without altering its typeform and affecting its impression of quality. Both company engineers and consultant designers worked closely with Alcoa's chief industrial designer, Samuel Fahnestock, to produce an excellent example of industrial design at its best. The camera subsequently won Alcoa's Annual Industrial Design Award. Another happy result for Graflex was the fact that the simplified camera began to appeal to amateur photographers. Graflex also ventured off in another direction by developing a stereo camera and viewer designed by F. R. Lovell. Although it was unique enough to be shown at the Triennale, it had no lasting appeal to the public. It would appear that part of the enjoyment of photography depended upon the group experience, which stereoscopic viewing could not provide.

*Theodore Clement's*
*Kodaslide projector.*
*Credit: (216).*

The Kodak Carousel slide
projector was a break-
through. This first model
had an exceptionally busy
base. Credit: Eastman
Kodak Company.

By 1966, the Kodak
Carousel had been sim-
plified and was ap-
proaching unity of form.
Credit: Eastman Kodak
Company.

Serious photographers wanted more than foolproof, easy-to-operate cameras, and only foreign manufacturers with low labor costs could make the precision instruments they demanded at prices they could afford to pay. While American companies were vying for their shares of the lower-priced consumer market, Japanese industry managed to come into the market over the top.

Edwin Land demonstrated his Polaroid process of instant photography at the 1947 winter meeting of the Optical Society of America. This dramatic instant-imaging process based on microelectronics and chemistry contributed to the revolution in communications that was bringing a wave of new challenges to designers to give the resulting products form and functional value. Edwin Land was particularly articulate on the subject of inventions. He believed that they must come into a world that was not prepared for them, and that it was "the duty of the inventor to build a new gestalt and to quietly substitute that gestalt for the old one in the framework of society. And when he does his invention calmly and equitably becomes part of everyday life and no one can understand why it wasn't always there." (33, 54)

The first Polaroid camera, Model 95, designed by Walter Dorwin Teague, went on sale for $89.75 at the Jordan Marsh department store in Boston in November 1948. It was an old-fashioned-looking bellows contraption, apparently put together from existing parts made by several subcontractors. Nevertheless, it was a marketing sensation. Shortly thereafter it was distributed to selected stores (not photographic-equipment stores) in major cities. Polaroid's Model 80 "Highlander," introduced in 1954, brought the price down to $60.00, within reach of the general public. Teague's second version of the "Highlander" was designed to eliminate the dated appearance of the first model. In 1961 Polaroid introduced Model J66, designed by Albrecht Goertz in the more contemporary configuration of 35-millimeter cameras. Then in 1963 James

*Peter Müller-Munk's firm redesigned the Graflex press camera, using aluminum to replace a mix of wood, magnesium, and cycolac parts. The new cohesiveness of form improved the camera's function as well as its appearance. Credit:* Industrial Design *(December 1958).*

Conner and William Purcell of the Henry Dreyfuss office refined the form further into Model 100, each time moving the product a step closer to a typeform that was unique to the Polaroid process.

While other manufactured products struggled to survive in open competition, which forced them to be responsive to technological, social, and psychological changes, the telephone existed in a near-monopoly situation. When Bell Laboratories decided in 1946 that technological advances justified a new telephone, it assigned its industrial design consultant, Henry Dreyfuss, to work with company engineers on the project. Robert Hose (1915–1977), who had begun his design career as a Bell employee and had left the company to become an associate of Dreyfuss, was given responsibility for the account. Not only would the new phone have to meet designers' and engineers' criteria for human factors and function; since the company charged a monthly fee for the "rental" of each unit long after its initial cost had been recovered, reliability and durability were also important.

The Model 500 desk set, introduced in 1951, became the near-inviolate typeform for the American desk telephone. It was said to have represented more than 2,000 hours of design and development in the Dreyfuss office, most of it devoted to analysis and human engineering. In appearance it presumed to be a neutral complement to any environment.

Over the years, however, the American telephone fell inexorably behind the increasing rate of evolution in other countries. Americans who traveled abroad or followed the progress of the arts of the environment in magazines began to realize that the Bell typeform was aging perceptibly. In the United States, a small Ohio manufacturer, the North Company, introduced a new telephone concept at the 1956 meeting of the independent telephone industry representatives in Chicago. The Ericofon, invented and designed by L. M.

Ericsson of Sweden, was a light one-piece product with a dial in the base of the handpiece. Although its virtue lay more in its uniqueness than in its utility, it helped open the way for a new generation of telephones.

Bell's product planners and designers began to bring forward ideas that had lain dormant. There was a belated realization that domestic needs for telephones were different from business needs and should be addressed with something more than wall phones and optional colors. Impending changes from analog to digital controls and microelectronics provided the company with additional incentive to make a change. What Bell did was transform the one-piece handset that had been used by telephone linemen into a consumer product. The "Trimline" telephone, which went on the market in 1965, had the dial (later, the buttons) in the handpiece. Although it was visually clumsy and awkward to hold and operate, it was a welcome change from the venerable handset. In the absence of alternative choices, it found ready acceptance. The Trimline broke Bell's resistance to change, and it was soon followed by the more compact "Princess" telephone.

It was evident that, less than a century after the invention of the telephone, satellites were making global communication possible. Sound and image could be transmitted, stored, and duplicated by means previously impossible. Rapid technological changes forced manufacturers of communications-related equipment to change their products almost annually. Designers were obliged to undertake even more careful analyses of the visual and aural interface between people and their machines.

The typewriter continued to dominate formal communication. Only it could put communication into a tangible form that could be handled, stored, and transmitted by other machines. In the immediate postwar period, most of the attention given to typewriters was devoted to reducing the drudgery of typing on

The original Polaroid
camera looked like a con-
ventional folding camera.
Credit: (39, 76).

The Polaroid Automatic
100, designed to be held
horizontally, was a hand-
some product. Credit:
(216).

The Bell Telephone company's Model 500 desk set was designed to be convenient and unobtrusive. Credit: (12).

The "Trimline" telephone was designed by the Dreyfuss office. Credit: (216).

Carl Otto's Voicewriter dictation machine was a successful attempt to restyle an existing disk machine to compete with the new magnetic-belt machines. Credit: (38, 136).

them and servicing them. The shape, spread, and angles of the keys came in for an extraordinary amount of attention, as did the problems of making duplicate copies with existing technology.

While the conventional typewriter was being reengineered from a mechanized apparatus to an electronic one, manufacturers and designers attempted to distract attention from its technological obsolescence by giving typewriters colorful, highly styled housings. Even the Italian-made Olivetti Lettera 22 portable—listed as the first choice from among the 100 best products in a 1959 survey of 100 architects, designers, and design educators—was only the same old mechanism cloaked in a new shape. Even after Olivetti purchased Underwood (a long-time American manufacturer of typewriters) in 1959, Olivetti's devotion to modern forms did not make much of a dent in the American market.

In 1961, the IBM Selectric typewriter came onto the market, introducing an entirely new technology involving "bread-boarded" transistorized circuitry (developed in the Bell Telephone Laboratories). This new circuitry revolutionized the form of the typewriter. Eliot Noyes, who had taken over the IBM account as consultant design director after working

on it while he was employed by Norman Bel Geddes and later sharing the account with Sundberg-Ferar, was responsible for the form of the Selectric. In a few years the typewriter itself would begin to disappear from business offices, leaving behind only its keyboard as the entry port of communication with the computer.

New concepts for copying machines appeared in the late 1940s and the early 1950s. The old methods of duplicating office correspondence and reports had been tedious and time-consuming. Carbon paper was the usual means of producing a small number of copies; if more were wanted, one had to rely on hectographic and mimeographic processes, which meant preparing gelatin in the first case and cutting a stencil in the latter.

The first breakthrough in terms of convenience was the process of transferring images by means of a chemically treated paper that was heat-sensitive. Generally known by its trade name, Thermo-Fax, the process took only a few moments and required little additional work. One Thermo-Fax machine, the Secretary, designed by Samuel Highberger of the Harley Earl office, won an award from the Industrial Designers Institute in 1958 because,

This portable typewriter designed by Dreyfuss shows early concern for human factors. The keys were shaped to fit the fingers, and crackle paint was used to reduce glare. Credit: (39, 95).

The IBM Executive typewriter, designed by Eliot Noyes in the mid 1950s, had a smooth sculptural form drawn rather awkwardly over an unyielding mechanism. Credit: (216).

The classic IBM Selectric typewriter, designed in 1961 by Eliot Noyes, illustrates the humanizing dominance of form over mechanism. Credit: International Business Machines.

Eliot Noyes (standing at right) and Walter Baermann (seated at right) posed in the shop of Normal Bel Geddes in the late 1940s. The model is a rough study for a new IBM typewriter. Credit: Vincent Foote.

aside from the fact that it had been carefully designed to fit into the office environment, its form was in the design idiom of the day: a black panel or "face" with a light, neutral shell cover. Other copiers that were on the market at the time used variants of the photographic negative to make duplicates of typed, printed, and drawn originals.

The major revolution in office copiers came from an unexpected source: the Haloid Company's xerography process, invented by Chester Carlson in 1938. When it first appeared in public in 1957 (as the Zerographic process), it was considered too complex and too expensive to be a real competitor in the office. It involved several separate machines, and the shop-made metal cabinets in which they were housed gave no hint of the form that was to come.

The company, renamed Xerox in 1958, was aware of the growing demand for a small, less expensive office machine that could make copies on ordinary paper, and it concentrated its design and engineering efforts on those goals. In 1959 Xerox introduced its Model 914, which set the typeform for a whole family of office machines and virtually swept away all competing processes. The fact that the machine was expensive was offset by Xerox's lease/use program, which brought it within reach of the average office. Within a decade copiers had flooded offices and schools with a tidal wave of paper, creating serious problems of confidentiality and copyright protection.

Similarly, an entirely new family of products was being developed around the capabilities of magnetic tape. Video tape would eventually virtually displace photographic film in many applications. The flexibility of a video camera, a video player, and a television screen offered possibilities well beyond those of any other means of technological communication for work, play, and artistic expression.

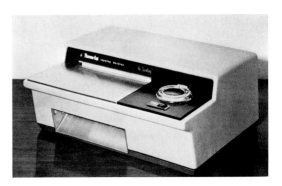

This Thermo-Fax copying machine, designed by Samuel Highberger of the Harley Earl office, helped establish the typeform for copying machines. Credit: Industrial Design (May 1957).

The now-classic Xerox 813 copier, designed in 1964 by Armstrong, Balmer and Associates. Its dignified form elevated the product from a back-office appliance to front-office status. Credit: (216).

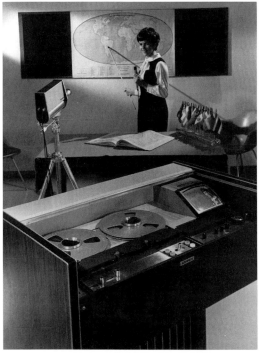

The VR-303 Videotrainer, designed in 1965 by Frank Walsh and his staff for the Ampex Corporation. Credit: Frank T. Walsh, Ampex Corporation.

The Ampex VR-303 Videotrainer in use. A complete closed-circuit television recording system was introduced in 1965, complete with camera and monitor. It and its descendents revolutionized educational and professional presentations. Credit: Frank T. Walsh, Ampex Corporation.

*We bear in mind that the object being worked on is going to be ridden in, sat upon, looked at, talked into, activated, operated, or in some other way used by people individually or en masse.*

Henry Dreyfuss, 1955 (11, cover)

*Henry Dreyfuss's calling card suggested that man was the focus of design. Credit: Henry Dreyfuss.*

One of the most elusive dreams of the postwar era was that somehow the automobile and the airplane would be crossbred into a winged hybrid that could drive off a roadway, spread its wings, spin its pusher propeller, and take off to fly directly to its destination, ignoring the congestion below. Although prototypes were built and flown, the dream faded when it was realized that congestion in the air could be even more difficult to police or service than that on the ground.

The promise of personal aircraft, however, persisted. Cessna, Beechcraft, Piper, Ryan, Fairchild, Stinson, and other companies that had designed and built small aircraft for military service simply spruced up their interiors and paint jobs and put them on the market with assurances that anyone could learn to fly. Industrial designers were often called in to develop appropriate interior schemes. Henry Dreyfuss redesigned the Stinson Voyager, and Raymond Loewy developed the civilian version of the Fairchild F47.

Beech Aviation, however, decided to break for the lead in the postwar race with an entirely new small airplane for civilian flyers. Its prototype soloed in 1945, was certified by the Civil Aeronautics Administration, and was put on the market in 1947 as the Beechcraft Bonanza 35. In a bold move that gave the Bonanza a distinctive appearance, the traditional empennage, consisting of vertical and horizontal stabilizers and rudder, was replaced with a V tail, which was lighter, safer in a spin, and easier to manufacture. The Bonanza also introduced a tricycle landing gear, which made takeoffs and landings easier. Twenty years later there were 10,000 Bonanzas in service, and improved versions were still in production in the 1980s.

In 1945 the Civil Air Administration projected that there would be between 500,000 and 2 million private planes in the air by 1955. However, in 1946 only 33,000 were sold, and that total was never reached again. In a few cases the original airframes, now half a century old

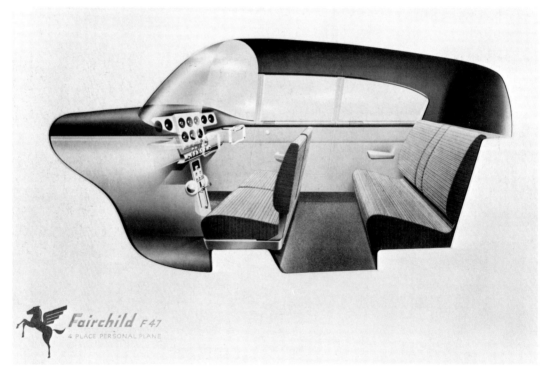

Fairchild F47
4 PLACE PERSONAL PLANE

Raymond Loewy's office
produced this sketch of a
civilian version of the Fairchild F47. Credit: (216).

This rendering of the
interior of the F47 was
strongly suggestive of an
automobile interior—per-
haps as much for psycho-
logical as for practical
reasons. Credit: (216).

*The first Beechcraft
Bonanza Model 35.
Credit: Beech Aircraft
Corporation.*

*The Learjet 23, the world's
first private jet. Credit:
Smithsonian Institution.*

in design, are still being manufactured (with improvements mandated by experience and regulations). In other cases entirely new aircraft, such as the Learjet, were put into service.

The late 1940s and the 1950s saw a great surge in the popularity of power boats, particularly outboards. An outboard motor could be hung over the transom of practically anything that floated. In 1947 the Scott-Atwater company of Milwaukee put on the market (often under the private brand names of various dealers) an outboard motor designed by Brooks Stevens Associates. Johnson Motors of Waukegan, Illinois, assigned the task of securing its position in the fast-moving outboard-motor industry to the combined forces of its advertising agency, J. Walter Thompson, and the design office of Dave Chapman. The two firms' research studies showed that 62 percent of the new outboard motors were being purchased by blue-collar workers who were spending their discretionary income on boating rather than on a second automobile or television set. Dave Chapman characterized boating as providing a necessary release for everyone, blue collar or white collar, and J. Walter Thompson built a successful promotional program on that theme. Chapman's collaboration with Johnson was reported as indicative of a broadening of the relationships between designers and their clients.

The involvement of the Eliot Noyes office with power boating was motivated primarily by the search for forms that were expressive of the boating environment. The Cummins C/235 HydroDrive, designed under Noyes's direction by Robert Graf, had an eloquent sculptural form that combined hydrodynamic principles with functional needs.

Some manufacturers of boats, however, were unduly influenced by the automotive styling of the era. Fins, speed lines, chrome trim, and other decorative elements were added on the presumption that the public would buy in a boat what they had been conditioned to put up with in automobiles. This was not always

Brooks Stevens described his design goal for the Hiawatha outboard motor as "compactness, complete enclosures, and accessability to functional parts." "Streamlining, eye appeal, [and] long, low, sweeping contours" were, said Stevens, "of secondary consideration but equally important to point of sale acceptance." Credit: (216).

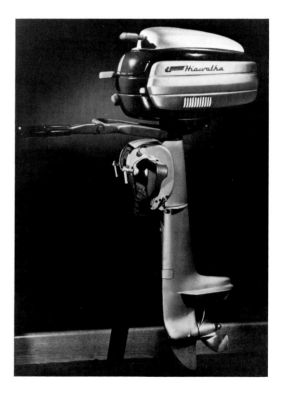

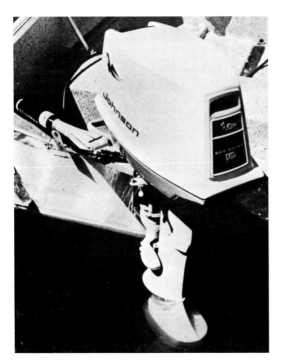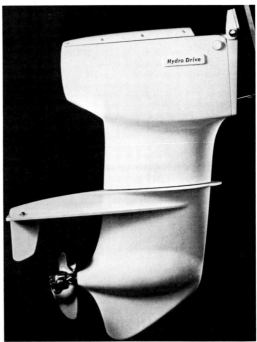

The Johnson Motors
design project combined
the services of an adver-
tising agency (J. W.
Thompson) and an indus-
trial design office (Dave
Chapman). Its goal was to
appeal to a growing mid-
dle class looking for
power, status, and attractiveness in boating.
Credit: (10).

The marine outdrive unit
designed for the Hydro
Drive company by the
Noyes office had a hand-
some form that stood as
an art form apart from its
function. Credit: Industrial
Design (December 1964).

This fiberglass boat for
Evinrude Motors was
designed by Brooks Ste-
vens in 1963 to be excep-
tionally stable and smooth
riding. It was devoid of
obvious styling details yet
handsome as a total prod-
uct. Credit: Industrial
Design (December 1964).

the case, however. When the Evinrude Motors Corporation assigned Brooks Stevens to develop a small boat, the result was a 14-foot runabout with a fiberglass "gull-wing" hull with sponsons and a broad bow for stability and better riding characteristics. Its form had a clean nautical character that set it well apart from automotive forms. On a larger scale, Norman Bel Geddes for the Gar Wood Boat Company, Donald Deskey Associates for the Wheeler Shipbuilding Corporation, and others designed superstructures and interiors for the production-line manufacture of larger cruisers to provide the kind of comfortable living afloat that was previously available only in custom-built craft.

There was little doubt that travel in one form or another would be more and more popular among Americans in the postwar era, and of course travel requires luggage. In the late 1940s, Robert Briers Wemyss patented a construction system for light, moderately priced luggage that was admirably suited to the needs of travelers. Wemyss's concept called for a die-cast or extruded aluminum frame, fitted with hinges, locks, and handles, to which shells made of drawn aluminum or molded plastic would be attached. It transformed what had previously been a craft-based product, dependent upon the skills of leather, sheet-metal, and wood workers, into a modern manufactured puroduct that could be assembled by unskilled workers on a production line.

Within five years this innovative system had been adapted for transporting Dictaphone dictating machines by William O'Neil. The Dictaphone cases had cast magnesium frames and Royalite plastic shells. John Hauser used a similar approach, with Melamine-impregnated fiberglass frames and phenolic shells, in his successful Tri-Taper luggage for the American Tourister company.

In 1957, the Shwayder company expanded on the Wemyss concept to create its own major entry into the field of rigid lightweight

In the sense that a successful design, unlike an invention, may have several parents, this landmark line of luggage owes a debt to Wemyss, Hauser, Best, and Fujioka. Mel Best's Samsonite "Silhouette" of 1957 brought it all together. Credit: Mel Best.

The stainless-steel "Pal" razor, designed by Henry Dreyfuss in 1961, sought to make permanent a product that was increasingly being treated as expendable. It had the appearance of fine modern flatware. Credit: (13).

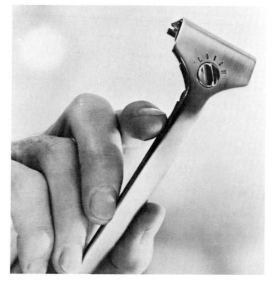

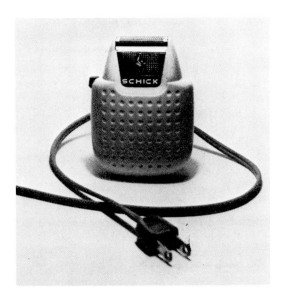

*This 1950 electric shaver by Carl Otto made a strong break from the previous typeform—it was intended to be held in the palm rather than gripped with the fingers. Credit:* Industrial Design *(July 1959).*

luggage. Mel Best Associates, with Clair Samhammer, developed the Shwayder luggage, which was first marketed in 1958 as the Samsonite Silhouette line. Its construction was based on extruded aluminum frames and vinyl-laminated shells. A quarter of a century later, Samsonite, as it became popularly known, was still the leading hard-sided luggage on the market, with numerous imitators around the world.

Luggage continued to evolve, however. Many people came to regard soft luggage as more suitable for automobile and air travel. There are still those travelers, however, who prefer a rigid and presumably impregnable protective case for their belongings.

Manufactured products for personal use do not disappear from the market quickly, even after their successors have been introduced by social or technological changes. For example, although electric shavers began to come onto the market in the 1930s, many still preferred Gillette's replaceable-blade razor of 1895, and there were even a few who insisted on using the straight razor of the nineteenth century.

Razors using disposable blades continued to come onto the market in new forms, with increasingly clever devices for changing the blade. The American Safety Razor company tried to combine permanence and disposability in the Pal razor, designed by Henry Dreyfuss and Associates in 1951. While the blades were replaceable, the handsome stainless-steel handle was guaranteed for life. Its days, however, were numbered. Gillette opted for disposability of both handle and blade, going against the conventional wisdom that condemned products designed for a short lifespan as wasteful of energy and materials.

Electric shavers began to hit their stride after the war with Schick's Model 20. Designed by Carl Otto, who took over the account after he left Raymond Loewy, this shaver changed the basic form of the electric shaver from a finger-held to a palm-held machine. The handsome form that resulted was very successful on the market—400,000 units were ordered in the first week, and some 6 million were eventually sold. Jay Doblin called this product "typical of commercial design assignments initiated to motivate consumption" (9, 83).

The increasing popularity of air travel led to the need for better seating in airline terminals. Expanding and rapidly changing gate accommodations for passengers called for seating systems that could be modified quickly. In contrast with railroad and bus terminals, airport accommodations were the responsibility of each airline and were often modified with the seasons.

Airline managers considered the sight of passengers lying down to sleep across several seats between delayed flights bad for business. They wanted their waiting areas to accommodate passengers for not more than half an hour. It was also considered important that the seating be as modern as the airplanes, with no evidence of wear and tear.

Furniture manufacturers, especially those producing office furniture, were particularly interested in the potential market in airport seating. Charles Eames undertook to solve the problem of airport seating for the Herman Miller company by modifying a system of cast-aluminum furniture that he and Don Albinson had apparently developed for leisure rather than transient seating. Adapted for use at Chicago's O'Hare Airport in 1962, this seating (which came to be known as "O'Hare") consisted of cast and polished aluminum side frames that were supported on a T-shaped steel bar, which was held up by cast-aluminum floor pieces. Interchangeable seats and backs covered in black vinyl were stretched between the side frames and held in tension across the back by horizontal die-cast aluminum bars. "O'Hare" was comfortable for sitting, but it was virtually impossible to lie across the individual units.

*Charles Eames's leisure seating was transformed into "O'Hare" airport seating. Credit: (43, 98).*

## School and Work

*If you are going to . . . really involve people and not teach them, you must open the door in an intriguing and fascinating way.*

Charles Eames, 1958 (148)

Around 1950, the wave of postwar children began to enter the public schools. During the 1930s and the 1940s, with the American school population relatively static at around 25 million, there had been little pressure for new schools or equipment. Except for maintenance and repair, durability and inflexibility were the rule. School furniture was heavy and bolted to classroom floors. However, as the school population rose, schools and their furnishings had to change. The rigid academic environment gave way to experimental teaching and to flexible, more open classrooms.

Companies that had not previously manufactured school furniture looked upon the growing market as fair game and strove to develop new furniture concepts. Unlike the established manufacturers, they recognized that adaptability to match different subject activities and classroom sizes and shapes would be important. They also noted that school furniture should be fitted to the changing sizes of school children.

In 1952 the Brunswick-Balke-Collender company decided to add school furniture to its established lines of billiard and gym equipment and asked the Dave Chapman industrial design organization to develop the new program. Within a year after the design development got underway, the new line (consisting of eleven basic units) was ready for public display. The desks and the chairs had tapered legs of steel tubing, with pivoting floor glides. Desk tops, seats, and seat backs were of laminated wood with plastic surfaces. By changing the angle of the leg units, seat height could be adjusted. With the success of this line, the Brunswick company moved into second place in the industry. The furniture had a light, sprightly appearance that belied the fact that it was sturdy and strong enough for the schoolroom.

*This structurally innovative school furniture was designed by Dave Chapman for the Brunswick-Balke-Collender company. Credit: Dave Chapman, Inc.*

Brunswick and Chapman were subsequently involved in a landmark case of design-patent infringement when a subcontractor, who had been given a basic set of drawings to bid on, proceeded to manufacture copies of the Chapman design. Even though the designs had been modified somewhat, the courts ruled that the intent to defraud was evident and ruled against the subcontractor. The outcome of the case was of particular importance to designers because, in the past, court rulings on design-patent infringement has most often gone against the original designers when minor details had been altered.

Another interesting foray into classroom furnishings by the Chapman organization was its contract from Educational Facilities Laboratories, Inc. (a nonprofit corporation established by the Ford Foundation) to make an in-depth study of classroom facilities and layouts from the viewpoint of using television as a teaching tool. The firm's report, Design for ETV: Planning for Schools with Television, published in 1960, was an extensive overview of alternative classroom arrangements for the use of television to teach different subjects to pupils of various ages. The study was distributed widely and had a useful impact on the use of television in the nation's schools, and the Industrial Designers Institute cited it for having opened up the broader field of design research to industrial designers.

In the postwar spirit of celebration and hope for the future, it seemed nothing was too good for American children. They were to be pampered, perhaps as no generation of children had ever been. The potential market for products for children did not escape the attention of manufacturers who believed they had new concepts for furnishings and toys to add to those already in existence.

Harry Sundheim, a buyer of infant products at Sears, was aware that the company had developed a market for round playpens but had been obliged to drop them because of mechanical problems. In 1951 he left Sears to join the entrepreneur-manufacturer John Bur-

ton Tigrett, who made it his business to seek out, develop, and market innovative ideas. Tigrett took on the assignment on his usual terms: He paid no development fees, preferring a royalty system that returned a percentage for each unit that was sold when and if the product came to market. Tigrett passed Sundheim's proposal to the design firm Designers, Inc., which after more than a year of effort canceled its agreement with Tigrett without solving the problem. Then he approached Charles Eames, who was also, after months, unable to solve the problem. Eventually, the mechanical problem of the circular playpen was solved by Tigrett and his own staff. Sears accepted the revised playpen and placed an order, as did Marshall Field. The Play-A-Round pen was a success. In 1955 Tigrett sold 10,000 units. This increased to 50,000 units by the end of 1956, at which time Tigrett turned the product over to the Thayer company and went on to other products.

Another folding nylon net playpen, in a square shape, was developed around the same time by James Fulton, who was working in the office of Harley Earl in Detroit at the time. The product, conceived as an exploratory assignment with Alcoa, was patented and manufactured by the Trimble company and went on to become the industry standard. Other innovative children's furniture and furnishings appeared during that fertile period, including strollers, baby carriers, portable beds and bassinets, and bathing and changing facilities.

Charles Eames continued to present child-oriented products for John Tigrett's consideration. One was a set of colorful 3-by-3-foot panels, with a box of brass clips, that could be used to build various structures. At Tigrett's suggestion, Eames agreed to reduce the size of the panels, and on his way back to California by train he hit upon using the slotting system familiar in egg and beverage cartons. The result was the "House of Cards," a set of 54 decorated plastic-coated cards that sold for 98 cents a pack when Tigrett introduced them in 1953. A year later Eames added a second set of small cards with photographs of architectural features printed on them. A "Giant House of Cards" was also introduced at the same time, made up of twenty 7-by-11-inch cards with bright designs and patterns. These cards became a status product for adults—a form of play sculpture for sophisticates.

Eames's Sun Machine was designed as a contribution to Alcoa's Forecast program in 1958. Its underlying message—the promotion of solar energy—was as rich as the quality of its expression. Eames noted that "if you are going to . . . really involve people and not teach them, you must open the door in an intriguing and fascinating way" (148).

Play experiences based on construction systems continued to be a source of immediate aesthetic, psychological, and physical satisfaction for children. New ones were developed using postwar materials and processes. Giant popbeads of polyethylene made a particularly pleasant sound when small hands snapped them together into a string and a rewarding pop when they were pulled apart. The Lego system was based on plastic blocks that could be pressed together to form virtually anything. Other new construction toys echoed the larger world around them. The national highway program inspired kits of miniature highway elements, including straight and curved road segments, cloverleafs, overpasses, and toll stations. With them came small blocks representing automobiles, school buses, ambulances, airplanes, and racing cars, all with colorful pegs representing people.

The rush of manufactured products for home and work saw its toy manifestation in simplified wooden or plastic representations of telephones, clocks, phonographs, television sets, radios, cameras, typewriters, and the like that children could assemble and pretend to use as adults did, and little trucks and tractors that they could ride. The little girl was presumed to be delighted when her presents included toy irons, washing machines, stoves, refrigerators, vacuum cleaners, and mixers;

*John Tigrett's idea for a playpen made of modern materials was rejected by buyers as unorthodox when it was proposed in 1955. After a sample was shown to the public, acceptance skyrocketed. The round, nylon-net play-pen became the new typeform. Credit: Industrial Design (April 1958). Photograph by Hank Parker.*

The architecturally inno-
cent eloquence of the
House of Cards and the
eclectic choice of patterns
were a near-perfect sum-
mary of the range and
quality of Charles Eames's
interests. Credit: Ray
Eames. Photograph by
Charles Eames.

Like other contributors to
Alcoa's Forecast Pro-
gram, Charles Eames was
challenged to say some-
thing interesting with aluminum. His Sun Machine
accomplished nothing,
but demonstrated that the
world is bathed with free
energy. Credit: Ray
Eames. Photograph by
Charles Eames.

the little boy revved up his racing car, put his truck to work, "operated" his drill, and defended his territory with an atomic cannon.

After the USSR beat the United States in the race to launch an artificial satellite by orbiting Sputnik I in 1957, America's schools placed greater stress on the so-called hard sciences. Toy manufacturers were quick to get on the bandwagon. Gyroscopes, telescopes, and planetariums were promoted as never before. The Lionel company, well known for its electric trains, introduced kits for meteorology, electronics, and plastics and a series on the work of famous inventors. General Electric and other companies not normally associated with the world of toys put out kits that purported to make science fun and fascinating for children. The promises on the boxes often far surpassed the value of the contents.

Playgrounds still had swings, slides, and seesaws; however, in the late 1950s they were apt to be named "space swing," "rocket slide," and so forth. There were play structures based on Fuller's Dymaxion dome, as well as obstacle courses and jungle gyms. Architects began to design constructivistic playground apparatus, and sculptors to create amorphous play surfaces. They were developed in handsome model form, presented to school boards and government officials, and put up in schoolyards in suburbia and abandoned building sites in cities—more often than not to be ignored by children, who were fascinated by less sophisticated things.

In the adult world, an important step in education was taken in the early 1950s when the federal government decided to build an Air Force Academy. Skidmore, Owings, and Merrill, the architects, were charged with developing a facility intended to be on the same scale of importance as the other service academies.

Walter Dorwin Teague Associates was selected to work with S.O.M. after presentations by some thirty design firms; it was decided that "the large industrial designer

*Victor Schreckengost's 1953 juvenile tractor and trailer for Murray Ohio Manufacturing were safe, sturdy, and realistic. Credit: (38, 26).*

*These aluminum play sculptures were designed by David Aaron in 1958 for Alcoa's Forecast Program. Credit: Industrial Design (July 1958). Photograph by Wingate Paine.*

*This classroom furniture designed for the Air Force Academy by the Teague office had structural pieces of extruded and anodized tubing and seats and tabletops of plastic. Credit:* Industrial Design *(April 1958).*

*The dormitory rooms and furnishings at the Air Force Academy, also designed by the Teague office, were handsome and simple. Credit:* Industrial Design *(April 1958).*

with broadest background [was] best qualified in breadth of experience . . . and in depth of established capacity'' (95). It was estimated that the assignment, for which a $70 million overall budget was set, would require the selection of 60,000 different pieces of equipment and fittings, of which 1,500 called for special design. The design guidelines emphasized function, economy, standardization, and durability. WDTA established a team of twelve designers stationed in Denver under project director Carl Conrad and another group working in New York under John Lee. The result was a clean and effective (if somewhat formalistic) system of furnishings that conveyed little of the romance, challenge, and daring that was at one time associated with aviation.

The business environment underwent a dramatic change in the postwar era. In 1963 the Herman Miller company described its new Action Office as a system of office furniture based on a study of the office environment and its procedures. Inspired by the *Bürolandschaft* [office landscape] planning system (invented in Germany by Everhard and Wolfgang Schnelle), George Nelson, with designers R. Beckman and L. Blodie and with Robert Probst, the head of research for Herman Miller, created an office system that eliminated permanent walls and enclosures. Their stated goal was to create a system that permitted employees to work sitting or standing and to provide them with display spaces for work in progress and with adequate storage facilities. The result was a series of modular units that could be arranged in various configurations. Since the ceiling area was to be open, aural privacy was to be provided by ''white noise'' machines. Probst's basic proposals were given form at Nelson's office, and Robert Blaich at Herman Miller transformed the ideas into manufactured products. The final results brought a warm informality to the office.

In the same spirit of openness and democracy that was suggested by the Action Office system and other ''landscape'' office plans, it was considered appropriate that bank officers should sit out in the open, in full view of their depositors. To this end, Manufacturer's Trust's offices in mid-Manhattan were planned by Skidmore, Owings, and Merrill as an open, glass-walled demonstration of a trustworthy organization that had nothing to hide. Its most conspicuous symbol was the bank vault door designed by the Henry Dreyfuss office for the Mosler Safe Company. The massive door was kept open during the day as a public attraction and closed at night. What was not commonly known was that it was only a symbol. The actual access to the vault was more conveniently and inconspicuously located near the center of the bank.

The same designers appear again and again as the source of innovative solutions to problems. For example, Henry Dreyfuss insisted to the Honeywell company as early as 1937 that the thermostatic control it manufactured at the time as a vertical thermometer would be more effective functionally and psychologically if it were to be reengineered as a circular dial resembling a clock. Furthermore, he suggested that it would be more acceptable if the outer ring of the cover were painted or otherwise finished to blend into the wall it was mounted on. Although the idea was rejected at first, the public response to prototypes built and tested during the war was promising enough to justify production in 1953. Once on the market, the Honeywell thermostat quickly became the new typeform.

The postwar building boom and the growth of suburbia brought a surge in the use of power tools. Many prospective homeowners found that they could stretch their dollars by subcontracting the finishing of some or all of the interior or by having the attic or the basement left unfinished so that they could do it themselves later. Some developers even offered to throw in power tools for the homeowner to use in completing the house.

The first power tools were designed for use in the building trades. Generally clumsy and expensive, they were the products of a static

The "Action Office,"
manufactured by the Her-
man Miller company.
Credit: (43, 104).

Henry Dreyfuss's massive
vault door seems to float
in space behind the glass
wall of Manufacturers
Trust's offices in Manhattan. Credit: Ezra Stoller,
Esto Photographics, Inc.

*Henry Dreyfuss's round thermostat for Honeywell, which began its evolution in 1942. Credit: Honeywell, Inc.*

industry that had not been pushed to improve them for the benefit of operators. Moreover, they were designed for continuous heavy use. It was not unusual for the contractor rather than the individual workers to own the tools (especially those that were stationary rather than portable) and to be responsible for their servicing and storage between jobs.

This changed dramatically at the height of the building boom when carpenters realized that they could be more independent and sell their services at a higher rate if they owned their own power tools. And power-tool manufacturers foresaw a much larger market for their products if they could tap the interest of prospective homeowners in doing their own work. The idea hit the mark with the man of the house who saw himself as a modern homesteader making a home for his family with his own hands. There was a touch of ego involved. The suburban family man wanted to keep up with his neighbors by improving his house—and perhaps, in the process, to set an example for his son. Eric Larrabee was amused by the thought that power tools were not destroying skills, but rather putting them into the hands of unskilled householders.

Manufacturers competed for shares of the new market in several ways, the most important being to bring prices down. The obvious way to lower prices was to lower the quality of existing tools by lowering standards of reliability, performance, and safety. Another way was to provide saws with smaller blades, sanders with smaller pads, drills with smaller chucks, and so on. Some manufacturers were able to lower costs by combining several machines into one versatile product, such as the Shopsmith and the Cummins Do-it-Shop, that could perform different operations using the same motor.

Toward the end of the 1950s a new generation of power tools began to appear that were eminently suited to the needs of the amateur. One of the first was a double-insulated drill, designed by L. Garth Huxtable for the Millers Falls company, that virtually eliminated the danger of electrical shock by using plastic for

L. Garth Huxtable's small drill for Millers Falls (1960) introduced double insulation. *Credit:* Industrial Design *(December 1960).*

Harper Landell designed the U-130 circular saw in collaboration with Black and Decker engineers in 1965. *Credit:* Industrial Design *(December 1964).*

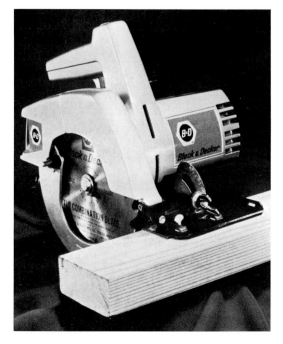

Three double-insulated power tools, with cycolac housings, designed in the late 1960s by Pulos Design Associates for Rockwell. Credit: author's collection. Photograph by Harry Beach.

These "Surform" hand tools were designed in the late 1960s by Laird Covey for the Stanley Tool Company. Their handsome shapes were conceived with sound consideration for the operator's convenience and safety. Credit: Laird Covey Industrial Design.

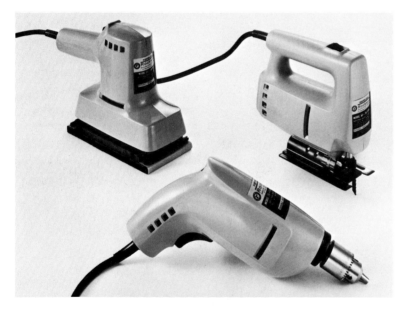

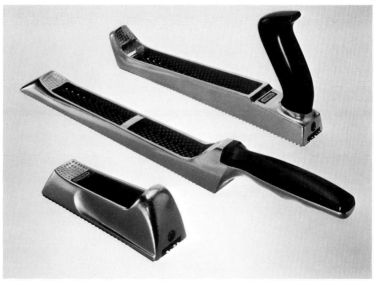

the body and for a gear between the spindle and the motor. Other companies continued to produce highly styled and polished aluminum shells until they were obliged to change by consumer pressure.

The new power tools were not only safer to use; they were also as much as 60 percent cheaper than their predecessors. One reason for this is that they designed to be assembled by automation, without many of the screws and clips essential to hand assembly. This was done as much for the protection of the consumer as to save manufacturing costs; if there was any malfunction, the purchaser was advised to return the product for a replacement at no cost rather than to try to fix it. These were disposable products, with product life predetermined to give the consumer a good return on his investment. At this point, portable power tools began to reach the price level of gift items. As the market began to level off, manufacturers increased their marketing efforts, often devoting more attention to appearance and packaging than to performance.

Even before the boom in power tools began to subside, it was evident that the rush to build housing was slowing down and that the market for power tools would reach saturation. As a result, tool manufacturers went on a search for new products. Yard and garden tools proved to be a logical next step for most manufacturers of portable power tools. The mechanisms of drills, circular saws, sanders, and jigsaws were easily adaptable to grass trimmers, edgers, hedge clippers, and shears.

At the National Hardware Show in New York in November 1957, two entire floors were devoted to outdoor equipment. Some eighty different manufacturers had power lawn mowers on display. The rotary mower, on the market for only 10 years, was outselling reel-type mowers four to one. The overall sale of power mowers had increased thirtyfold, from about 100,000 units a year to more than 3 million.

Power tools for outdoor use developed a character that was distinctly consumer-oriented. They were carefully designed, with clean

*This rotary lawn mower designed by Brooks Stevens in the early 1950s was an assemblage of parts rather than a total design. Credit: (38, 164).*

*A riding lawn mower designed for the Porter Cable machine company in 1960 by Pulos Design Associates. Credit: author's collection.*

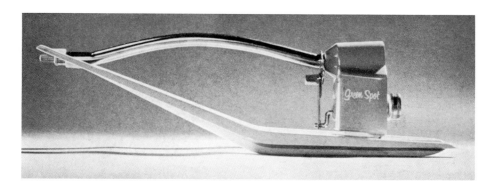

*Dave Chapman's office designed a series of water sprinklers for Scovill Manufacturing Company in the late 1950s. The sled-like base allowed this one to be dragged easily across a lawn. Credit: Industrial Design (February 1958). Photograph by Frank Carioti.*

shapes and a certain liveliness, to transform tasks that had once been considered distasteful into attractive experiences. When carelessness on the part of a manufacturer or a user led to an injury, the cause was identified and reduced by redesign (sometimes spurred by legislation).

Computers posed a formidable task for industrial designers because there were no precedents for their forms. The process by which they evolved their forms was mainly one of packaging and repackaging components in a race to keep up with technology while also considering human factors. In the beginning, the size and complexity of machines such as IBM's Selective Sequence Calculator dominated the human operators. However, with miniaturization the computing monster was tamed into a less fearsome assemblage of consoles, processors, and printers. In the process, the intermediate operating step whereby instructions had to be punched into cards, which were then used to communicate with a machine that did its thinking with vacuum tubes, was eliminated as transistors replaced both the tubes and the cards. As a result, operators were able by design to gain physical and intellectual dominance over computers such as the IBM 1440 Data Processor.

Equally important to the electronic processing of information for industrial and business purposes was the development of new tools for research and analysis. The new scientific instruments were more compact yet more accurate and easier to read. Their new forms were appropriate to their functions and were carefully conceived to avoid association with consumer electronics.

Robert Quandt and colleagues developed a distinctive character for the Corning company's diagnostic instruments, using die-cast or fabricated rectilinear aluminum shells with dark matte surfaces, bright bezels, large controls, and white dial surfaces with bold markings. (Dark surfaces with white or lighted markings were more popular in consumer

electronics.) The new instruments were designed for heavy laboratory use and for easy calibration and repair. Limited production required special attention to cost savings without jeopardizing reliability. A similar design process was followed by David Malk for Beckman Instruments, by Theodore Youngkin for Consolidated Electrodynamics, and by Carl Clement for Hewlett-Packard.

The extension of laboratory design to medical and dental instruments, office and hospital equipment, specialized furniture, and prosthetics opened up new fields for industrial designers.

Some dentists designed their own equipment, then patented their ideas and saw them through to production. Dr. Sanford Golden, for example, developed a dental chair that enabled the patient to be rotated comfortably into a position that was low enough to enable the dentist to sit down while working. Golden produced a prototype for his own use. The Ritter company of Rochester, which specialized in dental equipment, learned about the chair and funded further research at the University of California at Los Angeles, where Golden was on the faculty. With design assistance from Walter Dorwin Teague, Jr., David Deland, and Benjamin Stansbury, a version of Sanford's chair was brought onto the market under the name Euphoria. Teague worked with Ritter's engineers to develop a central dental unit to complement the new chair. All of its elements were housed in a single structure, and most of the instruments and controls were covered when not in use by a sliding panel. The colors and forms were soft; however, the unit had a robotic character that may have made it less comforting than it was intended to be.

A notable example of the industrial designer's service to the medical profession was the development of a new autopsy suite for the Institute of Pathology of Case Western Reserve University. Sophie Koch-Weser, working under the direction of Leon Gordon Miller, planner and design consultant to medical affiliates of the university, designed the suite

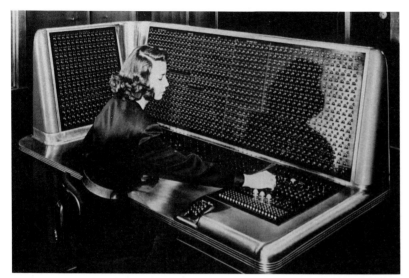

*Sundberg and Ferar worked with IBM in 1948 to design the console for the Selective Sequence Electronic Calculator. All stages of the computation process were indicated by lights. Like a setting for a science fiction movie, the machine dominated the operator. Credit: (216).*

*IBM's 1440 Data Processing System, designed in 1962 by Walter Furlani, J. W. Stringer, and Eliot Noyes, illustrates the shift to dominance of the machine by the operator. Credit: American Iron and Steel Institute.*

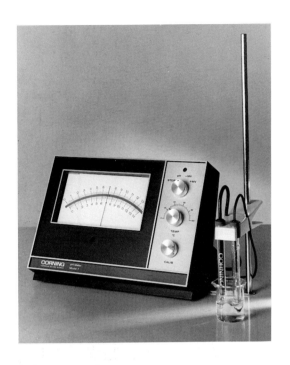

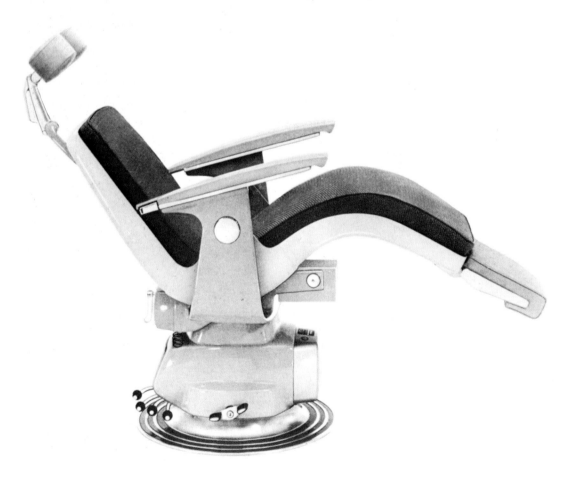

Corning Glass Works
produced this pH meter,
designed by Robert
Quandt and C. Minot
Dole, in 1964. A dark gray
epoxy coating and bright
metal details gave it a scientific character. Credit:
(43, 92).

The "Euphoria" dental
chair was honored in 1960
by the IDI as a "product of
finely sculptured form,
compatible with human
anatomy, and with a rare
completeness of detail to
ease the tensions of both
patient and dentist" (114).
Credit: Industrial Design
(June 1959).

Walter Dorwin Teague
Associates designed the
housings of the Ritter Dental Unit to be efficient,
attractive, and calming.
The diverse operations of
the unit were organized
into a cohesive, almost
anthropomorphic whole.
Credit: (38, 119).

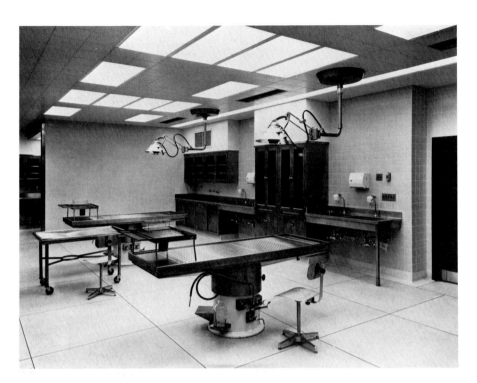

A pathology suite and
autopsy tables designed
for Western Reserve Uni-
versity by Sophie Koch-
Weser. Credit: (216).

to serve as a demonstration and teaching unit as well as a functioning facility. The stark drama of the design was entirely appropriate.

Harold Van Doren was considered the most scholarly of the first-generation designers. His book *Industrial Design,* published in 1940, was both a text for practice and a guide for planning and management. One of Van Doren's first clients was the Toledo Scale Company, which assigned him in the early 1940s to facilitate a transition from heavy cast metal to plastic construction. Whereas the original scale's case had more than a dozen cast parts that had to be ground down, sanded, fitted together, and then filed and painted repeatedly, the new scale's cover was built out of eight elements made of Plaskon, a urea thermosetting resin, that could be used as they came out of the molding machine, with little or no finishing.

The Van Doren scale was one of the first major products to make the shift from being shop-built and bound to its invented form to having a shell that was separate from its structure. Now the shell and the structure were free to serve their own functions—the shell to mediate the relationship between the product and the consumer, the structure to do the work. Such transitions in the building of products provide fascinating but relatively easy assignments for designers because of the fundamental shifts in materials and in manufacturing technology. For many products—especially those that serve the needs of various industries, trades, and professions—modifications are expected to be made as new information, new materials, and new processes become available or as the methodology of a product's use changes. Attempts to subject such products to the whims of fashion or styling generally meet with ridicule or disaster. Industrial design has an important role to play in these product areas, but the design of a product must conform to the product's character.

Unlike most consumer goods, industrial capital goods are usually evaluated for purchase

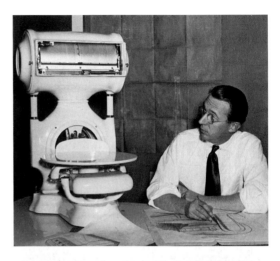

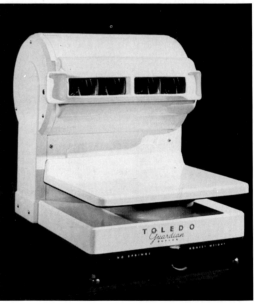

*Harold Van Doren analyzing the thoroughly time-worn Toledo Scale. Credit: J. M. Little.*

*The redesigned Toledo "Guardian" scale. Credit: (39, 90).*

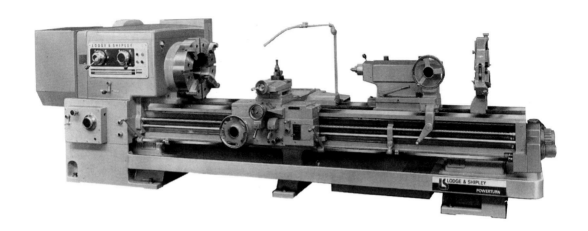

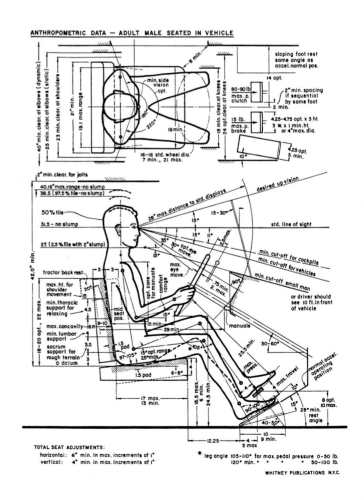

ANTHROPOMETRIC DATA — ADULT MALE SEATED IN VEHICLE

TOTAL SEAT ADJUSTMENTS:
horizontal: 6" min. in max. increments of 1"
vertical: 4" min. in max. increments of 1"

* leg angle 105-110° for max. pedal pressure 0-50 lb.
   120° min. " " " " 50-100 lb.

WHITNEY PUBLICATIONS N.Y.C.

*Productivity and efficiency are the most important factors facing the designer of machine tools. Peter Müller-Munk's design for this Lodge and Shipley lathe achieved these goals with easier-to-operate controls and better-organized information for the operator. Credit: Lodge and Shipley Company.*

*The commitment of Henry Dreyfuss and his associates to the importance of human factors in industrial design resulted in anthropometric diagrams that were published for all designers to use. Subsequently, Niels Diffrient developed the Humanscale series, published by The MIT Press. Credit: Henry Dreyfuss.*

by several persons. One may judge a product in terms of its return on investment, another in terms of operation and maintenance, and a third in terms of safety. Their responsibility is to find a reason *not* to buy a given product. The Lodge and Shipley lathe is an example of such a product. In working on improvements in its design, Peter Müller-Munk's group was obliged to respect the machine's essential character as a heavy piece of equipment that was expected to produce precise results. With that obligation in mind, the designers worked to make the controls more convenient, to make the charts and guides easier to follow, to reduce the set-up time, and to facilitate maintenance.

Henry Dreyfuss had built his career primarily on the designing of products that were not considered to be in the normal run of consumer goods. After Dreyfuss left the firm he had founded, William Purcell, Don Genaro, Niels Diffrient, and Jim Conner carried on the firm's commitment to design what Purcell has characterized as "quality products which called for longer lasting or more classic design approaches than products in the higher style categories" (199).

One employee of the Dreyfuss firm, Alvin Tilley, was a trained engineer who made human-factors analysis a major focus of attention in the company. He had served as the technical author of the Dreyfuss *Measure of Man* books. The *Humanscale* guides, which became essential tools for industrial designers, also owe a technical debt to Tilley.

The Dreyfuss firm also relied upon Dr. Janet Travell as a consultant. She had directed x-ray research on appropriate body positions relative to comfort. With her assistance as well as Tilley's, Henry Dreyfuss Associates were able to strike a balance between human factors, aesthetics, and appropriate technology.

The lift trucks that Dreyfuss Associates designed for the Hyster company in the early 1960s embodied the best principles of indus-

*Henry Dreyfuss's design for this Hyster lift truck integrated the tilt cylinders with the overhead guard, providing additional protection for the operator. Credit: (43, 77).*

*This Utility Loader, designed by C. Hermes and L. Hall for Sperry New Holland, had a sturdy form and was highly versatile. Credit: C. Hermes, Sperry New Holland.*

*This fork-lift truck, designed in 1972 by John Adams and David Tompkins of the Richardson/ Smith design firm, is an example of good product form achieved through strict adherence to functional and human-factors considerations. Credit: Richardson/Smith.*

trial design. Every reasonable consideration was given to the operator's convenience and safety, and the trucks were carefully adapted to the demands of their working environment. Their forms were organized into a cohesive whole that took into account the use of welded heavy plate steel, which was natural to such products.

Another series of work vehicles, manufactured by Sperry New Holland, followed similar principles of design. The engineer L. Hall and the designer C. Hermes directed the development of "Utility Loaders" with imaginative mechanical linkages that enabled them to perform mechanical actions that were almost human in their movements. In 1973 the Sperry New Holland L-35 Utility Loader was selected by the American Iron and Steel Institute as the year's best-designed farm machine.

Richardson/Smith Associates of Worthington, Ohio, worked with the Crown company of New Berlin, Ohio, on the development of fork-lift trucks for use in factories and warehouses. These working vehicles were considerate of the operator's safety and efficiency. Their clean, compact forms respected the tight aisle spaces in which they had to operate, and the absence of protrusions reduced the hazard they presented. More than the preoccupation with style and volatile expression, these products represented the best in American industrial design.

Another area in which industrial designers had an increasingly important role to play was that of "environmental design." Their involvement included membership in community betterment associations and participation in seminars on professional responsibility for the aesthetic quality of the man-made environment. In one such seminar organized by architects in 1966, the subject was "Why Ugliness." The lecture of the industrial designer F. Eugene Smith, "Why Ugliness, Why Not," became a rallying point for design action in the public interest over the next decade. Some products in this area were under private control; others (such as public

signs, urban furniture, street and highway lighting, power-transmission and water towers, and fire hydrants) were public property.

Oil companies that operated gasoline stations had been very conscious of their impact on the public and, from the beginning, had contracted with designers to develop their trademarks, signs, buildings, and pumps. During the 1960s the Mobil Oil Corporation employed Eliot Noyes Associates to develop its overall station-design program, and Chermayeff and Geismar Associates to provide graphic-design assistance. The result was a handsome program of coordinated elements.

Water towers also received design attention. The Saarinens' water tower for General Motors became a landmark. One outstanding public water tower is the polyspheroid one erected by the Chicago Bridge and Iron Company for the city of Carbondale, Illinois. In 1965 the Committee of Steel Plate Producers of the American Iron and Steel Institute commissioned Peter Müller-Munk Associates to develop a series of concepts for steel water-storage tanks that would stimulate public thinking about the possibility that such tanks could also serve other purposes. It was proposed that water tanks serve as public sculpture. It was also suggested that they be expanded to include public meeting places, restaurants, and observation platforms. In short, designers hoped to make visual features rather than eyesores out of them.

Henry Dreyfuss Associates worked with Southern California Edison to develop recommendations for power-transmission poles, and Donald Deskey Associates developed new light poles for New York City. Cornelius Sampson and Associates took on the formidable task of redesigning the fire hydrant, whose existing form seemed so well entrenched as to defy any attempt to change it. The result was a good-looking product that met excellent acceptance. By 1962 it was being produced by three factories for installation in communities across the country.

A Mobil gas station—a
classic example of col-
laborative design between
graphic designers (Cher-
mayeff and Geismar
Associates) and industrial
designers (Eliot Noyes
and Associates). Credit:
(44, 20).

*Environmental sculpture at its best, achieved in a 750,000-gallon water tank erected in 1964 by the city of Carbondale, Illinois.*
*Credit:* Industrial Design *(December 1965).*

In 1965, Peter Müller-Munk Associates came up with this imaginative water-tower concept for the American Iron and Steel Institute. Credit: (216).

No product escapes the attention of industrial designers. The ubiquitous fire hydrant was transformed into handsome sculpture with no additional cost or loss in efficiency by Cornelius Sampson and his associate Donald Baldocchi for the East Bay Municipal Utility District. Credit: (216).

## Chariots of Chrome

*If these products have been designed specifically for transitory beauty according to an expendable esthetic, then they will fall not into ridicule, but into a calculated oblivion where they no longer embarrass their designers.*

Reyner Banham, 1960 (113)

In June 1939 a motorcade of small automobiles in bright colors with red wheels and chrome hubcaps, driven by a team of young women, made its way across George Washington Bridge on its way to be displayed in the Crosley Pavilion in the Communications section of the New York World's Fair. The destination was unusual, considering the fact that the other automobile manufacturers had built their pavilions in the Transportation section. However, Powell Crosley, Jr., already well known as a manufacturer of refrigerators, radios, and other appliances and as the owner of a major radio station, saw the small automobile as just another product in his array of consumer products. At the fair, Crosley's automobiles were put on display alongside his radios and his other appliances.

Crosley's attitude toward manufactured products was parallel to Henry Ford's: he felt that such products should be available at prices that those who made them could afford. His "Forgotten Man's Car" (as he called it) was sold through department stores as well as through a network of dealers. The two-seat coupe was priced at $325—$65 under its only competitor, the American Bantam. It was a spartan product, with tube-framed fabric seats, hand-operated windshield wipers, and sliding windows. Even so, it was considered comfortable, convenient, and a reasonable buy.

When the manufacture of private automobiles was halted in 1942, interest in Crosleys increased dramatically—some were being resold for as much as four times the original price. This convinced Crosley that the preferred postwar automobile would be small, reasonably priced, and economical to operate.

In actual fact, however, neither the Crosley nor the American Bantam attracted enough serious interest to survive.

In 1940 the promise of the future was that everyone could look forward to owning an automobile as soon as the unpleasantness was over. Advertisements promised that the car of everyone's dreams would be delivered promptly at war's end at a price within the veteran's reach. People were warned that the first postwar automobiles might be more like slightly improved 1942 models than like "cars of the future," but this did not put them off. If the dream car was not quite ready, anything that looked like an automobile and had four wheels and an engine would do.

By the end of the war, half of America wanted to buy a Jeep—in part because of the romance attached to it, but also because many thought that Jeeps would be the first vehicles to become available. At war's end, some Jeeps were made available for purchase by military personnel in Europe, and some of these were dismantled and shipped home privately.

Those who were not able to get automobiles, used or new, made do with bicycles. Americans who had been in Europe as part of the Army of Occupation or who had been in the first wave of tourists to go abroad came back with romantic stories of the bicycles that filled the streets from Copenhagen to Milan. Some were able to purchase and bring back European bicycles; others purchased American bicycles at home. For a while it was fashionable for a young couple to go visiting or shopping on two bicycles, with a baby in the father's basket. American manufacturers quickly began producing more bicycles; however, they followed the heavy-bodied streamlining of automobiles rather than the lean forms of European bicycles.

There is reason to believe that a substantial number of Americans would have paid a good price for a small automobile if it had been well made and elegantly designed. The major manufacturers, however, preferred to believe

Carl Sundberg may have counseled Powell Crosley on the first Crosley car in 1939; however, it was mostly Crosley's design. The cars were assembled on Crosley's production line from parts manufactured elsewhere. Credit: Crosley Auto Club.

A sketch of a street scene in postwar Milan by Constantino Nivola. Source: Interiors (December 1947).

that the public wanted larger and lower automobiles festooned with celebratory chrome.
Perhaps they saw any movement toward
smaller cars as a threat to their profits. They
began to respond to public pressure by ini-
tiating small-car programs, but these were
abruptly canceled in 1948—supposedly because of a shortage of materials and appropriate facilities. (Their preliminary work was not
entirely wasted. The GM small car appeared in
Australia as the Holden, and Ford's came onto
the market in 1948 in France as the Vidette.)

There were eight active automobile manufacturers at war's end: Ford, General Motors,
Chrysler, Studebaker, Nash, Packard, Hudson,
and Kaiser-Frazer. The demand for automobiles was so great that it was estimated
that even three years of full production would
not be able to meet it. This encouraged
smaller manufacturers to enter the market,
and by 1948 they had taken over nearly 20
percent of it.

Though some consumers may have found
smaller cars acceptable, there was also some
activity in the development of larger cars.
Preston Tucker's Torpedo, which weighed
over 3,000 pounds (some 500 pounds more
than the average car of the time), had several innovative features, including a center-
mounted headlight that turned with the front
wheels, a pop-out windshield, and an easily
removable rear-mounted engine. Styled by
Alex Tremulis, who went on to work for Ford
as a consultant, the Tucker Torpedo went out
of production when Preston Tucker was taken
to court on stock-fraud allegations. Though
Tucker was exonerated several years later,
production of the car never was resumed.

The first automobiles to reach the market after
the war were a small number of worn prewar
cars that were reluctantly put up for sale by
their owners and some vehicles that were
released from government and military motor
pools. They were followed by production of
new automobiles (actually made from prewar
tooling with superficial changes) when that
was authorized by the War Production Board.
In the case of the Ford Motor Company, the

WPB set a quota of slightly over 39,000 cars for 1945. Yet by the time they were introduced, the company had orders for 300,000. It turned out, however, that not even 39,000 could be manufactured by Ford, because of a series of strikes in the industry. In addition, the Office of Price Administration had set prices for the cars at the 1942 level in order to avoid a surge of postwar inflation. When the Ford Motor Company realized that at this price it was losing $400 on each automobile, it applied to the OPA for an increase. However, even that was not enough to stem the company's losses. In this light, it is understandable that the major manufacturers (Ford, General Motors, and Chrysler) were not in much of a hurry to increase production.

During the war, Henry Ford's son Edsel had secretly arranged for a small team of designers and engineers to work on Fords for the future. The project was not authorized by the War Production Board, nor was it known to Henry Ford. After Edsel died in 1943, his son Henry Ford II, who had been released from the Navy to help his grandfather run the company, was told about the clandestine project; though he wanted to go ahead with it, his grandfather heard about it and scrapped it. Henry Ford II was determined to steer the company away from bankruptcy, and in 1946 he hired a new corporate vice-president, Ernest Breach, to set up separate styling studios for the development of the company's various automobiles.

The Studebaker company had contracted with Raymond Loewy Associates in the 1930s in an attempt to reverse the decline in its share of the market. Loewy had set up a separate office close to the factory in South Bend, Indiana, and appointed Virgil Exner to manage the project. After the successful introduction of the Studebaker Champion in 1939, Loewy had been under contract to work on a new Studebaker for postwar production. Since the operation was entirely outside Studebaker, it was beyond the control of the War Production Board.

Loewy's directive to Exner and the South Bend office had been to make the car look agile, whether in motion or stationary. Furthermore, since Loewy was convinced that weight was the enemy of economy and performance, he had insisted that every effort be made to reduce bulk and conserve materials. Exner had made a number of small models in clay and reviewed them with Loewy, and one had been selected and turned over the the Budd company in Philadelphia to be executed in full scale in wood. Studebaker's management had approved the design, and drawings had been prepared for production tooling so that the new car could be manufactured as soon as circumstances permitted.

When the 1947 Champion was introduced in late 1946—two years before the other automakers could bring out their postwar models—it drew considerable attention. Its bold styling represented a complete break with that of prewar automobiles and set the characteristic form for the postwar period. The rear deck of the coupe was as long as the hood, and the rear window was of a daring wraparound design. The sides of the body had been flattened by widening the body to 60 inches. The car was just over 60 inches high; however, no headroom was lost because the chassis had also been lowered. Overall, the car looked leaner and lighter than its predecessors. In short order, public acceptance snowballed as word got around that the first really modern American automobile was on the market at a price that middle-class citizens could afford. Between 1946 and 1949, Studebaker broke all its records for sales and profits and emerged from receivership to fourth place in the industry.

The success of the 1947 Studebaker was cultural as well as financial; designers had proved that they could sense what the next typeform of an American automobile should be. The car's success also substantiated the idea that, although a product that deviates from the norm represents a great risk, such a product stands to win many converts if it is better suited to its physical environment than

*Norman Bel Geddes demonstrating to executives how a bolder striping pattern will give the Nash a lower and wider appearance. He served as a design consultant to Nash until the war stopped production. The 1946–47 Nash 600 carried his styling recommendations. Credit: Library of Congress.*

its competitors and if its designer has anticipated the psychological desires of consumers.
(If a deviation fails, the design is not always
forgotten. It is often the failed aberrations that
catch the attention of historians, collectors,
and museum curators.)

Eliot Noyes, in his *Consumer Reports* series
"The Shape of Things," praised the 1947
Studebaker Champion as so refreshing that it
made other cars (which he called "inept and
trashily decorated") look out of date. Noyes
also—prophetically—criticized corporate
automotive designers whose chief function
was "to create superficial eye appeal and
readily controlled obsolescence in appearance" (67).

Not all of Studebaker's postwar models were
successful in the marketplace. (One notable
failure was the 1950 model.) However, Loewy
and Exner had managed to jolt the American
automobile industry back to life.

The automobile that Ford introduced in 1947
was unchanged for all intents and purposes
from its prewar car. However, after the new
vice-president, Ernest Breech, drove what
company engineers and stylists had proposed
for the 1949 Ford, he decided that it was inadequate and went outside the company for
help. He brought in George Walker, a former
designer for Nash, to redesign the 1949
model. It was to be the Ford Motor Company's
fourth totally new car—the others having been
the Model T, the Model A, and the V8. Like the
Studebaker, the new Ford had flatter sides, no
running boards, improved visibility, and more
seating room. The entire design process, from
sketches to a full-scale final clay model, was
completed in three months. With management's approval, the car was rushed into
production.

The all-new 1949 Ford made its trade debut at
the Waldorf-Astoria Hotel in New York. It was
introduced to the press and to dignitaries at
an extravagant party and then seen by hundreds of thousands who lined up around the
block outside the hotel waiting their turn. At
the time, the length of such a line was consid-

ered the most important indication of the success of an automobile's introduction. If the line was long enough, it would attract more people and the *New York Times* would deem it sufficiently important to print a photograph of the mob scene on its front page—taken in the trade as ultimate proof of public acceptance.

The most distinguishing element of Walker's new Ford was its armored and chromed front end. (*Time* magazine called Walker "The Cellini of Chrome.") A heavy molding swept down in an arc to the gravel deflector. A chrome bar was mounted across the arc, with a circular "spinner" in the middle. This stylistic detail became quite prominent on other postwar products, reflecting perhaps a head-on view of the piston-driven fighter plane which was identified in many minds with the victories of the Allies in World War II. This same motif showed up on small and large appliances.

Another aircraft motif had appeared in 1948 as a design feature on a General Motors automobile. It was reported that Harley Earl had been inspired by the twin vertical stabilizers of the P-38 fighter to add a small, rather innocuous bump atop each rear fender of the 1948 Cadillac. In the 1950s these bumps were to grow into large fins, not only on Cadillacs but also on many other automobiles.

In addition to keeping designers busy with annual model changes, the automobile manufacturers maintained separate studios for the exploration of advanced ideas in styling and engineering. Beginning in the 1950s, models and prototypes of experimental vehicles (which had previously been studied in the privacy of the styling studio) were brought out for public display. Such showings attracted thousands of people eager to get a taste of the future.

Harley Earl (who in 1936 had created the so-called Y-Job, the first "dream car") had two unorthodox experimental cars built at General Motors in 1951: the XP-300 and the LeSabre. They were, in effect, laboratories on wheels, one exploring technological concepts and the other exploring ideas for functional and aesthetic improvements. Both vehicles were enthusiastically received, attracting the public's attention and whetting its appetite for vehicles to come. It was not long before some of the new ideas, such as the curved windshield of the LeSabre, appeared on production cars.

Aside from Earl's aircraft-like Firebirds of the mid 1950s, GM's "dream cars" were rather orthodox technologically. Presumably they were exhibited in order to test new ideas on the public. In fact, however, by the time a feature appeared on a "dream car," it had already been readied to appear in production two or three years in the future. In such cases, the automakers were really preparing the public for an idea that was indeed going to be used.

The public was flattered at first by all the attention that was being paid to it by American automobile manufacturers. The attention was hardly necessary, however, because the supply of automobiles could not begin to catch up with demand. In a way, perhaps, automobile stylists used the public as an audience before which they could exercise their talents so long as they attracted attention. Stylists in the automobile industry preferred to believe that the public wanted automobiles that were flashier and more powerful. It may also be that the forms of the automobiles were the result of the stylists' sketching techniques. A side elevation looked better if drawn in sweeping "highlight" lines suggesting sleekness and speed, even if the forms that resulted were little more than skin deep. In contradiction, the front end of an automobile, also developed in elevation, was expected to suggest power and thrust, if not meanness and aggression. Most often the two elevations met disastrously at the corners. To paraphrase McLuhan, the stylists' medium controlled the message while the real form of the automobile cowered underneath.

At the time, the stylists may have been right in presuming that consumers would be willing to pay more for highly styled cars than for more modest and economical ones. Undoubtedly the public had come away from a period of peril and austerity with celebration on its mind. Perhaps exuberant and baroque automobiles suited the period. Not even the outbreak of the Korean War could stem the mood of enthusiasm—in fact, 1950 turned out to be a boom year for the auto industry, with over 6.5 million vehicles manufactured and sold.

The implications of stylists and publicists that automobiles were being styled to reduce wind resistance were not supported by automotive and aeronautical engineers, who pointed out that a research study had shown that the differential in power required to overcome drag between the boxy cars of the 1920s and the smoother shapes of the postwar cars at speeds under 100 miles per hour was relatively small. It seems that the real reason for the promotion of aerodynamics as a factor in automotive design was (as it still is) simply to sell more cars.

In June 1950, the Museum of Modern Art held a symposium on "The Esthetics of Automobile Design," which was organized by Philip Johnson, director of the museum's department of architecture and design. Seven men (the majority of whom were automobile enthusiasts, and only one of whom was involved in the actual practice of automobile design) were called upon to comment on the aesthetic quality and character of a selected group of automobiles. Most of the automobiles discussed were custom built rather than mass produced. This put Raymond Loewy, the only member of the symposium who had direct experience with mass-produced American automobiles, on the defensive. He came prepared, and he retaliated against the criticism of production models with illustrations showing what would happen to custom vehicles if they had to conform to considerations of comfort, safety, and commercial production.

In 1951 the museum held an exhibition intended to show "how form, line, and proportion, combined with function, produce beauty in cars as well as other objects" (143). The brochure for the exhibition acknowledged that, even if the expensive sports car was an easier design problem than the family automobile, the principles of good design were applicable to all automobiles. A Jeep was exhibited outside, apart from the other vehicles—perhaps to keep visitors from comparing the more self-conscious designs with its no-nonsense presence.

When the Korean war ended in 1953, all controls were taken off and full-speed production was resumed. The auto manufacturers and their stylists were riding high—relatively free, in a seller's market, to follow their own initiative, with few reservations about public acceptance. If any real concern was given to consumers, it was the realization that women were making a majority of the buying decisions. Harley Earl, vice-president of styling at General Motors, bragged that he had added nine female stylists to his staff to provide the "woman's touch" to the detailing, materials, colors, and finishes of automotive interiors. George Walker, director of styling at Ford, told *Time*: "Beauty is what sells the American car. And the person we're designing it for is the American woman. . . . It is the woman who likes colors. We've spent millions to make the floor covering like the carpet in her living room." (186)

Styling, along with annual model changes, increased sales substantially, hastening the turnover of cars and putting more consumers into the sequence of ownership of each one. Moreover, stretching the life of an automobile earned more for insurance companies and repair shops.

The General Motors "dream cars" were presented publicly in 1953 at the first of a series of annual Motoramas. At these extravagant presentations, staged at the Waldorf-Astoria Hotel, barkers, models, entertainers, and dancers were employed to focus the visitors' attention on the latest dream cars and, per-

George Walker's first automobile design for the Ford
company was the 1949
Tudor sedan. The wide,
rounded body absorbed
the fenders. Credit: Henry
Ford Museum and Green-
field Village.

The Cadillac coupe of
1948 had its taillights
mounted in slightly raised
housings, which set off the
tailfin trend. Credit: General Motors.

haps not quite so incidentally, on current production automobiles. Beginning in 1954, the
Motoramas also included "kitchens of tomorrow" and the latest products from the
Frigidaire division.

At the 1953 Motorama, GM exhibited the Corvette, a sports car with a body of glass-fiber-
reinforced polyester resin. The Corvette was
intended to gauge and perhaps stimulate
public desire for an elegant, high-performance
small car. General Motors had intended to put
it into production with a metal body; however,
the demand for the plastic version was so
great that the company was forced to change
its plans, and Corvettes have had plastic
bodies ever since. Within a decade the Corvette had evolved into a true luxury sports car.

The same year, 1953, also saw the introduction of another classic: the Studebaker Starliner, designed by Raymond Loewy. Like the
Corvette, the Starliner was the result of a conviction that there was a place in the American
market for a smaller, more European-style personal automobile that was more than an economy model. Loewy had developed his concept
for a sportier personal car on his own and
arranged for Studebaker's management to see
it "by accident." They approved it on the spot,
without making changes. The Starliner (built
as a show car in 1951) found a unique position alongside such foreign classics as the
Cisitalia, the Alfa-Romeo 1900, and the
Porsche 1500 coupe. Like them, it had a taut
form without a conventional front grille. Its
only weakness was a curious indented back-
lash on each side (variations of which later
appeared on other American automobiles).
Despite a deteriorating automobile market in
late 1953, as production came up to full
capacity, the relatively expensive Starliner
sold as fast as it could be produced. In fact, it
accounted for 40 percent of Studebaker's
1953 sales, and it was expected to help the
company even more in 1954.

The post–Korean War period, however,
brought a fierce selling situation and a strong
buyer's market. A number of the independent
auto companies that had flourished a few

The 1953 Chevrolet Corvette was conceived as an American response to imported sports cars. Its distinctive body was virtually devoid of superficial decoration. Credit: General Motors.

The 1963 Corvette Stingray. Credit: General Motors.

Raymond Loewy's 1953 Studebaker Starliner coupe was acclaimed by the Museum of Modern Art not as a design but as a work of art. Credit: (216).

years earlier went into bankruptcy or had to abandon the production of certain models. Studebaker found it necessary to merge with Packard in order to survive. Hudson and Nash merged to become American Motors, and Kaiser-Fraser merged with Willys-Overland.

Elegant, prestigious automobiles continued to appeal to the status-conscious. Others, however, were attracted to the more practical station wagon, which suited the needs of suburban families. Even though it was estimated in 1954 that the automobile market was saturated, station-wagon sales—which had represented only 2 percent of the market in 1954—would increase to 14 percent by 1958.

Ford's vice-president and general manager, Lewis Crusoe, responded to the challenge of the Corvette and the Starliner by ordering a rush program for a small two-passenger open car with a canvas top. In this case, haste proved to be a benefit to design. There was no time to follow the complicated process of market analysis and conferences, which tended to dull the imagination. Nor was there time to go through the stylist's labyrinth of form configurations and decorative embellishments. Rather, the designers followed without question a Ford edict that there should be a

straight line from headlight to taillight that would contrast with the curved forms of the Corvette and Starliner.

Ford's plain but handsomely proportioned Thunderbird was brought to market in 1954. Despite its relatively high base price of $2,695, it was an immediate success, with sales of 16,000 units in its first year. In 1954 and 1955 the attention that the Thunderbird attracted helped Ford pass Chevrolet in sales for the first time in years. However, as is so often the case with automobiles, success bred failure. For 1958 the Thunderbird became a gaudy four-seater, and the classic Thunderbird was gone.

The Chrysler Corporation had not fared as well as its competitors in 1954, because it had carried over its 1953 styling with only minor cosmetic changes. Moreover, Chrysler management continued to insist on a rational approach to automotive design. The company claimed that its products were smaller on the outside but bigger on the inside, that passenger convenience came first, and that its cars could be more readily repaired. Meanwhile, General Motors and Ford promoted flashier cars that looked bigger on the outside only. In

self-defense, Chrysler launched a hasty, dramatic redesign program in 1954 under Virgil Exner, its director of styling. This program resulted in a set of finned 1955 models that fell into aesthetic line behind their competitors while being promoted as having "The Forward Look." However, Chrysler did not sustain its styling momentum, and by 1959 its market share had slipped back to a little more than 11 percent.

Except for Chrysler's aborted attempt to hold the line for sanity in automobile design, safety was being almost ignored by the automobile industry despite the increasing public concern. A gnawing suspicion that the problem might not be entirely the fault of the driver brought the problem to Congressional attention, and in 1956 Congress ordered a $200,000 study on "The Federal Role in Highway Safety." The first sessions of the House subcommittee on the subject of automobile design hazards drew spirited resistance from the automobile industry and its traffic-safety establishment. Even so, the forbidden subject had finally been brought to the surface. It would be discussed and fought over for a quarter-century before a sense of mutual responsibility would begin to alter the tragic record of a product system that preys upon the people it serves.

The safety investigations were balanced by discussions on a federal level that led to approval for the building of a 45,000-mile system of interstate superhighways, estimated to cost $100 billion. It was estimated that some 70,000 new road-building machines would be needed to supplement the existing national army of 144,000 earthmovers. Existing manufacturers of heavy highway machines, such as the Clark Equipment Company and Hyster, geared up to meet the challenge. The smaller LeTourneau company was bought out by Westinghouse, which, with the industrial design firm of Painter, Teague and Petertil, developed a variety of highly specialized off-road trucks, embankment compactors, and super earthmovers that had a massive elegance. They were essentially custom-built of welded steel plates, which demanded slab construction. Although the machines differed radically in function and appearance, each had to have a radiator-engine unit. "This was a critical focal point," James Teague writes. "Establishing a basic 'family look' here and simplifying the rest of the units when possible, a new overall identity to the entire line was achieved." (205)

It became evident that a new generation of automobiles would be needed to meet the demands of sustained speeds. In spite of the automotive industry's callous position that, if the public wanted safer automobiles, it would have to pay more for them, it was painfully evident that the public was already paying for unsafe cars. As a result, public agencies, with the support of insurance and health organizations, pressed the industry for safer automobiles. The automobile manufacturers, most of them convinced that safety did not pay, reluctantly began to provide seat belts and other accessories as optional equipment for those who insisted on, and were willing to pay extra for, protection. It was unfortunate that the design community as a whole did not take a position on the issue of styling versus safety. Those designers inside the industry either would not or could not admit publicly that their commitment to styling was related to safety. Those outside the industry largely ignored the issue as being beyond their area of responsibility.

In an important public move to promote automotive safety, the Liberty Mutual Insurance Company had been sponsoring a research project on auto safety (conducted by the Cornell Aeronautical Laboratory). The Cornell-Liberty Safety Car, introduced in 1957, had more than fifty new features directed toward passenger safety. This prototype was sent on tour around the United States in the hope that public interest would encourage the automobile industry to pay as much attention to safety as it was paying to styling. Twenty-five years later, all of its safety features had become standard on American automobiles.

The decline in automobile sales in 1956 may have been due in part to the public's concern about safety. It was also evident, however, that the automakers had overproduced in 1955. George Walker's response to the decline was that Ford would be making styling changes annually rather than every three years. With sales at General Motors down 25 percent, Harley Earl took the position that the public could be brought back into the show and sales rooms through increased attention to styling. In a 1958 GM paper, "Styling—The Auto Industry's Cinderella", it was stated that "dynamic obsolescence caused by the annual model change is the lifeblood of the auto industry and a key factor in the national economy" (246). As if to prove this point, in 1959 the Cadillac tailfin reached its apogee and the Motorama show was the most extravagant ever. The actions of GM and Ford were undeniable evidence that styling rather than safety and product quality was the principle device being used by the major companies as a marketing tool. Styling was as familiar to Detroit as it is to the garment industry in New York. It was the cheapest thing about a product to change and the easiest and most visible thing to promote on the runway, in the print media, or on television.

The Ford Motor Company was aware that the biggest gain in sales of its competitors had been in medium-priced cars, because people tended to trade lower-priced cars for larger and more expensive ones made by the same company. Whereas GM had three medium-priced cars, Ford had only the Mercury. As a result, Ford decided to initiate a research-and-development program that would produce a new contender for brand loyalty at the medium price level. The result was the most exhaustive product-analysis program the industry had ever seen. It would eventually cost the company $250 million.

David Wallace, manager of market research for this so-called E program, worked with Columbia University's Bureau of Applied Social Research to establish a character for the new automobile. The bureau's recommendation

The machines that built the superhighways were the antithesis of the vehicles that would use them. Painter, Teague, and Petertil designed this 30-ton off-the-road truck. Credit: James Teague.

The C450A Embankment Compactor was developed by H. Harbke of Hyster with Dreyfuss Associates. Its two basic units, each with its own power, were integrated by design into a simple, direct, and powerful whole, with concern for ease of operation and safety. Credit: (216).

With some perspective, it is obvious that this 1959 Cadillac coupe had its own aesthetic expression—more rococo than gothic. Credit: General Motors.

*A scene from General
Motors' 1959 Motorama,
with the company's 1959
models in the background
and Harley Earl's experi-
mental Firebird III in the
foreground (under a
"space shape" and a
satellite). Photograph by
James Pirkl.*

was that it should be designed to compete with mid-priced automobiles then offered by General Motors and Chrysler. Wallace and his staff also considered some 18,000 possible names for the new car, relying in part on a *Chicago Tribune* study of the "personalities" of existing automobiles and the degree to which they shaped and were shaped by their owners. The main recommendations were that Ford's new product should be brash, ambitious, and highly visible, and that it should be, as Wallace said, "the smart car for the younger executive or professional family on its way up" (90).

The name chosen for the car was Edsel, honoring Henry Ford's son. Asked about the appropriateness of the name, David Wallace shrugged off the question by saying that the car's personality would be shaped by the merchandising and advertising program (for which the sum of $10 million was allocated).

Roy Brown (the chief stylist of the Edsel studio) and his staff came up with something for everybody. The vertical grill was one design, the vigorous scallops on the sides another, and the horizontal taillights yet another.

In a way, the Edsel proved to be an agglomeration of all that the public was tiring of. Eric Larrabee noted that Americans had become uneasy with the vulgar ostentation, the superfluous size, and the brute power of American automobiles and would have welcomed a practical, safe, and reasonably priced vehicle. Instead they were offered the opposite.

The first Edsels appeared in the showrooms of 1,160 new dealers early in September 1957. By the end of the month it was evident that the car was in trouble. It attracted a great deal of attention, most of it for the wrong reasons. To many potential buyers it was the opposite of what they had been expecting. Ford's promotional coyness only added to the public's disappointment. Late in 1959 (after the 1960 model had been introduced), Ford gave up hope of turning public opinion around and discontinued production. The Edsel was a

disastrous blunder in automotive merchandising, and it raised serious questions about the value of market analysis and research.

The Edsel was only symptomatic of a malaise that was spreading throughout the automobile industry. There was a general feeling that the industry had lost contact with consumers, and that, with GM, Ford, and Chrysler moving in concert, there was little the consumer could do about the problem.

The American public, however, was becoming increasingly unhappy about American automobiles. Fairing fenders into bodies had made repairs more expensive, as had the use of curved glass in windshields and rear windows. Cars had less headroom, and getting into and out of them had become difficult. The new cars did not fit into garages built for shorter and narrower ones. Excessive overhangs, both front and rear, meant that the cars could not negotiate the abrupt angles that often existed between streets and driveways. Reduced ground clearance had made it virtually impossible for the new cars to use unpaved or partially paved secondary roads. Nevertheless, it appeared that such cars were here to stay, and that, if anything, buildings, driveways, and other elements of the man-made environment would have to change to accommodate them. People were asking for smaller, plainer, safer, and more efficient automobiles. What they were being offered were ever larger, longer, and lower cars, loaded with convoluted forms and hung with chrome ornaments.

While the "Big Three" were celebrating the impact of their product on American lifestyles and the potential for increased sales as a result of the highway program and scrambling for shares of the market for medium-price and high-price cars, and while stylists were preoccupied with extravagant forms and baroque ornamentation, scant attention was paid to the fact that, in 1957, for the first time, the United States was importing more automobiles than it was exporting. Europeans claimed that American cars cost too much and could not navigate European streets and roads. Further-

*The 1958 Oldsmobile was a veritable billboard for decoration. An advertisement claimed that "its precedent-breaking beauty fully deserves all the applause owners are giving it," and spoke of "style that will stay in style" (185). Credit:* Saturday Evening Post *(May 3, 1958).*

*The 1958 Plymouth station wagon, advertised as the longest on the road. Credit:* Saturday Evening Post *(May 3, 1958).*

*The 1958 Edsel. Credit: Ford Motor Company.*

**FIVE BIG REASONS WHY YOUR NEXT STATION WAGON SHOULD BE A** *Plymouth*

more, European automakers had substantially increased production and could now export cars to the profitable American market.

In 1949, a pair of amusing little foreign cars were unloaded at a dock in New York. The two had been imported officially to be shown as part of an exhibition of German goods arranged by the U.S. military government to encourage trade with West Germany. They were, of course, Volkswagens. On July 10, 1950, twenty VWs were unloaded at a Brooklyn pier. Thus the strange little "Beetle," without benefit of size, sweep, or glamor, invaded to raise havoc with the smug American styling establishment. In 1955, 1 million VWs were produced, of which some 29,000 were sent to the United States. By 1960, Volkswagen's annual sales in the United States had increased to 160,000. Daniel Boorstin notes that the Volkswagen's "refusal to change" became "a valued 'special feature' with a sales appeal that was itself quite novel" (4, 554).

The European automobile manufacturers were not the only ones who were interested in the U.S. market. In August 1957, Toyota sent two Toyopets—top sellers in Japan—to test their potential in the American market. They were not well received. Americans said that they were "overpriced, underpowered and built like tanks" (176). Although Toyota took them back, the company later returned with a vengeance to virtually capture, with other Japanese manufacturers, the small-car market.

By 1959, an unprecedented demand for smaller cars had developed in the United States. Foreign automobiles were believed to be of higher quality than American cars. Moreover, they were valued as status symbols—a foreign car was a prestigious stablemate in the suburban garage for a large American sedan or station wagon. Auto imports went from 55,000 in 1955 to more than 500,000 (better than 10 percent of the American market) in 1959.

There were only two relatively small American cars in 1959: the Rambler and the Lark. That year, their manufacturers—American Motors and Studebaker, respectively—shared about 8 percent of the market and showed profits for the first time in years. The Big Three had been halfheartedly importing cars from their foreign subsidiaries. General Motors imported the German Opel and the British Vauxhall, Ford brought over the Taunus models made by its German subsidiary, and Chrysler began importing the Simca after buying into that French company. As the volume of imports continued to increase (owing in part to the sale of the aforementioned cars), the American manufacturers began to ask for protectionist legislation and quotas to protect their market. They argued that they could not afford the investment that would be required to produce small automobiles in the United States. In fact, one company took the position that it would take an assured market for 500,000 small cars to justify the venture. Their greater fears seem to have been of the reduction in profit that smaller cars would bring and of the possibility that the sales of small cars would cut into the sales of larger ones.

However, while the Big Three were protesting imports and resisting pressure to produce their own small automobiles, hoping perhaps that the small-car market would peak and then disappear, they had been developing their own "compact cars" since 1958. For the 1960 model year, Ford introduced the Falcon, Chrysler the Plymouth Valiant, and GM the Chevrolet Corvair.

The press for economy under which all three American "compacts" were designed forced them into simpler forms with little of the "jewelry" that decked out their larger and more expensive siblings. This gave them a foreign air that helped make their entry successful. Although they pulled some sales away from the larger models, they reduced the imports' market share from 10 to 5 percent. As a result, a number of foreign manufacturers who had not taken the time or paid the cost to develop solid service systems were forced out of the American market. Only Volkswagen, which had established a strong support system, prospered in the United States.

The first Volkswagen to be imported. Credit: Volkswagen of America.

The first Toyopets en route to the United States. Credit: Toyota Motor Sales, U.S.A., Inc.

*The 1960 Chevrolet Cor-
vair had a modest form
that made a clean break
with other automobiles.
Credit: General Motors.*

*The 1967 Corvair had been refined into one of America's most handsome automobiles. Credit: General Motors.*

The Ford Motor Company decided in 1961 to produce a sporty four-seater. Three of Ford's design studios were assigned by Eugene Bordinat, director of styling, to compete on this project. The studio directed by Joseph Oros won with a proposal for a long-hood/short-deck car based on the Falcon chassis but having its front seats set 9 inches farther back. Despite false air scoops, an awkward dashboard, and an amateurish bas-relief of a horse in the middle of the grille, the Mustang, introduced in 1964, was a huge success. Orders for 63,000 were received the first day it was offered for sale. Jay Doblin calls it "one of the great marketing decisions of our time," noting that "the entire venture was intelligently conceived and executed" (9, 121).

Also in early 1961, Sherwood Egbert, president of Studebaker, called Raymond Loewy at his Palm Springs home and asked him to come up with a concept for an expensive small car to be built of fiberglass on an existing chassis. Unlike the Mustang, which was designed and developed through established practices and took three years to come to market, the Studebaker Avanti was introduced a little over a year later. Loewy's design featured a long hood and a short rear deck, a wedge-shaped silhouette, and a pinched-in "Coke-bottle" effect on the sides. A special design task force was set up to execute the design. Two weeks later a quarter-scale clay model was shown to management and approved; then a full-size clay model was built at Studebaker's South Bend factory and accepted for production by management. The entire process of design took less than two months, and the Avanti was introduced in the spring of 1962 at the New York Automobile Show.

*The 1964 Ford Mustang was designed to reach a market for a low-priced sporty car. Its success demonstrated again that designers can anticipate public aspirations. Credit: (43, 58).*

*Raymond Loewy's dramatic Avanti, like his earlier successful designs for Studebaker, had a European character and was almost free of chrome trim and decoration. Credit: (43, 181).*

# Titanium Skies

*We are born in haste; we finish our education on the run; we marry on the way; we make a fortune at a stroke, and lose it in the same manner, to make and lose it again ten times over, in the twinkling of an eye. Our body is a locomotive, going at the rate of twenty-five miles an hour; our soul, a high-pressure engine; our life is like a shooting star, and death overtakes us at last like a flash of lightning.*

unknown American author, 1839 (5)

Advances in transportation made possible by wartime technology opened up new horizons for travel. Rising standards of living provided average Americans with the resources and the time to travel for the experience itself, in order to satisfy their curiosity, or in order to visit their ancestral homes. For many other countries, American tourism became an important industry. With that went a demand for all of the appurtenances and conveniences associated with comfort and safety on the go. The services of industrial designers were essential to meeting the demand.

Moreover, physical communication between members of the business and industrial communities became as essential as paper and electronic correspondence. Manufactured products for affluent Americans increasingly found their sources in other countries that had less expensive natural and human resources. It became common for foreign and American professional people to travel abroad as product design and development became a global activity.

Within a decade after the war the number of Americans traveling abroad by air had exceeded those traveling by ship. Yet in their planning for the postwar era, the owners of the great steamship lines did not see much of a threat from the infant airlines. After all, the passenger capacity of a ship far exceeded that of an airplane. Moreover, the leisurely experience of getting there was still considered to be half the fun. As late as 1949, listings of daily arrivals from Europe in New York showed as many as thirty major ships a day and only twelve airliners. The American companies Pan American and Trans World Airlines competed with British Overseas Airlines and the Dutch airline KLM for the few passengers who were willing to fly. Yet their combined total could have been carried several times over by the *Queen Elizabeth* or the *Mauritania*. Considering the relative capacities of airliners and ocean liners, at the time it would have taken more than 200 airline crossings to equal one ship crossing.

Opportunities to design interior accommodations and furnishings for both ships and airliners were offered to industrial designers. It seems that they were preferred over architects or interior decorators at the time because ships and airplanes were, with the exception of the airframe or the hull, products. Furthermore, they needed to be furnished with products that would be designed and manufactured exclusively for each vessel. Another important point was the fact that industrial designers, some of whom came out of the world of display and theater design, were still being credited with much of the success for exhibits at the New York World's Fair and came naturally to mind. In a way, transportation interiors could be taken as settings for participatory theater.

The American industrial designers contracted to design the accommodations and furnishings of major ocean liners included Donald Deskey, who converted the *Argentina* from a troop ship back to its original function as a cruise ship, and Raymond Loewy and his associates, who were commissioned to design ticket offices, staterooms, and public areas of the *Pacific Liner* for Matson Lines. American Export Lines retained the Henry Dreyfuss group to design the public rooms and cabins of its new ocean liners, the *Independence* and the *Constitution*. Their assignment was to provide the passengers with the best features of American living as well as the utmost in comfort and convenience in a designed environment that was between the regal opulence of prewar ocean liners and modern, more democratic comforts.

*A sun deck designed by the Dreyfuss office for the S.S. Independence. The glass enclosure could be opened in fair weather. Credit:* Interiors *(April 1951). Photograph by Gottscho-Schleisner.*

Another nautical challenge to industrial designers was an assignment undertaken in the early 1950s by the office of Gordon Lippincott and Walter Margulies. As one of three industrial design firms under contract to the Navy for studies in habitability, they were assigned to design the interior of the *Nautilus,* the world's first atomic-powered submarine, whose almost inexhaustable power source created new problems of endurance without loss of efficiency. Lippincott and Margulies worked with personnel of the Electric Boat Division of the General Dynamics Corporation to design accommodations for a crew of 90, whose living quarters were on two decks. Their task was to make this underwater home comfortable. Design attention was given not only to furnishings and equipment but also to less tangible yet equally vital aspects of the artificial environment. Controlling noise, vibration, and odors was considered to be just as important as lighting, air movement, temperature, and humidity. Colors, textures, and materials were selected and varied to be comfortable without becoming boring. It was also essential that they be tested under lowered light, simulating battle conditions. In many ways, the assignment anticipated design problems that would have to be solved in the coming space age.

Public travel on land was in a situation similar to that of ocean travel. Although railroad companies had recognized the threat of the growing airlines before the war and had rebuilt some of their special trains to make them more attractive to passengers, they now began to spend much more heavily to modernize their equipment. New furnishings were designed for special luxury cars: lounges, bars, and observation, snack, buffet, and dining facilities. Other cars were ingeniously conceived so that they could be converted into movie theaters, dance floors, or family cars with nurseries.

The General Motors Corporation built an entire "Train of Tomorrow" to demonstrate advanced ideas for comfort and safety to rail-

*Atomic submarines opened up a new area of service for industrial designers. Because they could remain underwater for long periods, they presented special challenges in habitability. This photo shows the launching of the* Nautilus. *Credit:* Design *(January 1970).*

The main dining room of General Motors' prototype Train of Tomorrow (1947). The stairs led to an "Astra Dome." Credit: General Motors.

A cutaway view of the Astra Dome car of GM's Train of Tomorrow. Credit: General Motors.

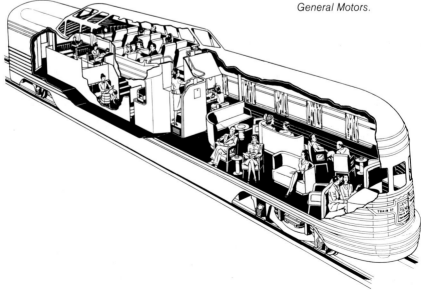

road companies. Though GM was not about to go into the railroad passenger car business, it did manufacture locomotives, and thus it was protecting its own interest. The company invited manufacturers and other suppliers to contribute new ideas to the prototype train. In turn, the company suggested that those whose proposals were included in the train were free to sell similar services and equipment to railroad companies. The GM train had an observation car with a raised glassed-in seating area called the Astra Dome.

The Budd company built its own "Vistadome" observation cars, following designs by Brooks Stevens, for the twin Zephyrs of the Burlington Line. It also designed and built a modern all-stainless-steel kitchen for the New York Central company. New York Central also added stainless-steel observation cars and cocktail-lounge cars to its all-coach Pacemaker between New York and Chicago. Henry Dreyfuss and his associates worked with both New York Central and the Pullman Standard company to develop the latest comforts and conveniences. Dreyfuss stated that although the Twentieth Century Limited his firm had designed in 1938 was still in fashion, improvements could still be made.

However, no matter how much Dreyfuss and other designers contributed to postwar trains, the public was being increasingly attracted to the airlines, which were expanding their routes as fast as new commercial aircraft could be built. The railroads acknowledged the inevitable and began to shift their attention from passenger traffic to freight. They reconciled their loss of prestige by noting that while passenger trains got all the publicity, company dividends were paid by freight. Despite the fact that the United States had half of the world's railroad mileage, the private owners of the railroads and the short-sighted government permitted this valuable national resource to deteriorate in the face of developing competition from airplanes and automobiles.

Bus manufacturers and transportation companies also attempted to hold their own passenger traffic by adding features and comforts in an attempt to keep up with changes in railroad coach travel. As a result, buses became much more convenient and hospitable. Those designed for longer runs now had lavatories, vending machines, better seats, and other amenities. Raymond Loewy's initial assignment from the Greyhound company, in the 1930s, had been a modest but challenging one: to improve the graphics and the general appearance of existing buses. This he did with a new silhouette of a leaner greyhound and with sweeping paint shapes that echoed the wheels, suggesting speed. Later, in 1944, he and his associates had been contracted by Greyhound to develop an entirely new double-deck bus for postwar use that would be suitable for high-speed, long-distance travel and able to carry 50 passengers instead of 37. Loewy and his staff had built a full-scale mock-up to solve problems of space and human factors, from which two prototypes were built for road testing. After changes were made, an early pre-production model was put on the road before 1950. The final vehicle, the Scenicruiser, built by the Greyhound company, went into scheduled service in 1954.

By 1960 it had become evident that traffic congestion in American cities, brought on by commuters who either had no choice or insisted on driving their own automobiles to work, was leading to urban gridlock. This rekindled interest in mass-transit systems, which had served cities well in the past and yet had been happily abandoned by many in favor of automobiles and suburban living. Resistance to public transportation was based in part on memories of aging equipment (the last totally new mass-transit system had been built in 1907) and in part on the fact that suburbanites did not want to leave their cars in the suburbs (where cars were necessary) and then pay the cost and suffer the presumed inconvenience of mass transit when they had to get to the city.

The "Scenicruiser,"
designed by Raymond
Loewy in collaboration
with Greyhound and GM
engineers. GM conceived
the corrugated stainless-
steel exterior, while the
Loewy office resolved the
complex problems of pas-
senger seating and con-
venience with a full-scale
mock-up of the interior.
Credit: Greyhound.

Nevertheless, the problem of commuting was becoming acute, and something had to be done. One "solution" that was already underway was the decay of city centers as business, industry, and commerce followed the people to outlying areas. However, mass-transit systems were looked upon with favor by those who had a vested interest in stemming the exodus from the cities. There was some hope that the public could be lured back to mass-transit systems if they could be made faster, more comfortable, and more attractive, with no more inconvenience and cost than the private automobile. It was suggested that simply adding more buses would not solve either the physical or the psychological problems.

The obvious answer was to provide an elevated rail system. It was a familiar mode, associated in the public mind with applications at Disneyland and at various theme parks. It was felt that, despite the rattling steel elevated trains of the earlier part of the century, new elevated systems with electrical propulsion, rubber tires, and new lightweight materials would not threaten the visual or the aural environment.

The federal government thought well enough of the prospects for elevated mass-transit systems to invest more than 7 million dollars studying the feasibility of the system proposed by the San Francisco Bay Area Rapid Transit District. As this was to be the country's first new elevated line, it was considered important that a thorough study be made before construction began. In an unprecedented concession to comfort and aesthetics, the BART authorities called in an industrial design firm to work on the project from the beginning. The firm was the Sundberg-Ferar organization of Detroit, which not only had an excellent reputation in the profession but also maintained substantial model-building facilities. The firm's first contract was for $275,000 to develop, with the St. Louis Car Company, a full-scale prototype car to be displayed in the San Francisco area in order to stimulate public enthusiasm. The car was built in Detroit, trucked to San Francisco, and exhibited in 1965. Sundberg-Ferar was also retained to design BART's graphics and all the station hardware. The stations themselves were to be designed by local architects.

Montgomery Ferar proudly described his company's design for the basic BART car as offering "a sense of fleetness and sophistication that is unconsciously translated by the viewer into a feeling of security" (212). His firm and BART provided the typeform for modern mass-transit rolling stock. Its essential identifier was the polyester-reinforced control pod, which was originally designed so that it could be moved from one end of the car to the other.

On a smaller scale than BART but equally important to the long-range evolution of elevated transit systems was the Westinghouse company's Skybus project of 1964, for which Eliot Noyes Associates were contracted to design the elevated structures and a prototype of an electrically propelled car that would run on a pair of elevated concrete tracks. As with BART, the first priority was to build a full-scale model of the proposed car to be used to attract public support. The prototype was first shown in New Canaan, Connecticut, close to the Noyes office, and was then moved to a more complete demonstration site in South Park, near Pittsburgh. Subsequently a fully operational system was erected at Morgantown, West Virginia. In 1968 the Skybus system would be installed as an elevated shuttle between the main terminal and satellite departure gates at the new Tampa airport. Eliot Noyes described his firm's approach to the Skybus project as follows: "The design of an electric-powered, rubber-tired, automatic transit vehicle involved complex problems of engineering, human factors, and appearance. As industrial designers we tried particularly to solve the human problems of comfort, circulation, and delight for the passengers along with the other more mundane but equally complicated aspects of the problem." (219)

The BART and Skybus vehicles ran on conventional tracks. The Europeans, however, experimented with monorail systems, such as the German Alweg (in which the car straddled the rail) and the French Safege (in which the car was suspended from the rail). An Alweg system was erected in Seattle for the Century 21 exposition of 1962, and a Safege system was used (under franchise from the French) at the 1964–65 World's Fair in New York. Teague associates were consultant designers for the Safege system.

Other American cities also considered monorails and other novel systems. However, in the end they elected to upgrade existing facilities. Boston, Chicago, and Washington rehabilitated their subway and surface systems and extended them to serve their major airports. In fact, every major city took whatever steps local politics and resources permitted and worked with engineers and industrial designers to improve its mass-transit system with new cars, ground equipment, signs, and maps.

There was considerable attention in the 1960s to the prospects for the development of high-speed transit systems along heavily traveled "corridors" between major cities. Despite heavy federal support for planning (under the High Speed Ground Transportation Act of 1963), very little came of this. For a time it was hoped that such a system would make an appropriate gift from the United States to its people on the occasion of its upcoming bicentennial. Unfortunately, the promised grand scheme was never realized. In all likelihood, its failure was the result of lobbying in Washington by the automobile and highway-construction industries.

One compelling conclusion is that, in their self-serving hold on intercity transportation, the automobile industry and the highway builders had stimulated the growth of airlines and the lowering of air fares to the point where air travel was threatening to take the place of public surface transportation.

The Civil Aeronautics Act, signed in 1938 by President Roosevelt, brought order out of confusion and encouraged the rapid growth of commercial aviation. By providing financial assistance for the building of ground facilities, it helped air travel become an important part of the nation's transportation system. The federal government's justification for becoming involved was that it was in the national interest for the government to support the development of larger passenger planes that could be adapted for military service if necessary.

After its twin-engine DC-3 established a reputable position in commercial aviation in the United States and abroad, the Douglas company decided to build large four-engine commercial airliners. The DC-4 and the DC-6 became flagships for the company in the postwar era.

The original development of the interiors of the Douglas DC-4 and Boeing's competing Stratoliner had been a joint effort, with several airline companies pooling their finances to share the development costs. This ensured compatibility in passenger accommodations and services, which was considered essential to the growth of the industry. At the time, it was considered important that some passenger space be set aside for sleeping accommodations. A public accustomed to such amenities on trains was expected to demand them on aircraft as well.

For the Douglas DC-6, E. Gilbert Mason and Associates designed the seating, the washrooms, the galley, and provisions for converting part of the interior into upper and lower berths.

The design firm of Walter Dorwin Teague served Boeing for many years in a similar capacity as Mason did Douglas. By 1946 Teague had a satellite design office at the Boeing plant in Seattle, with Frank Del Guidice as resident consultant designer. The group developed prototype interiors for the Stratoliner and the Stratocruiser. In addition, they customized the interiors of Boeing aircraft sold to various airlines. Teague proposed that airline passengers should be able to move about freely once the aircraft was at cruising al-

This full-size mock-up of the BART rapid-transit vehicle (designed by Sundberg and Ferar) was displayed in the San Francisco Bay area to stimulate support for the program. The control pod could be mounted at either end of the basic car. Credit: (216).

A sketch rendering of the Skybus system designed by Eliot Noyes and Associates (Allan McCroskery and Allen Hawthorne). Credit: Design (April 1963).

The interior of the Skybus mock-up showed evidence of sensitive attention to all components. With windows curving into the roof, the interior was unusually well-lighted. Credit: (216).

titude, and that they should be able to play games and obtain refreshments in a lounge. He also suggested that music and movies would help passengers pass the time. Another designer, Howard Ketchum, suggested placing observation lounges in the noses of future airplanes and making some of the seats removable so that passengers could dance.

Although foreign auto manufacturers were threatening to take over the American auto market, the American aviation industry was heading for world dominance in commercial air transportation. The end of the 1940s saw Boeing's Stratocruiser, the Douglas DC-6, and Lockheed's Super Constellation competing for sales to the airlines of the free world. All three companies depended upon industrial designers to develop aircraft interiors and accommodations that would keep them in the race. For a while, it appears, the Constellation had the advantage. Besides having a unique form and claiming to be the quietest plane in the air, the "Connie" had interiors designed by Henry Dreyfuss. "It also introduced something else that pleased the passengers—compartmentalization and eye appeal," writes Douglas Ingalls in his book on the Lockheed company. "The long fuselage was broken up with cabin dividers and different color schemes to break up the monotony of 'riding in a tube.' Famous designer Henry Dreyfuss . . . added smart lively colors, wood paneling, diffused lighting, and other touches that offered a new mode for luxury aloft." (19, 82)

The Jet Age had already been ushered in by fighter aircraft that had taken to the skies in the final battles of the Second World War. By the mid 1950s, Lockheed, Consolidated Vultee, Douglas, and Boeing were racing to produce the first jet-driven airliner suitable for non-stop intercontinental flights. Boeing came in first with the 707, which it had derived from its KC-135 (an Air Force tanker). The Douglas DC-8 was a close second, the Convair 880 a distant third. Consolidated Vultee and Lockheed were in a separate contest to build and put into service smaller turbo-prop aircraft for short-haul routes.

*In the early 1950s, Lockheed's dolphin-shaped Constellation held the lead in the commercial airliner field. It was acclaimed as the fastest and quietest airplane in service. Credit: (216).*

*The interiors of the TWA Constellations were designed by Henry Dreyfuss Associates, who divided the fuselage into compartments in order to give a feeling of comfort and security. Credit: (216).*

Given similar performance specifications as well as fares under federal controls, the allegiance of the public to one airline over another depended upon the character and quality of accommodations and services. Thus, in the total environment in which a commercial airliner was to be conceived and operated, the designer became an important surrogate for the traveler. He had, in effect, three clients to satisfy: the aircraft manufacturer, the airline company and, most important, the ultimate passenger. He was expected to be able to vary functional arrangements, services, and decorative treatments. All of this was to be done without offending the passenger's sensitivity or jeopardizing his comfort and safety. The designer had to be prepared to work with dozens of subcontractors on the design and development of the scores of individual products that made up the interior. In a way it was as though one were to design not only the interior of a house but also all of its furnishings, fixtures, tablewares, textiles, and major and minor appliances.

What is more, the industrial designer was expected to adapt his pattern of work to the patterns of his client manufacturer. The Douglas company, for example, had an internal design group consisting of designers and engineers. They, in turn, collaborated with designers under contract to a client airline company. For example, in the case of purchases of DC-6B Mainliners from Douglas by United Airlines, Raymond Loewy's office was engaged by the airline to work with Douglas's internal design staff. In the same way, Consolidated Vultee contracted with Harley Earl Inc. to provide design and consulting services for its prototype Convair 880 jet airliner.

Henry Dreyfuss had been working with Lockheed for a number of years as consultant designer for the Constellations. His firm continued to carry overall responsibility for keeping the company's aircraft interiors up to date and customizing them for purchasers. To this end, Dreyfuss had a satellite design group of six working under William Purcell at the Lockheed plant in Burbank. In working on the inte-

rior of Lockheed's new short-range Electra turbo-prop airliner, the Dreyfuss group had a full-scale wooden mock-up built, complete with lighting and air conditioning. This was used for study purposes and also as a sales tool. Later, when American Airlines came to Lockheed for its own Electras, the Dreyfuss group worked with the airline's own consultant, E. Gilbert Mason, and his design group. Jane Travell contributed to the design of the seats, using data from x-ray studies on appropriate body positions relative to passenger comfort.

Over the years the Dreyfuss office brought a higher level of design to the airline industry. The "on-board art" program brought in the talents of Helena Hernmark, Jack Larsen, and Norman La Liberte, who set themes that did not treat the interior as a living room or an art gallery but rather gave it a unique and yet calming character. Also successful was the design team's development of handsome new dinnerware and flatware for on-board use. Unfortunately, cost-cutting programs subsequently displaced the handsome products developed by James Ryan and Niels Diffrient, with Charles Mauro as a consultant.

Niels Diffrient was in charge of Dreyfuss's American Airlines program from 1969 until he opened his own office in 1980. He, with Jim Ryan and others, designed graphics, interior layouts, and seating as well as food-service items for American's Boeing and Douglas aircraft. According to Diffrient, through the use of human factors "we could, at long last, present our concepts to engineers with more than an aesthetic rationale. . . . We gained stature and a new power." (195) (While he welcomed the use of human factors as a design resource, Diffrient cautioned designers not to assume the role of experts in this area.)

When the Boeing company asked Walter Dorwin Teague to design the interior of the 707, he convinced management to let him build a full-scale mock-up. The agreement called for a flat design fee of $500,000 plus cost, and it contained a proviso that management would not visit the mock-up until it was ready for pre-

*The most handsome stainless-steel flatware produced for airline use was that designed in the early 1970s by the Dreyfuss office for American Airlines. Credit: Niels Diffrient.*

*Walter Dorwin Teague and his associate Danforth Cardozo confer in 1956 on seat design and placement in the full-scale model of the interior of the Boeing 707. Credit: Walter Dorwin Teague Associates.*

sentation. The mock-up was built in seven months under Frank Del Guidice, the director of the WDT Boeing Task Force, with the assistance of Robert Harper, Robert Ensign, and Walter Teague, Jr. It consumed 16,000 man-hours of design and 26,000 hours of construction. Several hundred individual products, to be produced by 54 separate subcontractors and manufacturers, had to be designed or modified. When the mock-up was ready to be presented, Boeing executives were invited to New York to take a "trip" back to Seattle in it. They entered a waiting room and gate complex where they were assigned a seat and boarded the aircraft interior. Doors were closed, take-off announcements were made, and the plane "took off" to the sound of jet engine noises. The view and lighting from the windows changed as the executives "flew" in real time to Seattle. After refreshments and a meal, the comfort and safety features of the new interior were demonstrated. "Arriving" in Seattle, the Boeing executives approved the interior with no reservations. Another full-scale mock-up, built in Seattle, was used for years as a sales tool by redesigning the interior to meet the requirements of representatives of client airlines, who were also given a "ride" in an interior designed to their specifications.

Pan American inaugurated the age of commercial jet service on October 26, 1958, when its 707 jet clipper America took off from New York's Idlewild Airport for Paris. It carried over 100 passengers and eleven crew members in the comfort and convenience developed by the Teague organization.

Other design offices concentrated on providing graphic design services to national and international airlines, which were competing for passengers with airplanes drawn from the same small pool of manufacturers. Two industrial design offices that were particularly successful in this field, Lippincott and Margulies and Walter Landor Associates, broke away from pictorial tradition to introduce bold bands of color and abstract trademarks.

*Robert Smith and Joseph Rinaldi of Lippincott and Margulies developed a new exterior paint scheme and graphics program for Eastern Airlines in 1965. Their solution sent airline graphics off into bolder, more dramatic, and more abstract directions. Credit: (216).*

*Alitalia retained Landor Associates to create its new identification program. Credit: Landor Associates.*

In 1963, President John F. Kennedy announced that in order to enhance American prestige abroad and to maintain international air supremacy, the United States would build a supersonic transport (SST) to compete with the Concorde, which was under development by an Anglo-French consortium. The Federal Aviation Agency called for bids to be presented on September 6, 1966, for an airplane to carry between 250 and 300 passengers, compared to the Concorde's 136. The American SST was to fly at a speed of 1,800 miles per hour as compared to the Concorde's limit of 1,450. The lower speed of the Concorde was due to the fact that its aluminum sheathing could not endure the high temperatures developed by friction at a higher speed. The SST was to be sheathed in titanium, which could withstand the 630° that would be generated on the leading edges and the sheathing.

Even though the federal government had agreed to pay up to 75 percent of the costs of the design competition, only two manufacturers, Lockheed and Boeing, submitted bids and specifications. By the end of October 1966, both companies had unveiled full-scale mockups of their proposals.

The interiors for the Lockheed SST were designed by the Sundberg-Ferar office, which had put together a team of sixty specialists to explore the use of lightweight materials in seat construction. Boeing's interiors were designed by Walter Dorwin Teague Associates. Both design groups had opted for interior schemes that sought to allay passengers' qualms rather than to accent the adventure of supersonic air travel.

At year's end, General Maxwell Taylor, speaking for a selection committee that included military and aviation experts as well as representatives of domestic and foreign airlines, announced that the Boeing SST, the 2707, had been chosen and that Boeing was being contracted to build two prototypes. It was anticipated that some 2,000 SSTs would be in service by 1990.

The Concorde was test-flown in 1968 and put into scheduled service in 1971—the same year as the Soviet Union's TU-144. Taking their cue from Boeing's successful use of a model of the 707 as sales tool, the British built a full-scale model of the Concorde in 1967 at BAC's Filton Works. It, too, had interiors designed by an American firm, Charles Butler and Associates. The French Concorde was built by Sud-Aviation, with the interiors designed in collaboration with Raymond Loewy's Paris office.

The Boeing 2707 was never to fly. Although it was scheduled to be test-flown in 1968 and to go into scheduled service by 1974, its development was aborted by widespread public fears about sonic booms and the depletion of the ozone layer. Despite valiant efforts by Najeeb Halaby of the FAA to save the program, a coalition of environmentalists and budget-cutters led to a withdrawal of funds. (Lockheed went on to develop the L-1011 and Boeing the 747, the long-range "jumbo jet" transports of the following two decades. Again their consultants designed and built prototypes, interiors, and equipment.)

The National Aeronautics and Space Administration's plans for space stations that would be occupied for extended periods posed new challenges in the area of habitability for industrial designers. Lippincott and Margulies had worked on the habitability of the submarine *Nautilus,* and Raymond Loewy's office had provided consultation to the Merchant Marine Association on the habitability of nuclear-powered surface vessels. Now Loewy's firm was called upon to apply its experience to improving the safety, efficiency, and comfort of the occupants of space stations.

Walter Dorwin Teague Associates designed a full-scale mock-up of Boeing's entry in the competition to build an American supersonic transport. Boeing won the competition, but the project was canceled. Credit: Industrial Design (November 1966).

Raymond Loewy's Paris office projected this interior for the French Concorde in 1973. Credit: (23, 243).

*Walter Dorwin Teague's recommendation for motion picture systems to be used on Boeing 747: a wide screen in first class (bottom), rear-projection screens in the aisles of the middle class seating, and a cabin screen in economy class. Credit: (216).*

*The cover of a habitability study for space stations prepared for NASA by Loewy/Snaith. The studies reviewed problems of work, hygiene and recreation. Full-scale foamcore mock-ups were built for research. Credit: (23, 212).*

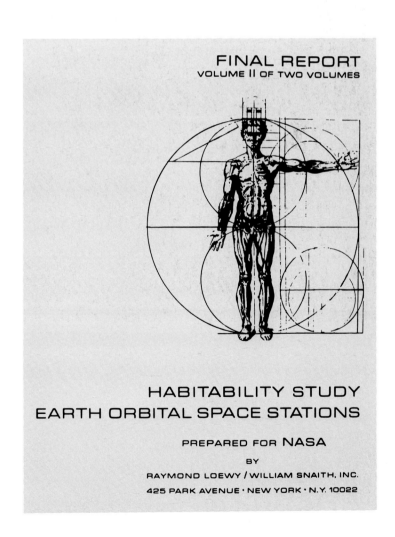

FINAL REPORT
VOLUME II OF TWO VOLUMES

HABITABILITY STUDY
EARTH ORBITAL SPACE STATIONS

PREPARED FOR NASA

BY

RAYMOND LOEWY / WILLIAM SNAITH, INC.
425 PARK AVENUE · NEW YORK · N.Y. 10022

# The Form of Tomorrow

*The things we live with, the things we fashion for ourselves to make our work, our leisure, our homes, and our public places conform to our standards of what is right and acceptable . . . will inevitably form a pattern for future historians as to what we stood for and whether the shape and tempo of our world was worth perpetuating.*

Peter Müller-Munk, 1955 (235a)

For most of the twentieth century, the dominant design ideology conformed to the classical canons of Euclidean geometry. It was evident in the forms of Gustav Stickley's furniture that straight lines were better suited to machine-driven production. Frank Lloyd Wright noted in his autobiography that he preferred the clean-cut straight-line forms that "the machine can render far better than would be possible by hand." This aesthetic dogma affected all the arts in one form or another, but most particularly the arts of design—architecture and manufactured products—because they were bound to forms conceived at the drawing board primarily with the instruments of the draftsman, the straight edge and the compass. The arts of design in the past that were dependent upon the free hand of the artist and sculptor were left to the nineteenth century. The same drawing instruments in the hands of the engineer also gave form and linear and circular action to mechanical equipment. In the process, geometry, which had in the past been the skeleton of form, came to the surface to dominate expression. Its mathematical shapes, heralded as rational and inviolate, were christened Modern Design —the true dogma of the machine age.

Modern architecture proudly displayed its naked structure of industrially rolled or extruded linear elements. Modesty was provided by curtain walls of planar materials—glass, metal, and composites—manufactured in standardized rectangular sizes. Even natural materials, such as stone and wood, were subjected to the dimensional standards. Buildings became "erector sets"—prefabricated structures assembled from manufactured parts that could be duplicated *ad infinitum* if the noble ethic of architecture would permit it.

In the same obeisance to geometric form, what Walter Gropius called the trilogy of form (the sphere, the cone, and the cube) also dominated modern furnishings and the decorative arts. Furniture, lamps, lighting fixtures, surface patterns, glass, pottery, and metal and plastic tablewares and accessories were bound to Euclid. Yet within that severe discipline, virtually every decade of this century had its own particular character. Those characters are now enjoying attention as the residue of a fading avant-garde.

Mass manufactures whose forms also came off the drawing boards of engineers followed the same theorems of geometry. If the engineer's responsibility was to see to the relationship between the manufactured product and the work it had to do, it was left to the industrial designer to solve the relationship between the product and those who would use it. His obligations were to help make the product convenient and safe, to clarify the dialogue between the machine and its human operator, to give the product a form that would be consistent with its function and its user's expectations, and to make the product attractive to consumers in a competitive marketplace. As a result, modern buildings, furnishings, and products all contributed to the Modern Design movement.

Beginning in the 1960s, Modern Design was challenged by rebellious design theories that were seeking new aesthetic territory on which the aesthetic character of the approaching century might be built. The rebels claimed that the mechanical purity of modernism had resulted in a contrived aesthetic that was devoid of social value. It was claimed that the self-serving formalism of Modern Design had been posing as functionalism while ignoring human needs and desires. Modern Design, which had been honored as aesthetic conviction, was demoted and thus made vulnerable to a new generation of tastemakers.

Herwin Schaefer observed in 1970 that "modern design . . . no longer [had] the convincing prestige of a ruling style" and that we were entering "what might be called the post-modern era in design" (36, 199–200). Post-modernism, the American recessionist movement, offered to bring new life to design by borrowing elements from past styles. However, what Richard Meier called a rich collage of meaning, symbol, and metaphoric image resulted in stage settings with yesterday's props that were likely to be even more ephemeral than Modern Design. Nevertheless, beneath all the polemics about metaphors, ironic references, and puns on historic style, there still lay the eternal conflicts between form and function, between expression and utility, and between art and service. At the very least, post-modernism called attention to the failure of modern formalism that had led design into the current slough of nostalgia.

Reyner Banham reprimanded museums for expecting expendable objects to have eternal values. Well-meaning institutions that had tied themselves to Modern Design were left defending their treasures as the word "modern" itself became démodé and was obliged to court a new clientele among collectors and historians. Nevertheless, modern museums were to be commended for championing the philosophy that precious materials and aristocratic uniqueness were not the only criteria upon which cultural values could be based. They proposed that manufactured products dependent upon modest materials could also have eternal aesthetic value.

Russel Wright, in his search for a lifestyle that was uniquely American, proposed that it be based upon casual living, with the conviction that Americans should not be bound to outmoded cultural patterns. Better living suggested to him that good design could be democratic and called for furniture and accessories to be made of humbler materials—aluminum and stainless steel rather than silver, maple and birch rather than mahogany, earthenware and plastic rather than porcelain, and so on. His proposal was a wise one, even

though it seemed daring at the time. It did not, moreover, threaten the traditionalists' hold on products for formal and ceremonial occasions. It seemed reasonable to allow that some products with distinct social and cultural values would continue to reflect historical form and thus conform to the character, if not the expensive substance, of their predecessors.

The challenge for designers was to develop increasingly sophisticated manufactured products to the point that their service, not their substance, was important. Reyner Banham called it a "throw-away aesthetic." This was the challenging legacy of R. Buckminster Fuller's rather disarming philosophy, "more with less," which appealed to manufacturer and consumer alike. The manufacturer saw in the shorter lifespan of his product a self-renewing market. The consumer was convinced that technology was constantly improving products and expected such improvements to be evident in the operation as well as the appearance of each succeeding generation of a product. The public, in fact, was flattered by the attention paid to it by industry as evidenced not only in the product but also in its packaging and promotion. Companies, well aware of their dependence on consumer faith, saw to it that their corporate identities were positively presented to consumers.

It is evident from the perspective of time that the expansion of industry to serve a predominant middle class would lead to materialism for which industry would be held accountable. The result was criticized as a shift from concern for humans to a callous disregard for the public's well-being. By the 1960s it was being suggested that designers were themselves unwitting agents of materialism. Alexis de Tocqueville, a little more than a century earlier, had observed in *Democracy in America* that materialism was to be dreaded among a democratic people because it encouraged men to believe that all was matter only. He called this propensity "the fatal circle within which democratic nations are driven round."

Nevertheless, the support of a large middle class that is characteristic of a democracy is essential for mass-produced products. Technology, as one of the fruits of knowledge, knows no boundaries. It is infinitely divisible without diminishing in value, and as it becomes increasingly sophisticated, it becomes imperative that everyone must share its costs and benefits. The essential value of mass production is that it can provide thousands with services that might otherwise be denied them.

It may, in fact, be argued, that, as the United States and other countries learn to balance production and consumption, they are advancing to a state of post-materialism in which everyone is entitled to the comfort and security made possible by modern technology. Moreover, it is inevitable that manufactured products should become universal in character. Irrespective of national or geographical origins, they serve needs that humans everywhere have in common. Beginning in the 1950s, as products developed international rather than national typeforms, they began to move across national borders almost at will. Their manufacturers became multinational corporations or entered into global alliances. Industrial designers took to the air for their clients, traveling between the United States and other countries to assist in the development of products. Since then, design leadership, technological and cultural, has been shifting from country to country in a competitive drive to keep up with onrushing technology and changing lifestyles. The result has been an inexorable move toward universal forms. This suggests the emergence of a new global identity—one richer and deeper than that constrained in the past by narrower horizons.

Some will argue that the globalization of design will result in homogenization or a post-historic state as products shed ethnic memory and historic affiliations. The fear is that products will enter an evolutionary plateau from which there will be no escape. There is no evidence, however, that technological products can be held back in an open society. It is true that earlier man-made products that had strong cultural or stylistic inheritance often found it necessary to go through a period of historical pretense before their own identities became strong enough to shed such camouflage. However, modern technological products have no such history to hold them back. It is inevitable that such products will continue to evolve richer forms. Instead of arriving at universal generic forms, it is more likely that products will be designed to meet the particular needs and desires in various parts of the world. There is no single mass market for any product, but rather an infinite variety of demographic groups that will determine the final configurations, features, qualities, and price levels of the products that are offered to them.

Since World War II the United States has been serving as the proving ground of a global society in which ethnic, social, economic, and cultural principles have been tried and tested and have been approaching equilibrium. Although the United States has had a common market since the eighteenth century, it is really during these last few decades that American markets have been opened to the world. Thus, American culture may be an early manifestation of an emerging world sensitivity that was sparked by this "promiscuous breed," as Hector de Crevecoeur called the Americans in 1782.

A new morality is emerging by which the tyranny of runaway production may be displaced by a democracy of quantity and quality that will be more sensitively and humanely matched to human needs and desires. Designers the world over seek to tame the products of higher technologies and to train them for human benefit. Manufactured products are, in the end, the true artifacts of this society. As the now separate nations of this planet become one, it is inevitable that manufactured products will echo their historic amalgamation.

# Bibliography

1 Ambasz, Emilio. *Italy: The New Domestic Landscape.* Florence: Centro Di, 1971.

Arens, Egmont. *Color in the War.* General Printing Ink Corporation, 1943.

2 Banham, Reyner. *Design by Choice.* New York: Rizzoli, 1981.

3 Banham, Reyner. *The Aspen Papers.* New York: Praeger, 1974.

Bayley, Stephen. *The Conran Directory of Design.* New York: Villard, 1985.

Bel Geddes, Norman. *The Miracle in the Evening.* Garden City: Doubleday, 1960.

4 Boorstin, Daniel. *The Democratic Experience.* New York: Vintage, 1974.

Burchard, John, and Albert Bush-Brown. *The Architecture of America.* Boston: Little, Brown, 1961.

5 Chevalier, Michel. *Society, Manners and Politics in the United States.* Boston: Weeks, Jordan, 1839.

Cohen, Arthur A. *Herbert Bayer.* Cambridge: MIT Press, 1984.

Consumer Reports Editors. *I'll Buy That.* Mount Vernon: Consumer Reports Books, 1986.

6 Council of Industrial Design. *Design in the Festival.* London: His Majesty's Stationery Office, 1951.

7 DePree, D. J., and F. Knoll. *A Modern Consciousness.* Washington: Smithsonian Institution Press, 1971.

8 Dichter, Ernest. *Motivating Human Behavior.* New York: McGraw-Hill, 1971.

Diffrient, Niels, with A. R. Tilley, David Harman, and J. Bardagjy. *Humanscale.* Cambridge: MIT Press.

9 Doblin, Jay. *One Hundred Great Product Designs.* New York: Van Nostrand Reinhold, 1970.

10 Dorfles, Gillo. *Gute Industrieform und ihre Ästhetik.* Verlag Moderne Industrie, 1964.

11 Dreyfuss, Henry. *Designing for People.* New York: Paragraphic, 1967.

12 Dreyfuss, Henry. *Industrial Design: A Pictorial Accounting 1929–1957.* New York: Henry Dreyfuss, 1957.

Dreyfuss, Henry. *Industrial Design: A Progress Report.* New York: Henry Dreyfuss, 1952.

13 Dreyfuss, Henry. *Industrial Design.* Volume 5. New York: Henry Dreyfuss.

14 Dunn, Alan. *The Last Lath.*

15 Farr, Michael. *Design in British Industry.* New York: Cambridge, 1955.

16 Galbraith, John Kenneth. *The Affluent Society.* Boston: Houghton Mifflin, 1958.

Giedion, Sigfried. *Space, Time and Architecture.* Fifth edition. Cambridge: Harvard University Press, 1969.

Graff, R., H. William, and R. Matern. *The Prefabricated House.* Garden City: Doubleday, 1947.

17 Harrison, Helen H. *Dawn of a New Day.* New York University Press, 1980.

18 Henrion, F. H. K., and Alan Parkin. *Design Coordination and Corporate Image.* New York: Reinhold, 1967.

Herbert, Gilbert. *The Dream of a Factory-Made House.* Cambridge: MIT Press, 1984.

Heskett, John. *Industrial Design.* New York: Oxford University Press, 1980.

Hiesinger, Kathryn B., and George H. Marcus III. *Design Since 1945.* Philadelphia Museum of Art, 1983.

Hopfinger, K. B. *Beyond Expectations.* London: G. T. Foulis, 1956.

19 Ingells, Douglas J. *L-1011 Tristar and the Lockheed Story.* Fallsbrook, Calif.: Aero, 1973.

Jones, Cranston. *Architecture Today and Tomorrow.* New York: McGraw-Hill, 1961.

Keats, John. *The Insolent Chariots.* New York: Lippincott, 1958.

20 Larrabee, Eric. *Knoll Design.* New York: Abrams, 1981.

21 Lescaze, William. *On Being an Architect.* New York: Putnam, 1942.

Lifshey, Earl. *The Housewares Story.* Chicago: National Housewares Manufacturers Association, 1973.

22 Lippincott, J. Gordon, *Design for Business.* Chicago: Theobald, 1947.

23 Loewy, Raymond, *Industrial Design.* Woodstock, N.Y.: Overlook, 1979.

24 Loewy, Raymond. *Never Leave Well Enough Alone*. New York: Simon and Schuster, 1941.

Lynch, Vincent, and William Henkin. *Jukebox: The Golden Age*. New York: Putnam, 1981.

25 Lynes, Russell. *The Tastemakers*. New York: Harper, 1955.

26 Marks, Robert W. *The Dymaxion World of Buckminster Fuller*. New York: Reinhold, 1960.

McAusland, Randolph. *Supermarkets: 50 Years of Progress*. Washington: Food Distribution Institute, 1980.

27 McCoy, Esther. *Case Study Houses, 1945–1962*. Los Angeles: Hennessey and Ingalls, 1977.

28 McLuhan, Marshall, and Quentin Fiore. *The Medium is the Massage*. New York: Bantam, 1967.

Meggs, Philip B. *A History of Graphic Design*. New York: Van Nostrand Reinhold, 1983.

Meloan, Taylor W. *Mobile Homes*. Homewood, Ill.: Irwin, 1954.

Melson, H. R. *Collected Writings of Alvin Lustig*. New York: Thistle.

29 Miller, R. *Design in America*. New York: Abrams, 1983.

30 Moholy-Nagy, Laszlo. *Vision in Motion*. Chicago: Theobald, 1947.

Nader, Ralph. *Unsafe at Any Speed*. New York: Grossman, 1965.

31 Nash, Ben, *Developing Marketable Products and Their Packages*. New York: McGraw-Hill, 1945.

Nelson, George, and Henry Wright. *Tomorrow's House*. New York: Simon and Schuster, 1946.

32 Nelson, George. *Chairs*. New York: Whitney, 1953.

Nelson, George. *The Herman Miller Collection*. Zeeland, Mich.: Herman Miller Co., 1950.

33 Olshaker, Mark. *The Instant Image*. New York: Stein and Day, 1978.

Pulos, Arthur J. *American Design Ethic*. Cambridge: MIT Press, 1983.

Pulos, Arthur J. *Opportunities in Industrial Design*. Skokie: National Textbook Co., 1978.

34 Rogers, Meyric C. *Italy at Work*. Rome: Istituto Poligrafico Dello Stato, 1950.

Rohde, Gilbert. "Aptitudes and Training for Industrial Designers." In *Art in American Life and Education*. Bloomington, Ill.: Public School Publishing Co., 1941.

35 Russell, Gordon. *Designer's Trade*. London: Allen and Unwin, 1968.

36 Schaefer, Herwin. *Nineteenth Century Modern*. New York: Praeger, 1970.

37 Society of Industrial Designers. *51 U.S. Industrial Design*. New York: Studio Publications, 1951.

38 Society of Industrial Designers. *Industrial Design in America*. New York: Farrar, Strauss & Young, 1954.

39 Society of Industrial Designers. *U.S. Industrial Design 1949/1950*. New York: Studio Publications, 1949.

Suhonen, P. "Artek—A Short History." In *Artek: 1935–1985*. Helsinki Museum of Industrial Arts, 1985.

40 Teague, Walter Dorwin. *Design This Day*. New York: Harcourt, Brace, 1940.

41 Van Doren, Harold. *Industrial Design*. New York: McGraw-Hill, 1940.

Wallance, Don. *Shaping America's Products*. New York: Reinhold, 1956.

Wessel, Joan, and Nada Westerman. *American Design Classics*. New York: Design Publications, 1985.

White, Lawrence. *The Automobile Industry Since 1945*. Cambridge: Harvard University Press, 1971.

Wilson, Richard Guy, Diane H. Pilgrim and Dickran Tashjian. *The Machine Age in America 1918–1941*. New York: Abrams, 1986.

42 Wright, Russel, and Mary Wright. *Guide to Easier Living*. New York: Simon and Schuster, 1950.

Wurts, Richard. *The New York World's Fair 1939/1940*. New York: Dover, 1977.

*Culture and Technology of the Italian Furniture 1950/1980*. Rome: Italian Foreign Trade Institute, 1981.

*Design Concepts: Water Storage.* New York: Iron and Steel Institute, 1965.

*Design for ETV: Planning for Schools with Television.* New York: Educational Facilities Laboratory, 1960.

43 *Design in America.* New York: McGraw-Hill, 1969.

*Design in Finland 1986.* Helsinki: Finnish Foreign Trade Association, 1986.

*Design Process Olivetti 1908–1978.* Milan: Grafiche Milani, 1979.

44 *Design Today.* New York: Iron and Steel Institute, 1968.

*High Styles: Twentieth Century American Design.* New York: Whitney Museum of American Art, 1985.

45 IDEA 54 International Design Annual. New York: George Wittenborn, Inc., 1953.

46 *Industriele Vormgeving in Amerika.* Gravenhage: Contactgroup Opvoering Productiviteit, 1954.

47 *Laszlo Moholy-Nagy.* Paris: Centre National d'Art et de Culture Georges Pompidou - CCI, 1976.

*Alumni Review,* California Institute of Technology, June 1942, p. 2.

*American Business,* September 1946, p. 42.

*American Heritage,* December 1960. "The Mighty Jeep," pp. 39ff.

*American Merchandising,* September 1943, pp. 279–285.

**Architectural Forum**

48 March 1940, pp. 187–188.

49 October 1941, p. 34.

50 December 1942, p. 3.

51 January 1943, p. 98.

52 February 1943, p. 34.

53 March 1943, p. 11.

54 June 1943, p. 50.

55 September 1943, p. 4.

56 September 1943, p. 116.

"Greatest House-Building Show on Earth." March 1947, pp. 105–112.

"House Equipment Packaged." February 1946, pp. 81–96.

Kelley, Burnham. "Politics and the Housing Crisis Since 1930." January 1943, p. 60.

Pulos, Arthur J., "The Restless Genius of Norman Bel Geddes." July 1970, pp. 46, 51.

**Architectural Record**

57 June 1940, p. 87.

58 April 1943, p. 131.

Dunnett, H. "Furniture Since the War." March 1951, pp. 150–166.

Gueft, Olga. "Edward J. Wormley: A Portrait." November 1956, pp. 90–105.

**Architectural Review**

October 1946, pp. 93–119.

Kaufmann, Edgar Jr. "Borax or the Chrome-Plated Calf." August 1948, pp. 88–92.

**Art and Industry**

59 March 1958, pp. 86–87.

Dutton, N. "British Industry can Lead the World. . . ." January 1946, pp. 2–6.

**Art Digest**

60 August 1940, p. 16.

April 1949, p. 35.

**Arts and Architecture**

"Styling, Organization, Design." August 1947, pp. 24–27.

"House in a Factory." September 1947, pp. 31–35, 49–50.

February 1954, pp. 13–16.

61 *Atlantic Monthly,* January 1941, p. 23.

**Automobile Quarterly**

62 Volume 14, no. 4 (1976), p. 431.

"Austin and Bantam Story." Volume 14, no. 4 (1976), pp. 404–429.

Better Homes and Gardens, April 1947, p. 43.

Bush-Brown, Albert. "A Designer's Manifesto for Leadership." *Industrie und Kunst Linz* (date unknown), pp. 115–118.

### Business Week

63  January 13, 1940, p. 35.

October 29, 1949, p. 25

February 25, 1950, p. 64.

*California Arts and Architecture,* September 1946, pp. 30ff.

64  *Carnegie,* March 1960, p. 89.

65  Chiles, James R. "Titanium: For When You Care to Use the Very Best." *Smithsonian,* May 1987, pp. 86–95.

Clement, Theodore. "Industrial Design in the U.S.—1966." *American Designer,* February 1967, pp. 13–14.

*College Art Journal* 8, no. 3 (1949), p. 222.

### Consumer Reports

66  May 1947, p. 176.

67  May 1948, p. 204.

68  January 1949, p. 26.

69  January 1950, p. 45.

70  February 1967, p. 114.

Caplan, Ralph. "It's the Curve that Counts." April 1965, p. 185.

71  Noyes, Eliot. "The Shape of Things." July 1949, p. 314.

Noyes, Eliot. "The Shape of Things." September 1949, p. 392.

### Craft Horizons

72  July-August 1958, p. 30.

Brown, C. "ICA's Technical Assistance Team. . . ." July-August 1958, pp. 28–36.

*Cue,* February 1944, pp. 5, 11, 12.

### Design

73  November 1951, p. 1.

74  March 1964, p. 38.

75  December 1965, p. 25.

76  January 1970, p. 46.

77  January 1970, p. 84.

Blake, J. "Jubilee Celebrations for the Men from DRU." January 1943, p. 26.

78  Grafly, Dorothy. "Industrial Design." January 1947, p. 16.

Kabaker, Alvin. "Better Design for America." December 1935.

### The Designer (London)

79  September 1969, p. 6.

80  September 1969, p. 7.

### Design Quarterly

81  No. 29 (1954), pp. 5–6.

82  No. 51–52 (1960), p. 3.

Dreyfuss, Henry. "The Industrial Designer and the Businessman." *Harvard Business Review,* November 1950, p. 80.

*Economist,* December 23, 1944, p. 832.

*Esthetique Industrielle* (Paris), no. 7 (1953)

### Everyday Art Quarterly

83  Fall 1946, p. 12.

84  Summer 1947, preface.

85  Autumn 1947, p. 1.

86  Winter 1949–50, p. 4.

### Fortune

87  December 1942, supplement.

88  February 1949, p. 204.

Doblin, Jay. "The 100 Best Designed Products." April 1959, pp. 135–141.

Freedgood, S. "Odd Business, This Industrial Design." February 1949, pp. 130ff.

McQuade, Walter. "Charles Eames Isn't Resting on His Chair." February 1975, pp. 96ff.

Nelson, George. "Business and the Industrial Designer." July 1949, pp. 92–98.

Nelson, George. "The Furniture Industry." January 1947, pp. 107–111.

"That Lustron Affair." November 1949, pp. 92–94.

*Frequent Flyer,* March 1987, pp. 65–75.

**89** Goldsmith, Maurice. "Design Research Unit." *Graphis,* no. 23 (1948), p. 258.

*Graphis,* 1950, No. 201, pp. 136–147.

**Harpers**

August 1958, pp. 66–75.

Blake, Peter, and Jane Fiske McCullough. "Very Significant Chair." August 1958, pp. 66–75.

**90** Larrabee, Eric. "The Edsel and How It Got That Way." September 1957, p. 73.

Larrabee, Eric. "The Six Thousand Houses that Levitt Built." September 1948, pp. 77–88.

Perry, John. "New Products for Post-War America." February 1943, pp. 330–332.

**House and Garden**

**91** July 1939, p. 15.

**92** July 1947, p. 26.

"1947: Design Year in the USA." July 1947.

**House Beautiful**

"This House Plus Garage Equals." April 1947, pp. 106–130.

Gordon, Elizabeth. "Museum Objects Belong at Home." December 1947, p. 121.

**Industrial Design**

**93** October 1955, p. 98.

**94** December 1955, p. 39.

**95** April 1956, p. 12.

**96** October 1956, p. 20.

**97** January 1957, p. 12.

**98** February 1957, p. 53.

**99** February 1957, p. 39.

**100** June 1957, p. 75.

**101** July 1957, p. 60.

**102** January 1958, p. 80.

**103** May 1958, p. 49.

**104** July 1958, p. 21 (originally in *Business Week,* April 12, 1958).

**105** July 1958, p. 51.

**106** January 1959, p. 57.

**107** January 1959, p. 70.

**108** March 1959, p. 73.

**109** March 1959, p. 58.

**110** April 1959, p. 47.

**111** November 1959, p. 80.

**112** January 1960, p. 68.

**113** March 1960, p. 65.

**114** June 1960, p. 14.

**115** July 1960, p. 70.

**115a** November 1960, p. 73.

**116** August 1961, p. 63.

**117** April 1962, p. 74.

**118** March-April 1982, p. 44.

Allen, D. "Power Tools: The Newest Home Appliances." February 1954, pp. 30–37.

Burrey, S. "John Burton Tigrett's Business Has No Barriers." April 1957, pp. 66–75.

Conway, Patricia. "Smith vs. Ugliness." May 1966, pp. 38–45.

"Design as Economic Diplomat." August 1956, pp. 68–73.

Ferrebee, Ann. "U.S. Design Abroad." February 1963, pp. 26–47.

Fleishman, Avrom. "Design as a Political Force." April 1957, pp. 44–60.

Freeman, John Wheelock. "The Studebaker Story." February 1954, pp. 38–45.

Larrabee, Eric. "Machines that Make Music." June 1954, pp. 22–31.

Larrabee, Eric. "The Great Love Affair." October 1955, pp. 95–97.

Pile, John. "The Black Box." April 1954, pp. 43–51.

"Plastics on the Table." April 1954, pp. 63–69.

Sorkin, Michael. "Just a Phone Call Away." March-April 1983, pp. 3–4.

Sterling, David. "Kitchen of Tomorrow." July-August 1982, pp. 44–47.

"The Continuities of Jens Risom." October 1959, pp. 150ff.

## Interiors

**119** October 1945, p. 16.

**120** April 1946, p. 8.

**121** January 1947, p. 12.

**122** February 1947, p. 18.

**123** July 1947, p. 101.

**124** July 1947, p. 102.

**125** July 1947, p. 103.

**126** July 1947, p. 105.

**127** December 1947, p. 83.

**128** December 1947, p. 92.

**129** December 1947, p. 112.

**130** January 1948, p. 129.

**131** July 1948, p. 71.

**132** September 1948, p. 10.

**133** December 1948, p. 14.

**134** April 1949, p. 14.

**135** April 1949, p. 18.

**136** April 1949, p. 166.

**137** July 1949, p. 78.

**138** November 1949, p. 67.

**139** May 1950, p. 166.

**140** November 1950, pp. 145, 194, 196.

**141** March 1951, p. 100.

**142** September 1951, p. 122.

**143** September, 1951, p. 125.

**144** November 1951, p. 152.

**145** February 1953, p. 85.

**146** March 1954, p. 90.

**147** February 1955, p. 12.

**148** April 1958, p. 183.

"Best of the New Furniture." October 1948, pp. 92–101.

Chermayeff, Serge. "The Case of a Unique Building Plan." September 1948, pp. 96–119.

"Goldmine in Southeast Asia." August 1956, pp. 94–101.

Gueft, Olga. "Edward J. Wormley: A Portrait." November 1956, pp. 90–105.

"Industrial Design: From England sans Curlicues." May 1948, pp. 113–117.

Nelson, George. "Blessed are the Poor. . . ." July 1948, pp. 70–120.

Nelson, George. "Modern Furniture." July 1949, pp. 76–111.

Nelson, George. "Problems of Design, Ends and Means." May 1948, pp. 84–87.

Teague, W. D. "Italian Shopping Trip." November 1950, pp. 144–149, 194–201.

"Their Fine Italian Hands." July 1947, pp. 80–83.

Jordan, Michael. "Looking Backward." *Car and Driver,* March 1983, pp. 55–58.

*Machine Design,* July 26, 1979, p. 34.

**149** *Metal and Alloys,* January 1945, p. 84.

**150** *Modern Plastics,* June 1945, p. 6.

## Museum of Modern Art Bulletin

**151** November 1940, pp. 12–13.

**152** May 1942, p. 2.

**153** December 1942–January 1943, p. 6.

**154** December 1942–January 1943, p. 10.

**155** December 1942–January 1943, p. 18.

**156** December 1942–January 1943, pp. 6–7.

**157** December 1942–January 1943, p. 9.

**158** Fall 1946, p. 3.

**159** January 1948, p. 13.

**160** "The House in the Museum Garden." Fall 1946, p. 1.

**161** Kaufmann, Edgar Jr. Preface. Fall 1946.

*The Nation,* October 11, 1958, pp. 211–213.

Nelson, George. "Chairs." *Holiday,* November 1957, pp. 137–142.

**Newsweek**

November 25, 1957.

August 29, 1966, pp 48–55.

**New York Times**

162 January 1, 1939, IX, p. 9.

163 February 3, 1940, p. 9.

164 May 5, 1940, p. 9.

165 October 4, 1941, p. 28.

166 March 15, 1942, II, p. 2.

167 March 22, 1942, X, p. 2.

168 September 26, 1943, VI, p. 14.

169 September 26, 1943, VI, p. 15.

170 July 12, 1944, p. 16.

171 November 14, 1945, p. 16.

172 November 21, 1945, p. 18.

173 December 16, 1947, p. 58.

174 September 25, 1949, XX, p. 14.

175 June 6, 1984, p. C-19.

176 May 6, 1986, p. 9.

"Electrical Goods Set New Sales Figures."
August 4, 1940, p. 7.

"Equipping New Homes." August 25, 1940,
p. 12.

Friedlander, Paul. "The Threshold of the
Supersonic Travel Age." October 9, 1966, X,
pp. 1, 17.

**Package Design**

177 May-June 1968, p. 29.

178 May-June 1968, p. 30.

179 May-June 1968, p. 31.

180 May-June 1969, p. 29.

**Pencil Points**

181 April 1939, p. 238.

182 [Month?] 1940, p. 439.

183 *PM,* August-September 1939, foreword.

*Printer's Ink,* January 1959, p. 30.

*Product Engineering,* October 21, 1957, pp.
32–33.

*Progressive Architecture,* September 1964, p.
222.

**Sales Management**

July 1, 1943, pp. 40–47.

April 15, 1953, pp. 18–19.

**Saturday Evening Post**

184 July 17, 1943, p. 98.

185 May 3, 1958, p. 45.

*Society of Automotive Engineers Transactions,* July 1946, pp. 325–328.

*Stile Industria,* October 1960, p. 5.

*This Week,* December 1955 (reprint).

**Time**

October 31, 1949, pp. 66ff.

186 November 4, 1957, p. 100.

*Tools,* October 1945, p. 28.

187 *Ulm Journal,* April 1968, p. 14.

**Vogue**

188 February 1939, p. 71.

February 1939, p. 99.

**Interviews**

189 Dreyfuss, Henry. Tape interview with Ray
Spilman, March 18, 1969.

190 Kostellow, Rowena Reed. Interview by author,
November 17, 1983.

191 Zeller, Herbert. Taped interview with Rudy
Krolopp. Transcript, July 1984, pp. 10–11.

**Correspondence**

192 Blauensteiner, Charlotte. Letter to author,
October 23, 1984.

193 Clement, Theodore G. Letter to author, July
17, 1963.

194 Cushing, George. Letter to author, July 31, 1963.

195 Diffrient, Niels. Letter to author, September 5, 1984.

196 Graser, C. F. Letter to author, January 25, 1983.

197 Gunn, William N. Letter to PDC members, June 22, 1971.

198 Müller-Munk, Peter. Letter to author, July 23, 1962.

199 Purcell, William F. H. Letter to author, November 9, 1982.

200 Reinecke, Jean. Letter to author, November 29, 1982.

201 Russell, Gordon. Letter to Antonin Heythum, February 22, 1951.

202 Sandin, Raymond S. Letter to author, June 24, 1963.

203 Spilman, Raymond. Letter to author, September 13, 1963.

204 Stevens, Brooks. Letter to author, December 7, 1982.

205 Teague, James. Letter to author, August 5, 1986.

206 Teague, Walter Dorwin. Letter to Richard Bach, June 28, 1946.

207 Warner, Sidney. Letter to author, March 24, 1976.

**Syracuse University, George Arents Research Library**

208 Albini, Franco. Letter to Society of Industrial Designers, June 24, 1950.

209 Amendment to New York State Education Law, Section 1270, Article 48-A.

210 American Designers Institute meeting minutes, April 2, 1945.

211 American Designers Institute National Board meeting minutes, January 26, 1950.

American Designers Institute meeting minutes, 1942–1950.

BecVar, Arthur. Letter to Robert Hose, September 15, 1953.

212 Ferar, Montgomery. Statement for *Design in America*.

213 Flank, R. *History of the American Designers Institute,* 1962, p. 10.

214 Gueft, Olga. Letter to Peter Müller-Munk, May 3, 1954.

Antonin Heythum Papers.

ICSID Summary Reports: "The Education of Industrial Designers," 1965–1967.

ICSID Working Group on Education meeting minutes, 1963–1969.

215 Industrial Designers Institute. Letter to ASID, August 7, 1959.

216 Industrial Designers Society of America Papers.

217 Industrial Designers Society of America Papers, Box 33.

William Lescaze Papers.

Müller-Munk, Peter. Letter to Olga Gueft, April 30, 1954.

218 Nash, Benjamin. Definition of Industrial Design. Box 33.

Nelson, George. Proposal for *Design in America*. Box 103.

219 Noyes, Eliot. Statement for *Design in America*.

Pulos, Arthur. ICSID Report to UNESCO: "Industrial Design Education in the United States, 1960–1966," 1966, pp. 14–17.

220 Society of Industrial Designers Book Committee. Statement by Robert Hose, October 21, 1953.

221 Society of Industrial Design Archives. Proposal dated May 1944.

Society of Industrial Designers Education Bulletins 1–3, 1946–1948.

Society of Industrial Designers meetings minutes, March 1946–October 1949.

Teague, W. D. Letter to prospective exhibitors, May 14, 1957.

222 Teague, W. D. (office). Meeting minutes, February 7, 1944.

223 Vassos, John. Letter to J. Streichler, February 27, 1962.

John Vassos Papers.

## Miscellaneous Publications

Akron Art Institute exhibition catalog, November 2–December 2, 1947.

**224** Amendment to New York State Education Law, Section 1270, Article 48-A.

*Journal of the American Hospital Association,* August 1960 (reprint).

**225** American Management Associates. "American Business and Industrial Design," 1947, p. 20.

American Society of Industrial Designers Newsletter, August 1956.

*The Anatomy of Design* (monograph). London: Royal College of Art, 1951.

Bach, Alfons. "Shopping Centers" (paper for *Distribution Age*), 1946.

Black, Misha. "Notes on Design Education in Great Britain," 1970, p. 4.

Black, Misha. "The Training of Industrial Designers in Great Britain." Lecture to Symposium at The Hague, April 1960.

**226** Black, Misha. "History of ICSID." Brussels, ICSID Secretariat, 1975, p. 3.

California Graduate School of Design catalog, 1940–41.

**227** Conference on Industrial Design, a New Profession. Museum of Modern Art, for Society of Industrial Designers, 1946 (typescript), p. 1.

**228** Ibid., p. 46.

**229** *Design Sense* (Lippincott & Margulies publication), no. 23, p. 2.

"Design Since 1945" (exhibition catalog, Philadelphia Museum of Art), p. 112.

"Design USA" (exhibition catalog, U.S. Department of Commerce with IDSA and Package Designers Council, 1965).

Donald Deskey Archives, Cooper-Hewitt Museum, New York.

*Encyclopedia Americana* Annual, 1951, p. 334.

"Eva Zeisel: Designer for Industry" (catalog, Le Chateau Dufresne, Montreal, Canada, 1984).

"Evening Courses in Industrial Design, Fall Term, 1948–1949" (New York University flyer).

"Exhibition for Modern Living" (catalog, Detroit Institute of Art, 1949).

**230** Glace, Margaret, and Florence Beeley. "Conference of Schools of Design," Metropolitan Museum, June 22–23, 1944 (pub. 1946).

**231** "Good Design is Your Business" (exhibition catalog, Albright Art Gallery, 1947), p. 9.

ICSID Constitution, adopted at First General Assembly, Stockholm, Sweden, September 17, 1959.

"Industrial Design: An International Survey" (ICSID/UNESCO Report, March 1967).

**232** "Industrial Design Education in America" (report, ICSID Congress, Paris, 1963). p. 29.

"Industrial Design Education in the United Kingdom." London: Design Council, 1977.

**233** "Industrial Design in the U.S." (Project No. 278, European Productivity Agency, OEEC, Paris, 1959), p. 10.

**234** Ibid., p. 80.

IDSA newsletter, April 1965, p. 1.

IDSA newsletter, July-August 1967, pp. 2–3.

*Knoll au Louvre* catalog, 1972.

Koike, S. "The Evolution of Industrial Design in Japan." *Journal of World History* 9 (1965), pp. 394–395.

**235** McConnell, P. "Society of Industrial Designers" (1945), pp. 5–6.

**235a** Müller-Munk, Peter. "The Dynamics of Industrial Design." SID Eleventh Annual Meeting, Washington, D.C., 1955.

Museum of Modern Art press release, spring 1951.

**236** *News Chronicle Souvenir Book,* London, 1951, p. 5.

*New York World's Fair Official Guidebook,* 1940, p. 58.

Package Designers Council newsletters, June 1961–Winter 1982.

**237** Package Designers Council newsletter, winter 1982, p. 1.

**238** Package Designers Council publicity release, January 1971.

**239** Parkhurst, Charles, Jr. "A Consumer Looks for Good Designs" (Albright Art Gallery, 1947), p. 32.

**240** Photograph, courtesy of Randall Bond.

**241** Pratt Institute catalog, 1936–37, p. 29.

Pulos, Arthur J. "William Lescaze and the Machine Age." *Courier* 9 (spring 1984), pp. 9–24.

Royal College of Art, School of Industrial Design (Engineering), catalog, 1965.

Shipley, James R. "Industrial Design at the University of Illinois" (1947).

**242** Small Business Administration. *Design is Your Business.* (Washington: U.S. Government Printing Office, 1953), p. 2.

Small Business Administration. *Developing and Selling New Products.* Washington: U.S. Government Printing Office, 1955.

Society of Industrial Designers newsletters, 1956.

"The Story of GM" (General Motors brochure).

**243** "Summary of the Educational Conferences held by the IDSA" (typescript, 1968), p. 12.

**244** Ibid., pp. 14–15.

**245** Ibid., pp. 13–14.

**246** "Styling—The Auto Industry's Cinderella" "General Motors paper, 1958), p. 1.

**247** *Teague* v. *Graves,* 27 NYS 2nd Series (1941), p. 762.

**248** Ibid., p. 763.

**249** "Tupper, Earl S. Kitchen Containers & Implements, 1945–56" (collection, Museum of Modern Art, New York).

"20th Century Design: USA", Buffalo Fine Arts Academy, Albright Art Gallery, 1959–1960.

University of Bridgeport Industrial Design flyer, March 1949.

U.S. Department of Commerce. "Design USA" (catalogue, 1965), foreword.

**250** U.S. Supreme Court Reports, volume 260, October term, 1922, p. 692.

**251** U.S. Supreme Court Reports, volume 316, October term, 1941, p. 205.

"Victory Model 850" (Wurlitzer flyer). Author's collection.

# Acknowledgments

Graham Foundation for Advanced Studies in the Fine Arts, Grant, 1987

National Endowment for the Arts, Distinguished Designer Sabbatical Fellowship, 1984

The following colleagues in design were kind enough to share their valuable experiences about industrial design practice and education in the United States. (The letter I follows the names of those who provided tape-recorded comments or allowed the author to interview them.)

C. Joshua Abend (I); James Alexander; Dale H. Beck (I); George Beck (I); Arthur BecVar; Mel Best (I); Carl Bjorncrantz; Robert Blaich; Eugene Bordinat; Francis Braun; Peter Bressler; Kent Brown; Joseph Carriero; Dave Chapman; Theodore Clement; Harold Cohen; James Conner; Laird Covey; Arthur Crapsey (I); Pierre Crease; George W. Cushing; Frank Del Guidice; Thomas David; Niels Diffrient; Jay Doblin; H. Creston Doner; Henry Dreyfuss; John Duddy; Ray Eames; Elwood P. Engel; John Ensor; Lawrence Feer (I); Montgomery Ferar (I); William A. Fetter; Henry Finkel; Vincent Foote; Robert Fujioka; Walter Furlani; James Fulton (I); Carroll Gantz; Thomas H. Geismar; Wim Gilles; Channing Wallace Gilson; Henry Glass; William Goldsmith (I); Cal Graser; Lurelle Guild (I); Robert J. Harper; Richard Hollerith; James Hvale; Gifford Jackson; George Jergensen; Leo Jiranek, Edgar Kaufmann, Jr. (I); Douglas Kelley (I); Rudolf H. Koepf; Irv Koons; Rowena Kostellow; Rudolph Krolopp (I); Thomas Lamb; Harper Landell; Walter Landor; Monte Levy; Luke Lietzke; J. Gordon Lippincott (I); Raymond Loewy; Sam Maloof; Ellen Manderfield (I); Joseph R. Mango; Leon Gordon Miller; Peter Müller-Munk (I); C. Stowe Myers (I); John Najjar; George Nelson (I); Eliot Noyes; Roy Parcels, James Pirkl (I); William F. H. Purcell; Jean O. Reinecke; Raymond C. Sandin (I); Viktor Schreckengost (I); James Shipley; Joseph Sinel (I); F. Eugene Smith; Robert G. Smith; Ray Spilman (I); Brooks Stevens; James Teague; Walter Dorwin Teague, Jr.; Herbert Tyrnauer; John Vassos (I); Don Wallance; Frank Walsh; Sidney Warner (I); Ray Wheeler; Arnold Wolf; Edward J. Wormley; Russel Wright (I); Eva Zeisel; Herbert Zeller (I).

These museums, galleries, and institutions were of invaluable assistance in providing guidance and photographs:

Akron Art Museum (Jane E. Falk); American Craft Council (Susan Harkavy); Buckminster Fuller Institute; Cooper-Hewitt Museum; Detroit Institute of Arts (Kay S. Young); Detroit Public Library (Margaret Peters); Fifty-50 Gallery (Ralph Cutler); Hagley Museum and Library (Daniel T. Muir); Henry Ford Museum; Isamu Noguchi Garden Museum (Bonnie Rychlak); Levittown Public Library (Janet Spar); Library of Congress; Museum of Modern Art (Thomas D. Grischkowsky and Cara McCarty); National Air and Space Museum (Larry Wilson); National Bowling Hall of Fame and Museum (Bruce Pluckhahr); Package Designers Institute; Philadelphia Museum of Art (Marjory Cafone and Conna Clark); Queens Museum; Solomon R. Guggenheim Museum (Regine O'Brien); United States Patent Office; University of Texas, Hoblitzelle Theater Arts Library; Wharton Esherick Museum (Mansfield B. Bascom); Whitney Museum of American Art (Nancy Princenthal).

Special mention is merited by Randall I. Bond, Associate Librarian of the Fine Arts Library at Syracuse University, and by the George Arents Research Library, which, with the generous assistance of Associate Librarian Carolyn Davis, provided access to the important archives of American Industrial Design. The papers of the following designers were researched: Dave Chapman, William Lescaze, Russel Wright, Ray Spilman, Walter Dorwin Teague, and John Vassos. In addition, the special archival collections of the ADI/IDI, the SID/ASID, and their successor organization, the Industrial Designers Society of America, provided professional details and a sense of continuity.

The following corporations were of assistance in obtaining information and/or photographs about their design activities and products:

Albert Kahn Associates, Inc. (Joe Bedway); Bell and Howell (Lois Robinson); Brunswick Corporation (Ross Stemer); Chrysler Corporation; Dazey Products; Dunbar Furniture Company; Esto Photographics (Erica Stoller); Gates Learjet (Terryl Mack); General Mills (Kim Dickey); General Motors Corporation (John Dickey); Herman Miller, Inc. (Linda Folland); Hoover Company (H. E. Buker); Howard Miller Clock Company; Knoll International (Carol Kim and Donald Rorke); Lever Brothers Company (Shirley Loxley); Maytag Company (Ron Krajnovich); Monsanto Company; Polaroid Corporation (Naorin Rohani); Rudolph de Harak and Associates (Barbara J. Carnana); Rudolph Wurlitzer Company; Salton Company (Lewis Salton); Joseph E. Seagrams & Sons (Carla Caccamise Ash); Tigrett Industries (Frances Tigrett); Volkswagen of America (Maria N. Mader and Camille Paluscio); Waring Products Corporation (William Dugar); Wearever/Proctor Silex (Marshall B. Johnson); Winchendon Furniture Company.

Special mention must be made of David Broda, who took most of the photographs from miscellaneous documents and publications.

Personal gratitude is extended to the following staff members of Pulos Design Associates, Inc., for their assistance in research and in the organization of photographs and the preparation of the manuscript: Jeanne Bianchine, Michael Cridland, Martha Heald, Margaret Leo, and Paul Sweeney. Without their patience and dedication this book would not have been possible.

# Index